The Cambridge Handbook of
Religious Epistemology

The Cambridge Handbook of Religious Epistemology, the first to appear on the topic, introduces the current state of religious epistemology and provides a discussion of fundamental topics related to the epistemology of religious belief. Its wide-ranging chapters not only survey fundamental topics but also develop non-traditional epistemic theories and explore the religious epistemology endorsed by non-Western traditions. In the first part, Faith and Rationality, readers will find new essays on Reformed epistemology, skepticism and religious belief, and on the nature of evidence with respect to religious belief. The rich second part, Religious Traditions, contains chapters on Hindu, Buddhist, Islamic, Jewish, and Christian epistemologies. The final part, New Directions, contains chapters ranging from applying disjunctivism and knowledge-first approaches to religious belief, to surveying responses to debunking arguments. Comprehensive and accessible, this Handbook will advance the field for years to come.

Jonathan Fuqua is Assistant Professor of Philosophy at Conception Seminary College. He is the co-editor of *Faith and Reason: Philosophers Explain Their Turn to Catholicism* (2019) and *Classical Theism: New Essays on the Metaphysics of God* (2023).

John Greco is the Robert L. McDevitt, K.S.G., K.C.H.S. and Catherine H. McDevitt L.C.H.S. Chair in Philosophy at Georgetown University. He is the author of *Putting Skeptics in Their Place* (Cambridge, 2000), *Achieving Knowledge* (Cambridge, 2010), and *The Transmission of Knowledge* (Cambridge, 2020).

Tyler Dalton McNabb is Associate Professor of Philosophy at St Francis University. He is the author of *Religious Epistemology* (Cambridge, 2018) and *God and Political Theory* (Cambridge, 2022). He has also co-authored *Plantingian Epistemology and World Religions* (2019) and *Classical Theism and Buddhism* (2022).

T0382588

Cambridge Handbooks in Philosophy

Cambridge Handbooks in Philosophy are explorations of philosophical topics for both students and specialists. They offer accessible new essays by a range of contributors, as well as a substantial introduction and bibliography.

Titles published in this series
The Cambridge Handbook of Information and Computer Ethics
Edited by Luciano Floridi

The Cambridge Handbook of Cognitive Science
Edited by Keith Frankish and William Ramsey

The Cambridge Handbook of Artificial Intelligence
Edited by Keith Frankish and William Ramsey

The Cambridge Handbook of Evolutionary Ethics
Edited by Michael Ruse and Robert J. Richards

The Cambridge Handbook of the Just War
Edited by Larry May

The Cambridge Handbook of the Ethics of Ageing
Edited by C. S. Wareham

The Cambridge Handbook of Religious Epistemology
Edited by Jonathan Fuqua, John Greco, and Tyler McNabb

The Cambridge Handbook of
Religious Epistemology

EDITED BY

Jonathan Fuqua
Conception Seminary College, Missouri

John Greco
Georgetown University, Washington DC

Tyler Dalton McNabb
St Francis University, Pennsylvania

Shaftesbury Road, Cambridge CB2 8EA, United Kingdom

One Liberty Plaza, 20th Floor, New York, NY 10006, USA

477 Williamstown Road, Port Melbourne, VIC 3207, Australia

314–321, 3rd Floor, Plot 3, Splendor Forum, Jasola District Centre,
New Delhi – 110025, India

103 Penang Road, #05-06/07, Visioncrest Commercial, Singapore 238467

Cambridge University Press is part of Cambridge University Press & Assessment,
a department of the University of Cambridge.

We share the University's mission to contribute to society through the pursuit of
education, learning and research at the highest international levels of excellence.

www.cambridge.org
Information on this title: www.cambridge.org/9781316517710

DOI: 10.1017/9781009047180

First published 2023

A catalogue record for this publication is available from the British Library.

Library of Congress Cataloging-in-Publication Data
Names: Fuqua, Jonathan, editor. | Greco, John, editor. | McNabb, Tyler Dalton, editor.
Title: The Cambridge handbook of religious epistemology / edited by Jonathan Fuqua,
    John Greco, Tyler McNabb.
Description: Cambridge ; New York, NY : Cambridge University Press, 2023. |
    Includes bibliographical references and index. | Summary: "The Cambridge Handbook
    of Religious Epistemology, the first to appear on the topic, introduces the current state
    of religious epistemology and provides a discussion of fundamental topics related to the
    epistemology of religious belief. Comprehensive and accessible, it will advance the field
    for years to come"– Provided by publisher.
Identifiers: LCCN 2023010597 (print) | LCCN 2023010598 (ebook) | ISBN 9781316517710
    (hardback) | ISBN 9781009048354 (paperback) | ISBN 9781009047180 (epub)
Subjects: LCSH: Knowledge, Theory of (Religion) Classification: LCC BL51 .C3234 2023
    (print) | LCC BL51 (ebook) | DDC 210–dc23/eng/20230406
LC record available at https://lccn.loc.gov/2023010597
LC ebook record available at https://lccn.loc.gov/2023010598

ISBN 978-1-316-51771-0 Hardback
ISBN 978-1-009-04835-4 Paperback

Contents

Tables

Contributors

Charity Anderson is an Associate Professor of Philosophy at Baylor University.

Max Baker-Hytch is a Tutorial Fellow in Philosophy at Wycliffe Hall, University of Oxford.

Michael Bergmann is a Professor of Philosophy at Purdue University.

Laura Frances Callahan is an Assistant Professor of Philosophy at the University of Notre Dame.

Terence Cuneo is Marsh Professor of Intellectual and Moral Philosophy at the University of Vermont.

Christina H. Dietz is a Research Fellow at the Dianoia Institute of Philosophy at Australian Catholic University.

Enis Doko is an Associate Professor of Philosophy at Ibn Haldun University, Turkey.

Katherine Dormandy is a University Professor of Philosophy at the University of Innsbruck, Austria.

Thomas A. Forsthoefel is a Professor of Religious Studies at Mercyhurst University.

Victoria S. Harrison is a Professor of Philosophy at the University of Macau, China.

John Hawthorne is a Professor of Philosophy at the University of Southern California and at the Dianoia Institute of Philosophy at Australian Catholic University.

Daniel Howard-Snyder is a Professor of Philosophy at Western Washington University.

Elizabeth Jackson is an Assistant Professor of Philosophy at Toronto Metropolitan University.

Lorraine Juliano Keller is an Assistant Professor of Philosophy at Saint Joseph's University.

Samuel Lebens is an Associate Professor of Philosophy at the University of Haifa, Israel.

Kevin McCain is a Professor of Philosophy at the University of Alabama at Birmingham.

Daniel J. McKaughan is an Associate Professor of Philosophy at Boston College.

Sandra Menssen is a Professor of Philosophy at the University of St. Thomas.

Duncan Pritchard is UC Distinguished Professor of Philosophy at the University of California, Irvine.

Kegan J. Shaw is an Associate Professor of Philosophy at Anderson University.

Thomas D. Sullivan is a Professor of Philosophy Emeritus at the University of St. Thomas.

Joshua C. Thurow is an Associate Professor of Philosophy at the University of Texas at San Antonio.

Jamie B. Turner is a doctoral researcher at the Centre for Philosophy of Religion at the University of Birmingham.

John Zhao is a PhD Candidate in Philosophy at the University of Macau, China.

Introduction

Jonathan Fuqua and Tyler Dalton McNabb

Religious Epistemology Matters

The questions of faith and reason, taken up in this book in great detail, are universal across time and place; nor have they gone away with the Enlightenment, the rise of modern science, or the epistemological cynicism of postmodernism. One finds extensive and serious philosophical discussion of things divine, of God and the gods, throughout the history of philosophy, East and West, down to the present day. The human being is an animal, but in most cases is also a "believer." In a nod to the extensive body of scientific work on humanity's religious proclivities, some have even called the human being "the believing primate" (Schloss and Murray 2009). As the "believing primate" designation suggests, religious belief seems to bear an interesting and unclear relationship with reason. For one thing, without reason, no one could have any religious beliefs nor engage in any religious practices based on those beliefs. To be a believing primate, you have to be a rational animal (the latter designation being, of course, Aristotle's famous definition of the human person). In *that* sense, at least, religion is rational: To be religious you have to be rational.

On the other hand, the objects of religious belief, principally God or the gods, typically transcend the mundane world of ordinary, medium-sized objects accessible to us through perception and upon which our reason normally operates. God, for example, is a very different sort of being than is the book you are holding in your hands, or the computer on your desk or lap. God, if real, is also very different from the objects we contemplate when we think at high levels of abstraction, such as strings, quarks, waves, numbers, functions, and so on. Revealed religions, moreover, often claim to bear a message from God or the gods, telling us of divinely unveiled truths inaccessible to mere human reason. Reason thus confronts two mysteries in revealed religion: the strangeness of the Object(s) and the otherworldliness of its message.

But is it rational to believe in, say, invisible beings? Or to believe in strange-sounding, allegedly miraculous things? Is it sensible to think that an invisible being can act in the material world in ways that seem to "violate" the laws of nature, or to somehow govern the whole cosmos by an omnicompetent providence? And if human beings are indeed rational by nature, why are they so prone to form beliefs about beings and events that go far beyond what reason can say? Why not stay within the safer, more terrestrial confines of what our reason alone can say? Don't we have our rational hands full with such recondite matters as physics and mathematics? Why go gallivanting into theological terrain, which literally transcends our space-time continuum?

The key, perhaps, to understanding why beings equipped with reason are so prone to form beliefs about matters that transcend the mundane world lies in seeing that the human person is also, as some recent moral philosophers have emphasized, the "meaning-seeking animal" (McPherson 2020). The human person wants to know not only what happened, but also *why* it happened; to know where, if at all, the universe came from – Why is there something rather than nothing? Why this universe and not some other? And what does it all mean? Where is it all going? Is there a point to it all? A point to *my* life? A way I am supposed to live in which I might be more perfectly united to beauty, truth, and goodness? And what happens when we die – annihilation or life after death? Is there any way to be redeemed from the wretched aspects of our condition, such as our proneness to immorality, physical corruption, and death? Is there an Author of life who made me and loves me or is it all just a cosmic accident?

In trying to answer these questions we seem bound to look "beyond" the mundane world upon which reason normally operates and to try and find out whether there is a transcendent, supernatural, extra-mundane Author(s) of our world and our lives. This seems to make sense: If there is an answer, or an Answer, to our questions about meaning, it probably won't be found simply by looking around at the items in the universe, for it is their existence and meaning which we are asking about. And if there is an Author of all things, surely it or he or she (or whatever) must be very different from us and the terrestrial objects with which we are familiar. So, our capacity for rationality seems to set us on a meaning-seeking journey, and yet, as we progress on this quest, we realize that the Object(s) we are questing about is something that, by the very nature of the case, seems bound to transcend our terrestrial rationality: Reason, paradoxically, appears to point beyond itself – or so, at least, it has sometimes been argued. Hence, the human person, a rational animal, is also, by virtue of being a meaning-seeking animal, the believing primate.

But maybe, in fact, there is no purpose or teleology and thus maybe reason doesn't point anywhere – maybe nothing points at anything. Or maybe reason points at something that isn't there or at something it can't access at all, and so it wouldn't be rational to believe in it. One thing seems clear, at least: Insofar as human beings are rational, meaning-seeking animals, we cannot ignore the question of religion nor the important philosophical questions about the rational status of religious belief and practice. We will either think about these questions explicitly and reflectively or we will simply imbibe answers to them from those that happen to have our ear. As G. K. Chesterton once remarked, "Philosophy is merely thought that has been thought out. It is often a great bore. But man has no alternative, except between being influenced by thought that has been thought out and being influenced by thought that has not been thought out" (2011: 291). Religious epistemology can be thought of as the attempt to think these things out, using all the tools of philosophy at its disposal; the only alternative to it, given that we are rational, meaning-seeking, religion-prone animals, is being influenced by thought that hasn't been thought out.

Epistemology – often known as the "theory of knowledge" – is a branch of philosophy that asks questions about the nature of knowledge, rationality, and reasonable belief; about the sources of these things, such as perception, intuition, testimony, and reason; and about the very possibility of answering the skeptical challenge that we are largely, if not totally, in the dark about the real truth of things. Like the meaning-seeking questions of faith and reason, its questions go back to the dawn of philosophy and stretch throughout the history of philosophy.[1] Contemporary religious epistemologists make careful use of all the philosophical and epistemological tools at their disposal to inquire about, among other things, whether religious belief can be rational or perhaps even rise to the level of knowledge; to ask about the very nature of faith; to consider the sources of religious belief, such as testimony, religious experience, sacred writings, alleged miracles, and philosophical arguments (e.g., the "proofs" for God's existence); and to consider possible objections to the truth or rationality of religious belief, such as those posed by religious disagreement, or evolutionary debunking arguments, or the problem of evil. In this volume, you'll encounter a fairly comprehensive, cutting-edge sampling of this literature by a variety of philosophers and philosophical perspectives. We hope they will help you think things out.

Overview of the Chapters

This volume is divided into three parts. Part I, "Faith and Rationality," centers on what is typically considered the heart of religious epistemology, the rationality of religious belief. This section of the volume is broken up into seven chapters. In Chapter 1, "Natural Theology and Religious Belief," Max Baker-Hytch explores and defends the project of natural theology. Roughly, natural theology's aim is to discover whether or not God exists, apart from the aid of divine revelation. Baker-Hytch argues that natural theology gives us a neutral space where believers and non-believers can reason together about religion. Baker-Hytch then explores various types of arguments utilized in natural

---

[1] For an overview of the history of epistemology in the West, see Hetherington (2019). For a historical anthology of primary sources discussing faith and reason, one that stretches from Greek philosophy down to the present day, see Helm (1999). For resources on epistemology in non-Western philosophy, see Forsthoefel (2002) and Westerhoff (2009).

theology. Specifically, he focuses both on traditional deductive-style arguments and the more recent inductively styled arguments for God. Finally, Baker-Hytch looks at two problems that proponents of natural theology will have to face. First, he engages the problem of the gaps. Even if we can prove that a first cause or source of all being exists, why think that this cause is God? Second, even if there are successful arguments from natural theology, there is an accessibility problem. How can technical arguments from natural theology justify religious faith for the everyday believer? Baker-Hytch points to solutions for both of these problems.

In Chapter 2, "Evidence and Religious Belief," Kevin McCain looks to show that evidentialism, even about religious belief, is still a live option for epistemologists today. McCain begins by clarifying what evidentialism is and is not. He does this by looking at two types of objections. The first is that evidentialism is too demanding, while the other objection is that evidentialism is too weak. Regarding the former, McCain makes clear that evidentialism does not entail the view that in order for evidence to be admissible, the evidence must take the form of an inference or an argument. This should help those who are concerned with the evidentialist thesis being too strong. In response to the latter objection, McCain ends up developing what he calls Phenomenal Explanationism. While this view takes primary insights from the phenomenal conservatism tradition, McCain offers his new model with further constraints so as to address the standard worries epistemologists have when considering phenomenal conservatism. McCain then explores the application of Phenomenal Explanationism to the epistemology of religious belief.

In Chapter 3, "Reformed Epistemology," Michael Bergmann defends the central thesis of Reformed epistemology, namely that religious belief can be rational apart from being based on reasoning or arguments. For example, why can't religious belief be rationally based on experience? Bergmann takes a look at what he considers to be the three main stages of how the Reformed epistemology project developed. After this developmental overview, he looks at various recent developments in the related literature, such as how Reformed epistemology has accommodated the recent social turn in religious epistemology and how Reformed epistemologists have synthesized their views with contemporary cognitive science of religion. Finally, in the last section of Bergmann's chapter, he looks at key objections to the Reformed epistemology thesis, such as the classic Great Pumpkin Objection and an objection from epistemic peer disagreement. Bergmann finds these objections wanting.

In Chapter 4, "Rationality and Miracles," Charity Anderson argues that miracle claims can be rationally accepted through the means of testimony. Usually, when skeptics reject religious testimony, they do so for one of two reasons. Either they downplay the sort of knowledge that can be obtained through the means of testimony, or they argue that the probability of a miracle is so improbable that it is never rational to believe that one occurred. Both elements can be found in Hume's famous argument against miracles. Anderson pushes back on Hume and argues that defining miracles as extraordinarily improbable stacks the deck against the faithful. Anderson then develops epistemological models for testing testimonial truth claims.

In Chapter 5, "Pragmatic Arguments for Theism," Elizabeth Jackson looks at whether, from a practical point of view, one should try to believe that God exists. Even more specifically, is it rational for practical reasons to commit oneself to a specific religious tradition? Jackson surveys various pragmatic arguments for believing that some set of religious claims is true, with a special focus on Pascal's Wager. Jackson looks at various versions of the argument, including versions that focus on infinite and non-infinite utilities. She ends her chapter by engaging various objections to pragmatic arguments, including an objection that argues that pragmatic considerations entail that one should endorse fundamentalism about religious dogma.

"Fideism" is an umbrella term used to cover an array of views relating to the permissibility of assenting to religious claims that are in tension with reason. In Chapter 6, "Skepticism, Fideism, and Religious Epistemology," Duncan Pritchard puts forth his own model of fideism, what he calls "Quasi-Fideism." Following Wittgenstein's "hinge" epistemology, Pritchard argues that religious faith can be understood as an arational hinge commitment – that is, a commitment that is neither rational nor irrational. On this view, faith is not in opposition to reason. Rather, faith operates as a kind of arational background, against which rational evaluation takes place. Pritchard ends his chapter by engaging with concerns that one may have by endorsing his model.

In Part I's final chapter, Chapter 7, "The Problem of Faith and Reason," Daniel Howard-Snyder and Daniel J. McKaughan tackle the question of whether faith conflicts with reason. Their novel approach to this question involves a detailed examination of the nature of faith. Traditionally, when philosophers analyze the question of faith and reason, they assume that faith entails belief. Thus, the central question, on the traditional understanding, is whether one can rationally believe some religious claim while also being aware of sophisticated objections to the truth of that claim. Howard-Snyder and McKaughan avoid this discussion altogether as they develop an account of faith that rejects the "faith entails belief" claim. Instead, the authors opt for an account of faith that considers faith to primarily be a resilient reliance on some promise or person rather than a belief in some set of propositions.

While the religious epistemology literature has been dominated (and perhaps for good reason) by questions relating to the rationality of faith in general, one underdeveloped area in the literature relates to how specific religious traditions understand and model religious epistemology. Part II of this volume, "Religious Traditions," attempts to rectify this gap. In Chapter 8, "Jewish Religious Epistemology," Samuel Lebens argues that Jewish epistemology, at its roots, is a communal epistemology. Lebens starts his chapter by developing what is known as the Kuzari Principle. Roughly, the idea behind the principle is that if some proposed event is unforgettable, is claimed to have been witnessed by a significant portion of a nation or people group, and has been allegedly passed down from generation to generation ever since, then probably, that event actually occurred in history. Various versions of this principle are then used to justify belief in important historical events, such as the events surrounding the Exodus. Religious knowledge is, then, connected to group testimony and collective knowledge. Because of this, we shouldn't think that the individual can reach her full religio-epistemic potential without her community. She depends on others for her religious knowledge.

In Chapter 9, "Christian Religious Epistemology," Sandra Menssen and Thomas D. Sullivan briefly introduce models for understanding religious epistemology from the Christian tradition. They then move on to develop their own unique Christian religious epistemology, arguing that the great-making features of a proposed revelation, such as extraordinary degrees of unity, beauty, intelligence, and originality, can make it reasonable to believe that the revelation is true. Menssen and Sullivan go on to use Thomas Aquinas's work to illustrate one way they think a case might begin to be built for the contention that the Christian revelation possesses the aforementioned great-making features. Menssen and Sullivan then look at various objections to their view, such as whether there are other proposed revelatory claims that possess some or all of the same great-making features as Christian revelation allegedly does.

In Chapter 10, "Islamic Religious Epistemology," Enis Doko and Jamie B. Turner look to map out the various epistemological traditions contained within the overall Islamic tradition and put them into conversation with contemporary epistemology. They begin by explicating the rationalist or kalām tradition, specifically through examining the thought of thinkers like Al-Maturidi and al-Ash'arī. Those who consider themselves hard evidentialists will find a home in this tradition. In contrast, those who are committed to Reformed epistemology will appreciate the Traditionalist school surveyed. Here, there is special attention given to the thought of Ibn-Taymiyya.

After addressing religious epistemologies from the Abrahamic tradition, we have two final chapters to close out this section. In Chapter 11, "Hindu Religious Epistemology," Thomas A. Forsthoefel argues that epistemology is intimately connected to soteriology and metaphysics within the Hindu tradition(s). Looking specifically at the Advaita Vedanta tradition, Forsthoefel argues that in order for some subject S to know the fundamental truth about reality, S needs properly cognitive functioning faculties, properly functioning Gurus, and the Vedas. These will enable her to get into the mental space where she can obtain the right internal access to achieve knowledge (or knowledge beyond knowledge) about Brahman and, thus, achieve genuine liberation.

In the final chapter of Part II, Chapter 12, "Buddhist Religious Epistemology," Victoria S. Harrison and John Zhao show how Buddhist epistemologies are tied to soteriology. The aim of religious knowledge is the escape of suffering. However, as Zhao and Harrison demonstrate, there is no "one" Buddhist epistemology. The chapter explicates three Buddhist traditions. First, they discuss early Buddhist epistemology, which is rather mundane and oriented toward empiricism. This contrasts with the Pramāṇavāda tradition, which relies on knowledge of the particulars and fictional universals through inference and perception. Finally, the chapter surveys the anti-realist epistemology of the Madhyamaka tradition. Here, they discuss the two-truth theory and the role the interdependence thesis plays in religious epistemology.

Part III of this volume, "New Directions," includes seven chapters on cutting-edge topics within religious epistemology. Taken together, they attempt to apply recent work in epistemology and philosophy of religion to the questions of religious epistemology, thereby pushing the conversation in new and stimulating directions.

In Chapter 13, "Trust, Testimony, and Religious Belief," Laura Frances Callahan makes use of recent epistemological work on trust and testimony to explore (i) the place of trust and testimony in the formation of religious belief and (ii) the rationality of using testimony to form and sustain religious belief. Callahan notes that religious belief and practice is social-epistemological, in the sense that it is shot through with epistemic dependence on others. Though this might seem epistemically regrettable, Callahan argues otherwise. She gives both epistemological and theological reasons for thinking that relying on others to help us form our religious beliefs is far from being an epistemically bad thing. Callahan's discussion of these matters engages current debates in the epistemology of testimony. In addition, she considers the contemporary philosophical literature on trusting others. Using these resources, Callahan explores the epistemic and nonepistemic benefits of trusting others and then applies relevant insights to religious epistemology. For example, she concludes, trust is a pervasive feature of thinking and doing things together, in the religious domain but also more widely.

In Chapter 14, "Religious Disagreement," Katherine Dormandy brings recent work in the epistemology of disagreement literature to bear on the potential problem posed by religious disagreement. She explains and then challenges the dominant framework for understanding disagreement generally and religious disagreement more specifically. This framework roughly relies on a trio of possible views one can take toward disagreement: steadfastness ("it's rationally okay to stay where you are in the face of disagreement"), Conciliationism ("rationality demands lowering your confidence in your belief"), and the Total Evidence View ("in cases of disagreement whether P, you must take into account your total evidence: your own evidence regarding

P and your evidence regarding what your peers think about P"). Dormandy challenges the dominant framework in two ways. First, she argues that we should view religious disagreement as an opportunity to learn rather than as a problem to be solved. Second, she makes a distinction between impartialist evidence (roughly, public, shareable evidence) and partialist evidence (roughly, private, non-shareable evidence) and, from there, argues for a new view she dubs "egalitarianism," according to which we should give equal weight to each type of evidence.

In Chapter 15, "Franciscan Knowledge," Lorraine Juliano Keller explains and defends Eleonore Stump's account of Franciscan knowledge, a type of knowledge that Stump claims is important in both knowing God and in responding to the problem of evil. Franciscan knowledge is characterized as nonpropositional knowledge, meaning that it is not reducible to propositional knowledge; it includes, by way of example, knowledge of oneself, second-personal knowledge of other persons as persons, and knowledge of music and pictures. Franciscan knowledge is plausibly an important avenue of knowing God: if God is personal and relates to us personally, then some of our knowledge of God will be second-personal, and thus knowing God won't be limited to propositionally knowing facts about God. It will include, additionally, knowing God personally, the way you know, say, your mother. Keller defends this view against recent objections and explains its potential importance for responding to the problem of evil, and for elucidating the compatibility of apophaticism (the idea that any knowledge of God is really just negative knowledge of what is not true about God) and the sort of rich knowledge of God (putatively) available in heaven.

In Chapter 16, "Liturgically Infused Practical Understanding," Terence Cuneo uses recent work in epistemology to tackle a religious problem involving liturgy. Religious practice in many religious traditions involves liturgical rituals. One problem with liturgical rituals, which Cuneo refers to as the "alignment worry," is that there is often a gap between the rote, mechanistic performance of these rites and what they are supposed to express and inculcate, which is certain religious attitudes like faith, hope, and love. Cuneo responds to this worry from within the perspective of the religious tradition he knows best: Eastern Christianity. Cuneo argues that the epistemological value of Eastern Orthodox liturgy lies in part in its ability to inculcate the liturgically infused practical understanding of a certain "Maximian" worldview, that is, a theological worldview based on the writings of St. Maximos the Confessor. Cuneo's innovative chapter includes an exposition of practical understanding and an explanation of how liturgical rites can help infuse such understanding in their practitioners.

In Chapter 17, "Knowledge-First Epistemology and Religious Belief," Christina H. Dietz and John Hawthorne explore the implications of taking a knowledge-first approach to epistemology for religious epistemology. They hone in on two themes of knowledge-first epistemology: (i) the idea that our evidence is just what we know (E = K) or, more weakly, the idea that our evidence is a subset of what we know (E to K); and (ii) the idea that other positive epistemic statuses, such as justification, should be understood in terms of knowledge. After explaining and exploring these two themes, Dietz and Hawthorne turn their attention to Reformed epistemology and attempt to delineate what a knowledge-first Reformed epistemology would look like. Crucially, it would include the idea that God's existence is part of the theist's evidence. The authors go on to discuss two further issues from the perspective of a knowledge-first Reformed epistemology: putative defeaters for theistic belief, such as the existence of seemingly pointless evil, and the relationship between religious commitments, public reasons, and democratic liberalism.

In Chapter 18, "Epistemic Disjunctivism and Religious Knowledge," Kegan J. Shaw argues for a view he calls "religious epistemological disjunctivism." This view is an application of disjunctivism about visual perception to putative cases of mystical or theistic perception. According to epistemological disjunctivism, in a good case of visual perception that P, one knows that P because one sees that P is the case and, moreover, one's grounds for P are both factive and reflectively accessible. Shaw both explains and defends epistemological disjunctivism. He then applies epistemological disjunctivism to cases of theistic perception. Here too, he argues, in a good case one has factive and reflectively accessible grounds for thinking that God is thus and so. Shaw argues that this disjunctivist theory of religious perception has advantages not shared by standard externalist and internalist accounts of religious experience.

Finally, in Chapter 19, "Debunking Arguments and Religious Belief," Joshua C. Thurow utilizes recent epistemological work to investigate the prospects for formulating a successful debunking objection to the rationality of religious belief. Debunking arguments against religious belief attempt to "explain away" the presence of religious belief as the product of non-rational factors. They are "You just believe that because" objections. Thurow explains debunking arguments and details several that have been made against religious belief. Thurow then turns his attention to an investigation of the cogency of these arguments, including how critics of debunking arguments have utilized recent developments in epistemology to answer them.

Part I

Faith and Rationality

1 Natural Theology and Religious Belief

Max Baker-Hytch

1.1 What Is Natural Theology?

Natural theology has traditionally been defined in contradistinction to revealed theology. Since at least as far back as the ancient Greek philosopher Parmenides (Clark 2013: 11–13), one finds various expressions of a distinction between two quite different ways of arriving at beliefs about God or gods: one which appeals to allegedly divinely inspired and revealed sources of knowledge and the other which relies only on the natural human cognitive apparatus, unaided by putative revelation.[1] The latter approach hasn't been consistently referred to with the label "natural theology" until relatively recently, but it is clear that earlier thinkers such as Augustine and Aquinas were familiar with this basic distinction.[2] There appears, then, to be a longstanding recognition of an intellectual activity that involves an attempt at rationally establishing religious truth claims using methods that are in some sense religiously neutral. This activity might be thought to serve several interrelated goals: (1) to provide a methodology for those wishing to investigate the truth or falsity of a religious worldview prior to having committed to its tenets; (2) for those who are already committed to the tenets of a religious worldview to be able to investigate how much rational justification their religious beliefs would have if they were to base those beliefs solely on sources that are recognized by skeptics and believers alike; (3) for those already committed to the tenets of a religious worldview to have a means of trying to persuade those not already committed, without appealing to sources that the unpersuaded don't recognize.

Given that these are the central goals that natural theology seeks to fulfill, we can identify a couple of crucial features that a piece of reasoning needs to have in order to count as a natural theological argument. Firstly, it must presuppose only those cognitive faculties and belief-forming methods that

---

[1] For some contemporary expressions of this distinction, see Craig and Moreland (2009: ix), Parsons (2013: 247), Plantinga (1974: 219–220).

[2] Augustine makes a distinction between those religious propositions that can be demonstrated by rational proof and those that cannot (1991 [400]: 6.5). Aquinas makes a similar distinction when he distinguishes "philosophical science built up by reason" from "sacred science learned through revelation" (1981 [1272]: 1a, q. 1).

are available in principle to any rational agent. It cannot invoke alleged special faculties or sources of insight that only some individuals possess or whose existence is contested by adherents of competing metaphysical world-views. This doesn't rule out appealing to scientific discoveries that rely on technologies and conceptual frameworks not possessed by humans in all ages or places. The point is that human beings in all eras of history and all parts of the globe have had the same basic cognitive apparatus that would have enabled them to grasp those scientific discoveries if they had been taught the relevant conceptual frameworks and provided with the requisite technology. Secondly, an intellectual activity that seeks to fulfill one or more of (1)–(3) cannot treat religious texts as sources of properly basic belief, which is to say, it cannot assume that the assertions of religious texts are likely to be true simply in virtue of their being asserted *by those texts*.

It is worth considering two sorts of intellectual activity that provide interesting test cases for the foregoing characterization of natural theology. The first is the project of trying to establish the historicity of events that are described in religious texts, the most prominent example of which is the effort to argue for the historicity of Jesus' alleged resurrection (Swinburne 2003; McGrew and McGrew 2009; Licona 2010). This project typically involves applying standard historical methods to argue for the reliability of certain key portions of the historical narrative in the Pauline epistles (e.g., 1 Corinthians 15:3–8) and the New Testament Gospels (e.g., Mark 16:1–8) and then goes on to argue that a bodily resurrection is the best explanation for the events described in those portions of the narrative. This seems to be straightforwardly an instance of natural theology in that the New Testament texts at issue are not being treated as sources of properly basic belief. Rather than being assumed, the historicity of the relevant portions of the narrative is being argued for on the grounds that those portions allegedly exemplify properties that a secular historian will recognize as evidence of authenticity. So whilst this approach in some sense "appeals to" religious texts, it does so in a way that is fully consistent with the goals of natural theology outlined above.

A second test case is the project of seeking to establish the logical coherence of the central doctrines of a specific religious tradition, which is one of the key tasks (though by no means the only one) that the burgeoning field of analytic theology aims to undertake (Rea 2009). Typically, the way this project is undertaken is that an author presents a description of a doctrine such as the Trinity that is drawn from religious texts and traditions, and then proceeds to try to show that the doctrine is logically coherent by appealing to analogies or thought experiments. I am inclined to think that even though this in some sense involves "appealing to" religious texts or traditions, it too is an instance of natural theology. To see why, consider an analogy with *a priori* knowledge. Let us grant that no one would ever acquire the concepts of *bachelor* or *unmarried man* apart from having various kinds of sensory experience of the world. Still, it doesn't follow that one's knowledge of the proposition *bachelors are unmarried men* is not *a priori*. Whilst one's acquisition of the requisite concepts occurs through experience, one's epistemic justification for the belief that *bachelors are unmarried men* comes simply from reflecting on the meanings of the words, and hence is *a priori*. Similarly, whilst analytic theologians may derive their descriptions of the doctrines they study from religious texts and traditions, the epistemic justification they offer for believing in the logical coherence of these doctrines derives exclusively from the application of methods that are available in principle to both believer and nonbeliever alike: rational intuition, thought experiments, arguments from analogy, and so on.

1.2 The Varieties of Natural Theology

In this section we turn to consider the landscape of contemporary natural theology. As the remarks at the end of the previous section indicate, natural theology can be argued to encompass more than just arguments for the existence of God. However, given that arguments for the existence of God are still in many ways the central focus of the project of natural theology, I shall restrict my focus in this section to considering just these arguments. Moreover, I shall be concerned just with those arguments that offer reasons for thinking theism is true (or probably true) as opposed to arguments that offer merely pragmatic reasons for believing in God, Pascal's Wager being the most notable example of the latter.[3]

Immanuel Kant (1998 [1781]: A590/B618–A591/B619) claimed that there are only three ways to argue for the existence of God, which he termed the ontological argument, the cosmological argument, and the physico-theological argument. Kant distinguished these three arguments on the basis of the way in which the premises of each argument are allegedly known: purely *a priori,* on the basis of indeterminate experience, and on the basis of determinate experience, respectively. Whilst Kant's classification of natural theological arguments has been very influential,[4] it is by no means the only way to carve up the landscape, and it arguably misses a large amount of important nuance. For example, moral arguments typically appeal to the intuition that there are objective moral values and duties, which could be seen as a kind of *a priori* intuition. But it would be very odd indeed to lump moral arguments in with ontological arguments, considering the vast differences between these two families of arguments. Indeed, it is striking that Kant doesn't even recognize moral arguments in his taxonomy. To take another

---

[3] For more on pragmatic arguments for theism, see Chapter 5 of this volume.

[4] See, for example, the Stanford Encyclopedia of Philosophy entry on "Natural Theology and Natural Religion" (Chignell and Pereboom 2015), which wholly adopts Kant's mapping.

example, contemporary arguments from consciousness frequently appeal to a combination of introspection and empirical observations from the field of neuroscience. It is again unclear where these arguments would fit in Kant's schema.

A more adequate approach might be to consider several families of arguments, which is to say, loose groupings, each of which have enough cohesion for us to be able to note some interesting things about their common structural features. The vast majority of natural theological arguments (henceforth NTAs) that have been studied to date can be grouped into the following eight families:[5] (A) ontological, (B) cosmological, (C) teleological, (D) historical-experiential, (E) metaphysical-explanatory, (F) axiological, (G) noological (having to do with mind), and (H) epistemological. I shall suggest that (F) and (G) are sub-families of (E), but they have enough distinctive features to warrant separate discussion.

(A) Ontological Arguments

Ontological arguments can be thought of as arguments for theism from the nature of greatness or perfection. Anselm of Canterbury (1979 [1078]) argued that a thing is greater if it exists not only as a concept in the mind but also in reality. According to Anselm's argument, if the greatest conceivable being existed only as a concept in the mind, then there would be something conceivably greater than it (namely, something that also existed in reality), but that would of course result in a contradiction. Hence, the greatest conceivable being must exist not only in the mind but also in reality. In a somewhat similar vein, René Descartes (1988 [1641]: 63–71) argued that since existence is a perfection, a supremely perfect being cannot lack existence, hence there must actually exist such a being.

These arguments have been accused of treating existence as a property. Most philosophers, following Kant (1998 [1781]: A592/B620–A602/B630), hold that existence is not a property (or at any rate not a first-order property) but rather the precondition of something's being the bearer of any properties at all. The development of modal logic and modal metaphysics in the twentieth century has helped to sharpen the issues here. It is now quite widely recognized that whilst a thing's merely existing is not among its properties, its *necessarily* existing is. Indeed, some authors have claimed to find hints in the direction of a second kind of ontological argument in both Anselm and Descartes (Malcolm 1960; Leftow 2007, 2022), namely, a *modal* ontological argument, which contends that a perfect being cannot fail to have the property of *necessary* existence, which is greater than the property of merely contingent

---

[5] The labels "axiological" and "noological" are borrowed from Craig (2001b).

existence. If it is genuinely possible for a perfect being to exist, then such a being exists necessarily, and hence actually exists.

Modal ontological arguments are the subject of intense discussion in contemporary analytic philosophy of religion, having been defended by Charles Hartshorne (1962), Alvin Plantinga (1974: ch. 10), and Yujin Nagasawa (2017: ch. 7), among others. There is something of a consensus among contemporary metaphysicians that the modal rule upon which most modal ontological arguments rely – the S5 rule, which states that if it is possible that it is necessary that p, then it is necessary that p – is highly plausible (Lowe 2002: 116–120). Everything thus hinges on whether a perfect being genuinely is possible, where the possibility at issue is metaphysical (or absolute) possibility. Graham Oppy (2007: ch. 12) contends that no one who isn't already a theist has good reason to affirm that such a being is possible. Several authors, however, are exploring novel ways of supporting the possibility premise, some of which even appeal to the content of religious experience (Pruss 2001, 2010; Nagasawa 2017: 202–205; Bernstein 2018).

(B) Cosmological Arguments

Cosmological arguments have been perhaps the most popular of all NTAs in the history of Western philosophy. One can find cosmological arguments in ancient Greek philosophy, in medieval Christian, Jewish, and Islamic philosophy, in the early modern period, and in the writings of a number of contemporary analytic philosophers (Craig 2001a). There are two characteristics that are particularly distinctive of cosmological arguments.

Firstly, the datum with which cosmological arguments begin is some metaphysically contingent and yet highly general feature of the cosmos. One of Aquinas's Five Ways (1981 [1272]: 1a, q. 2, a. 3) begins with the fact that objects undergo change, and another with the fact that there are causes and effects. An argument that Edward Feser (2017: ch. 2) attributes to Plotinus starts with the observation that some objects are wholes that are composed of parts. The cosmological argument developed by the kalām school of medieval Islamic philosophers and revived by William Lane Craig (1979) begins with the premise that the universe had a temporal beginning. A cosmological argument defended by Gottfried Leibniz (1991 [1714]: secs. 32–40) and Samuel Clarke (1998 [1705]) starts from the fact that there is a totality of things that exist contingently.

A second distinctive feature of cosmological arguments is that they invoke a principle according to which all the members of a particular class of things require a cause or explanation by something that is outside of that class. For example, the kalām cosmological argument has a principle stating that everything that begins to exist has a cause (external to itself) for its existence. The class that is said to require an external cause, in this case, is the class of all things that have a temporal beginning. In general, the wider the class that is singled out as needing explanation, the harder the argument is to defend. God, of course, would need to fall firmly outside the class of things that are said to require an explanation by something external to themselves, otherwise God will not constitute a legitimate terminus of explanation. Some defenders of cosmological arguments contend that their favored explanatory or causal principle needs no justification; its truth is obvious and is knowable simply via *a priori* intuition (Craig 1979). Others offer what might be termed a "transcendental" argument for their preferred principle, contending that some such principle is a presupposition of all scientific and philosophical reasoning (Feser 2017: 149–151).

It is striking that cosmological arguments don't typically purport to establish the existence of a being with all the classical divine attributes but instead something more minimal: a first cause or a necessary being. With that said, some defenders of cosmological arguments offer follow-up arguments that seek to show why the first cause or the necessary ground of everything must in fact have a range of other divine properties, which we shall consider later in this chapter.

(C) Teleological Arguments

Teleological arguments take as their data some empirically observable, contingent feature(s) of the structure of the universe. Typically, this consists in some pattern or configuration of parts or circumstances that is striking and seemingly improbable and that exhibits value of some sort, whether it be the instrumental value of making possible the existence of complex life or the intrinsic value of being beautiful. The empirical data that such arguments invoke may be observable by virtually anyone or may be accessible only to scientific experts. Examples of the former include the argument from the apparently purposive structures of living organisms put forward by William Paley (1802); Aquinas's Fifth Way (1981 [1272]: 1a, q. 2, a. 3), which begins with a claim about the apparently goal-directed behavior of various objects that lack intelligence of their own; Richard Swinburne's (2004: 154–166) argument from temporal order (i.e., the regularity of nature); and the argument from natural beauty (Tennant 1930; Wynn 1997). The argument from cosmic fine-tuning (Collins 2009; Hawthorne and Isaacs 2018) is an example of a teleological argument that invokes empirical data that are only accessible to scientific experts. The fine-tuning argument begins with the observation in recent physics that in order to be life-permitting, the fundamental physical constants and initial conditions of a universe need to fall within a tiny range out of all the possible values they could take. There is another teleological argument whose empirical premise is similarly difficult for laypeople to assess, though is rather more scientifically contested than the empirical premise of the fine-tuning argument. It begins with the claim that certain structures in the biological world display a kind of complexity that cannot have been produced by a series of incremental evolutionary steps (Behe 2003).

It is seldom claimed by advocates of teleological arguments that the allegedly designed feature at issue is *impossible* to explain in naturalistic terms. Hence, teleological arguments are almost always framed nondeductively. Paley's argument was cast in terms of an analogy between living organisms and human-made machines – an analogy that David Hume (1990 [1779]) had already subjected to intense criticism. Most modern teleological arguments, by contrast, invoke no such analogy but instead employ a Bayesian probabilistic framework. Where F is the feature of the universe under consideration, teleological arguments are usually framed in terms of a comparison of likelihoods, the claim being that F is much more likely given theism than given naturalism, and hence F powerfully confirms theism over naturalism; put more formally, $Pr(F|\text{theism})$ $>> Pr(F|\text{naturalism})$. The grounds offered in support of this comparative claim are twofold, corresponding to the two values that make up the comparison. On the left-hand side, it is alleged to be at least moderately probable that if God exists, then God would want a universe containing embodied, rational creatures (like humans), and F is either necessary for the existence of such creatures or is as at least as good a way of bringing about such creatures as any other way available to God (given other things God might be trying to bring about). On the right-hand side, the probability of F on naturalism is alleged to be very low, owing to the lack of mechanisms that a naturalist can legitimately invoke which would make it remotely likely that F would come about.

As one would expect, critics of such arguments tend to focus on defending the plausibility of naturalistic mechanisms that would make F at least moderately probable – for example, a multiverse in which vastly (if not infinitely) many different combinations of fundamental physical constants and initial conditions are tried out at random (Bostrom 2002: ch. 2). Another angle of attack, one pursued by some theists (Halvorsson 2018), is to cast doubt on our ability to have knowledge of divine psychology, which is something that seems to be presupposed by claims about what God would want the universe to contain.

(D) Historical-Experiential Arguments

What are commonly known as arguments from religious experience and arguments from miracles have a significant amount in common, such that it makes sense to discuss them together.[6] It is noteworthy that arguments in this

---

[6] The label "argument from miracles" is an unhelpful misnomer, in that the arguments in question don't begin with the premise that a miracle has occurred – that would obviously beg the question against the nontheist.

category have the potential, if successful, to lend support not just to generic theism but also to particular versions of theism, such as Islam or Christianity. The project of trying to argue for religiously specific claims about God from such data is sometimes known as ramified natural theology.

Arguments from religious experience fall into two broad categories. One sort begins with reports of religious experiences and argues that the existence and character of these reports lends evidential support to the hypothesis of theism or some specific version thereof (Gutting 1982; Mawson 2005: ch. 10). The other sort argues that a person who has a religious experience of such-and-such character under such-and-such conditions would be justified in having beliefs about God on the basis of that experience (Alston 1991; Swinburne 2004: ch. 13). The latter doesn't purport to establish any conclusion about God's existence directly, whereas the former does.

What is common to arguments from religious experiences of the first sort and arguments concerning alleged miracles is that they both begin with some testimony describing experiences whose character is alleged to be such as to lend support to the hypothesis that God exists and is the cause of the experiences in one of the following three senses: (i) God acted miraculously to bring about a publicly observable event that is the external stimulus of the experiences;[7] (ii) God acted miraculously in order to bring about private experiences in the individual; or (iii) the experiences are the result of the operation of a genuine extra-sensory perceptual ability via which the individual perceived God or some other supernatural reality (whether or not the workings of that perceptual ability involved miraculous intervention). Arguments that seek to establish Jesus' resurrection from certain items of historical testimony are typically seeking to establish (i). Arguments that contend that God or some supernatural reality is the best explanation for widespread reports of religious experiences are usually seeking to establish (ii) or (iii).

As with teleological arguments, because it is generally granted that the experiences at issue could in principle be explained naturalistically, these arguments are well suited to probabilistic formulations: the claim is that the reported experience E is much more probable given theism (perhaps of a specific variety) than naturalism; put more formally, $\Pr(E|\text{theism}) \gg \Pr(E|\text{naturalism})$.

Famously, Hume (2000 [1777]) argued that miracles are by their very nature maximally improbable events by virtue of their being maximally counter-inductive, so that even testimonial evidence of the highest quality is insufficient to overcome the prior improbability of the alleged miracle. This argument struggles to find many contemporary defenders. John Earman (2000), no friend

---

[7] In this case the evidence needn't be limited to testimony but could also include physical traces of the event. For helpful discussion on this point, see (Swinburne 2003: 14–15).

of theism, calls the argument an "abject failure." In particular, Hume's way of assigning epistemic probabilities to events has been severely criticized in view of the way that it makes it virtually impossible to have justified beliefs in hitherto unobserved event-types, an implication which would threaten to undermine the scientific enterprise (Hájek 2008). Others have noted that Hume's estimate of the prior probability of an event pays attention exclusively to the observed frequency of the event-type and thus totally ignores the way in which evidence for theism can indirectly raise the prior probability of certain kinds of miracles, whose very purpose would be to stand out as unique, revelatory events (Swinburne 2003: 25–26). In short, an in-principle argument against the occurrence of miracles of the sort that is often attributed to Hume is very likely an overreach. As such, there is no principled barrier to arguing from an experience that is sufficiently difficult to account for naturalistically that theism is the best explanation for the experience's occurrence, in one of the three senses outlined above.

(E) Metaphysical-Explanatory Arguments

In this category belong a wide range of arguments whose common characteristic is that they involve essentially the following two steps: the first step is an argument for metaphysical realism about a certain kind of entity; the second is an argument, usually cast as an abductive inference, to the conclusion that theism is better able to account for or accommodate the entity in question than any rival theory. Examples of entities that have served as the bases of such arguments are abstract objects in general (Feser 2017: ch. 3), mathematical entities such as natural numbers (Goldschmidt 2018) and sets (Menzel 2018), propositions (Keller 2018b), and possibilities (Leftow 2012: ch. 23).

The abductive inference to theism as the best explanation turns on the claim that theism has superior explanatory resources to be able to accommodate metaphysical realism about the entities in question. Three specific aspects of God's nature seem to afford rich resources for grounding or accommodating the aforementioned entities: firstly, God's mental life, and hence, representational abilities, afford the resources to accommodate those entities that seem to be representational in nature (e.g., propositions); secondly, God's unlimited causal powers satisfy the apparent need for some of the aforementioned entities to stand in causal relationships with the material world in a way that, for example, the Platonic realm of Forms is unable to do; thirdly, God's unlimited perspective means that, in contrast to attempts to ground some of the aforementioned entities in limited human mental activity, a theistic account faces no similar limits.

Let us now turn to consider two families of arguments that can be seen as species of metaphysical-explanatory arguments.

(F) Axiological Arguments

Like other metaphysical-explanatory arguments, axiological arguments involve basically two steps: first, an argument for objectivism, in this case, about some aspect of the moral or aesthetic domain; second, an argument – sometimes deductive but, increasingly, abductive in form (Baggett and Walls 2016: ch. 2) – that theism offers the best or only way to make sense of such objectivity.

Some such arguments contend that both objective moral values (e.g., the badness of pain) and objective moral obligations (e.g., that one ought not to kill innocent persons) are difficult or impossible to reconcile with nontheistic metaphysics (Craig 2008: ch. 4; Baggett and Walls 2016). Other proponents of axiological arguments are willing to grant that objective moral values may not need to be grounded in God, but contend that objective moral obligations have a number of features that make them especially difficult to square with a godless metaphysical picture, most notably, their sense of inescapable authority and their allegedly irreducibly social nature, or in other words, the way in which moral obligations are always ultimately owed *to someone* (Adams 2002: chs. 10-11; Evans 2013). A typical approach is for proponents of such arguments to work through a range of nontheistic accounts of moral obligations – including social contract accounts, secular natural law theories, and Kantian approaches – arguing that none are adequately able to do justice to the aforementioned features of moral obligations (Ritchie 2012).

(G) Noological Arguments

Noological arguments are a species of metaphysical-explanatory arguments that focus specifically on features of our mental lives that are alleged to sit uneasily with a naturalistic metaphysics. The features highlighted by such arguments include all of the following: the very fact that we have subjective, conscious experiences at all (Adams 1987: ch. 16; Moreland 2008; Page 2020); that mental states have the property of intentionality or aboutness (Reppert 2009); that the so-called psycho-physical laws that map brain states to conscious experiences would appear to need to be incredibly complex and numerous (Swinburne 2018); and that thoughts cause other thoughts in virtue of their representational properties, not merely in virtue of physical pushes and pulls, so to speak (Reppert 2009).

As with other metaphysical-explanatory arguments, the heart of these sorts of arguments is the claim that theism has much greater metaphysical resources than naturalism for accommodating the reality of conscious experience, intentionality, mental-to-mental causation, and so on. Whereas naturalism has to somehow get these phenomena out of fundamentally nonconscious, nonintentional building blocks, theism entails that these phenomena are at the bedrock of reality.

(H) Epistemological Arguments

Finally, epistemological arguments are those arguments that begin with a skeptical challenge to our supposed knowledge of some domain of reality and seek to convert the challenge into an argument for theism by defending the claim that theism offers the best or only way of getting around the skeptical challenge under consideration. Some such arguments seek to do this with global skeptical challenges, contending that naturalism leads to skepticism about *all* our cognitive faculties, whereas theism does not (Plantinga 2011: ch. 10). Others are more modest in scope, alleging that theism has a far easier time than naturalism of making sense of how we could have knowledge of some specific domains – for example, knowledge of metaphysically necessary truths (Koons 2018; Rogers 2021) or knowledge of objective moral truths (Ritchie 2012: chs. 2, 7; Baggett and Walls 2016: ch. 6).

There are basically two forms that an epistemological argument for theism can take. One approach is to grant that theists and nontheists alike are entitled to take themselves to have knowledge of the domain at issue, and then to argue that theism offers the best explanation for how we have such knowledge. The other approach is to claim that the naturalist has a defeater for all her beliefs in the domain in question (or *all* her beliefs, period, if the skeptical challenge is global in character). In response to local skeptical challenges, one option for the naturalist is to bite the bullet and admit that we lack knowledge of the sort in kind. But in response to global skeptical challenges, admitting the lack of *any* knowledge is a vastly less palatable option.

1.3 The Problem of the Gap(s)

In this section we consider the first of a pair of problems confronting the natural theologian. Even many enthusiastic proponents of NTAs tend to admit that there is a real sense in which no single NTA is enough on its own: there is a gap. Indeed, there seem to be at least two sorts of gap, one pertaining to content and the other pertaining to evidential strength. As for the former, most NTAs purport only to establish a proposition whose content falls some way short of full-blown theism with the whole range of classical divine attributes. As for the latter, there is a fairly widespread feeling that no single NTA is sufficiently powerful to carry the justificatory load for religious belief all by itself.

One strategy for dealing with this problem is to offer follow-up arguments that try to show why the fairly limited conclusion of some NTA (e.g., a cosmological argument for a necessary being) can be seen upon further reflection to entail a range of other divine attributes. One might call this the Thomistic approach, in view of the way that Aquinas follows up his Five Ways with a series of reflections intended to draw out most of the classical divine attributes from his earlier conclusions (1981 [1272]: 1a, qs. 3–13). Feser (2017) offers just such follow-up arguments purporting to deduce virtually all the classical divine attributes from the conclusions of his NTAs, most of which are cosmological arguments of one kind or another. Craig (1979: 149–153) offers a version of this approach that follows up his Kalām cosmological argument by inferring that the cause of the universe must also have the attributes of timelessness, immateriality, and personhood, and must be extremely knowledgeable and powerful. Joshua Rasmussen (2009) seeks to move from the conclusion that the universe has a necessary being as its foundation to the further conclusion that the necessary being must be a perfect being. The benefit of this approach is that it may allow one to establish full-blown theism via a single chain of deductive argumentation. The downside is that it is vulnerable in the way it depends on the success of one or two arguments. Even if we put that concern aside, this approach doesn't secure specific religious claims of the sort that are in contention between the Abrahamic faiths, for example.

The most popular approach to the problem of the gaps (with respect to both content and strength) is to offer what is known as a cumulative case: a framework that seeks to harness the combined power of a range of distinct NTAs to try to establish the existence of a God with the various classical attributes. Arguably, there is no alternative to offering a cumulative case if one is seeking natural theological justification for a religiously specific form of theism that makes claims about how God has acted in history; one will need a cumulative case that involves some historical-experiential arguments. There is no single agreed-upon framework for how a cumulative case should be constructed and evaluated. Broadly speaking, we can distinguish between informal and formal approaches, and among the latter we can distinguish between deductive and probabilistic approaches.

R. Douglas Geivett (1995: chs. 6 and 7) develops a cumulative case in which different deductive arguments secure different divine attributes. On this approach there could be multiple arguments offered for a given attribute, so that there would be justificatory overdetermination. The main challenge for this approach is how to establish that one and the same being is the bearer of all the different attributes purportedly established by the various deductive arguments. It would seem that at this point, things cannot stay strictly deductive. Some kind of inductive or abductive argument is required to make the case that one and the same being is the bearer of all the different attributes that have allegedly been established by deductive arguments. T. Ryan Byerly (2019) and Justin Mooney (2019) have developed a framework that purports to show that a single bearer of attributes is a superior explanation for the conclusions of a range of NTAs than multiple bearers of these various attributes.

Turning to probabilistic approaches, it is typical to employ the framework of Bayes theorem. There are several different (mathematically equivalent) ways to state Bayes theorem, but perhaps the most intuitively accessible is the odds form:

Ratio of posteriors   *Ratio of priors*   *Ratio of likelihoods (Bayes factor)*

$$\frac{Pr\,(H1|\,E_{1\ldots n})}{Pr\,(H2|\,E_{1\ldots n})} \;=\; \frac{Pr\,(H1\,)}{Pr\,(H2\,)} \;\times\; \frac{Pr(E_{1\ldots n}|H1)}{Pr(E_{1\ldots n}|H2)}$$

The odds form supplies a formula for calculating what is known as the ratio of posteriors: how much more probable some hypothesis H1 is conditional on some body of evidence $E_{1\ldots n}$ than a rival hypothesis H2 is conditional on that same body of evidence. This ratio is equal to the product of two other ratios. Firstly, there is the ratio of priors: how much more probable H1 is than H2, logically prior to $E_{1\ldots n}$ being taken into account. Secondly, there is the ratio of likelihoods (also known as the Bayes factor): how much more likely $E_{1\ldots n}$ is given the truth of H1 than given the truth of H2. This latter ratio is a measure of how strongly $E_{1\ldots n}$ supports H1 over H2. In the context of natural theology, H1 is usually the hypothesis of theism, though sometimes it is the hypothesis of a particular version of theism, such as Christianity or Islam. Usually, H2 is the hypothesis of naturalism. And $E_{1\ldots n}$ is some collection of evidence that is alleged to support theism over naturalism. A cumulative case is constructed by taking the conclusions of various arguments to constitute the different items of evidence that make up $E_{1\ldots n}$. Provided that E_1 and E_2 are two genuinely independent pieces of evidence, each of which lend support individually to H1, then the probability of H1 conditional on both pieces of evidence is greater than the probability of H1 conditional on only one of these pieces of evidence.[8] By aggregating a large number of items of evidence (i.e., a large number of independent NTAs) that each lends some degree of support to theism, the aim is to build a case that supports theism far more strongly than any argument taken in isolation is capable of doing (see Poston 2018).

One challenge for this framework is how to capture the force of deductive arguments, given that the Bayesian approach only works if one grants a nonzero probability to E given the falsity of H, whereas deductive arguments are usually seen as issuing conclusions that are certain if the argument is sound. A way around this might be to see deductive arguments as yielding conclusions that have an epistemic probability of less than 1, specifically, as having a probability that is no greater than the probability of the argument's least certain premise.[9]

---

[8] Brandon Fitelson (2001) offers an account of independence of evidence according to which two pieces of evidence, E_1 and E_2, are confirmationally independent of one another just in case the degree to which E_1 confirms H is unaffected by whether or not E_2 is known, and the degree to which E_2 confirms H is similarly unaffected by whether or not E_1 is known.

[9] Note that it is common to hold that one can legitimately assign an epistemic probability between 0 and 1 to a proposition that is either metaphysically necessary or metaphysically impossible.

There are yet other challenges to this framework. One is the so-called problem of the priors, the issue of how one is supposed to work out the prior probabilities of theism and its rival hypotheses. Perhaps the most popular way of trying to settle on estimates of the priors is by evaluating the simplicity of a hypothesis, though this is by no means a straightforward issue (Swinburne 2004: ch. 5; Miller 2016). Perhaps the biggest challenge, however, is as follows. There is considerable difficulty in achieving consensus over the extent to which individual items in the cumulative case lend support to theism, and when the case gets large and complex, there are increasingly many points at which disagreements can enter in, all of which raise the question: Is the formal apparatus really helping us get clearer on things at the big picture level, or are we ultimately thrown back on something more impressionistic? Do we ultimately still have to resort to a holistic judgment about which metaphysical picture makes best sense of everything?

This brings us to informal approaches to developing a cumulative case. Advocates of such approaches are usually motivated by concerns of the sort just outlined regarding the inescapability of employing some sort of holistic, sense-making judgment. Defenders of such an approach include Basil Mitchell (1973) and William Abraham (1987). Paul Draper (2010) has sketched the outlines of what he calls an "emergent" cumulative case, which similarly lacks a formal framework. Draper's approach asks us to consider whether, when one steps back from the details and surveys a whole range of striking phenomena (consciousness, morality, cosmic fine-tuning, religious experience, etc.), it is more plausible to regard them all as being ultimately illusory, as naturalism requires, or instead to take them at face value. The advantage of an informal approach is that it can incorporate evidence of any kind – including non-propositional evidence, if such a thing exists – owing to the absence of a formal apparatus that may or may not be well suited to appreciating the force of various types of evidence. The obvious concern is that such an approach lacks the precision that philosophers are so keen on. But perhaps the lack of precision is simply an appropriate acknowledgment of the artificiality of attempting to fit a vast array of considerations regarding the nature of ultimate reality into a neat, formal framework. At any rate, an informal approach to constructing a cumulative case is surely the truest to how we do, in reality, choose a worldview.

1.4 The Problem of Accessibility

Being able to evaluate NTAs requires a measure of philosophical training. If one needs to be able to evaluate NTAs in order to gain any epistemic benefit from them, then those without such training – the majority of religious believers – are not in a position to derive any epistemic benefit from NTAs.

This is an unfortunate situation, because even if one can have justified religious beliefs that are not based on NTAs – and the debate about that issue rumbles on[10] – it is highly plausible that the justification for one's beliefs can be substantially increased by NTAs. This is what might be termed the problem of accessibility.

One can discern three basic responses to this problem. The first is simply to affirm it: those without philosophical training cannot benefit from NTAs. The second is to hold that laypeople can gain epistemic justification derivatively from philosophical experts in their communities. A third position is to view laypeople as being able to have an intuitive grasp of the data to which many NTAs appeal, and thus as being able to gain epistemic justification from having cognitive contact with the features of reality that are the basis for NTAs. The first of these positions needs little elaboration. Let us consider in more depth the second and third positions.

It is natural to think that laypeople can be justified in holding some beliefs for which they themselves are not able to evaluate the evidence – the belief that electrons exist, for example – provided they are aware of the existence of experts in the relevant fields who do understand the evidence and view it as supporting the belief in question. The vast majority of a typical layperson's scientific beliefs are like this. Some have suggested that something similar might hold for religious beliefs (Wykstra 1998, 2002).[11] The obvious challenge to this position is that there is known to be substantial disagreement among the relevant body of philosophical experts concerning the cogency of NTAs. That is not to deny that some of the premises of some NTAs enjoy a wide consensus of expert opinion – for example, the S5 rule in modal logic, which is a premise of the modal ontological argument. But it is also fairly clear that no such consensus exists when it comes to the overall evaluation of any given NTA's success or failure. It should be emphasized that this is also the case for the vast majority of interesting philosophical debates that one could care to name.[12] All in all, it is hard to see the situation for religious beliefs as being closely parallel to the situation for belief in electrons when it comes to the potential for gaining justification simply by trusting experts. With that said, whereas the barriers to a layperson gaining firsthand acquaintance with the evidence for electrons are very high, they are somewhat lower when it comes to evaluating some (though not all) of the arguments for God's existence.

---

[10] See Chapter 3 of this volume.

[11] Wykstra's position is a nuanced one, in which believers need some firsthand contact with evidence that supports their beliefs, but believers can legitimately rely on experts to help them counter certain kinds of defeaters.

[12] Indeed, theism could be said to be in a better situation than many philosophical views under consideration today in terms of the sheer quantity of distinct arguments that have been put forward in its defense (Poston 2018).

The basic idea with the third position is that the data which serve as the premises for NTAs are in fact widely accessible to ordinary people, even if the technical formulations of those data developed by philosophers are not. The foremost defender of this view, C. Stephen Evans (2010), highlights several examples of what he terms "natural theistic signs," that is, experiences that the vast majority of people have, which bring them into cognitive contact with the data that serve as the basis of various NTAs: a sense of "cosmic wonder" that there should exist a world at all (cosmological arguments); the apprehension of apparent providential order in the world (teleological arguments); and an awareness of objectively binding ethical obligations and of the infinite worth of human persons (moral arguments). I would add another: awe at the fact of conscious experience, and its oddity in contrast to the world of unfeeling physical matter (arguments from consciousness).

There are a couple of suggestions on offer as regards how exactly it is that someone who is aware of one of these theistic natural signs might thereby gain epistemic justification for her religious beliefs. One suggestion is that an experience of a natural theistic sign might serve as the trigger for someone to form a basic belief in God (i.e., a belief that involves no inference at all), which arises spontaneously in something like the way that a belief that your friend is sad is triggered by your experience of seeing her tear-stained face. The possibility of gaining justification in this way depends upon the truth of a theory of epistemic justification on which there are such things as properly basic beliefs (beliefs that are justified despite not being based on inferences) and on which experiences of the sort at issue can serve as an appropriate stimulus for a properly basic belief.[13] Another suggestion is that someone might make an informal inference (perhaps unconsciously) from a natural theistic sign, akin to the sort of quick and unconscious inference we make in everyday life all the time, for example, upon observing that a home's curtains are drawn and the driveway is empty, one concludes that the occupants are away. The possibility of gaining justification in this way depends upon the truth of a theory of epistemic justification on which an inferential belief can be justified even if the person does not fully grasp the way in which the evidence supports the belief, provided that it does in fact support it.[14] Given that both of these suggestions comport with views in contemporary epistemology that are fairly widely held, the prospects for this sort of response to the problem of accessibility look bright.

---

[13] The view known as phenomenal conservatism, which is an increasingly popular version of internalism about justification, holds that if it strongly seems to you that *p*, then you are *prima facie* justified in believing that *p* (see Tucker 2013). Phenomenal conservatism is compatible with someone's having a properly basic belief that is non-inferentially prompted by awareness of a natural theistic sign.

[14] Conee and Feldman's (2004) influential version of internalist evidentialism allows that someone can be justified in believing *p* on the basis of evidence E without grasping the evidential support relation between E and *p*, so long as such a relation does exist.

2 Evidence and Religious Belief

Kevin McCain

2.1 Evidentialism

Evidentialism is the position in epistemology that justification supervenes on the evidence that one has. More precisely, the two most prominent contemporary Evidentialists, Earl Conee and Richard Feldman, formulate the key thesis of Evidentialism this way:

EJ Doxastic attitude *D* toward proposition *p* is epistemically justified for *S* if and only if having *D* toward *p* fits the evidence that S has at *t* (1985: 15).

Importantly, EJ is a principle of *propositional justification* rather than *doxastic justification*. Propositional justification concerns the justification one has for a particular doxastic attitude regardless of whether one has that attitude or not. For instance, it may be that believing that God exists is justified for Jones even though Jones is agnostic. Doxastic justification concerns the status of one's actual doxastic attitudes. If Jones suspends judgment about God's existence when her evidence on the whole supports believing that God exists, Jones's suspending judgment is unjustified.

Often those who oppose Evidentialism when it comes to religious beliefs take aim at Evidentialism as a theory of something other than propositional justification. Some might attack Evidentialism on the grounds that more than just having sufficiently strong evidence is required for doxastic justification. However, Evidentialists agree that in addition to having sufficiently strong evidence, doxastic justification requires basing one's doxastic attitude on that evidence, which many think involves one's evidence causing the doxastic attitude in the appropriate way.[1] Others might fault Evidentialism as an account of warrant (where "warrant" refers to whatever is needed to turn true belief into knowledge). Of course, this too misses the mark. After all, presumably for a true belief to amount to knowledge, that true belief must be doxastically justified, and we have seen already that Evidentialism allows that more than evidence is required for doxastic justification. Additionally, the lesson of Gettier's famous examples is that justified true beliefs might fall short of being knowledge.[2] Thus, Evidentialists will readily admit that in

---

[1] See McCain (2012) and Korcz (2021).   [2] See Gettier (1963).

addition to a belief fitting sufficiently strong evidence and being based upon that evidence in the appropriate way, warrant requires satisfying some condition that can block Gettier cases.

With these clarifications in hand, we can state more clearly what Evidentialism about religious beliefs says. According to Evidentialism, right now Jones has justification for believing that (G) God exists if and only if believing that G fits the evidence that Jones has now. What about a case where Jones has the belief that G? Evidentialism says that it is *necessary* (but not sufficient) for Jones's belief that G to be justified that she has sufficient evidence for it. Similarly for warrant and knowledge, Evidentialism insists that Jones can have a warranted belief that G or knowledge that G *only if* she has sufficiently strong evidence for believing G. To sum up, if Evidentialism is true, then Jones has propositional justification for G just in case G fits the evidence she has at the time in question. Evidentialists add to EJ that if G fits Jones's evidence and she bases her belief that G in the appropriate way on that evidence, her belief is justified; and, if Jones's justified belief that G satisfies whatever is required to block Gettier cases, that belief is warranted (and if true, knowledge).[3]

The reader will have noticed that two key terms in EJ need to be spelled out before we can properly evaluate Evidentialism: evidence and fit.[4] As we will see, some objections to Evidentialism arise because of mistaken views about the former and others because of mistaken views about the latter.

2.2 Evidentialism Requires Too Much?

Perhaps the most common objection to Evidentialism applied to religious beliefs is that it requires too much for justification. The gist of this objection is that once we spell out what counts as evidence for religious beliefs, we find that most ordinary believers simply cannot satisfy the requirements imposed by Evidentialism. It is widely accepted that the religious beliefs of many ordinary believers, even if false, can be justified. Hence, the objection concludes that Evidentialism must be false. One of the most prominent expressions of this objection comes from Alvin Plantinga (2000b: 70, emphasis in original), who says, "Evidentialism is the view that belief in God is rationally justifiable or acceptable only if there is *good evidence* for it, where good

---

[3] If Moon (2012) is correct that warrant entails truth, then the parenthetical remark is superfluous.

[4] Another central issue concerns what it is for S to "have" something as evidence. Fortunately, this issue will not be a concern for our purposes, so we can set it aside here. For those interested in evidence possession, McCain (2014: ch. 3) is a good starting point for exploring the issue.

evidence would be arguments from other propositions that one knows."[5] Unsurprisingly, after explaining Evidentialism in this way, Plantinga persuasively argues that this has extremely skeptical results – both for religious beliefs and even general beliefs about the world around us. After all, even if there are two dozen or so good arguments for God's existence, as Plantinga has claimed, it is likely that many ordinary believers are not familiar with most of them.[6]

Many Evidentialists readily acknowledge that Plantinga is right in arguing against the view that he calls "Evidentialism" because they deny the view of evidence that Plantinga assumes in making his argument.[7] Nevertheless, Plantinga's argument is very helpful in that it highlights that Evidentialists should not accept that evidence only consists of arguments from propositions one knows. In response to this sort of objection, Evidentialists insist on different accounts of evidence, the most prominent of which we will turn to now.

2.3 Evidentialism Requires Too Little?

Many Evidentialists seek to avoid the problem highlighted in the previous section by claiming that justifying evidence is much easier to come by than arguments from what one knows.[8] These Evidentialists suggest that we should understand evidence as consisting of seemings/appearances.[9] In other words many Evidentialists follow Michael Huemer (2007: 30) in accepting Phenomenal Conservatism (PC):

If it seems to S that p, then, in the absence of defeaters S thereby has some degree of justification for believing that p.

The general idea here is that PC can be understood as a theory of evidence and evidence possession – evidence consists of seemings, and one has a particular item of evidence when one has a particular seeming.[10] Many of these "PC Evidentialists" hold that strength of justification is just a matter of the strength

---

[5] See also VanArragon (2020).
[6] See Walls and Dougherty (2018) for Plantinga's original lecture about the "two dozen or so" arguments as well as recent discussions of those arguments.
[7] See Long (2010) and Dougherty and Tweedt (2015). Wykstra (1989), (2001) defends a version of Evidentialism that is close to the target of Plantinga's critique. However, Wykstra's "sensible evidentialism" doesn't require that individual believers have arguments for their religious beliefs but only that such arguments are available in the community. See Tucker (2011) for criticism of Wykstra's view from an Evidentialist perspective.
[8] See Tucker (2011), Dougherty (2020), Gage and McAllister (2020), and McAllister (2020).
[9] I use "seeming" and "appearance" interchangeably throughout this chapter.
[10] See Tucker (2011).

of one's seemings.[11] In other words, the more strongly it seems to Jones that *p*, the more justification Jones has for believing that *p*.

In order to get a handle on PC, it will be helpful to say a bit about what exactly seemings are. While there is some controversy as to the exact nature of seemings, most proponents of PC accept the view that they are a particular kind of experience.[12] A seeming is an *experience* that has *propositional content* or some type of *accuracy conditions* that allows that experience to *represent* mind-independent states of affairs with a particular sort of forcefulness – that is, the feel of a mental state whose content reveals how things actually are. So, when Jones has a seeming that *p*, she has a particular experience which represents the content that *p* in a way in which that content feels true. For example, when looking out her window Jones may have a seeming that (*s*) the sun is shining. Jones's seeming in this case is a perceptual experience that presents the content *s* to her in a way that is very different from how she might host the content *s* while sitting in a dark room imagining a sunny day. In the case of Jones's perceptual experience, *s* strikes her as true and something that is imposed upon her by the way the world is; imagining *s* lacks this forcefulness.[13]

Now that we have a clearer picture of the nature of seemings, it is easy to see how PC allows Evidentialists to avoid the charge of requiring too much for justification. According to PC Evidentialists, all that is required for Jones to have justification for believing that (*G*) God exists is that it seems to Jones that *G* and she lacks defeaters (she doesn't have good reason to think that *G* is false or good reason to think that her seeming that *G* is produced in an untrustworthy manner). PC Evidentialists argue that these conditions are easy to meet, and so they claim that Evidentialism doesn't preclude ordinary believers from having justification for religious beliefs.

Admittedly, invoking PC clearly avoids the problem of making the justification of religious beliefs too difficult. However, some argue that it avoids this problem by landing squarely in another one – it makes the justification of religious beliefs too easy. Thomas Senor (2020: 153, emphasis in original) forcefully presses this objection:

Suppose I look at my leaf-covered lawn and it *really* seems to me that there are precisely 2,397 leaves there. I haven't counted the leaves, and I have no special leaf-counting perceptual faculty. If [PC] is correct, then I have very good reason – good evidence – for thinking that there are 2,397 leaves in my lawn. But if that

---

[11] See Dougherty (2020) and Gage and McAllister (2020).

[12] See the essays in Tucker (2013) for various views about the nature of seemings. See McCain and Moretti (2021: ch. 3) for criticisms of views of seemings contrary to the one described in this chapter.

[13] Supporters of PC contend that there are many kinds of seemings in addition to perceptual seemings: a priori, mnemonic, moral, and perhaps others. See McCain and Moretti (2021: ch. 1) for discussion.

is all there is to justification, then there's no reason to be interested in it since *anything* can be justified for anyone if only it *seems* to them to be true.[14]

There are a few responses to this objection that PC Evidentialists have offered. The first is simply to bite the bullet and allow that justification is really this easy.[15] Of course, many find this response unpersuasive. Another response is to insist that seemings such as Senor's leaf seeming wouldn't be very strong, so such a seeming would only provide minimal justification.[16] Of course, there's no in principle reason for thinking that such crazy seemings couldn't be strong. Hence, this response fares little better than the previous. A much better response is to emphasize that PC says that seemings provide justification in the *absence of defeaters* and then insist that in cases like Senor's, the person is apt to have defeaters.[17] While this response is better by far than simply biting the bullet or insisting that crazy seemings can't be strong, it's still not very compelling. After all, it isn't hard to see how someone like Senor might respond: "What if it strongly seems to me that there are 2,397 leaves in my lawn and I don't have defeaters for this?" Again, there's no in principle reason for thinking that this couldn't happen. In such a case it seems that the PC Evidentialist is forced to admit that Senor is not only justified in believing that there are 2,397 leaves in his lawn in this case, but also that he is *strongly justified*.

Some, particularly those sympathetic to PC Evidentialism, may be inclined to say that in the case just described it isn't counterintuitive to think that Senor really does have justification for believing that there are 2,397 leaves in his lawn since he has the relevant seeming and no defeaters. Others, however, will find this result unacceptable. Hence, they will insist that PC Evidentialism fails to provide a plausible account of how Evidentialism can be true of religious beliefs (or beliefs more generally). While there are additional serious problems facing PC Evidentialism, the details of those problems aren't important for present purposes.[18] It is enough to recognize that the success of PC Evidentialism is dubious.

Where does this leave Evidentialism about religious beliefs? We might be inclined to think that Evidentialism is in dire straits. The most popular way of avoiding the charge that Evidentialism requires too much for justification runs

[14] I have put "PC" in place of "RC*" (which is a particular version of PC Evidentialism) in this quote. The exact details of RC* are irrelevant since the general concern is a challenge for PC Evidentialism more broadly. See also DePoe (2020) and VanArragon (2020) for similar objections.

[15] Dougherty (2020) suggests this response. Also see McNabb (2019), who suggests that beliefs based on such seemings might be warranted.

[16] See Gage and McAllister (2020).

[17] See Gage and McAllister (2020). There is a concern, however, that PC Evidentialism requires supplementation in order to really deliver on this result because it lacks an account of defeat. For more on this concern see McCain (2018) and McCain and Moretti (2021: ch. 2).

[18] See McCain and Moretti (2021) for discussion of the most pressing of these problems.

smack into the problem of making justification far too easy. Before despairing, Evidentialists would be advised to see if there is an Evidentialist theory that lies between these two extremes. Fortunately, there is.

2.4 An Evidentialism That Is Just Right

In the previous section we saw that PC Evidentialism seems incapable of addressing the challenge facing Evidentialism concerning religious beliefs. Importantly, as we will see in this section, the problem with PC Evidentialism isn't that PC is totally misguided. PC Evidentialists are on the right track in claiming that seemings are evidence, but they are mistaken in insisting that justificatory differences boil down to differences in how strong seemings are.[19] Evidential fit is more nuanced than simply strength of seemings. To see how realizing this can help Evidentialism meet the challenge of not requiring too much or too little for the justification of religious beliefs, let's look at a more plausible seemings-based Evidentialist theory.

Phenomenal Explanationism is an Evidentialist theory that combines PC as a theory of evidence with an explanationist theory of evidential "fit."[20] Roughly, explanationist theories in general hold that propositions are supported by a body of evidence when they are part of the best explanation of that evidence. Let's take a look. [21]

Phenomenal Explanationism (PE)

Believing p is justified for S at t if and only if at t:

(1) S has total evidence, E (where this is ultimately constituted by seemings);[22]
(2) either
    (i) p is the best (sufficiently good) explanation of e (where e is a subset of E),
       or

---

[19] The monolithic view of seemings that many proponents of PC accept, where the only thing that makes a difference when it comes to justification is a seeming's strength, is mistaken. In fact, there are importantly different kinds of seemings and these differences can yield differences when it comes to justification regardless of the strength of the seemings. For more on this, see McCain and Moretti (2021: ch. 3).

[20] The need for a pairing of PC and explanationism to yield *PE* is explored much more fully in McCain and Moretti (2021).

[21] For a more in-depth discussion of PE see McCain and Moretti (2021), particularly ch. 4.

[22] S's evidence "ultimately" consists of seemings in the sense that seemings are evidence, and beliefs are evidence when and only when they are justified (either directly by seemings or indirectly on the basis of seemings by way of other beliefs whose justification ultimately depends upon seemings).

(ii) p is an explanatory consequence of the best (sufficiently good) explanation of e (i.e., the relevant explanation of e would provide an explanation of p's truth that is significantly better than the explanation it would provide of $\sim p$'s truth);[23]

(3)   it is not the case that p fails to satisfy (i) and (ii) with respect to e because of the additional evidence included in E.

It will be helpful to elaborate *PE*. First, *disbelieving p* at t is justified for S, on *PE*, if and only if at t believing $\sim p$ is justified for S. Furthermore, *withholding belief/suspending judgment* about p and $\sim p$ at t is justified for S, on *PE*, if and only if at t neither believing p nor believing $\sim p$ is justified for S.[24]

Second, *PE* is a general account of propositional justification – it applies to inferential justification and noninferential justification. Indeed, *PE* admits of noninferential, immediate justification. Thus, it is not a necessary condition of *PE* that in every case (or even in most cases), S must make an inference in order to be justified in believing that p. Instead, *PE* simply requires that p bear certain explanatory relations to S's evidence – whether the latter is made up of appearances, beliefs, or a combination of the two – for believing p to be justified for S.

Third, although there are many different accounts of the nature of explanation, it is not necessary to settle the issue to understand *PE*.[25] A promising general approach to explanation that can be assumed here is Jaegwon Kim's idea that "explanations track dependence relations" of all kinds – causal relations, mereological relations, the relation of constitution, and so on.[26] Importantly, "explanation" in *PE* should be understood to mean *potential* explanation (an explanation that would *if true* explain the phenomena in question) rather than *actual* explanation. The reason for this is that it seems

---

[23] When an explanation makes p more probable than $\sim p$, that explanation provides a better explanation of p than it does of $\sim p$, all other things being equal. When an explanation entails p, it provides no explanation at all of $\sim p$. Hence, logical consequences of the best explanation of e are explanatory consequences of that explanation in at least a minimal sense.

[24] This captures the intuition that withholding belief/suspending judgment about p and $\sim p$ is justified whenever p and $\sim p$ are *equally supported* by the relevant available evidence. There may be other senses of withholding belief/suspending judgment, such as when one does not believe or disbelieve p because one has *no evidence* relevant to p and $\sim p$ at all. Further, there may be other conditions that are required for one to count as suspending judgment, but whether there are or not won't affect the discussion in this chapter (see Friedman (2017) for more on suspension of judgment).

Though focused on course-grained attitudes (belief, disbelief, and withholding), *PE* can be adapted to discussions of degrees of confidence/credence as well. The general idea is that *PE* yields that the more evidence and the better the explanation that p provides of that evidence, the higher the credence in p that is justified for S.

[25] In fact some (e.g., Poston 2014) argue that "explanation" is a primitive concept that cannot be given a full analysis at all. We can remain neutral on this issue though.

[26] See Kim (1994: 68). For more on how this ecumenical approach captures the relations that the most prominent theories of explanation deem explanatory, see McCain (2015).

plausible that in at least some cases, one can be justified in believing things that are false. A falsehood is never the best explanation of some evidence in the sense of being the *actual* explanation, but it may be the best *potential* explanation when one is not aware that it is a falsehood.

Fourth, for an explanation p of e to be the *best*, all that is required is that there is no equally good rival explanation of e. Suppose p explains e. q is a rival explanation of e if and only if p and q each offer an explanation of e and they cannot both be true. Hence, it is possible that p is the best explanation even if there are multiple explanations of e that are tied for best. What matters is that p is a nonredundant part of *all* of the best explanations of e. If there exists an explanation of e that is tied for the best explanation, and this explanation does not include p as a nonredundant part, then p is not the *best* explanation. This is the case because there is an equally good explanation of the evidence that does not include p as a nonredundant part.[27] Of course, it is difficult to spell out exactly what it takes for one explanation to be as good as, or better than, another. Fortunately, it is not necessary to settle this issue here. It is enough to recognize that this will be determined by the sorts of virtues typically appealed to in discussions of inference to the best explanation – things like explanatory power, predictive power, simplicity, and so on.[28]

Fifth, there is a direct link between the quality of an explanation and the strength of the justification provided by it. As we have seen, *PE* maintains that S has some justification for believing p on the basis of e only if p is the best *sufficiently good* explanation of e, or p is an explanatory consequence of the best *sufficiently good* explanation of e. Furthermore, we have seen that p is an explanatory consequence of the best explanation of e only if the best explanation of e would provide a *significantly better* explanation of p than of $\sim p$. The reason for these clauses is that it is not enough that an explanation simply be the best for p to be justified; it must also be a sufficiently good explanation. After all, it could be that all the explanations, including the best, are very poor explanations. Additionally, for S to have some justification for believing p because it is an explanatory consequence of the best explanation of her evidence, p must not only be explained slightly better than $\sim p$ by the best explanation of S's evidence, it also must be explained *significantly better*.

---

[27] An interesting variety of this sort of case arises when there are multiple equally good explanations of e and almost all of them contain p, but some small minority (perhaps just one) does not. Does this make it so that believing that p is not justified? Yes. After all, there is an explanation that is as good as all the others that does not include p. That said, in such a case it is likely that the best explanation for why there are multiple explanations that include p and only a small number that do not is that the probability of p is n (where 'n' is perhaps above .5). Hence, while believing that p is not justified, believing that p has a particular (perhaps high) probability may be justified. This sort of case is analogous to ones in which one has purely statistical evidence for p.

[28] See McCain (2022) for further discussion of important explanatory virtues.

Now that we have *PE* firmly in hand, let's look at why it is an Evidentalism that is just right. To begin with, *PE* doesn't fall prey to the sort of objection that Plantinga raises. *PE* doesn't make the justification of religious beliefs too hard because it doesn't restrict evidence to arguments from what one knows. Instead, it allows that seemings are evidence and that they can justify beliefs when the truth of the belief is the best explanation for S's evidence. *PE* doesn't make justification too easy either. Recall Senor's case of it seeming to him that there are 2,397 leaves in his lawn. In such a case *PE* delivers the intuitive result that Senor isn't justified in believing this. Importantly, it does so even in the case where Senor's seeming is particularly strong and he lacks defeaters. How is this? Even in a case where Senor has a strong seeming that there are 2,397 leaves in his lawn, without appropriate background evidence concerning having such a faculty, having counted the leaves, etc., the fact that there are 2,397 leaves in his lawn isn't the best sufficiently good explanation of his evidence. In such a case there are several rival explanations that are just as good given the evidence – Senor is suffering from some sort of mental illness, he is engaging in strange wishful thinking, and so on. Hence, *PE* says that Senor isn't justified in believing that there are 2,397 leaves in his lawn.

Before concluding that *PE* delivers on the promise of accounting for the justification of ordinary believers may have for religious beliefs, it is important to at least briefly consider what sort of evidence ordinary believers are apt to have and how it is that *PE* says they can have justification. Consider Jones's belief that (*G*) God exists. Plausibly, it seems to Jones that *G*. However, as we've seen, given *PE* it is likely that Jones's mere seeming isn't sufficient on its own to justify her belief. The reason for this is that it is likely that there are rival explanations for her seeming that are as good, or nearly so, as that *G* is true (we return to the issue of rival explanations in the next section). Nevertheless, this doesn't mean that *PE* will yield the result that Jones lacks justification for believing that *G*. For one thing, it is possible that Jones has had a religious experience of God. Such an experience would itself be a seeming, but of a special sort. It is more than just the seeming that God exists. This kind of seeming includes an apparent truth-maker for that content – something in Jones's experience apparently represents God's existence. To appreciate the difference between this sort of seeming and the mere seeming that God exists, let's consider an analogy. In a case where Jones has a perceptual seeming of a horse partly behind a fence post, it seems to Jones that the horse has a middle (even though the horse's middle isn't presented in her experience because of the presence of the fencepost). It also seems to Jones that the horse has a tail, but that seeming comes with an accompanying presentation of the tail – it is actually presented to Jones in her experience. Though Jones may have justification for accepting both that the horse has a middle and that it has a tail, the seeming itself appears to provide sufficient justification for believing the horse has a tail but not for believing that the horse has a middle (Jones will need to rely upon background evidence to justify believing the horse has a middle).[29] Similarly, if Jones has a seeming that includes a presentation of God's existence in the seeming itself, that seeming can justify believing G because the best explanation for an awareness of God is that G.

Of course, one might worry that most ordinary believers haven't had these sorts of experiences of God. So, it is likely that Jones simply has the seeming that G without having an awareness of God's existing. It is still plausible that Jones can have justification for believing G though. Ordinary believers, even if they aren't aware of good arguments for God's existence, have a tremendous amount of evidence from the testimony of others. This testimony might simply be in the form of knowing that many intelligent people believe that God exists, or it might be testimony concerning the occurrence of miracles, or a number of other sorts of relevant information.[30] Given this wealth of evidence, it isn't implausible to think that the best explanation of Jones's *total evidence* is that G. Hence, *PE* secures the result that ordinary believers can have justification for religious beliefs without lowering the standards for justification to the point that justification is uninterestingly easy to obtain.

2.5 Are There Other Explanations Though?

At this point one might worry that *PE* leads to skepticism about religious beliefs. After all, there are a number of explanations for why it seems to Jones that (G) God exists, and many of these explanations don't include G's truth. For instance, a potential explanation of Jones's seeming is that she really wants God to exist, and her seeming is a result of wishful thinking. Another potential explanation is that humans have evolved to believe in God because the mechanisms that produce seemings like Jones's conveyed a survival advantage upon ancient humans who possessed those mechanisms. Either of these possibilities could explain why it seems to Jones that G even though G is not true. Hence, one might think that *PE* is committed to denying that ordinary believers have justified religious beliefs.

This worry is partly correct. There are cases where *PE* will yield the result that religious beliefs are unjustified. But, of course, this is exactly as it should be. Let's assume that Jones merely has the seeming that G without any experience of God's presence, any testimonial evidence about God's existence, any knowledge of arguments for God's existence, any ties to a religious community, and so on. In this case *PE* yields the result that believing G is

---

[29] See Chudnoff (2013) and McCain and Moretti (2021).
[30] See Anderson and Pruss (2020) on the evidence that testimony provides for miracles.

not justified for Jones because the truth of *G* isn't the best explanation of Jones's very sparse evidence. As we noted there are other potential explanations (wishful thinking, the evolutionary story, and so on) that appear to account for Jones's minimal evidence as well as *G* does. Notice, however, that the case just described is very different from the evidential situation of most ordinary believers. Many ordinary believers have had seemings of God's presence or perhaps other religious experiences. And even those who have not had such experiences themselves are aware of the testimony of those who have. Ordinary believers also tend to have a wealth of additional evidence, from arguments for God's existence to evidence from the teachings of their religious community to simple reflection on the way God has seemed to be active in their lives. Plausibly, in the cases of ordinary believers with all this evidence, *G* is the best explanation of their evidence.

One might still worry – *what if* it turns out that an evolutionary story (without God) or wishful thinking or some other nonreligious hypothesis is the best explanation of the evidence had by ordinary believers? In that case, *PE* says that ordinary believers aren't justified in believing *G*. Again, this seems exactly the right thing to say though. After all, if wishful thinking really is the best explanation of all of one's evidence concerning God's existence, then one doesn't have a good reason to believe God exists. *PE* doesn't guarantee that religious beliefs are justified, nor does it guarantee that they aren't. Rather, *PE* offers a plausible account of when there is sufficient evidence to justify believing that applies to religious beliefs.

2.6 Is This Really Evidentialism?

Phenomenal Explanationism lies in the sweet spot between requiring too much for justification and requiring too little. One might worry that this is too good to be true though. In this case the worry is apt to come from other Evidentialists. Some may worry that *PE* is not internalist enough because it only requires for justification that *p* is the best explanation of one's evidence; it doesn't require that one is aware of this explanatory relation. Consequently, some might think that *PE* avoids the challenges the justification of religious beliefs pose for Evidentialism by giving up on Evidentialism!

In order to appreciate this objection and why it is misguided, it is important to say a bit about the difference between internalist and externalist theories of justification. All internalists about justification are committed to mentalism – the idea that any two subjects who are mentally alike are alike with respect to justification. So, if S_1 and S_2 are mental duplicates, then for any proposition, if believing that proposition is justified for S_1, believing it is justified for S_2, and vice versa. Some internalists are inclined to add further requirements beyond mentalism, such as, for example, the requirement that one is always able to reflect and determine whether believing p is justified.[31] It is this latter sort of access internalist who is apt to object that *PE* isn't really Evidentialism. Let's look at two responses to this objection. First, there can be both internalist and externalist versions of Evidentialism.[32] Hence, even if *PE* were an externalist theory of justification, that wouldn't entail that it isn't a kind of Evidentialism. Second, *PE* is in fact an internalist form of Evidentialism. Admittedly, *PE* doesn't have strong access requirements for justification, but it is nevertheless a form of mentalism. In other words, given *PE*, any two subjects who are mentally alike must be alike with respect to justification. So, *PE* may not be as internalist as some would like, but it's internalist enough.

2.7 Concluding Remarks

We have seen that *PE* is a promising Evidentialist theory that can account for the justification of ordinary believers' religious beliefs. Of course, there may be other Evidentialist theories that can meet the dual challenge of requiring neither too much nor too little of ordinary religious believers. What matters for the present purpose, though, is that the Evidentialist has at least one plausible way of accounting for the justification of religious beliefs. In light of this and the intuitive plausibility of Evidentialism, it would be premature to dismiss Evidentialism when it comes to religious beliefs (or beliefs more generally). Further, it would be a mistake to think that sufficient reason has been given for thinking that evidence isn't necessary for the justification of religious beliefs.[33]

---

[31] See Pryor (2001) for helpful discussion of internalism and externalism.

[32] See Bergmann (2018) for discussion of various externalist forms of Evidentialism.

[33] Thanks to Jonathan Fuqua, John Greco, and Tyler McNabb for helpful comments on an earlier draft of this chapter.

3 Reformed Epistemology

Michael Bergmann

The key idea of Reformed Epistemology is that religious beliefs can be rational even if they are formed and sustained noninferentially, that is, not on the basis of arguments.[1] The contrary view – that religious beliefs can be rational only if held inferentially on the basis of arguments – has, at times, been a popular and even a dominant view in various academic communities. Thus, Reformed Epistemology is controversial and has been a minority position in philosophy of religion, even among certain groups of religious believers who endorse the rationality of their own religious beliefs. But since its inception (in its contemporary incarnation) a little more than forty years ago, it has grown in influence to become one of the more prominent positions, in analytic philosophy of religion, regarding the rationality of religious belief.

Section 3.1 of this chapter will say more about what Reformed Epistemology is and how it has developed. Section 3.2 will review several objections to Reformed Epistemology, along with some responses to them.

3.1 What Is Reformed Epistemology?

3.1.1 The Main Ingredients of the View

As noted above, the main idea of Reformed Epistemology is that religious beliefs can be epistemically appropriate even if they are held noninferentially – that is, not on the basis of inference or argument. Unfortunately, the term 'Reformed Epistemology' as a name for that view can be and has been misleading. The rationale for the name is that the view, at least in the form in which it was introduced into the contemporary discussion four decades ago, was inspired by thinkers in the Reformed tradition in Christianity.[2] But although it is certainly true that the Reformed tradition provides inspiration for the key thesis of Reformed Epistemology, there is nothing in that key thesis that is incompatible with non-Reformed or non-Protestant Christianity, or even

---

[1] Although I will speak most often in this chapter of rationality, Reformed Epistemologists also make this same point about other epistemic virtues such as knowledge, justification, warrant, and entitlement.

[2] See Plantinga (1980, 1983) and Wolterstorff (1983b). Both Plantinga and Wolterstorff are themselves part of the Reformed tradition.

non-Christian religion: Pentecostals, Catholics, and Muslims can adopt Reformed Epistemology's key thesis.[3] For this reason, some have (quite understandably) resisted the 'Reformed Epistemology' label.

Would another name for the view be better? Perhaps. We could distinguish between Inferentialism and Noninferentialism with respect to religious belief: The former says that religious beliefs can be epistemically appropriate only if they are held inferentially (on the basis of arguments); the latter says that religious beliefs can be epistemically appropriate even if they are held noninferentially. Then the name 'Reformed Epistemology' could be replaced with 'Noninferentialism with respect to religious belief.' But the shorter name has become entrenched, so I'll continue to use it.

A simple account of Reformed Epistemology says it *just is* the view that there can be noninferentially rational religious belief. But there are two difficulties with this simple account. To understand the first difficulty, consider *Noninferentialism about belief in electrons*, the view that belief in electrons can be noninferentially rational. One version of this view says that belief in electrons can be noninferentially rational but only if it appropriately depends via testimony on someone else's inferentially rational belief in electrons.[4] For example, according to this version of the view, ordinary high school students can have rational *noninferential* belief in electrons (via testimony from their teachers), but only if someone in the testimonial chain leading to their belief in electrons (e.g., those in the scientific community) rationally believes in electrons *inferentially* on the basis of good arguments. This sort of Noninferentialism applied to religious belief – call it 'Weak Noninferentialism with respect to Religious Belief' (WNR) – says that there can be *noninferentially* rational religious belief, but *only if* it appropriately depends via testimony on someone else's inferentially rational religious belief formed on the basis of good arguments. The difficulty, for our purposes here, is that Reformed Epistemology disagrees with WNR by insisting that S's religious belief that p can be noninferentially rational *even if it's not the case* that there was someone in a testimonial chain leading to S's religious belief that p who rationally believed p inferentially (and even if S's religious belief that p isn't based on testimony at all).[5] Thus, the simple account of Reformed

---

[3] See Baldwin and McNabb (2018) for discussion of non-Christian employment of the key ideas of Reformed Epistemology.

[4] There are two main positions in the epistemology of testimony: reductionism (inspired by Hume), which insists that rational belief via testimony must be inferential (using other belief sources to infer the reliability of testimony before believing its outputs), and nonreductionism (inspired by Reid), which allows for rational belief via testimony to be noninferential. See Leonard (2021) and Lackey (2017) for some discussion of these differing views on testimony. The discussion of testimony in this chapter takes for granted the truth of nonreductionism.

[5] Wykstra (1998) opposes Reformed Epistemology so understood, even though he allows for the truth of WNR.

Epistemology is problematic insofar as it classifies WNR as an instance of Reformed Epistemology when in fact Reformed Epistemologists reject WNR.

To understand the second difficulty with the simple account of Reformed Epistemology, note that some opponents of Reformed Epistemology allow that (contrary to WNR) there *can be* noninferentially rational religious beliefs that don't depend testimonially on inferentially rational religious beliefs.[6] But they add (quite reasonably) that this can occur only if it's *false* that the person holding those noninferential religious beliefs *is or should be* aware of an undefeated defeater for them.[7] The problem arises because this view – which we can call 'Moderate Noninferentialism about Religious Belief' (MNR) – can be endorsed by those who insist that all reflective and informed people *are, or should be,* aware of undefeated defeaters for their noninferential religious beliefs, which keeps all such beliefs from being rational. But Reformed Epistemologists deny that we have good reason to believe that all informed and reflective people are prevented from having noninferentially rational religious belief. Given that MNR is compatible with opposing Reformed Epistemology in this way, it does not adequately capture what Reformed Epistemology is, even though MNR (like WNR) allows that there *can be* noninferentially rational religious belief.[8] Thus, another reason that the simple account of Reformed Epistemology is problematic is that it classifies MNR as an instance of Reformed Epistemology despite the fact that one can endorse MNR while rejecting Reformed Epistemology.

In light of these two difficulties for the simple account of Reformed Epistemology, consider what I'll call 'Strong Noninferentialism about Religious Belief' (SNR):

SNR: (1) A person S's noninferential religious belief that p *can be* rational *even if it's not the case that* that there was someone in a testimonial chain leading to S's belief that p who rationally believed p inferentially (in fact, even if S's belief that p wasn't based on testimony at all); and (2) we have no good reason to deny that there are many *actual cases* of noninferentially rational religious beliefs held by well-informed and reflective people in which it's *false* that these people are or should be aware of an undefeated defeater for these beliefs.[9]

---

[6] So the problem with these opponents, from the perspective of Reformed Epistemology, isn't the same as the problem with WNR.

[7] A defeater for a belief is, roughly, a good reason for thinking that belief is either false or formed in an untrustworthy way. An undefeated defeater is, roughly, a defeater that isn't *itself* defeated by an awareness of good reasons for thinking that defeater is mistaken or untrustworthy.

[8] Goldberg (2014) allows, at least for the sake of argument, that MNR may be true but still opposes Reformed Epistemology in just this way.

[9] We could add that, according to SNR, some of the beliefs that clause (1) says *can be* rational are also beliefs that clause (2) says *actually are* rational (or at least that we have no good reason to deny that they actually are rational).

SNR is closer to what actual Reformed Epistemologists hold. Thus, Reformed Epistemology in this chapter will be understood as equivalent to SNR.[10]

Because the most influential Reformed Epistemologists (i.e., William Alston and Alvin Plantinga) are renowned *externalists* in epistemology, some people have been misled into thinking that Reformed Epistemology is tightly tied to being an externalist in epistemology. (Externalists in epistemology are those who think that our beliefs can be rational *even if we aren't* aware of what those beliefs have going for them; internalists are those who think our beliefs can be rational *only if we are* aware of what they have going for them.[11]) However, Chris Tucker (2011) has shown that Reformed Epistemology can flourish in internalist soil.[12] Thus, some Reformed Epistemologists (both internalist and externalist) think that noninferential religious belief is epistemically appropriate in virtue of being based not inferentially on other beliefs via argument but noninferentially on some sort of *conscious experience*, which is also what many epistemologists (internalist and externalist) think about perceptual belief.[13] Other Reformed Epistemologists – typically externalists – think that noninferential religious belief (like other kinds of noninferential belief) can be epistemically appropriate even if not based on any conscious mental states at all.

In the cases where Reformed Epistemologists think rational noninferential religious beliefs are based on conscious mental states, on which sorts of conscious mental states do they think they are based? One kind of experiential evidence for noninferential theistic belief is dramatic religious experience, including, in particular, perceptual experience taken to be of God.[14] Another more mundane kind of experiential basis for theistic belief consists, in part, of theistic seemings. (A seeming is the conscious experience you have when it seems to you that something is the case; it has the feel of a mental

---

[10] With the proviso, noted earlier, that in place of rationality, some Reformed Epistemologists might speak instead of other epistemic virtues, such as warrant, justification, or entitlement.

[11] For more details on what internalism and externalism in epistemology are, see Bergmann (2006: ch. 1) and Alston (1986a).

[12] Given Wolterstorff's focus (see his 2010) on noninferential *entitlement* for religious beliefs – which requires, mainly, that they are held in accord with the believer's epistemic duties and obligations – his version of Reformed Epistemology might also be construed as internalist (at least by those who think that we generally are or can easily become *aware* of whether we are believing in accord with our epistemic duties and obligations).

[13] Where these externalists and internalists differ from each other is that *externalist* Reformed Epistemologists will think these sorts of noninferential religious and perceptual beliefs are rational in virtue of facts such as that they were formed reliably or in accord with proper function, whereas *internalist* Reformed Epistemologists will think they are rational in virtue of facts such as that they fit the believer's (internally accessible) evidence.

[14] This sort of experience is the focus of Alston (1991).

state "whose content reveals how things really are."[15]) Ordinary theistic seemings – that is, commonly experienced seemings about God – can be triggered by many things.[16] They might be triggered by things causally upstream from and distinct from conscious experience, including things such as the direct activity of God (this is one way of thinking about at least some instances of what the Christian tradition calls 'the testimony of the Holy Spirit'). But they can also be triggered by other experiences, such as feelings of guilt or being forgiven or desperate fear or gratitude; other triggers can be experiences of awe upon perceiving the grandeur and majesty of oceans, mountains, or sky.[17] Another way theistic seemings can arise is in response to the spoken or written testimony of others: we encounter the testimony, and what is said simply seems right.[18] Theistic seemings can also result from ruminating upon what we have learned about the complexity, mysteriousness, and possible origins of the natural world and of the human mind.[19] Thus, the evidence for this sort of noninferential theistic belief needn't consist *solely* of theistic seemings. It can also include observations, experiences, testimonial evidence, and reflections, as well as memories of these in response to which theistic seemings emerge noninferentially. In this way, noninferential belief in God can be like noninferential belief in the mental states of others: in each case, there is the relevant seeming (about God or about the mental states of others); and in each case there are often other kinds of experience that trigger those seemings (i.e., the experiences just mentioned that trigger theistic seemings; or perceptual experiences of facial expression, body language, and tone of voice that trigger seemings about the mental states of others).

---

[15] The quotation is from Tolhurst (1998: 298–9), who is emphasizing the *presentational phenomenology* of seemings, which is the feeling that their propositional content is being presented to you as true. For more discussion of what seemings are, see Bergmann (2021: 131–45).

[16] Plantinga seems to have theistic seemings in mind in his (2000b: 182–3) when he discusses the nature of the experiential evidence involved in the operation of the *sensus divinitatus*, which produces noninferential belief in God. There he notes that the common component of such evidence is doxastic experience, which appears to be the kind of experience involved in having a seeming. For Plantinga's views on doxastic evidence, see Plantinga (2000b: 110–11 and 1993a: 190–3).

[17] Plantinga (2000b:174).

[18] As Plantinga writes (2000b: 250): 'We read Scripture, or something presenting scriptural teaching, or hear the gospel preached, or are told of it by parents, or encounter a scriptural teaching as the conclusion of an argument (or conceivably even as an object of ridicule), or in some other way encounter a proclamation of the Word. What is said simply seems right; it seems compelling; one finds oneself saying, "Yes, that's right, that's the truth of the matter; this is indeed the word of the Lord."'

[19] Peirce (1965 [1908]).

3.1.2 Three Stages in the Development of Reformed Epistemology

The first stage of Reformed Epistemology (in its contemporary form) began in the late 1970s and early 1980s with work by Alvin Plantinga, Nicholas Wolterstorff, and William Alston. This quickly led to the first definitive statements of the view in the 1983 volume *Faith and Rationality*, with papers by the three just mentioned and several other authors as well.[20] One main goal of these early statements was, as Wolterstoff (2001a: 345) emphasizes, "brush-clearing" of the sort Thomas Reid provided in responding to his predecessors. Very roughly, Descartes and Locke insisted that the justification of perceptual beliefs required good deductive or probabilistic arguments for the reliability of perception, arguments that took only what is certain as premises (where what is certain is what we know best via introspection, a priori intuition, and perhaps clear short-term memory). Reid's reply was to highlight the implausible consequences of these views of Descartes and Locke and to insist that we can rely on perception as a source of justified noninferential belief apart from any independent verification of its reliability using other belief sources.[21] The application to the religious case was clear: Reformed Epistemologists claimed that the sources of our non-inferential religious beliefs can be rationally relied on to produce justified noninferential religious beliefs without first independently verifying their reliability using other belief sources. There was much discussion of the troubles associated with the classical foundationalism of Descartes and Locke and the connection between such classical foundationalism and opposition to Reformed Epistemology.[22] Thus, this early stage of Reformed Epistemology exposed the problematic assumptions of Inferentialism about religious belief and argued against them in order to make way for Noninferentialism about religious belief.

Once this negative brush-clearing work was completed, the way was prepared for the second stage of development consisting of several definitive positive accounts of Reformed Epistemology. The most influential and powerful of these were provided by Alston and Plantinga.[23] Alston's 1991 book, *Perceiving God*, defends the view that a kind of *perceptual* experience taken to be of God makes an important contribution to the justification of religious belief. The thought is that, in virtue of being seemingly aware (in a perceptual kind of way) of God's currently doing something or having some property, I can be justified in believing that God is doing that thing or that God has that property. And just as ordinary

---

[20] For helpful summaries of this early history, see Plantinga (1985: 55–64) and Wolterstorff (2001a: 334–45).

[21] See Wolterstorff (1996, and 2001b).   [22] See Plantinga (1983) and Wolterstorff (1983a).

[23] Wolterstorff worked out his version of Reformed Epistemology in Wolterstorff (1995a, 1995b, and 1999) and in other papers in his (2010). His account focused on entitlement rather than, like Plantinga, on warrant or, like Alston, on justification. Wolterstorff's version of Reformed Epistemology didn't get the same attention or have the same influence as the books by Alston and Plantinga discussed in the main text.

perceptual beliefs are noninferentially justified, so also these religious beliefs can be noninferentially justified. Plantinga lays out his positive account of noninferentially warranted religious belief in his 2000 book, *Warranted Christian Belief*, the third member of his "warrant" trilogy.[24] In it, he proposes a model (which he calls the "extended A/C model" because it is inspired by Aquinas and Calvin), according to which Christian belief is produced noninferentially by a cognitive process (i.e., the internal testimony of the Holy Spirit) that is functioning properly in an appropriate cognitive environment, in accord with a design plan successfully aimed at truth.[25] If the model is true, then Christian belief is warranted (i.e., it has enough of what is required to turn true belief into knowledge) – or at least this is so given the account of warrant defended in Plantinga (1993a). Moreover, although Plantinga defends merely the epistemic possibility of this model, he also claims that it is very likely that it or something like it is true, if Christian belief is true. Neither Alston (1991) nor Plantinga (2000b) explicitly emphasize that they are instances of "Reformed Epistemology"; but these books were clearly defending SNR (i.e., Strong Noninferentialism about Religious Belief), though they didn't use that label either.

The third stage of Reformed Epistemology consists of a variety of ways in which the view has been expanded and developed in greater detail since 2000. In the next section, I will briefly describe five such developments.

3.1.3 Five Recent Developments in Reformed Epistemology

First, the understanding of the relationship between Reformed Epistemology and traditional theistic arguments has become increasingly nuanced. Although there are supporters of Reformed Epistemology who express outright disdain for theistic arguments, the more standard approach for Reformed Epistemologists is to think of traditional theistic arguments as valuable even if not completely compelling or necessary.[26] The thought has been that their value lies in the

---

[24] See also Plantinga (1993a and 1993b), the first two members of his "warrant" trilogy, as well as his (2015), which is a shorter and more accessible version of Plantinga (2000b).

[25] This extended A/C model, which focuses on the work of the Holy Spirit, is discussed in Plantinga (2000: ch. 8). The non-extended original A/C model, which focuses on the warrant not of specifically Christian belief but more generic theistic belief, is discussed in Plantinga (2000b: ch. 6). The emphasis in the latter case is not on the testimony of the Holy Spirit but on the workings of a cognitive faculty that Plantinga (following John Calvin) calls the '*sensus divinitatus*'. The idea at work here is one inspired not only by Calvin but also by Aquinas and the New Testament letter of Paul to the Romans, according to which humans have a knowledge of God implanted in them by nature (although this knowledge is often confused and compromised in varying degrees).

[26] Plantinga (1983: 68–71) quotes Karl Barth as someone friendly to Reformed Epistemology who is *opposed* to reliance on theistic arguments. Plantinga's own moderately positive (even if not entirely enthusiastic) attitude toward theistic arguments is evident in his (2018 [1986]), which inspired Walls and Dougherty (2018) – a collection of papers developing two dozen (or so) theistic arguments identified in Plantinga (2018 [1986]).

assistance they provide in warding off objections to theistic belief and in showing skeptics that theism is at least a serious contender for our allegiance, given that the best arguments for it are about as compelling as philosophical arguments for controversial positions can be (which is to say, less than utterly compelling). However, a different Reformed Epistemologist perspective on theistic arguments has been developed by Stephen Evans (2010), Del Ratzsch (2003), and Plantinga (2011: ch. 8). Their suggestion is that many of the standard theistic arguments (e.g., design arguments, cosmological arguments, and moral arguments) take insights that are most powerful when they occur noninferentially and put these insights in the "inferential mode." Consider, as a parallel, the human ability to discern the emotions of others via perception of their facial expressions, tone of voice, and body language. Beliefs formed in this way about the mental states of others are widely viewed as both noninferential and rational. If an effort were made to translate what goes on when we form perception-based beliefs about the mental states of others into argument form – perhaps as arguments meant to prove the existence of other minds undergoing specific mental states – the result would be unimpressive. It would misrepresent what actually happens, given that such beliefs are formed noninferentially rather than inferentially; and it would undervalue the epistemic quality of the beliefs so formed, given that the resulting arguments would seem so weak (due to the fact that they would be unpersuasive to skeptics about other minds). The point made by Evans, Ratzsch, and Plantinga is that something similar is going on with traditional theistic arguments. Stated as arguments, they are far from knockdown proofs of their conclusions. But the best of them capture the central insights involved in the very natural *noninferential* theistic-belief-forming tendencies highlighted by Reformed Epistemologists.

Second, the cognitive science of religion (CSR) has been viewed as a potentially useful resource for examining, supporting, critiquing, and developing Reformed Epistemology. Both CSR and Reformed Epistemology posit that belief in God or gods is instinctively and non-reflectively produced via noninferential belief-forming mechanisms that are widespread and natural in humans. But within CSR, questions remain about the origin, reliability, and purpose of a possible faculty for producing beliefs in God or gods. There are ways to build upon results in CSR to raise objections to Reformed Epistemology.[27] Likewise, there are ways in which the results of CSR can be accommodated by Reformed Epistemology and perhaps even used to give accounts of how the belief-forming mechanisms posited by Reformed Epistemology work.[28] Both CSR research and the assessment of its implications for Reformed Epistemology are still in considerable flux and very much works in progress.

[27] See Marsh (2013), Davis (2020), and De Cruz and De Smedt (2013).
[28] See Clark and Barrett (2010, 2011), Murray (2009), Murray and Goldberg (2009), and Visala (2020).

Third, Michael Rea has proposed an account of noninferential theistic belief formation according to which we read the mind of God via perception of the natural world in much the same way that we read the minds of other humans via perception of their bodies.[29] Rea points out that some perceptual experiences seem to be cognitively impacted. For example, someone who has learned to read Russian sees Cyrillic letters as meaningful whereas others might see them as meaningless squiggles; likewise, a trained ultrasound technician experiences blotches on her screen as limbs of a fetus whereas others see only the blotches. In such cognitively impacted experiences, the way one spontaneously treats one's experience is affected by more than just the raw experience itself. Sometimes the added cognitive ingredient (affecting how we treat our sensory experiences) is provided by training, as in the examples of reading Russian text or ultrasounds. Other times, the added cognitive ingredient may be hardwired into our minds as when we (even as infants) seem to discern via perception the mental states of others; this hardwiring is clearly something in addition to raw experience, given that not everyone has this hardwiring (e.g., there are those on the autism spectrum whose social-emotional agnosia prevents them from effectively discerning emotions in others, despite preserving their raw perceptual experience). Rea suggests that just as our experience of the emotional states of other (possibly immaterial) human minds is due to cognitively impacted experience of purely natural stimuli, so also our experience of God's mind (which provides the basis for noninferential theistic beliefs) is due to cognitively impacted experience of purely natural stimuli.

Fourth, Bergmann (2017) offers an account of how epistemic intuitions play a significant role in accounting for the rationality of both noninferential religious beliefs and objections to such beliefs. (Epistemic intuitions are seemings about epistemic value – such as rationality – much like moral intuitions are seemings about moral value.[30]) In Plantinga's earliest work on Reformed Epistemology, he highlighted Roderick Chisholm's claim that our efforts to understand the nature of rationality are guided by the exemplars of rational belief that we have in mind when we start our theorizing: We consider examples of beliefs that strike us as rational and of beliefs that strike as irrational and we then try to identify what the former beliefs have in common that the latter beliefs lack.[31] Plantinga pointed out that, in doing this, many theists will, quite reasonably, include their noninferential theistic beliefs among the examples of beliefs that strike them as rational.[32] Bergmann

---

[29] See Rea (2018: chs. 6–7, esp. pp. 130–5). Note: This analogy is *not* intended to suggest that the natural world is the body of God.

[30] See the final paragraph of Section 3.1.1 for a discussion of what seemings are.

[31] Note that to say a belief strikes us as rational or irrational is to report an epistemic intuition – a seeming about epistemic value.

[32] See Plantinga (1980: 59–61 and 1983: 75–8) where he makes this point, citing Chisholm (1982).

(2017) emphasizes that these assessments – regarding which beliefs are rational and which aren't – play a crucial *evidential* role in responding to skeptical objections to religious belief and to disagreements on religious matters. Many (though not all) theists have epistemic intuitions, sometimes strong epistemic intuitions, in support of the rationality of their noninferential theistic beliefs. And just as skeptical objections to perception or memory or a priori intuition can be thwarted by strong epistemic intuitions in support of the rationality of noninferential perceptual, memory, and a priori beliefs, so also skeptical objections to the rationality of noninferential theistic beliefs can be undone by strong epistemic intuitions in support of the rationality of such theistic beliefs.[33] With this in mind, we can see that religious disagreement is partly explained by the fact that those involved in these disputes have *different evidence*: in particular, theists often have (as relevant evidence) epistemic intuitions about theistic beliefs that are quite different from the epistemic intuitions had by those who object to theistic belief as false or irrational; so this isn't a case where all relevant evidence is shared by those on both sides of the disagreement.[34] Thus, an understanding of the role of epistemic intuitions had by those with noninferential religious beliefs (and of different epistemic intuitions had by those objecting to such beliefs) can shed light on the cases to be made for and against Reformed Epistemology.

Last, consider the recent "social turn" in religious epistemology, highlighted by the work of John Greco and others.[35] In the early 1990s, Linda Zagzebski worried about what she viewed as Reformed Epistemology's individualistic emphases.[36] One of her concerns was that Reformed Epistemology wasn't sensitive to the social aspects of religious belief formation. But however justified those concerns were with respect to the particular presentations of Reformed Epistemology she had in mind, it's a mistake to think that SNR (i.e., Strong Noninferentialism about Religious Belief, which is how I'm understanding Reformed Epistemology in this chapter) is incompatible with treating the social nature of religious belief with full seriousness. Greco (2021: 162), for example, highlights the fact that testimony is absolutely central to religious belief formation in the Abrahamic faiths. For this reason, it is plausible to insist that any adequate religious epistemology must consider whether testimony-based religious belief can be rational (and both Greco and Zagzebski are right that this point has not been adequately emphasized in

---

[33] For discussion of the way in which strong epistemic intuitions can thwart radical skepticism about perception or memory or a priori intuition, see Bergmann (2021: chs. 6–8). For discussion of a similar dynamic with respect to religious belief, see Bergmann (2017).

[34] For further discussion, see Section 3.2.3 of this chapter. For an account of how conflicting epistemic intuitions of this sort play a similar role in disagreements over radical skepticism, see Bergmann (2021: ch. 12).

[35] See Greco (2009, 2021: ch. 9), Lackey (2017), and Zagzebski (2012).

[36] See Zagzebski (1993).

many contemporary discussions of Reformed Epistemology). However, any epistemology of testimony allowing (as Greco's does[37]) that, under certain conditions, *noninferential testimony-based* beliefs can be rational, can also allow that noninferential testimony-based *religious* belief can be rational, so long as the relevant conditions are satisfied. And Greco (2021: ch. 9) makes the case that the requisite conditions *can* be satisfied by such religious beliefs.

These five developments are just some of the many ways in which Reformed Epistemology has been elaborated in its third (post-2000) stage beyond what we find in the classic statements of the view offered in stage two.

3.2 Reformed Epistemology: Objections and Replies

Understandably, there are many objections to Reformed Epistemology. Space limitations will allow for brief discussion of only three of the more important problems.[38]

3.2.1 The Need for Independent Confirmation

It is widely believed that introspection (i.e., our ability to "look within" and tell what is going on in our own minds) can be rationally relied on without first independently verifying its reliability using other belief sources. And many think that Thomas Reid is right that perception can be treated in this same way. But some belief sources are not like this. Take, for example, the practice of interpreting a set of physical symptoms as manifestations of a particular disease (in a case where this isn't obvious before recent medical advances clarified this relationship). The first objection to Reformed Epistemology says that noninferential religious belief formation is less like introspection and perception and more like the case of belief about a disease based on perception of symptoms not obviously indicative of it.[39]

The reply is much like Reid's reply to Descartes and Locke with respect to perception. Just as epistemic intuition convinced Reid that noninferential perceptual belief is rational without first independently verifying the reliability of perception via other belief sources, so also epistemic intuition convinces many Reformed Epistemologists that noninferential religious belief is rational without first independently verifying the reliability of our noninferential

---

[37] See Greco (2021: chs 2–4).

[38] One of several important objections that I won't have the space to discuss in this chapter is the objection according to which Reformed Epistemology conflicts in important ways with the results of CSR. See notes 27 and 28 for references to work on this objection and responses to it.

[39] See Fales (2003) and Schellenberg (2007: ch. 8).

religious belief sources.[40] Moreover, as Plantinga has emphasized, if certain religions are true (which would mean that epistemically appropriate religious belief formation occurs in the way that those religions say it does – e.g., via the testimony of the Holy Spirit rather than via arguments), then having rational noninferential religious belief is exactly what we should expect.[41]

3.2.2 The Great Pumpkin Objection

The gist of this objection is that if we take seriously the Reformed Epistemologist's suggestion that there are rational noninferential religious beliefs, then (to be consistent) we should do the same with the suggestion that there are rational noninferential beliefs in claims that are clearly ridiculous, such as the claim that the Great Pumpkin exists.[42] And since it is clearly unacceptable to do the latter, we should refrain from taking seriously the Reformed Epistemologist's view that noninferential religious beliefs can be rational. This can be a tricky objection to get right; I won't take the time here to dig into the various ways of understanding it.[43] Suffice it to say that it's in the same neighborhood as objections to commonsensist responses to radical skepticism that say: "If we claim that perceptual beliefs are noninferentially rational, apart from any independent verification of their reliability, then (to be consistent) we would have to take seriously those who defend in a similar way beliefs formed via crystal ball gazing."[44]

Once this parallel is made clear, however, we can see a way for the Reformed Epistemologist to reply to the Great Pumpkin objection. Those defending commonsense endorsement of perception in the face of the "crystal ball" objection can say that even if defenders of crystal ball gazing can make philosophical moves exactly parallel to those of the commonsensist, commonsensists about

---

[40] See Bergmann (2017) for a development of this comparison. The point isn't that Reid and Reformed Epistemologists *explicitly thought of themselves* as relying on epistemic intuitions; rather, it's that they *did rely* on epistemic intuitions in the ways noted.

[41] See Plantinga (2000b: 188–90). For helpful modifications and improvements of this position, see Moon (2017).

[42] In Charles Schulz's *Peanuts* comic strip, the character Linus believes in the Great Pumpkin, a supernatural being with (presumably) the appearance of a large pumpkin who, after rising from the "most sincere" pumpkin patch, delivers gifts to well-behaved children around Halloween.

[43] See Plantinga (1983: 74–8 and 2000b: 342–51), Martin (1990: 266–76), and DeRose "Voodoo Epistemology," unpublished manuscript, presented to a 1999 meeting of the Society of Christian Philosophers https://campuspress.yale.edu/keithderose/voodoo-epistemology/. I'm not convinced that the difference DeRose highlights (between the allegedly easy-to-handle version of the objection that Plantinga considers and the more difficult version of the objection that DeRose lays out) amounts to a significant difference. At any rate, replies along the lines sketched below are just as effective for either version, and they are in the same vein as replies suggested by Plantinga.

[44] See Sosa (1997) and Bergmann (2008) for a discussion of this sort of objection to commonsensism.

perception have no good reason to take those defenses of crystal ball gazing seriously. It's true that the *form* of the reply is the same in each case. But the difference is that (in the normal circumstances in which we typically find ourselves) it is not rational for commonsensists to take seriously such a defense of crystal ball gazing, whereas it is rational for them to take seriously such a defense of perception; this is something they can determine via reliance on their epistemic intuitions about these cases. Similarly, the Reformed Epistemologist's reply to the Great Pumpkin objection is that whereas the *form* of the defense of noninferential belief in the Great Pumpkin is the same as that of the Reformed Epistemologist's defense of noninferential theistic belief, it is not rational for Reformed Epistemologists to take seriously such a defense of belief in the Great Pumpkin, whereas it is rational for them to take seriously such a defense of theistic belief. Once again, this is something they can determine via reliance on their epistemic intuitions about these cases.[45]

A more nuanced reply could grant that, under the right circumstances, the defender of Great Pumpkin beliefs and the Reformed Epistemologist (as well as the radical skeptic and the commonsensist about perception) could all have beliefs that are *internally rational*, where that means that the beliefs are epistemically appropriate responses to the believers' circumstances or evidence (which includes their seemings and epistemic intuitions). But this more nuanced reply could then insist that the relevant beliefs of Great Pumpkin followers and of radical skeptics are not *externally rational* in the way that the beliefs of Reformed Epistemologists and commonsensists about perception are. This is because to be externally rational involves being internally rational *and* being based on the sorts of evidence that one epistemically *should* have (including appropriate seemings and epistemic intuitions), and committed defenders of radical skepticism and of Great Pumpkin beliefs don't have the sorts of evidence they epistemically should have.[46]

3.2.3 The Problem of Peer Disagreement

The problem of peer disagreement focuses on your epistemic peers – that is, those whose evidence is approximately as good as yours and who respond to

---

[45] Obviously, radical skeptics have different epistemic intuitions about perception than commonsensists do; likewise, believers in the Great Pumpkin, if there were any, might have different epistemic intuitions about belief in the Great Pumpkin than your average theistic Reformed Epistemologist does. In addition, nontheists typically have different epistemic intuitions about noninferential theistic belief than do Reformed Epistemologists whose confidently held noninferential theistic beliefs strongly seem to them to be rational. Dealing with this sort of disagreement is the focus of Section 3.2.3 of this chapter and of Bergmann (2017 and 2021: ch. 12).

[46] For further discussion of internal and external rationality, see Plantinga (2000b: 110–12) and Bergmann (2017 and 2021: ch. 12).

evidence approximately as well as you do. The concern is that if those who appear to be your epistemic peers when forming beliefs on religious matters hold beliefs incompatible with your own, this suggests not only that one of you is mistaken but also that you have a defeater for these beliefs of yours. After all, given that the two of you are epistemic peers, how can you be sure that it is the one who disagrees with you (and not you) that is mistaken? In the context of Reformed Epistemology, the worry is that even if it's possible to have noninferential religious beliefs that are initially rational, this rationality is defeated upon recognizing that our epistemic peers disagree with us on religious topics (many times over).[47]

One way to reply to this objection is to start by considering other cases where we (seemingly rationally) maintain our beliefs in the face of disagreement. For example, consider disagreements about radical skepticism. Commonsensists notice that our strong epistemic intuitions in support of the rationality of our ordinary perceptual and memory beliefs seem to conflict with weaker epistemic intuitions in support of premises used in arguments for radical skepticism – premises saying what is required for a belief to be rational. Commonsensists think the rational thing to do in this situation is to maintain our ordinary perceptual and memory beliefs (and the epistemic intuitions that they are rational) and to reject the arguments for radical skepticism based on those weaker epistemic intuitions; those who think such commonsense responses fail and that the challenge of radical skepticism remains forceful disagree. There are two points that apply to both this example, concerning disagreement about commonsense responses to radical skepticism, and the case of religious disagreement. First, it's doubtful that the people who disagree in these examples have equally good evidence and are responding to such evidence equally well. After all, they don't have the same (or equally non-misleading) epistemic intuitions about the rationality of holding noninferential perceptual beliefs or noninferential religious beliefs. Or if they do, they aren't equally good at responding to that evidence (given how differently they respond). Second, even if they initially thought of each other as peers, their discovery of their disagreement can provide evidence that they aren't peers after all.[48] Both points remove the sting of this sort of disagreement-based objection to noninferential religious belief. For it's widely accepted that disagreement with those who *aren't our peers* – in particular, with those whose evidence is worse or who aren't responding as well to their evidence – needn't result in a defeater.

---

[47] See Goldberg (2014 and 2021) and Schellenberg (2007: ch. 8).

[48] For discussion of this kind of response to the objection from peer disagreement to noninferential religious belief, see Bergmann (2015 and 2017).

Again, there are other important objections to Reformed Epistemology not considered here. Moreover, there is much more to say (pro and con) both about the three objections that were considered here and about the replies to them that were mentioned. But this will have to suffice for the purposes of this chapter.[49]

[49] Thanks to Jeffrey Brower, John Greco, and Tyler McNabb for comments on previous drafts of this chapter.

4 Rationality and Miracles

Charity Anderson

Introduction

Can it *ever* be rational to believe that a miracle has occurred on the basis of a report? It is not difficult to find support for the idea that the correct answer to this question is no and that miracle reports always ought to be dismissed outright. Why might someone think it is *always* irrational to believe a miracle report? Two themes have dominated philosophical discussions concerning the rationality of believing a report of a miracle. The first relies on the idea that miracles are by definition massively improbable. Initial reactions of disbelief include expressions such as "What are the chances of *that* happening?" Miracles carry a built-in impression of implausibility. The second theme involves the thought that testimony is, in general, not a very reliable source of information. We are aware that people sometimes lie, are prone to mistakes or gullibility, and are at times subject to self-deception. On this line of thought, such factors reduce the evidential force of testimony, making it a weakened source of evidence. The result of combining these two themes is that it is very difficult – some suggest impossible – to rationally believe that a miracle has occurred on the basis of testimony: On its own, testimony is too weak to outweigh the improbability of a miracle. Both themes are addressed in Hume's famous essay on miracles. Philosophical discussion of the rationality of belief concerning miracles has become inextricably intertwined with Hume's argument. In this chapter, I examine each theme and critically discuss interpretations of and replies to Hume's argument.

The chapter unfolds in four sections: in Section 4.1, I clarify some central terminology. It is not a straightforward matter how to define *miracle* or *miracle report*. Various definitions have been proposed. I discuss some complications that entangle one commonly suggested definition, according to which a miracle is "a violation of a law of nature." Section 4.2 lays out an interpretation of Hume's argument and surveys several lines of response. Section 4.3 looks at the role of improbability and critically examines the idea that improbability alone is sufficient to ensure that the right response to a miracle report is disbelief. Section 4.4 briefly explores one factor relevant to a stance of moderate skepticism. Many miracle reports are often met with disbelief or skepticism, even by theists who otherwise believe that miracles occur. Background information and a careful investigation of particular details relevant in each case are essential to the evaluation of whether belief in any particular case is rational.

4.1 Preliminary Terminology

4.1.1 Definition of "Miracle"

A common conception of a miracle is such that a miracle involves a "violation of a law of nature." Hume (1975 [1748]) offers this as his first definition of a miracle in his essay *Of Miracles* (though he expands this definition in a footnote to add that an event that does not appear to us to be miraculous – the raising of a feather – may still be miraculous if it is caused by God and not through nature).[1] Aquinas (1975b) conceives of a miracle as an event "full of wonder."[2] Events are "full of wonder" for Aquinas when they are caused by a "divine power beyond the order commonly observed in nature." Aquinas ranks miracles: Those that are brought about by God but that nature "cannot do" are ranked the highest; those that nature could bring about, but that are nevertheless brought about by God, are ranked lower. The lowest rank are those that are "usually done by the operation of nature" but which, in a particular instance, are brought about by God and not via nature. Aquinas offers examples of rain and relief of illness: When either occur by divine power, rather than nature, they are miraculous events. In this way, Hume and Aquinas seem to be largely in agreement with respect to their conceptions of miracles.

It is a choice point whether, by definition, a miracle must be a very improbable event. It's worth considering whether we would continue to apply the term "miracle" to events that are presently thought of as paradigmatic miracles (healings or raising of the dead by a deity) if such events were commonplace and thus not massively improbable. Insofar as it seems plausible that we would still think of such events as miraculous, this suggests that the core idea of a miracle concerns the event's cause, not its frequency. But as it will not make a substantive difference to the ideas in this chapter, and as miracles are in fact infrequent, in this chapter I will think of miracles as very improbable events.

Another bit of terminology in need of preliminary comment is that of a "miracle report." A miracle could occur without being observed; a miraculous event could also be observed but not recognized as a miracle. For example,

---

[1] Hume's second definition of miracle is as follows: "A miracle may be accurately defined, *a transgression of a law of nature by a particular volition of the Deity, or by the interposition of some invisible agent.* A miracle may either be discoverable by men or not. This alters not its nature and essence. The raising of a house or ship into the air is a visible miracle. The raising of a feather, when the wind wants ever so little of a force requisite for that purpose, is as real a miracle, though not so sensible with regard to us." (1975 [1748], Sec. X, 90, n).

[2] Aquinas (1975b: C–CI).

someone ill might become well and God may have directly brought about the healing, but the latter fact may be unknown to any observer. I'll refer to a miracle report as a report that includes as part of its content the following: that some event occurred and that the event was caused by a deity or supernatural agent.

Most discussions of miracles and rationality focus on how one should respond epistemically when one hears a report that a miracle has occurred, rather than what one should believe if one were to observe a miracle firsthand. Plausibly, much of what is said about the rationality of believing a miracle report can be applied to the situation where one observes a miracle – after all, one's senses mess up from time to time, and this may give one some reason to reduce trust in them. This sentiment is expressed by Peter Annet (1744), who claimed that should it be that "a stone appeared to roll up a hill of its own accord to my sight, I should think that I had reason to doubt the veracity of my eye-sight, or of the object."[3] But although it's true that our senses are fallible, it does not follow from mere fallibility that the evidential force of our senses is weakened to such an extent that it is *never* rational to believe a miracle occurred if we directly observed the event.[4] More needs to be said to secure such a conclusion. But rather than debate this here, we will follow standard discussions and focus on miracle reports.[5]

Finally, it will be useful to raise and set aside one widely discussed issue concerning Hume's first definition – that a miracle is a violation of a law of nature. The combination of this definition with a conception of a law of nature as an exceptionless regularity threatens to rule out the occurrence of a miracle simply by definition. This makes an argument that it is irrational to believe a miracle report trivial. Despite the fact that this strategy would be question-begging, the line of reasoning has been attributed to Hume.[6] As others have noted, interpreting Hume in this way does not make sense of what Hume actually says. Moreover, it attributes to Hume a poor argument. One is hard pressed to comprehend why we need an argument that testimony cannot establish that a miracle has occurred if we know that such events are impossible. A principle of charity alone should give us pause here.

---

[3] Cited in Earman (2000: 135). Mackie (1982) similarly remarks: "but what, it may be objected, if one is not reduced to reliance on testimony, but has observed a miracle for oneself? Surprisingly, perhaps, this possibility does not make very much difference; it is always possible that I may 'misobserve' or 'misremember', or be 'deceiving myself.'" (p. 28).

[4] It is important to be careful in estimating the evidential impact of the fallibility of our faculties. In Section 4.3, we'll examine how imperfect sources of evidence can nevertheless have extraordinarily strong evidential force.

[5] As many philosophical discussions of miracles are concerned with repudiating or justifying belief in the central miracles of mainstream religions – with particular interest in the resurrection of Jesus – the focus on testimony is perhaps unsurprising.

[6] This view is attributed, for example, to Flew (1985) and to Johnson (1999).

Hájek (2008) rightly rejects the argumentative form sketched here as a suitable interpretation of Hume. Consider the following analogy, inspired by Hájek:

Step 1. A bachelor is an unmarried man. Thus, there's a contradiction in saying of any particular man that the man is married and the man is a bachelor.

Step 2. There is no credible testimony that someone is a married bachelor: Everyone who says they have seen a married bachelor is ignorant; we've never had enough people testify to the same married bachelor; people who believe such reports are led by their emotions or by "the love of wonder." In short, testimony of this kind has a bad track record.

Conclusion: We should be suspicious of all testimony that reports that some particular man is a married bachelor. All such testimony is unreliable and should be dismissed.

As Hájek correctly points out, if Hume's argument takes this form, we should be puzzled. Step 2 is obviously unnecessary once it is established that a married bachelor is a contradiction.

Moreover, had Hume intended to rule out miracles simply by definition, he could have drawn a stronger conclusion than he in fact draws. Hájek makes this point when he objects to (what he takes to be) Flew's (1985) reading of the argument:

Flew's reading [. . .] then becomes quite perplexing. It portrays Hume as regarding a miracle's occurrence as an *analytic* falsehood – on par with the death of an immortal being – as if he has simply defined miracles away. One is left wondering why Hume would settle for a merely epistemological conclusion, why he thinks he has merely ruled out rational belief in miracles, when really he has (on this reading) ruled out miracles themselves. Flew, then, implicitly attributes a glaring oversight to Hume . . ..[7]

We will hereafter set aside the idea that miracles are by definition impossible events, and the suggestion that Hume intended to advance this cheap argument. The topic has been widely discussed, and the problem it presents for belief in miracles is insubstantial. As we proceed, we'll draw on the conception of miracles found in Hume's footnote and in Aquinas: A sufficient condition for a miracle is that it is an event brought about by divine power.

4.1.2 Delineating the Topic

There are several distinct questions that we might wish to explore concerning miracles and rationality. The topic admits of nuance, and it is important to be

---

[7] Hájek (2008: 84).

clear what question is under investigation. For example, we can distinguish the question of whether it can be rational to believe that *some* miracle or other has occurred (that is, to believe that at least one miracle has occurred, even if we don't know which one) from the question of whether it can be rational to believe for some specific miracle that *it* occurred.[8] We might ask the question, "Do miracle reports provide any evidence for the occurrence of the miracle?" or the question "Do miracle reports provide evidence sufficient for rational belief that the miracle occurred?" Furthermore, we might be interested in whether it can be rational to believe that a miracle has occurred if all we have to go on is testimony (bracketing other evidence), or whether it can be rational to believe, with respect to the same miracle, that it occurred when the report is considered against some specific background information.

With respect to this last question, it will be helpful to make a few remarks about different investigative strategies. Typically, when we investigate a topic, we have reason to draw on all relevant information at our disposal. But it can sometimes be useful to isolate some bit of evidence, such as the testimony for a miracle, and evaluate the evidential significance of that piece alone – bracketing some of our relevant background information. Evaluation of our total evidence is a difficult task, and sometimes it's easier to examine one piece. Also, we might be interested to see what the result would be if we had less evidence or different evidence, such as the evidence of our interlocutors. (We'll return to this topic in Section 4.4 when we discuss the relevance of background information.)

One advantage of making distinctions within the family of questions we aim to investigate is that by bringing a specific question into focus, we can avoid offering a general response to questions that require more subtle treatment. The subject matter is complex, and an adequate investigation of the topic will be nuanced.

4.2 Hume's Argument

It is all but impossible to give a comprehensive overview of the rationality of believing a miracle report without discussing Hume's (1975 [1748]) essay, *Of Miracles*. Hume famously championed the idea that miracle reports ought to be dismissed outright, and his essay is arguably the most influential piece of writing on the topic. This section will be devoted to discussion of Hume's argument and subsequent interpretations and replies.

---

[8] See Sorensen (1983) for discussion. Sorensen argues that even if Hume establishes case by case skepticism for miracle reports, he does not establish that rationality requires us to withhold belief that at least one miracle report is true (even if we can't identify which one).

4.2.1 What Is Hume's Argument?

It is an understatement to say that Hume's essay has provoked much discussion. Many interpretations and responses have been advanced, and there is little to no agreement concerning how to reconstruct the argument. To make matters worse, there are tensions within the text that leave room for multiple plausible readings.[9] While interpretation of Hume's essay is contentious, in this chapter I will follow the reading offered by Robert Fogelin (2003), whose reconstruction strikes me as among the most promising. Fogelin's interpretation displays the merits of a close reading of the text and takes the entire essay (parts I and II) into account, rather than focusing solely on part I. His is not the only reading that bears these virtues, but it bears them particularly well. I will leave to one side issues concerning the internal coherence of what Hume says in this essay and his broader corpus. It is well noted that there appears to be a tension between Hume's views about induction and his reliance on laws of nature as the basis of his skepticism toward miracles reports. Since we are here concerned with the rationality of trusting a miracle report and not with Hume's internal consistency, or lack thereof, we will limit our discussion likewise.[10]

Fogelin makes several key points that will be instructive to highlight. First, Fogelin rightly observes that Hume is not disparaging of testimony in general. In this way, Fogelin avoids attributing to Hume the view that testimony is simply too weak a source of evidence to stand up against the strong inductive evidence that confronts any miracle. Hume is instead attentive to factors that reduce our trust in particular kinds of testimony – drawing attention to the character of the testifiers and the circumstances of speakers and hearers. Whether Hume is cynical in his evaluation of the relevant kind of testimony, we'll discuss in a moment; for now, we'll simply note that Hume does not set up a contest between *testimony* and *experience* and then conclude that testimony will always lose such a contest. Second, on Fogelin's interpretation, part II of the essay is not a superfluous add-on, but instead is integrated into the argument as a whole. The two parts work together to make one overall argument. This picture is both faithful to the text and avoids the "purely a priori" argument (discussed in Section 4.1) that some attribute to Hume. Finally, Fogelin assigns significance to a portion of the text that many

---

[9] Was Hume intentionally ambiguous in his presentation of the argument? Of course, it's hard to say with any certainty, but some have suggested that given the political and religious context in which he was writing and the risks of advancing an overtly anti-religious argument, it is not implausible that he would have had a motivation to be ambiguous. See Earman (2000) for further discussion.

[10] See Millican (2011) for a defense of Hume's consistency on this point (151–153). Millican further argues that even if Hume were inconsistent, it wouldn't be a problem for his argument concerning miracles.

interpretations either ignore or discount, namely, Hume's hypothetical case of eight days of darkness.[11] This is a key example in Hume's essay, as it is here that Hume makes clear that he thinks that testimony can, in principle, establish that a massively improbable event has occurred.

Hume's argument, then, according to Fogelin, involves two theses working in tandem. Miracles are incredibly improbable – but not impossible – events, and thus we require excellent evidence to establish that a miracle has occurred. Testimony can, in principle, establish very improbable events, but in the case of testimony for *religious miracles*, the testimony is heavily tainted and has lost the requisite strength: We should always be suspicious of such testimony. By contrast, a *nonreligious* miracle could be established on the basis of testimony, supposing that the testimony was sufficiently strong. Fogelin writes:

Yet, even if the standards for testimony in behalf of miracles are high, they remain, in principle, satisfiable. This is the point of Hume's example of the eight days of total darkness. The example shows what it would be like to meet such high standards. (2003:31)

I join Fogelin in thinking that the importance of Hume's case of eight days of darkness is that it shows that Hume thinks that, in principle, we could be rational to believe radically improbable events on the basis of testimony. Given enough credible testimony, we could rationally believe that an event occurred that has never before been observed and that is contrary to what we otherwise believe about the course of nature. Hume's argument has a decidedly more narrow target: He thinks testimony *of a certain kind* has a bad track record, namely, testimony to a religious miracle – more specifically, a miracle that forms "the foundation of a religion." Hume writes:

As the violations of truth are more common in the testimony concerning religious miracles, than in that concerning any other matter of fact; this must diminish very much the authority of the former testimony, and make us form a general resolution, never to lend any attention to it.... (1975 [1748]:99)

But while he advises skepticism concerning testimony for improbable events of a religious nature, Hume is extremely careful to delimit the space toward which his skepticism is directed; he does not extend it beyond a prescribed class that has a bad track record:

---

[11] Hume's example proceeds as follows: "...suppose, all authors, in all languages, agree, that, from the first of January 1600, there was a total darkness over the whole earth for eight days ... that all travellers, who return from foreign countries, bring us accounts of the same tradition, without the least variation or contradiction: it is evident, that our present philosophers, instead of doubting the fact, ought to receive it as certain, and ought to search for the causes whence it might be derived." (1975 [1748]: Sec X, 99).

I beg limitations here made may be remarked, when I say, that a miracle can never be proved, so as to be the foundation of a system of religion. For I own, that otherwise, there may possibly be miracles, or violations of the usual course of nature, of such a kind as to admit of proof from human testimony . . . . (1975 [1748]:99)

Little attention has been paid to Hume's appeal. But taking Hume at his word makes an important difference to how we understand the scope of his argument – and to how we reply to it. We'll next examine several replies to Hume's argument.

4.2.2 Replies to Hume

This section will discuss two types of replies to Hume's argument, the charge that Hume is defining his way to his conclusion by making miracles impossible events having been dealt with in Section 4.1. I'll discuss first the response that Hume was ignorant of the evidential strength that comes from multiple independent witnesses to a single event; and second, responses that accuse Hume of undue cynicism concerning testifiers to religious miracles.

4.2.2.1 Multiple Independent Witnesses

Early replies to Hume's essay emphasized the significance of the cumulative effect of the testimony of multiple independent witnesses. Since Hume's essay first appeared, readers have pointed out that given a plausible estimate of the probability of an event occurring in accordance with a law of nature, we can show that the number of independent witnesses required to establish that a miracle occurred is smaller than Hume seems to have anticipated. Some have suggested as few as five to seven independent witnesses would offset the unlikelihood of the event.[12] That is, it has been argued that the testimony of approximately five to seven independent witnesses would suffice to establish that a miracle occurred.[13] The exact number is not important here; what is important is the fact that there is some number which would be sufficient (and which is small enough to be plausibly attainable). Hume, it is thereby suggested, grossly underestimates how easy it would be for testimony to outweigh the evidence in support of a law of nature.

There is wide agreement that Hume did not have access to the probability calculus, which was being developed by Thomas Bayes at the time.[14] This fact offers a ready explanation for why Hume appears to overlook the significance

---

[12] Charles Babbage (2009 [1838]) places the number at six, arguing that six independent witnesses would make the probability of what they attest five times more likely than the event (where the event is the restoration to life of a dead man).

[13] See Ahmed (2015) for a dissenting argument.   [14] See Earman (2000).

of multiplying testifiers. Even J. L. Mackie, no friend of theism, suggests that Hume's essay would be improved by incorporating discussion of independent witnesses:

One further improvement is needed in Hume's theory of testimony. It is well known that the agreement of two (or more) *independent* witnesses constitutes very powerful evidence. (1982: 25)

Mackie continues, noting that in light of the powerful effect of multiple witnesses, it is of the upmost importance that we are correct about whether or not the witnesses are independent:

How have the witnesses managed to misobserve to the same effect, or to misremember in the same way, or to hit upon the same lie?' It is difficult for even a single liar to keep on telling a *consistent* false story; it is much harder for two or more liars to do so.... This is why the independence of witnesses is so important.... On the one hand, it means that a certain sort of testimony can be more powerful evidence than Hume's discussion would suggest. On the other, it means that where we have a plurality of reports, it is essential to check carefully whether they really are independent of one another.... (1982: 25–26)

Of course, since Hume did not think we can find even one respectable testifier, much less a handful, the reply misses the point. At least, Hume wouldn't have been impressed. Without a single credible witness, there's no hope of taking advantage of the strength of multiple witnesses. In this way, respondents to Hume who wish to make much of the force of aggregating independent witnesses must also address Hume's claims concerning the track record of testimony to religious miracles. We'll turn to this topic next.

4.2.2.2 Hume and the Track Record of "Religious Testimony"

As should by now be evident, Hume thinks the track record of testimony to religious miracles is very poor – so poor that we can adopt a general attitude of dismissal toward such testimony:

As the violations of truth are much more common in the testimony concerning religious miracles, than in that concerning any other matter of fact; this must diminish very much the authority of the former testimony, and make us form a general resolution, never to lend any attention to it...." (1975 [1748]: 99)

Though it is dubious whether testimony to miracles has a worse track record than *any* other type of testimony, Hume is surely right that testimony for miracles has a bad track record. Earman (2000), though he agrees with Hume's cynicism, objects that the question of whether "miracle enthusiasts" meet a minimal condition of reliability is an empirical question, and that Hume oversteps at this stage of the argument. Though there is certainly an empirical component to the question of how poor the track record actually is, there is also a philosophical claim here worth investigating.

Let's begin our discussion by addressing the general strategy of grouping together types of testimony and discrediting a testifier on the basis of their giving testimony of that type. Widely discussed problems involved in reasoning via a reference class arise here.[15] Events belong to many different classes; selection of the relevant class for any particular event is not straightforward. But there's something that may strike us as particularly odd about Hume's strategy here. Hume proposes to group testifiers together based on *what they say* (i.e., they are classified as the group of *those who have reported that a miracle has occurred*). And on this basis, Hume discounts their testimony and suggests we do likewise. Can it be rational to dismiss someone's testimony simply because reports of similar types of things have a bad track record? It's not immediately obvious how this reasoning should be evaluated.

We may begin by noting that there is subject matter about which people tend to lie or misreport more often than others – examples include a person's age, weight, how much TV they watch each week, etc. But the fact that people often lie about some subject matter does not make it rational to disbelieve testimony in *every* case of someone reporting about that subject matter. In some contexts, the fact that people often lie about some particular subject matter can be ignored: Suppose, for example, that a police officer asks you to state the date of your birth in a context where the consequence of lying is that you will be issued a significant fine. The fact that lots of people lie about their age in other circumstances will not lead us to expect you to lie in this context.[16] On the contrary, we would expect you to report accurately. We should not use the fact that people often lie about their age as a reason to distrust your testimony in this case.

Hume is correct to suggest that we ought to be sensitive to factors that raise suspicion of a person's testimony and that subject matter can be among those factors. The credence we give to various things said by one person often does vary along with subject matter.[17] But Hume's recommendation is to dismiss all such testimony in one fell swoop, and in doing so he indiscriminately groups together too broad a set of cases.

Placing all testimony to religious miracles in one reference class and noting that class has a bad track record does not make it rational to dismiss all miracle reports outright. The strategy Hume offers cannot rationally be applied across the board. Note, though, that this admission does not automatically secure

---

[15] For general discussion, see Hájek (2007).   [16] See Anderson (2018) for further discussion.

[17] Notice how differently we might treat, for example, the same person's testimony on the following two topics: their favorite color and how much work they completed over the summer. While we might expect them to report the first topic with near-perfect accuracy, if we know that they are prone to underestimate or overestimate their productivity, we are likely to think them less trustworthy with respect to the second report.

victory for theists. There is still substantial work to be done to demonstrate, in any particular case, that a miracle report is credible. Default skepticism may still be rational in many cases. Before we look at factors relevant to navigating particular cases, we'll examine more closely the role that the improbability of the event plays in determining the proper doxastic response.

4.3 Improbability

It's tempting to think that the improbability of a miracle alone makes it reasonable to dismiss a miracle report. On the one hand, it seems right to think that when an event is incredibly unlikely, we are right to be skeptical. But on the other hand, we in fact trust ordinary testimony to incredibly unlikely events with regularity. The lottery provides a straightforward example.

Suppose, on a particular date, the newspaper reports that the winning numbers of the New York Lottery were as follows: 88, 76, 15, 22, 91, and 56. The chance that this exact set of numbers is the winning sequence is roughly one in twenty-five million. But we would have no trouble trusting the newspaper report – even though we are aware that the newspapers report errors now and then. Are we rational to trust the newspaper report? For it to be more likely that the report is true than that the newspaper makes an error, the chance of a newspaper error would need to be small indeed. (And to make *belief* the rational response to hearing the report, the chance of error would have to be even smaller). Our supposed rationality in trusting the results would appear to hang on the newspaper having an *incredible* track record.

It's worth asking how Hume would recommend we believe. Hume's maxim suggests that for any case of testimony, we look at which is more likely: that S lies or is deceived or that the event S reports occurred. In his own words:

When anyone tells me, that he saw a dead man restored to life, I immediately consider with myself, whether it be more probable, that this person should either deceive or be deceived, or that the fact, which he relates, should really have happened. I weigh the one miracle against the other; and according to the superiority, which I discover, I pronounce my decision, and always reject the greater miracle. (1975 [1748]: 91)

We need to be careful how we understand this maxim. It's easy to misapply it.

As others have noted, comparing the chance that 88, 76, 15, 22, 91, and 56 is the winning sequence of numbers with *the chance that the newspaper contains an error* is not the right comparison to make.[18] Instead, we should compare the chance of 88, 76, 15, 22, 91, and 56 with the chance that *the*

---

[18] For further discussion, see Anderson & Pruss (2020) and Millican (2011).

newspaper errs by reporting precisely that these numbers (88, 76, 15, 22, 91, and 56) *are the winning sequence.*

With this comparison in mind, we can see how testimony can provide evidence for even extremely improbable events. Again, an illustration will help. Suppose that you receive a report of the winning lottery numbers from someone with a reputation of lying often – let's imagine the person lies one out of three times he gives a report and tells the truth two out of three times. Still, the chance that he will lie by choosing any particular sequence is quite low. When he reports that the winning sequence is 88, 76, 15, 22, 91, and 56, there is a 2/3 chance that he is telling the truth and a 1/3 chance that he is lying. But supposing that he chooses a sequence randomly when he lies, the chance that he would choose the sequence 88, 76, 15, 22, 91, and 56 is roughly 1 in 25 million. So, supposing that he randomly chooses a sequence when he lies, when he tells you that 88, 76, 15, 22, 91, and 56 is the winning sequence, his testimony is very strong evidence for the truth of what he asserts: It takes the probability that 88, 76, 15, 22, 91, and 56 is the winning sequence from ~1/25,000,000 to ~2/3. While .66 is not, in one sense, a very high credence, the testimony provides a significant boost in terms of a Bayes factor. And if we weren't interacting with a habitual liar, the boost would be even stronger.

We can compare this example with a case where the liar uses a different strategy to choose which sequence to report on the occasions when he lies. Holding other features fixed, suppose now that when the liar lies, he tends to choose a sequence that invokes surprise – the result being that he is more likely to choose some sequences than others. For example, let's imagine that he is more likely to choose a consecutive sequence, such as 10, 11, 12, 13, 14, and 15 when he lies than he is to choose a nonconsecutive sequence. Suppose the chance of him choosing any particular consecutive sequence is roughly 1/1,000. This supposition makes a difference to what we ought to think when we receive his report. Now, rather than the sequence he reports moving from a ~1 in 25,000,000 chance to a 2/3 chance of being the winning sequence, it moves only to 1/25,000.[19] The report is still evidence that 10, 11, 12, 13, 14, and 15 is the winning sequence (the report will increase the probability of the sequence from .00000004, to .00004), but .00004 is still a long way from making belief that *p* rational.

So, we should not think that it is rational to dismiss testimony to certain events *simply* because the events are improbable. There are two lessons here: Improbability alone does not do all the work; and even when the report is

---

[19] The relevant factor is that when he lies, he will more often choose the consecutive sequence than the nonconsecutive. Imagine, for example, that the lottery is run seventy-five million times. Two-thirds of the time he will report the winning number accurately; one third of the time he will lie. But rather than lying by reporting 10, 11, 12, 13, 14, and 15 once, on this setup he will report this sequence ~25,000 times.

offered by a testifier with a poor track record, the report still gets some – even if less – credibility. This highlights the importance of clarifying the question we wish to investigate. If what we want to know is simply *does testimony that M occurred provide any evidence at all for M?* the answer is straightforward: Given some plausible assumptions, typically it does. Questions concerning how strong the evidence is or whether it places one in a position to rationally believe that M occurred are more difficult to answer.

4.4 Moderate Skepticism

Most people (theists included) *do not* trust every miracle report they hear. There is a general attitude of skepticism toward such reports. The considerations laid out in this chapter suggest that if you think it is rational to dismiss *every* miracle report outright, you should not do so on the basis of the sheer improbability of such an event or the general bad track record of the testifiers. In closing, I'll suggest that we are not faced with a choice between total skepticism or foolish gullibility: Moderate skepticism concerning miracle reports is possible.[20] Here we have space only to gesture in the direction of further inquiry that needs to be undertaken to fully substantiate the claim that, in some cases, the rational response to a miracle report is belief.

Let's return to the distinction between whether a miracle report can constitute *evidence that* the reported miracle occurred and the report making it rational for a subject to *believe* that the miracle occurred. We've seen that testimony for a miracle (M) will typically provide *some* evidence that M occurred. Whether it is rational to believe that M occurred will typically depend on background information. This highlights the difficulty of arguing that it can be rational to believe that a miracle occurred *on the basis of testimony alone* – but also the pointlessness of thinking that it is problematic if testimony *alone* is insufficient to rationalize such a belief. Rarely do we believe anything strictly on the basis of testimony alone – our background information makes a contribution.

The importance of background information is not unique to the process of trusting testimony; background information plays a significant role in the process of belief-formation generally. It plays a significant role when we trust the deliverances of perception, memory, and other sources of knowledge – though this fact may often go unnoticed. Note that we are highly sensitive to the contexts in which we trust our eyesight – the lighting, our distance from the object of sight, whether it is moving or standing still, our expectations of what will be there, etc., all affect our reception of any given instance of

[20] The Catholic Church, for example, offers a model of how one might form criteria to guide investigation of alleged miracles; its regulations combine a cautious attitude toward miracle reports with willingness to believe should an investigation deliver a favorable report.

perception. And as the well-known example of Koplik spots demonstrates, even in a clear case of "seeing," our background information has a significant bearing on what we believe.[21] In the case of testimony for miracles, whether one's background information favors the existence or the nonexistence of a divine being, for example, will clearly often make a difference. As will one's prior expectations of the frequency of divine action. Additionally, the context and other details surrounding the report will be highly relevant. There is no blanket argument against miracle reports, but neither is there a blanket argument for them. Investigation of the merits of particular reports is beyond the scope of this chapter.[22]

In conclusion, we can in principle be in a position to trust miracle reports. We have here cleared some of the ground to make way for an argument in favor of particular reports, and suggested that some of the arguments that support a default dismissive attitude are not as sweeping as skeptics toward miracles might hope.

[21] Koplik spots are an indication of measles, but this fact was not known until discovered by medical science. Prior to this discovery, it would be unreasonable for someone ignorant of the connection to believe a patient had measles on the basis of seeing the spots. See Kelly (2014a).

[22] For discussion of the details surrounding reports concerning the resurrection of Christ, see Craig (1989), Habermas (1996), and McGrew and McGrew (2009).

5 Pragmatic Arguments for Theism

Elizabeth Jackson

Introduction

Theistic arguments fall into two main categories. *Epistemic* arguments, like the cosmological, ontological, and fine-tuning arguments, conclude that God exists. *Pragmatic* arguments, by contrast, conclude that you ought to believe in God, where 'ought' is the ought of practical rationality. Two of the most famous pragmatic arguments for theism are put forth by Blaise Pascal (1662) and William James (1896).[1] In the most basic form, pragmatic arguments for theism go like this: believing in God has significant benefits, and these benefits aren't available for the unbeliever. Thus, you should believe in, or 'wager on', God.

This chapter discusses different types of pragmatic arguments for theism and surveys their costs and benefits. Section 5.1 focuses first on Pascal's wager and discusses different types of wagers. These wagers differ on issues such as the benefits of wagering, the probability threshold required for wagering, and the actions involved in wagering. Section 5.2 turns to the epistemic-pragmatic distinction and discusses the nuances of James' argument, and how views like epistemic permissivism and epistemic consequentialism provide unique 'hybrid wagers'. Section 5.3 covers outstanding objections and suggests ways that the defenders of pragmatic arguments might respond. Section 5.4 concludes.

5.1 Types of Theistic Wagers

Let's begin by clarifying some terminology. It is natural to understand Pascal's wager in terms of *expected value*, which is the value of an action given uncertainty about some of the relevant facts. A common rule is that you should pick the action with the highest expected value; in a position of uncertainty, the action with the highest expected value is most likely to lead to the best outcome. For example, if I offer you a hundred dollars if a coin

---

[1] See Jordan (2007) and Duncan (2013) for comparisons between the Jamesian and Pascalian wagers, and Rota (2017) and Hájek (2018) for useful summaries of pragmatic theistic arguments. Also note that the Muslim philosopher and theologian Al-Ghazālī (12th century/ 1991) also proposed a version of the wager, and Al-Ghazālī's dates earlier than Pascal's.

Table 5.1 *The most basic wager*

	God exists (cr = n)	God doesn't exist (cr = 1 − n)	EV
Believe in God	ω	f1	ω
Don't believe in God	$-\omega$	f2	$-\omega$

lands heads but you have to pay me a dollar if it lands tails, it maximizes expected value for you to take my bet, even though there's a chance you could lose money. Put differently, if you were offered this bet over and over again, you'd make money in the long run (that is, in the limit). A second relevant term is *credence*, which is a measure of subjective probability – the confidence you have in the truth of some proposition, measured on a scale from 0 to 1, where 0 represents certainty a proposition is false and 1 represents certainty that it is true. For example, my credence that 1+1=2 is very close to 1; my credence that a fair coin will land heads is 0.5.

This leads us to the most basic form of Pascal's wager; the reasoning is as follows. There are two actions you can take – believe in God, or not believe in God – and two ways the world might be – God exists, or God does not exist. If you believe in God and God exists, you'll go to heaven, which is infinitely good. If God exists and you don't believe in God, you may go to hell, which is infinitely bad. If God does not exist, then whether you believe in God or not, whatever you gain or lose would be finite. Believing in God, then, has a higher expected value than not believing. Thus, unless your credence that God exists is 0, you should believe in God. As Pascal said, "Wager, then, without hesitation that [God] is," because "there is here an infinity of an infinitely happy life to gain," and "what you stake is finite" (1662: fragments 233–241). This basic form of Pascal's wager is represented by Table 5.1: cr stands for credence, ω and $-\omega$ represent negative and positive infinity, f1 and f2 are finite values, and EV indicates the expected value of each action.

That said, most wagers defended by philosophers – including the wager proposed by Pascal himself – are more complex than this simple gloss. This section outlines some of these different types of wagers for theism. While our focus is on Pascal's wager, some of these distinctions also apply to the Jamesian wager, discussed in the next section.

5.1.1 Finite and Infinite Values

The first distinction is between wagers that involve infinite values compared to wagers that merely involve finite values. Our initial gloss framed the wager in terms of infinite values, for at least two reasons. A natural benefit of theistic belief involves the afterlife, and heaven is plausibly infinitely good (and hell is plausibly infinitely bad). Second, wagers that appeal to infinite values only require your credence in theism to be non-zero and non-infinitesimal. (*Infinitesimal* credences are those that are infinitely close to zero, such as $1/\infty$.) So, infinite wagers get a strong result: even if your credence in theism is quite low (for example, 0.0001), you should wager because of the infinite values involved.

However, infinites also create problems. One of the biggest problems involving infinities is the many gods objection. Defenders of the many gods objection point out that many religions posit infinite gains (and infinite losses), and if you choose the wrong religion, believing in the God of that religion might prevent gaining the infinite goods of another religion (see Mougin and Sober 1994). So, simply believing in God doesn't guarantee an infinite good. Given this, it's not clear how to choose between religions, since all religions with infinite afterlives would seem to have the same, infinite, expected value. Thus, infinities put us at a standstill when trying to choose between religions.

Some have responded to this problem by keeping infinities in the wager but changing the way expected values are calculated (Bartha 2007; Jackson and Rogers 2019; Chen and Rubio 2020). The gist of the fix relies on the idea that not all infinities are created equal. For example, you should prefer a 90% shot at an infinite good to a 10% shot at the same good. This strategy provides the result that, all else equal, you should wager on the religion that you assign the highest credence. However, comparing infinities in this way gets technical and complex (especially when other things aren't equal).

Others propose that we move away from infinite values altogether. Instead, the outcome on which you believe in God and God exists is modelled with a very large, finite value. This is a simpler way to avoid the result that all religions have the same expected value (Jordan 2006; Rota 2016a, 2016b). While this provides a solution to the many gods objection, it also weakens the argument's conclusion. You should wager only if your credence that a religion is true is sufficiently high, since there's no infinite value to trump the finite values involved if God does not exist. What counts as sufficiently high depends on the value of belief in God if God exists. Michael Rota (2016a, 2016b), for example, argues that you should wager on Christianity if your credence in Christianity is at least 0.5. The threshold need not be this high, though, especially if we utilize very large finite values.[2]

---

[2] These fixes also answer the mixed strategies objection to Pascal's wager, raised by Duff (1986) and Hájek (2003). For discussion, see Jackson and Rogers (2019: sec. 4.4). Other responses to the many gods objection include Martin (1975), Lycan & Schlesinger (1989), Jordan (1991), Bartha (2012), and Lebens (2020).

5.1.2 Premortem and Postmortem Benefits

Not all pragmatic arguments for theism appeal to the afterlife. Broadly speaking, there are two kinds of benefits associated with taking the wager: premortem benefits and postmortem benefits. While traditionally, Pascal's wager appeals to postmortem benefits (e.g. heaven and hell), Justin McBrayer (2014) proposes a version of the wager that appeals to the premortem benefits of being a theist. He cites empirical evidence that "theists do better in terms of happiness, health, longevity, interpersonal relationships, and charitable giving" (130). On this version of the wager, even if universalism is true (that is, everyone goes to heaven), or there is no afterlife, you still have a reason to be a theist.

Note two things about premortem wagers. First, since wagers that appeal to premortem values are finite wagers, your credence in theism (or in a religion) plays a larger role. Whether you should wager will depend on your credences in both theism and atheism and how much better it is to be a theist rather than an atheist. Second, one worry for such arguments is that, on the teachings of several major religions, the religious person shouldn't expect their premortem life to be completely happy or without suffering, much less perfect. For example, in Christianity, the Bible teaches that "[you] must go through many hardships to enter the kingdom of God" (Acts 14:22) and "in this world, you will have trouble" (John 16:33). Judaism teaches that you cannot engage in idolatry, even to the point of death. Religious saints often live lives of poverty and significant sacrifice, and are even martyred for their faith. Those appealing to premortem benefits should be wary of the 'prosperity gospel', the position that once you become religious you will become happy, healthy, and protected from serious suffering (see Crummett 2023, "Paper That Argues Against Wagers That Appeal to Premortem Benefits," Unpublished).

5.1.3 Belief and Action

Third, wagers differ on what wagering amounts to. Note that we originally framed the wager in terms of whether you should believe that God exists. Let's call this the *doxastic wager*. While it may seem natural at first blush to understand the wager in terms of belief, this raises two key objections. First is the *impossibility objection*: Do you have the right kind of control over your beliefs in order to wager?[3] Second is the *irrationality objection*: Even if you can wager, is forming a belief for pragmatic reasons rational?[4]

In response to these objections, some have suggested we instead frame the wager in terms of action. Maybe Pascal's wager instead provides a reason to

---

[3] Those who discuss the impossibility objection include Mackie (1982: 201), Duff (1986: 108), Jones (1998: 173), and Jordan (1998: 173; 2006: 38).

[4] Those who discuss the irrationality objection include Clifford (1877), Flew (1976), Mackie (1982), Oppy (1991: 167), and Schroeder (2012: 266).

accept, or act as if, God exists (Rota 2016a, 2016b). Let's call this action-based wager the *acceptance wager*. This provides a way out of the impossibility and irrationality objections. First, you have control over whether you accept God's existence, as you can voluntarily engage in actions like going to church, praying, reading Scripture, and immersing yourself in a religious community. So, the impossibility objection doesn't apply to the acceptance wager. Second, standard theories of rational action appeal to pragmatic reasons, so it's rational to accept that God exists for pragmatic reasons. Thus, the irrationality objection also does not apply.

Choosing between the doxastic wager and the acceptance wager partially depends on what God desires of us. At least in certain religious traditions, God does not desire mere belief, but something more like commitment. This lends itself to the acceptance wager. However, even if insufficient, belief may be *necessary* for salvation, or weaker, an important aspect of a religious commitment, perhaps necessary in particular circumstances. Maybe wagering involves both belief and acceptance. If beliefs are involved in wagering at all, however, then the irrationality and impossibility objections again crop up. We'll consider a second response to both objections in the next section.

5.2 Epistemic and Pragmatic Reasons

This section addresses the distinction between epistemic and pragmatic reasons in light of pragmatic arguments for theism. *Epistemic* reasons are reasons connected to truth. The most common epistemic reason is evidence. *Pragmatic* reasons are reasons connected to your goals and/or your flourishing. You might have a pragmatic reason, but not an epistemic reason, to believe you're smarter than average. You have a pragmatic reason to believe this because it raises your self-esteem, but you don't have an epistemic reason to, assuming the belief is not supported by your evidence.

We'll cover three main topics in this section. First, we'll discuss a view called *epistemic permissivism*, and how permissivism provides a response to the irrationality and impossibility objections to the doxastic wager. Second, we'll cover two hybrid wagers – so called because they appeal to a combination of both pragmatic and epistemic reasons. The first involves a theory called epistemic consequentialism, and the second involves combining the wager with epistemic arguments for theism.

5.2.1 Permissivism and the Jamesian Wager

There are several differences between Blaise Pascal's wager and William James' wager. First, James appeals to finite values, whereas Pascal appeals to infinite values. Second, James argues that we should wager in cases where there is a 'forced choice' – meaning we cannot remain neutral. Third, on a common interpretation, Pascal argues that wagering on God is rationally *required*. In contrast, James argues that wagering on God is rationally *permissible*, as James is responding to Clifford's (1877: 289) claim that "it is wrong always, everywhere, and for anyone, to believe anything upon insufficient evidence."[5] Fourth, Pascal is more focused on the acceptance wager (or the acceptance wager as a means to the doxastic wager) as he suggests one should wager by taking holy water and attending mass, whereas James is more focused on the doxastic wager. Finally, and most important for our purposes, James argues that we should wager in cases where "reason cannot decide" (1896). He argues that if a matter cannot be settled by the evidence, we can exercise our will to believe and even do so 'lawfully', that is, without compromising epistemic rationality (see Adler 2002: 59–63).

James' idea that, on certain matters, 'reason cannot decide' suggests that our evidence is limited in certain ways. Of course, in some cases, our evidence clearly supports a certain proposition. For most of us, our evidence requires us to believe that $1 + 1 = 2$ and disbelieve that it is 75 degrees in Antarctica right now. However, some matters are more complicated. Consider highly controversial and complex issues in philosophy, politics, religion, or ethics: Should abortion be legalized? How much are we morally required to give to charity? What is the nature of epistemic justification? What political party is best for our nation? Does God exist? On matters like these, the evidence is complex and difficult to assess. These cases might be ones where, as James puts it, reason cannot decide. On matters like these, you might rationally believe p and I might rationally believe not-p, even if we are aware of the same evidence and arguments.

This suggests that a view in epistemology called *epistemic permissivism* is correct. Permissivism is the view that there are evidential situations that rationally permit more than one attitude toward a proposition. For example, epistemically rational paleontologists might share evidence but disagree about what killed the dinosaurs; epistemically rational jurors might share evidence but disagree about who committed a crime. Or consider a single juror: if she faces inconclusive evidence, then both belief that Smith is guilty and disbelief that Smith is guilty might be rationally available to her.

Plausibly, if permissivism is true, then many bodies of evidence are permissive regarding theism. Debates about God's existence have a long history, with powerful evidence on both sides. There is widespread disagreement about God's existence, and many atheists, agnostics, and theists appear to be epistemically rational, even when they are aware of the same (or similar) evidence that bears on God's existence.

[5] Thanks to Mark Satta.

If permissivism is true about theism, this provides an answer to both the impossibility objection and the irrationality objection (at least for those in permissive cases regarding theism, which I argue is a lot of us; see Jackson in press a). And this answer doesn't require us to move from belief to acceptance. First, consider the impossibility objection: because doxastic involuntarism is true, you don't have the right kind of control over your beliefs to wager at all. Here, note that many of the cases used to motivate doxastic involuntarism involve propositions that are either clearly true or false, given the evidence. Alston (1988), for example, considers offering you a large sum of money to believe that the US is still a colony of Great Britain. This seems extremely difficult, if not impossible to do, even if you want the money more than the true belief.

But consider instead a case where you're torn about whether theism is true, and where you know there are good arguments for and against, such that you could be rational to be a theist, atheist, or agnostic. It's much less clear that, in that case, you have no control over whether you believe in God. For example, in Peter van Inwagen's conversion story, he discusses how, during his conversion, he could both see the world as uncreated and see the world as created by God. He notes that "there was a period of transition, a period during which I could move back and forth *at will*, in the 'duck-rabbit' fashion" (1994: 35, emphasis mine). You have a more robust kind of doxastic control when your evidence is ambiguous about some matter, such that you are torn between two good explanations of your evidence. And for many, the evidence for theism is ambiguous in this way.

Permissivism also provides an answer to the irrationality objection. Suppose your evidence permits both theism and agnosticism, that is, either attitude is epistemically rational, given your evidence. Suppose you believe that God exists for a practical reason. It's not at all clear that this would compromise the epistemic rationality of your belief that God exists. By stipulation, theism is a rational response to your evidence! While these two responses are only briefly sketched here, I hope to have said enough to convince the reader that the advocate of the doxastic wager has a reason to take the Jamesian commitment to permissivism on board. (These arguments are further developed in Jackson in press a.) Thus, combining pragmatic arguments for theism with certain views in epistemology (e.g. permissivism) makes the wager more plausible.

5.2.2 Hybrid Arguments

Now we'll turn to two 'hybrid arguments' – arguments for theism that involve a combination of epistemic and pragmatic considerations. First, you might argue for the wager in conjunction with arguments that raise the probability of theism or of a particular religion. This style of argument often involves a pragmatic premise – a premise about what is practically rational (e.g. you should wager on the religion that is most likely to be true; or: you should wager on theism if it is at least 50% likely to be true) and an epistemic premise – a premise about truth or likelihood (e.g. religion X is most likely to be true; or: theism is at least 50% likely to be true).

Pascal himself (1662) arguably takes a route like this. Before Pascal presents the wager in the *Pensées*, he provides arguments for Christianity. Pascal takes these arguments to be strong enough to establish that, among religions, Christianity is the only 'live' possibility. This is the epistemic step. He then, in the famous wager, uses pragmatic considerations to establish that one should wager for Christianity rather than atheism – the pragmatic step.

More recently, Rota (2016b) also presents a hybrid argument. His argument can be summarized as follows (13):

1. If Christianity has at least a 50% chance of being true, then it is rational to commit to living a Christian life.
2. Christianity does have at least a 50% chance of being true.
3. Thus, it is rational to commit to living a Christian life.

Notice that premise 1 is the pragmatic premise – which Rota defends in the first half of his book, appealing to practical considerations – and premise 2 is the epistemic premise – which Rota defends in the second half of the book, appealing to, among other things, a version of the fine-tuning argument and the resurrection argument for Christianity. Of course, such hybrid arguments are not limited to Christianity in particular. Jackson and Rogers (2019), for example, provide arguments for a slightly different pragmatic premise – that you should wager for the religion (with an infinite afterlife) that is most likely to be true. (Note that it need not surpass the 50% threshold.) You could combine this with arguments that a particular religion is most likely to be true. Then, if it has an infinite afterlife, you should wager for that religion.

Note that, when compared to non-pragmatic arguments for theism, the epistemic step of these hybrid arguments relies on a much weaker premise. In Rota's argument, one would only need to establish Christianity's being 50% likely – but without the pragmatic premise, this likely won't convince you to wager on Christianity. For Jackson and Rogers, you simply need to identify the most probable religion with an infinite afterlife; then, you ought to wager on that religion, even if it is nonetheless unlikely in absolute terms. This is a particular strength of hybrid arguments: the pragmatic considerations take some of the burden off of the epistemic considerations. At the same time, the epistemic considerations block objections such as the many gods worry and make the wager more widely applicable (the arguments don't merely apply to those with, for example, antecedently sufficiently high credences in theism).

A second hybrid argument worth mentioning involves *epistemic consequentialism*. Epistemic consequentialism is the view that epistemic goodness is more fundamental than epistemic rightness, so 'rationality' and 'justification' should be understood in terms of conduciveness to epistemic goods (Ahlstrom-Vij & Dunn 2018: 2). Therefore, what makes a belief rational is the extent to which it causally contributes to future epistemic goods. Suppose that believing in God raises the probability that you go to heaven. But consider: the epistemic benefits of heaven are substantial. Imagine you had an unlimited amount of time to ask an omniscient being anything you wanted. The potential epistemic benefits would be enormous, if not infinite: endless pieces of significant knowledge/true belief/justified belief. Considerations like these point to an *epistemic* version of Pascal's wager. In other words: if epistemic consequentialism is true, then the epistemic benefits of heaven make theistic belief epistemically rational. This is a hybrid argument (rather than an epistemic one) because it appeals to the epistemic consequences of theistic belief, which is significantly different than, say, providing evidence or arguments for theism. On the other hand, epistemic considerations nonetheless have an important role to play in this non-traditional wager – and in fact this wager doesn't aim to establish that theism is practically rational, but rather that theism is *epistemically* rational. (See Jackson in press b, for further development of this argument.)

5.3 Outstanding Objections

Let's take stock. First, we've considered different types of wagers that have been proposed, which differ on issues such as the benefits of wagering, the probability threshold required for wagering, and the actions involved in wagering. Then, we turned to the epistemic-pragmatic distinction and discussed the nuances of James' argument, and how views like epistemic permissivism and epistemic consequentialism provide unique hybrid wagers. Along the way, we've touched on several objections to pragmatic arguments for theism, including the many gods objection, the impossibility objection, and the irrationality objection.

   In this section, we'll discuss some other objections to pragmatic arguments for theism. For the sake of covering new ground, I'll consider objections not addressed in my previous work.[6] After explaining each objection, I'll suggest some ways that the defender of the theistic pragmatic arguments might respond. My responses, however, should not be taken as the final word on the matter; defenders of pragmatic arguments for theism should take these objections seriously.[7]

---

[6] For responses to many objections to the wager, including objections concerning many gods, mixed strategies, impossibility, irrationality, infinite number of religions, bet-hedging, Pascal's mugging, the problem of hell, temporal discounting, and transformative experiences, see Jackson and Rogers (2019). For a response to the worry that taking Pascal's wager involves poor motives, see Jackson (in press c).

[7] Thanks to Amanda Askell for discussion of these objections and potential responses. See Askell (2012) for additional objections to Pascal's wager and replies.

5.3.1 Should I Take a Non-Religious Path to Infinite Utility?

An initial objection to pragmatic arguments for theism involves secular paths to infinite utility. Perhaps religions offer possible infinite utility, but religion isn't the only game in town. Consider *the singularity,* a potential point in the future of permanent and uncontainable technological growth. Artificial intelligence (AI) might develop the ability to improve on itself, and as it improves, it learns how to improve better and more quickly, causing an explosion in both computer intelligence and technological progress (Shanahan 2015). Technological advances such as these open up various possibilities for infinite utility, such as uploading your consciousness to a computer so that you can live forever. Even if this is unlikely, the objector may consider most religions unlikely. Then, it's not clear that one should wager on God rather than spending their time and resources supporting technological developments and advances in AI.

In response, note that non-religious paths to infinite utility are only a problem for pragmatic arguments for theism insofar as pursuing them is inconsistent with being religious. But you can be religious and also devote time and resources to support technological advances and progress toward the singularity. Pursuing AI research is consistent with believing in God and/or living a devoted religious life. Thus, let a thousand flowers bloom. Convert and support AI research!

If, for whatever reason, you have to choose between a secular path to infinite utility and a religious path, you ought to pick the one that is most likely to get you infinite utility. Even then, this wouldn't automatically mean you should reject the religious option. (However, this might be an advantage of infinite versions of the wager, as finite religious wagers mutually exclusive with secular infinite wagers would be trumped.) But I'm skeptical that, in most cases, you'd have to choose in the first place.

5.3.2 Do Infinite Values Always Trump Finite Values?

Infinite wagers normally rely on the idea that infinite expected values trump finite ones. This is part of what gives the wager its power and delivers the result that you should wager on a religion, even if your credence that it is true is quite low.

However, the idea that infinite expected values always trump finite ones seems subject to counterexample. Suppose someone offers you a 0.000001% chance at an infinite good if you are willing to be tortured for a trillion years. It seems like you should not take that offer, even though the former has a positive infinite expected value that should outweigh the finite negative expected value of being tortured. Oppy (2006: 255) provides a similar counterexample: "If there is a 1,000-ticket lottery for which the payout is positive infinite, and I already hold 900 of the tickets, what grounds are there for insisting that I should be prepared to betray all of my friends and family in order to obtain another ticket?"[8] These counterexamples suggest that infinite expected values may not always swamp finite considerations.

We'll consider three responses to this objection. The first bites the bullet but provides an error theory for our intuitions about the counterexamples. There is ample psychological evidence that we are terrible at reasoning with large numbers. For example, Kahneman (2011: 93) discusses the following study:

Participants in one of the numerous experiments that were . . . asked their willingness to pay for nets to cover oil ponds in which migratory birds often drown. Different groups of participants stated their willingness to pay to save 2,000, 20,000 or 200,000 birds. If saving birds is an economic good it should be a sum-like variable: saving 200,000 birds should be worth much more than saving 2,000 birds. In fact, the average contributions of the three groups were $80, $78 and $88 respectively. The number of birds made very little difference. What the participants reacted to, in all three groups, was a prototype – the awful image of a helpless bird drowning, its feathers soaked in thick oil. The almost complete neglect of quantity in such emotional contexts has been confirmed many times.

The numbers involved in this study were not even that large – ranging from 2,000 to 200,000. Yet people's estimates for the value of saving these birds were an emotional reaction to pictures of oil-covered drowning birds, and insensitive to the increase in numbers. In the same way, an emotional reaction to the badness of torture might skew our intuitions in the finite/infinite trade-off case, but we vastly underestimate the value of infinity. So maybe infinite expected values should always trump finite ones, and we should trust the mathematical principles over our intuitions about particular cases.

Some will find this response too much to swallow; we shouldn't be prepared to give up any finite good for a minuscule chance at an infinite one. An alternative response involves restricting the principles used in the infinite wager. So, perhaps, instead of the idea that infinite expected values always trump finite ones, maybe infinite expected values only trump finite ones when the chance at receiving the infinite good is sufficiently probable. Or maybe infinite goods don't trump finite ones if the finite ones involve doing

---

[8] Oppy's counterexample also raises the complex questions about the *social* aspects of pragmatic arguments for theism (and expected value reasoning in general). For example, should you wager on God if it has good consequences for you but negative consequences for others (or vice versa)? Do the pragmatic should and the moral should come apart? If so, how do we adjudicate between them? While there isn't space to address these questions here, note that some, such as Rota (2016b), have proposed *moral* versions of the wager, appealing to the well-being of close friends and family, or even considerations about what God would desire or require, if God exists. In principle, the positive consequences associated with wagering can be either practical or moral. Thanks to Mark Satta for helpful discussion.

something morally wrong (like betraying one's loved ones). While we don't have space to consider and refine various principles here, there are ways to have an interesting and strong version of the wager without committing to the idea that one should prefer infinite values to finite ones, *no matter what.* (This strategy may also help with other objections to the wager, such as Pascal's mugging; see Bostrom 2009.)

A third and final response involves relying on a version of the wager that only appeals to finite values. Finite wagers don't appeal to any principles – restricted or unrestricted – that involve infinite values swamping finite ones, so this worry would not arise in the first place.

5.3.3 Should I Commit to a Super-Religion?

Call a *super-religion* a religion that purports to have a much better heaven and/or worse hell than traditional religions. It seems easy to imagine or create super-religions. Of course, most of us will have a low credence in super-religions. But this low credence could easily be swamped by the fact that a religion has a significantly better heaven or much worse hell than other religions. After all, Pascal's wager teaches that what is lost in credence can be made up for in utility. Thus, it seems like pragmatic arguments for theism imply that you should commit to a super-religion.

In response, it may not be as easy to imagine or create a super-religion as you might think. Traditional religions normally don't assign numerical values to heaven or hell. Of course, they are generally thought to be infinitely good or infinitely bad, but the specific infinite cardinal or ordinal value is unspecified. For this reason, it may not be possible to create a super-religion: for any value you use to model a super-religion's afterlife, the afterlife of traditional religions can accurately be modelled with the same value.

Second, even if you can create a super-religion, there may be grounds to assign it an infinitesimal credence, especially if it is intentionally created to make a problem for Pascal's wager. As the claims about the afterlife become more fantastical (e.g. better heavens, worse hells), then your credence that a super-religion is true should lower in proportion. Given this mathematical framework, there may be no reason to commit to a super-religion in the first place.

5.3.4 Should I Follow the Most Exclusive Religion?

A final objection to pragmatic arguments for theism involves the extent to which you should hedge your bets when choosing which religion to practice. Suppose you become convinced that Christianity is true. Now you face another choice: convert to a mainstream denomination of Christianity or convert to an extremely conservative strand of Christianity. Suppose the latter teaches that if you drink alcohol, if women wear pants, or if you send your children to public school, you will not go to heaven. It seems like you should hedge your bets and follow the rules of the more exclusive strand of Christianity, despite your low credence that strand is true, since mainstream versions of Christianity don't prohibit teetotaling, private school, or wearing only skirts and dresses. This reasoning suggests that you should follow the strictest and most exclusive denominations of the highest-probability religion, as this maximizes your chance at infinite utility in the afterlife.

In response, it's not clear that following the strictest and most exclusive denominations would maximize expected value, all things considered. This is because joining such denominations has costs, which are also potentially infinite. Consider: if you joined a religion so strict that you could no longer wear pants, drink alcohol, or watch Netflix, this religion would be very burdensome and difficult to follow. This experience may raise the probability that you leave religion altogether. While your credence that this experience will cause permanent de-conversion may be low, your credence in the exclusive strand of Christianity is likely also quite low. For many people, the former credence is high enough to wash out the latter credence, so it will not maximize expected value to covert to the strict, exclusive denominations of a religion. Furthermore, other factors might give exclusive, rules-oriented denominations a bump down in expected value, including the fact that some religions warn against becoming rules-obsessed, as it leads to pride and judgment of others.[9] Thus, it's not clear that exclusivity wins out in expected value, all things considered.

5.4 Conclusion

We've surveyed different types of pragmatic arguments for theism and noted their costs and benefits. We focused first on Pascal's wager. We discussed different types of wagers that differ on issues such as the benefits of wagering, the probability threshold required for wagering, and the actions involved in wagering. Next, we turned to the epistemic-pragmatic distinction and discussed the nuances of James' argument. We also looked at two hybrid wagers. Finally, we discussed objections to pragmatic arguments for theism and ways that the defenders of pragmatic arguments might respond.[10]

---

[9] See Matthew 23.
[10] Thanks to Mark Satta, Brian Ballard, Anthony Rowden, Amanda Askell, Kyle Vollmar, John Greco, Jonathan Fuqua, and Tyler McNabb for helpful comments and discussion.

6 Skepticism, Fideism, and Religious Epistemology

Duncan Pritchard

Introduction

Our primary concern is with the relationship between skepticism and religious epistemology. There is both a positive and a negative side to this relationship. The latter is straightforward: just as skepticism is meant to undermine the positive epistemic standing of our beliefs, so one would expect it to undermine the putative positive epistemic standing of religious belief. Indeed, religious belief is usually regarded as 'low-hanging fruit' in this regard, in that it is a kind of belief that is thought to be particularly susceptible to skeptical challenges on several fronts (such as via its appeal to purely subjective experiences, or via its reliance on authority and custom).

As we will see, we can situate both Lockean evidentialism and fideism as being natural responses to this kind of skeptical challenge. In the former case, the overarching idea is to grant to the skeptic that religious belief stands in need of a particularly demanding kind of evidential basis (the very evidential basis that it is alleged to lack), but to contend nonetheless that this is an epistemic threshold that religious belief can clear. In the latter case, in contrast, rather than attempting to offer an epistemic response to the skeptical challenge, the fideist instead argues that the proper moral to be drawn is that religious belief is not to be evaluated epistemically at all, thereby making the skeptical challenge irrelevant. Skepticism is thus found to be lurking in the background with regard to two historically important ways of thinking about religious epistemology.

The negative relationship between skepticism and religious epistemology is not the complete story, however, for there has also been a long-standing tradition whereby skepticism has stood in a broadly positive relationship to religious epistemology. This is the more interesting part of our narrative, not least because it is the more surprising. Consider, for example, skeptical fideism. As just noted, it is natural (at least from a contemporary perspective) to think of fideism as being a way of responding to the skeptical challenge by exempting religious belief from being subject to epistemic assessment. But there is another way of thinking about the relationship between skepticism and fideism whereby they are much more entwined, such that fideism is, properly understood, the natural product of the application of skeptical reasoning.[1] Think, for example, of how Montaigne subjects his beliefs to a thoroughgoing critique via the employment of the Pyrrhonian skeptical modes, but in the process brings to the fore the manner in which the scope of one's commitments that are immune to such modes can take in one's religious commitments. Rather than fideism merely offering a route out of skepticism about religious belief, it is instead a wide-ranging skepticism that is generating the very rationale for fideism.

In light of skeptical fideism, we will contrast two contemporary uses of epistemic parity arguments, as they feature in reformed epistemology and a Wittgensteinian quasi-fideism. What underlies the reformed epistemologist's appeal to epistemic parity is precisely an *anti*-skeptical point – viz., that arguments against the positive epistemic standing of religious belief should trade on features that are distinctive of this kind of belief, and not be merely arguments that would undermine the positive epistemic standing of any belief, including those beliefs that are typically thought to be beyond epistemic reproach, insofar as any are (such as perceptual beliefs). Here we see the skeptical impulse turned back in on itself: for skepticism about religious belief to be compelling, it must be specific to religious belief, and not merely a generalized skepticism that, inevitably, also afflicts this doxastic domain.

Wittgensteinian quasi-fideism also incorporates an epistemic parity argument, but in an inverted form. In particular, whereas reformed epistemology trades on anti-skeptical claims in its use of an epistemic parity argument, quasi-fideism is closer in spirit to skeptical fideism in using skepticism in defense of religious commitment. The basic thought is that religious belief cannot be criticized for having arational commitments at its core, given that *all* belief has arational commitments at its core. The intended conclusion is not, however, the radical skeptical contention that all belief is lacking in positive epistemic support, but rather the thesis that it is in the nature of rationally grounded belief that it presupposes arational commitments, where these can include fundamental religious commitments. As we will see, quasi-fideism can be viewed as broadly aligned with skeptical fideism, in that it is a thesis that arises out of an engagement with skeptical considerations.

6.1 Lockean Evidentialism

Let's start with the idea that Lockean evidentialism and traditional fideism can both be regarded as responses to a certain kind of skepticism about the epistemic standing of religious belief. First, we need to consider the skeptical

---

[1] Although it would take me too far afield to explore this connection here, there are also important overlaps between skeptical fideism and apophatic theology. See Gutschmidt (2021).

challenge in play, as Locke conceives of it.[2] This is to account for the rationality of religious belief even despite the fact that it is often a kind of belief that seems to be essentially grounded in suspect epistemic sources, such as entirely subjective religious experiences or appeals to religious authority, as opposed to being grounded in sources that are held (by Locke at any rate) as epistemically sound, such as common experiences of a shared phenomenon or directly based on reason. In short, the skeptical challenge is that religious belief is epistemically problematic because it is not based on grounds that are available to all rational subjects, either via observations of a common reality or via reasoning that any rational subject could in principle undertake.

So construed, this is a skeptical challenge that is arising out of the scientific revolution and the new epistemic methods that this gave rise to. This wasn't the only impetus for Locke's interest in the rationality of religious belief, however, since he was also guided by a very practical concern regarding the proliferation of dangerous religious 'enthusiasts'. The availability of the Bible in English, along with the Protestant reformation that encouraged believers to develop their own understanding of biblical teachings, distinct from the guidance offered by a priest who is expounding the canonical teachings of the Church, inevitably leads to a situation where there are many individuals with strong religious convictions espousing radically different theologies. The result is a recipe for social anarchy.[3]

The skeptical response to this situation would be to cast religious belief as lacking an adequate epistemic basis. Locke's approach concedes the impetus behind the skeptical challenge – he certainly grants that the religious belief of the enthusiasts is irrational – but nonetheless regards it as a challenge that can be overcome. In particular, he concedes to the skeptic that one must proportion the strength of one's assent to a proposition, and thus one's belief in it, to the evidence that one has for its truth. This epistemic principle – the *principle of proportionality*, as it is known – plausibly frames the skeptical challenge for religious belief, given that it seems to be a kind of belief that involves a particularly strong form of conviction that is grounded on a relatively weak epistemic basis.[4] According to Locke, an upshot of this principle is that a subject's religious certainty that p demands either that p is itself certain (incorrigible or self-evident) or at least that p is probably true given only what is certain.[5]

Such an epistemic requirement sets a high hurdle for religious belief to clear. Nonetheless, Locke believes that such a hurdle can be cleared, albeit not by the

---

[2] Our principal focus for Locke's views in this regard will be chapter XIX of book 4 of his *An Essay Concerning Human Understanding* (Locke 1979 [1689]).

[3] See Mavrodes (1989).   [4] See Boespflug (2019).

[5] We thus get a kind of classical foundationalism, albeit of a slightly weaker variety than some other forms of classical foundationalism (e.g., those that demand that the nonfoundational elements should be deducible from what is certain). See Plantinga (1998, §2).

'enthusiasts' that he describes. For while Locke does believe that there can be such a thing as genuine divine revelation (he specifically mentions Moses and Gideon in this regard), he doesn't hold that in general relying on (what one takes to be) divine revelation can be an adequate rational basis for one's religious certainty, given how difficult it is to distinguish genuine divine revelation from the illusory kind. In particular, Locke claims that the evidence that is required for religious belief needs to be publicly available, which rules out appeals to one's subjective religious experiences. Similarly, in order to distinguish genuine from nongenuine divine revelation, one cannot appeal to only one's religious experiences, but one also needs an independent rational basis for treating this revelation as genuine, such as the direct perception of miracles (this is one crucial factor that sets Moses and Gideon apart from the enthusiasts).[6] Moreover, it is important to Locke that divine revelation cannot conflict with reason.[7] In the absence of such definitive evidential support as a miracle, however, the epistemically appropriate route to forming religious beliefs is by appeal to *a priori* arguments, such as arguments in favor of God's existence.[8]

Locke thus makes important concessions to the skeptic about religious belief but nonetheless argues that one can meet the skeptical challenge, and in the process differentiate rationally grounded religious belief from the irrational religious conviction of the enthusiast. Upon hearing Locke's description of what is involved in rational religious belief, however, it is tempting to respond by contending that the appropriate response is not this Lockean style of epistemic heroism but rather a very different kind of line, one that takes seriously how very different religious conviction is from ordinary belief. In its most straightforward form, this is the option offered by *fideism*. According to the fideist, religious faith is not to be evaluated along rational lines at all. Rather than trying to domesticate religious conviction and thereby turn it into an ordinary kind of belief that is subject to rational evaluation, we should instead take seriously the distinctive nature of religious conviction, and in particular its separation from the rational realm.

[6] It is interesting to situate Locke's claims in this regard alongside Hume's (1975 [1748]) later skeptical arguments regarding miracles. For even Hume could in principle accept that direct observation of a miracle can suffice to make it reasonable to believe that a miracle has occurred, as his skeptical concern about miracles is primarily regarding the propriety of forming such a belief on a purely *testimonial* basis. What Hume's argument would show, then, is not that someone like Moses could not reasonably believe that he has witnessed a miracle (thus confirming, on Locke's view, that his divine revelation is genuine), but that we could not rationally believe, on purely testimonial grounds, that Moses has witnessed a miracle (thus calling into question, from *our* epistemic perspective, the veracity of his divine revelation). For further discussion of Hume's treatment of miracles, see Pritchard and Richmond (2012).

[7] While divine revelation cannot be 'contrary to reason', Locke does allow that it can be 'above reason', in the sense of delivering truths that, while not in conflict with reason, cannot be established by purely *a priori* reasoning.

[8] See Rockwood (2020). See also Lowe (2010).

6.2 Fideism

Fideism is widely acknowledged to be a term of art that covers a range of proposals (the terminology only entered the lexicon in the nineteenth century, and only then as, initially at least, a pejorative description of certain views). The kind of fideism that interests us is a type of proposal that maintains that religious conviction is to be fundamentally understood in arational terms. This makes it distinct from moderate forms of fideism that merely depart from standard accounts of the epistemology of religious belief by denying the application of certain epistemic principles, without thereby treating religious conviction as being in essence arational.[9] It also makes it distinct from a particularly extreme form of fideism that views religious conviction as being in tension with rationality, such that religious faith calls one to accept, perhaps even passionately endorse, claims that one recognizes to be irrational. Such extreme fideism involves choosing faith over reason.[10] In contrast, fideism as we are understanding it is only committed to maintaining that a subject's religious convictions are not to be rationally evaluated. That is consistent with the idea that these convictions need not be in conflict with the subject's other (nonreligious) beliefs, which are to be evaluated rationally in the normal way. The overarching thought in play is not that faith and reason are in conflict, but rather that the realm of reason is restricted and doesn't apply to all of one's commitments.[11]

There is a natural route from skepticism to fideism of the kind that concerns us; indeed, one dominant form of fideism is explicitly described as *skeptical fideism* in recognition of its skeptical source. For how else would one discover the limitations of the realm of reason except by application of skeptical arguments? Consider someone who has religious conviction and who attempts, but fails, to offer the kind of rational support for this commitment that Locke demands, and yet discovers that this conviction remains unaffected. If that were so, it would reveal that the nature of this conviction is in fact very different from one's ordinary beliefs, as they tend to be such that they would be lost, or at least be held with much less conviction, were one to discover that they lack an adequate rational basis. It would be a natural next step to suppose that there is something amiss with the idea that religious conviction should be treated as akin to our ordinary ways of believing, and hence as subject to the kind of rational evaluation that is naturally applicable to our ordinary ways of believing.

Skeptical fideism of this kind comes most vividly to the fore in the work of Michel de Montaigne, especially his *Apology for Raymond Sebond* (2003 [1576]),

---

[9] For example, Penelhum (1983a; 1983b) has described reformed epistemology as a fideistic proposal because it denies the application of certain epistemic principles in the religious case. For a response, see Plantinga (1983, 87–91). See also Askew (1988).

[10] See especially Kierkegaard (1983/[1843]). For discussion, see Penelhum (1983a).

[11] For two overviews of fideism, see Carroll (2008) and Penelhum (2010).

the text that Richard Popkin (2003: 56) famously referred to as the "womb of modern thought." Through the employment of the Pyrrhonian skeptical modes, Montaigne is led to doubt whole swathes of his beliefs. And yet, in subjecting his beliefs to this trenchant skeptical critique, he discovers that his religious conviction is immune to these skeptical techniques. For rather than being based on reasons, it is instead a very different kind of commitment, which he describes as being more like breathing than an ordinary belief. Montaigne's intellectual innovation was to effectively expand the scope of our nondogmatic commitments that are immune to (Pyrrhonian) skeptical challenge such that they could include religious convictions. The defense of religious conviction is thus embedded within a wider skeptical stance that exposes the limitations of reasons, and which thus leads to a kind of faith that is entwined with a wider intellectual humility. This aspect of Montaigne's approach is nicely articulated by Brian Ribeiro:

We need to renounce our wicked pride and become humble – we need a good humiliation, in the literal sense. And Pyrrhonism is the means to this end. By showing us how worthless our powers are, we will be stripped down and "made ready" to accept the "finger of God" without high-handed resistance. This pattern – Pyrrhonizing acid-bath followed by ready acceptance of faith – is what scholars now call fideistic skepticism, of which Christian Pyrrhonism (Montaigne's form) is a specific variant. (2009: 13)

Note the contrast with a Lockean approach to religious epistemology. The goal is not to articulate the skeptical challenge in order to overcome it, but rather to employ the skeptical challenge to discern the limitations of rational evaluation, and thereby expose the arational nature of religious commitment.[12]

6.3 Skepticism and Epistemic Parity

The danger faced by fideism is that it can look like a mere epistemic capitulation, especially when contrasted with the epistemic heroism of Lockean

---

[12] Penelhum (1983a, 15–16) contrasts Catholic skeptical fideists like Montaigne with Protestant skeptical fideists like Pascal, describing the former as a 'conformist fideism' that identifies faith with loyalty to a tradition as opposed to the 'evangelical fideism' of the latter. See also Popkin (1992: 192). It's certainly true that Montaigne appeals to the idea of religious faith as custom as part of his defense of particular religious commitments, drawing upon similar remarks about custom and faith that one finds in Sextus Empiricus (the exact import of which is contested by scholars – see Bailey (2002: 193) and Annas (2012); see also the 'rustic Pyrrhonist' line described by Barnes (1997: 85)). But Montaigne's defense of religious commitment is not simply a matter of it being custom, however, as he seems to regard religious conviction as being, at heart, a primitive and natural response to the world rather than anything one might acquire by being part of a social practice. In this sense, his skeptical fideist treatment of religious conviction is similar to the quasi-fideism that we will be discussing below. See also Cardoso (2010), Ribeiro (2021), and Pritchard (2021).

evidentialism. In particular, the fundamental concern about fideism is that it leads to a kind of epistemic ghettoization of religious commitment, such that it is arbitrarily partitioned off from other, nonreligious, commitments. Why isn't the proper response to such a line to regard religious commitment as simply epistemically illegitimate, rather than as being immune to rational evaluation? In order to respond to these concerns, we need to consider the manner in which skeptical fideism can be in part motivated by an appeal to what is known as an epistemic parity argument.

In the contemporary epistemology of religious belief literature, considerations of epistemic parity are usually associated with reformed epistemology. This kind of proposal eschews the fideist route by effectively arguing for a lower rational bar for religious belief than that demanded by Lockean evidentialism. The appeal to parity concerns the claim that our ordinary beliefs are held to be perfectly in order from an epistemic point of view even while failing to satisfy the evidentialist rubric. For example, perception, at least in suitable conditions (and setting aside a radical skepticism that would call *all* belief into question), is thought to be epistemically in order even though we lack any independent rational basis for our perceptual beliefs. In particular, one's perceptual beliefs can amount to knowledge in the right epistemic conditions even though one lacks any supporting evidence for them, much less the kind of evidence that Locke demands. If one's perceptual faculties are functioning reliably, then that can suffice for knowledge, even though one has no noncircular evidential support for their reliability (one determines the reliability of one's perceptual faculties in a particular case by appealing to the outputs of one's perceptual faculties).

The crux of the matter is that if the evidentialist demand is not applicable to perceptual knowledge, then why should it be thought relevant to religious knowledge? For such an epistemic parity argument to work, it needs to be the case that religious knowledge is relevantly analogous to perceptual knowledge. This is where a second claim that is often associated with reformed epistemology kicks in, which is the appeal to a reliable religious faculty, the *sensus divinitatis*.[13] Just as one's reliable perceptual faculties can, in the right conditions, directly lead to perceptual knowledge even in the absence of supporting evidence, so one's reliable religious faculty can, in the right conditions, directly lead to religious knowledge, contra Lockean evidentialism. Now the epistemic parity argument is complete. Demanding that religious belief satisfies the constraints of Lockean evidentialism is to place it under an undue epistemic burden, one that wouldn't apply to everyday belief, such as perceptual belief, which, it is claimed, is relevantly analogous in epistemic respects to religious belief.[14]

[13] See especially Plantinga (2000b).

[14] See Wolterstorff (1976; 1983a) and Plantinga (1983; 2000b). See also Alston (1982; 1986b; 1991), whose work is often associated with reformed epistemology, though he never embraced this description of his view.

Of course, the defender of Lockean evidentialism – or, for that matter, the skeptic regarding religious knowledge – could dispute the particular epistemic story that the reformed epistemologist offers regarding the reliable religious faculty. But that kind of dispute is very different in orientation from one in which religious belief is simply lacking in the required epistemic fashion, as it is rather an internal dispute between rival accounts of the epistemology of religious belief. Our current interest, however, is in a very different kind of epistemic parity argument, one that aligns with skeptical fideism rather than with a positive account of the epistemic standing of religious belief like reformed epistemology.[15]

The epistemic parity argument offered by skeptical fideism involves showing that our ordinary beliefs are no less imbued with arational commitments than our religious beliefs.[16] Such a line of argument has natural affinities with Pyrrhonian thought, given that the application of Pyrrhonian skeptical techniques highlights the kinds of everyday nondogmatic forms of assent that are immune to skepticism in virtue of being, it turns out, commitments that are not based on reasons at all. Notice that a skeptical fideism that is allied to an epistemic parity argument in this way is not subject to the charge of defending an epistemic ghettoization that we noted earlier, for the simple reason that there is on this view no epistemic ghetto in prospect. Rather than the religious domain being delineated from the nonreligious domain, and thereby excluded from rational evaluation, the distinction between our rational commitments and our arational commitments is instead one that cuts right across our cognitive lives, taking in both religious and everyday domains of commitments.

6.4 Wittgensteinian Quasi-Fideism

There are thus two ways of thinking about fideism. A straightforward rendering insists that religious belief is to be evaluated in a completely different manner to all other forms of belief, with only the latter being subject to rational appraisal. Fideism of this kind faces the epistemic ghettoization challenge we noted earlier. In contrast, a second form of fideism is available that avoids this challenge by insisting that there is no sharp division between religious belief and everyday belief in this regard, in that the latter also includes commitments that are excluded from rational appraisal. This feature

---

[15] Reformed epistemology is not the only proposal in the literature that calls into question the epistemic demands made on religious belief by Lockean evidentialism. Moser (2008a; 2008b), for example, has offered an influential defense of the claim that the evidence that is relevant to the epistemic assessment of religious belief is not the 'spectator evidence' that is demanded by Lockean evidentialism, but rather a very different kind of evidence that he refers to as 'authoritative evidence'.

[16] See Penelhum (1983a) for an influential account of the epistemic parity argument at work in skeptical fideism, with particular focus on the work of Pascal and Kierkegaard.

of the view enables it to offer an epistemic parity argument. As we have seen, this second form of fideism is most naturally motivated by quite general skeptical concerns, which is why it is often known as skeptical fideism.

We can bring this latter form of fideism into sharper relief by considering the kind of hinge epistemology that Wittgenstein articulates in his final notebooks, published as *On Certainty* (1969). Although Wittgenstein's primary concern in these notebooks was not with religious belief, he does seem alert to the application of this view to the religious case. Moreover, there is independent evidence for thinking that one of the main influences of a Wittgensteinian hinge epistemology is the work of John Henry Newman, and in particular his *Essay in Aid of a Grammar of Assent* (1979 [1870]).[17] If so, then given the religious focus of this latter work, this would also support the application of a Wittgensteinian hinge epistemology to religious conviction. Elsewhere, I have described such a proposal as quasi-fideism in order to contrast it with the more straightforward form of fideism that is usually attributed to the later Wittgenstein.[18] In particular, while quasi-fideism is a genuine form of fideism, it differs from a straightforward fideism in holding that religious belief should be rationally evaluated in just the same way as nonreligious belief. As we will see, quasi-fideism is explicitly set out in the context of skeptical concerns, and hence has natural affinities with skeptical fideism.

Wittgenstein's overarching concern in *On Certainty* is to advance a radically different conception of the system of rational evaluation to the opposing picture that he claims is presupposed by both skepticism and traditional forms of anti-skepticism. According to this conventional picture, all of our commitments are subject to rational evaluation, including, in principle, all of them at once. We thus get the skeptical idea that our commitments as a whole can be rationally assessed and found to be wanting, along with the opposing anti-skeptical claim that such a wholesale rational evaluation of our commitments could in contrast find them in good order. Wittgenstein rejects both skepticism and traditional forms of anti-skepticism, which he claims mispresent the nature of rational evaluations.

Wittgenstein claims that once we reflect on the nature of rational evaluation, we come to realize that it is essential to any rational appraisal that it

---

[17] See Kienzler (2006) and Pritchard (2015b). See also Barrett (1997).

[18] The straightforward fideist reading of the later Wittgenstein has strong textual support, especially given the remarks on religious belief in Wittgenstein (1966). For critical discussion of this reading, see Nielsen (1967), Phillips (1976), and Bell (1995). I set out quasi-fideism in a number of places – see Pritchard (2011; 2015b; 2017a; 2018; 2022a; 2022b; in press a). For critical discussions of this proposal, see di Ceglie (2017; 2022), Ljiljanaa and Slavišab (2017), Bennett-Hunter (2019), de Ridder (2019), Gascoigne (2019), Boncompagni, "Religious Hinges: Insights from Pragmatism," (manuscript, 2021), Gomez-Alonso (2021), Smith (2021), and Williams (in press). For helpful discussion of Wittgenstein's philosophy of religion, see Whittaker (2010).

takes place against a backdrop of certainty that provides the framework for this appraisal. Since this background certainty supplies the framework for all rational evaluation, it cannot be itself rationally evaluated, and hence is arational (and therefore cannot amount to knowledge). Wittgenstein is thus maintaining that a fundamental requirement of the possibility of having rationally grounded beliefs is that one also has this arational certainty – *hinge certainty* – that provides the framework for rational evaluation. If that's correct, then all rational belief presupposes an arational hinge certainty. Hence, insofar as this idea is applied to the religious case (as quasi-fideism proposes), then there is no essential difference between the way in which religious belief and everyday belief involves commitment to arational certainties, as both necessarily require the existence of an arational hinge certainty. We thus get the fideistic kind of epistemic parity argument noted above.

The backdrop of certainty that Wittgenstein has in mind is essentially one's certainty in the fundamental veracity of one's world picture. This is manifest, in normal conditions, in a complete certainty in Moorean commonsense claims, such as 'I have two hands', 'my name is such-and-such', 'I am speaking English', and so forth. The overarching hinge certainty in one's world picture thus manifests itself in one being certain of particular propositions that express fundamental aspects of that world picture, in the sense that the falsity of these everyday commonsense propositions in normal conditions would call one's world picture as a whole into doubt. The overarching hinge certainty thus leads to hinge commitments to specific propositions.[19]

Wittgenstein argues that our hinge certainty is very different from the kind of commitment that is normally involved when one has a belief (and not just because one can believe something without being certain of it). Unlike our ordinary beliefs, our hinge commitments are not acquired via rational processes, nor are they responsive, at least in any direct sense, to rational considerations. This is what Wittgenstein (1969: §§359, 475, 559) means when he says that our hinge certainty is "animal," "primitive," and there "like our life." We acquire our hinge commitments by "swallowing them down" (Wittgenstein 1969: §143) as part of our induction into a social practice, and hence we are not persuaded of their truth; their truth is rather presupposed in the social practice itself. Once acquired, moreover, they are not directly responsive to rational considerations, in that this is a certainty that remains undiminished even once one recognizes that it is not grounded in reasons.

Consider one's hinge commitment, in normal circumstances, that one has hands. We do not normally consider the rational standing of such a claim, or indeed even consider it at all. But once we start to consider it, we might

---

[19] I've elsewhere described this overarching hinge certainty as the *über hinge commitment*, in contrast to the more specific hinge commitments that are manifestations of the über hinge commitment. See Pritchard (2015a, part 2).

naturally think that it is rationally grounded just like our other beliefs, such as being grounded in our sight of our hands or our memory of having them. Wittgenstein's contention is that once we consider the nature of this commitment, we realize that it doesn't function like this at all. One's certainty, in normal circumstances, that one has hands is not grounded in one's sight of one's hands, for example – one doesn't satisfy oneself that one has hands by looking to see if they are there. This certainty is rather part of the background against which one makes rational evaluations. Indeed, even once one becomes aware that one's hinge commitments are playing this role, this doesn't undermine one's confidence in them, as that confidence was never the result of rational considerations in the first place.[20]

The resulting picture that Wittgenstein offers of the structure of rational evaluation is thus very different from the standard view. The very idea that one can rationally evaluate all of one's commitments at once is on this proposal simply incoherent, as all rational evaluation presupposes hinge commitments that are not themselves rationally evaluable and hence are arational. If this is right, then it is part of the nature of all our beliefs that they presuppose arational commitments.[21] The application of hinge epistemology to religious belief would involve treating a subject's basic religious commitments as hinge commitments, and hence as essentially arational. One key advantage of such a proposal is that it would generate a kind of fideism that allows one to endorse the sort of epistemic parity line outlined above. The idea would be that there is essentially no difference between everyday belief and religious belief, in that both kinds of belief presuppose fundamental commitments that, as hinge commitments, are arational.

There are two further features of the quasi-fideist position that we should note. The first is its connection to skepticism, such that it arguably qualifies as a form of skeptical fideism (or, at least, can be construed in that spirit). Quasi-fideism is forged in the specific skeptical context that gives to an understanding of the limitations of reason. In particular, it arises in light of the realization that some of our commitments are immune to rational, and thus skeptical,

---

[20] I argue in Pritchard (2015a, part 2) that this feature of our hinge commitments makes them very different from the kind of propositional attitude that is a constituent part of knowledge, what I refer to as *K-apt belief* (in contrast to the more permissive folk notion of belief, which I claim does apply to our hinge commitments). Note that since religious hinge commitments do qualify as beliefs in the folk sense, it follows that quasi-fideism is incompatible with a fictionalist account of religious commitment. For discussion of the relationship between faith and belief, see Pojman (1986), Audi (1991), Alston (1996), and Howard-Snyder (2016).

[21] I develop this account of hinge epistemology in Pritchard (2015a). For the other main treatments of hinge epistemology, see Strawson (1985), McGinn (1989), Williams (1991), Wright (2004), Coliva (2015), and Schönbaumsfeld (2016). For a survey, see Pritchard (2017b).

evaluation, which then leads to a position whereby one's basic religious commitments are understood fideistically.[22]

The second feature of quasi-fideism that we should highlight is that it is not committed to treating all religious conviction as essentially arational. For just as one's ordinary beliefs can presuppose arational hinge certainties and be no less rationally grounded as a result, so one's religious beliefs can presuppose arational religious hinge certainties and yet also be no less rationally grounded. This is the sense in which this is a moderate, or quasi-, fideism, in that it doesn't involve treating religious conviction *en masse* as being arational, but only with regard to the most fundamental religious commitments. In particular, notice that quasi-fideism is able to advance an epistemic parity argument only because of the moderate nature of its fideism (as this tactic would be unavailable if it treated all religious belief as arational).

Whether quasi-fideism is compelling as an account of the epistemology of religious belief largely depends on two key issues. The first is whether the underlying hinge epistemology is plausible, as of course quasi-fideism will inherit all of the problems that afflict the more general proposal. The second concerns the application of hinge epistemology to the religious case. For even if hinge epistemology in general is compelling, it doesn't follow that quasi-fideism is credible, as that depends on whether fundamental religious commitments are suitable candidates to be hinge commitments.[23]

One issue that drives this second concern is that religious hinge commitments seem to be very different from the kind of Moorean commonsense claims that Wittgenstein cites. To begin with, fundamental religious commitments, as Wittgenstein himself notes elsewhere, seem to be quite unlike empirical commitments in that they express deeply held values.[24] But that makes them very different from claims about having hands or speaking English. One's fundamental religious commitments are different to one's quotidian hinge commitments in other ways too. For example, while one is not explicitly taught one's quotidian hinge commitments, one is explicitly taught one's religious hinge commitments. Relatedly, while one is not normally aware of one's quotidian hinge commitments in normal conditions, as they "lie apart from the route travelled by inquiry" (Wittgenstein 1969: §88),

---

[22] See Pritchard (2021). A further rationale in this regard concerns the Pyrrhonian impetus behind Wittgenstein's work – see Sluga (2004) and Pritchard (2019a; 2019b; in press b).

[23] A related issue in this regard is that whether one finds the transition from hinge epistemology to quasi-fideism compelling will depend to some extent on what kind of hinge epistemology one endorses. On some readings of hinge epistemology – for example, Wright (2004) and Coliva (2015) – fundamental religious convictions would not count as hinge commitments.

[24] Consider, for example, this passage: "It strikes me that a religious belief could only be something like a passionate commitment to a system of reference. Hence, although it's belief, it's really a way of living, or a way of assessing life. It's passionately seizing hold of this interpretation." (Wittgenstein 1980: 64)

one is usually aware of one's religious hinge commitments; indeed, they are typically explicitly affirmed as part of religious practices. Furthermore, while there is no normal context in which one would offer reasons in support of one's quotidian hinge commitments, it is quite common within religious contexts to offer reasons in support of one's religious hinge commitments.

The differences between religious and quotidian hinge commitments are thus quite significant. It follows that even if one is persuaded by hinge epistemology in general, one might not thereby be inclined to accept the application of hinge epistemology to the religious case represented by quasi-fideism. I think what is ultimately at issue here is whether one is willing to allow one's conception of a hinge commitment to extend beyond quotidian empirical claims about the world to encompass broadly axiological claims. If one takes this step, then one would likely end up with a form of hinge epistemology that doesn't just embrace religious hinge commitments but also other kinds of nonquotidian hinge commitments that incorporate axiological theses, like ethical and political hinge commitments. There is, however, a rationale for moving hinge epistemology in this direction, for if one's specific hinge commitments are manifestations of one's conviction in a particular worldview, then it is hard to see why those commitments would be limited to mundane claims about the world and wouldn't also take in large-scale axiological commitments.[25]

6.5 Concluding Remarks

We have witnessed how skeptical themes inform the debate regarding the rationality of religious belief. This occurs in both the expected manner of posing skeptical hurdles that religious belief is supposed to clear, and also in the more surprising manner of informing particular defenses of religious belief. On the former front, we've noted how Lockean evidentialism accepts a certain skepticism-friendly way of framing the issue (a framing that is rejected by reformed epistemology, for example), but nonetheless aims to defend the rationality of religious belief within this framing. On the latter front, we have been particularly interested in the formulation of skeptical fideism, especially insofar as this is allied to an epistemic parity argument that enables the view to avoid the charge of epistemic ghettoization. We also considered the prospects for a specific proposal that could plausibly be thought to be allied to this form of skeptical fideism, the Wittgensteinian quasi-fideism that attempts to apply hinge epistemology to the religious case.[26]

---

[25] I discuss some of the challenges facing quasi-fideism in Pritchard (2022a; 2022b; in press a). See also n. 18.

[26] Thanks to John Greco.

7 The Problem of Faith and Reason

Daniel Howard-Snyder and Daniel J. McKaughan

7.1 Faith-Conflicts-with-Reason Arguments

Any comprehensive textbook in the philosophy of religion contains a section on the problem of faith and reason, the contention that faith in God conflicts with reason. There are different ways to display the alleged conflict. Here's one way:

Argument 1

1. Faith in God requires always, or at least sometimes, believing on insufficient evidence that God exists.
2. Reason requires never believing anything on insufficient evidence.
3. So, faith in God and reason require incompatible things – in which case they conflict.

Here's another way:

Argument 2

1. Rational faith in God requires rational belief that God exists.
2. Belief that God exists is irrational.
3. So, faith in God is irrational – in which case it conflicts with reason.

Call these and their kin faith-conflicts-with-reason arguments.

Such arguments have borne the brunt of extensive criticism. In what follows, we evaluate three criticisms of these two arguments before we zero in on a crucial assumption, namely that you can't have faith in God unless you believe that God exists. Whether that's true depends on what faith is. We sketch a theory of faith that allows you to have faith in God even if you are in belief-canceling doubt about the matter. We then explain why that's a good thing about our theory, in contrast with Thomas Aquinas's theory. We close by assessing revisions of Arguments 1 and 2 that are in line with our theory, and we find them to be dubious, at best.

7.2 Fideism, Natural Theology, and Reformed Epistemology

The first criticism – a version of fideism – accepts the conclusion of each argument but observes that even if faith in God is at sword's point with reason, nothing of interest follows. For even if faith in God conflicts with reason, *so what?* Must those with faith in God tremble in their boots? Not at all. Unless reason has authority over faith in God, faith in God has nothing to fear in the conflict. Indeed, quite the opposite is true: faith in God has authority over reason.[1]

There are at least two problems with this fideistic criticism of the two faith-conflicts-with-reason arguments. The first problem is that, according to the first of the two Great Commandments – which is affirmed by the Abrahamic religions – we are to love God with all our heart, strength, soul, and mind (Deuteronomy 6:5, 10:12; Mark 12:30; Luke 10:27; Matthew 22:37; cf. Qur'an 8:22). But we can't love God with all our mind unless we allow reason to inform, influence, and regulate what we put our faith in, including faith in God. The second problem is that these traditions encourage the use of reason when it comes to relating to God by faith. For example, through the prophet Isaiah, God invites wayward Israel to "Come, let us reason together" (Isaiah 1:18), and the earliest Christians gave reasons to think Jesus was the Messiah, and Muslims are well known for prizing reasoned theological argumentation. So, the fideistic criticism of Arguments 1 and 2 will not satisfy people who aim to love God with all their mind, and who use reason to inform, influence, and regulate their faith in God, out of love of God.

A second criticism of these two faith-conflicts-with-reason arguments – a version of natural theology – affirms reason's role in relation to faith in God but denies that faith in God ever requires believing that God exists on insufficient evidence. After all, just as we can have faith in others while believing they exist on the basis of sufficient evidence, so we can have faith in God while believing that God exists on the basis of sufficient evidence. So, premise 1 of Argument 1 is false. More importantly, premise 2 of Argument 2 is false. That's because the publicly available evidence (e.g., certain general features of our world, or the moral, modal, and historical facts) is sufficient for rational belief that God exists; rational faith in God remains an option.[2]

A problem with this second criticism of Arguments 1 and 2 is that, even if faith in God never requires believing that God exists on insufficient evidence, the publicly available evidence is arguably insufficient for rational belief that God exists. In any case, when many people consider the publicly available evidence carefully – and when they give the best critical assessments of it their due weight – they judge that it is insufficient for rational belief that God exists.

Like our natural theologian's criticism of the two faith-conflicts-with-reason arguments, a third criticism – a version of Reformed epistemology – affirms reason's role in relation to faith in God but, unlike it, our Reformed

---

[1] The frame of mind characterized here resembles Tertullian's *Prescriptions Against Heretics*, chapter 7, and its heirs.
[2] Craig and Moreland (2012); Swinburne (2004).

epistemologist emphasizes private sources of belief in the existence of God (e.g., religious experiences) or the exercise of a dedicated capacity for forming beliefs that logically entail that God exists (e.g., a *sensus divinitatis*). And just as the private sources of mundane belief in the existence of objects in our immediate environment render such belief rational, so the private sources of belief in God's existence render it rational.[3]

One problem with our Reformed epistemologist's criticism of Arguments 1 and 2 is that, arguably, not only is there insufficient reason to believe that religious experience or the exercise of a dedicated God-belief-forming capacity *actually* renders belief in God's existence rational, but there are also undefeated undercutting-defeaters available, for example, not-implausible alternative explanations of these phenomena.

But a more important problem with both our natural theologian's and our Reformed epistemologist's criticism of the two faith-conflicts-with-reason arguments is that many people of faith identify with William Wainwright's self-description, according to whom it is difficult for him "to embrace *any* controversial [proposition] without *some* hesitation."[4] Nevertheless, he continues, theism seems "*more reasonable* to me, on the whole, *than its alternatives.*"[5] He concludes with these words:

My attitude is in many ways similar to T. S. Eliot's. Eliot appears to have combined a deeply serious faith with both irony and skepticism. (When asked why he accepted Christianity, he said he did so because it was *the least false of the options open to him.*) . . . I do not regard my stance as exemplary. If Christianity (or indeed any form of traditional theism) is true, a faith free from doubt is surely better. I suspect, however, that my religious life may be fairly representative of the lives of many intelligent, educated, and sincere Christians in the latter part of the twentieth century.[6]

Wainwright and Eliot lack *belief* that *God exists*, as do many other intelligent, educated, and sincere people of faith in the twenty-first century. Some theists accuse Wainwright, Eliot, and their kin of excessive skepticism or intellectual spinelessness. We protest. By our reckoning, they exhibit the virtue of intellectual humility, properly attending to and owning their intellectual limitations as they assess the grounds for believing that God exists.[7] In any event, they cannot join our natural theologian or our Reformed epistemologist in their criticism of Arguments 1 and 2. For them, the problem of faith and reason remains.

How might those who identify with Wainwright and Eliot view that problem? They might begin by observing that each of the two faith-conflicts-with-

---

[3] Alston (1991); Plantinga (2000b).   [4] Wainwright (1994: 78).   [5] Ibid. Emphasis added.
[6] Ibid.: 87. Emphasis added.
[7] For more on intellectual humility, see Whitcomb et al. (2017).

reason arguments has a premise that entails the Crucial Assumption: you have faith in God only if you believe that God exists.

But is the Crucial Assumption true? That depends on what faith is.

7.3 Resilient Reliance: A Theory of Faith

We propose that this is what faith is:

Resilient Reliance. For you to have faith in someone for something is for you to be disposed to rely on them to come through with respect to it, with resilience in the face of challenges to relying on them, because of your positive stance toward their coming through.

Several clarifications are in order.[8]

At a first approximation, a *positive stance* toward someone coming through is any of a variety of combinations of both positive cognitive states and positive conative states toward them coming through. Here's why we include it in our proposed theory.

Like fear, hope, anger and other complex psychological states, faith has built into it what's needed to make sense of behavior. For example, all you need to know to understand why Christina behaves in certain ways – confessing her sins, expressing gratitude to God, petitioning God, studying the Bible, gathering with Christians, relying on the two Great Commandments to make moral, social, and political decisions, receiving the sacraments, and the like – is that she has faith in Jesus as her Lord. However, Christina's faith can explain her relying-on-Jesus behavior only if it involves both cognitive and conative states. But we cannot explain her behavior by saying that she wants to follow Jesus as her Lord and she *believes* that he will *not* come through on that score, or by saying that she believes that Jesus will come through as her Lord and she *wants* him *not* to do so. Disbelief and disdesire are too "negative" to make sense of her behavior; more "positive" states are required.

At a first approximation, for Christina to be in a *positive cognitive state* toward Jesus coming through as her Lord is for her to be in some cognitive state or other that represents him as coming through and has three features: it has the content that Jesus will come through, it disposes her to take a stand on behalf of the truth of that content, and it is responsive to her evidence for its truth and/or is produced by a cognitive process or skill that aims at true positive cognitive states. *Belief* that Jesus *will* come through counts, but – crucially – there are other candidates, for example, a high-enough credence or confidence that he will come through or, depending on the details, accepting, trusting, hoping, or belieflessly assuming that he will; propositional reliance

---

[8] For more on faith and its relation to faithfulness, see McKaughan and Howard-Snyder (2022; in press a).

and imaginative assent might also be candidates.[9] One qualification. Just as you can put your hope in your spouse to remember your anniversary even though you lack belief of the "thick" proposition that they *will* remember, so Christina can have faith in Jesus as her Lord even though she lacks belief of the "thick" proposition that Jesus *will* come through, and instead believes a "thinner" proposition that it is *more likely than not he will come through*. We include belief in thinner propositions among positive cognitive states. Upshot: many states fall under the rubric of a positive cognitive state.

Note that the positivity involved in a positive cognitive state is a disposition to take a stand *on behalf of* its truth in contrast with taking a stand *against* its truth, or *no* stand at all. Nothing else. You can be in a positive cognitive state toward a proposition even when you regard its truth as bad or undesirable, as when you believe that you will be unjustly executed tomorrow.

For Christina to be in a *positive conative state* toward Jesus coming through as her Lord is for her to be in some conative state or other that motivates her to rely on Jesus to come through. Wanting him to do so counts but – crucially – there are other candidates. For example, imagine that, like the rich young ruler, Christina does not want to follow Jesus because it's too demanding but, unlike the rich young ruler, she wants *to want* to follow Jesus because she sees how much better her life might be if she were to submit to his Lordship. She has a second-order desire for her first-order desire to be changed. Nevertheless, she might yet have faith in Jesus as her Lord. For, although she lacks a first-order desire to follow him, it still matters to her since she wants to change her first-order desire (i.e., she wants to want to follow Jesus). In addition to first- and second-order desires, other options include looking with favor on Jesus coming through as her Lord, being for it, a felt attraction to it, caring about it, being emotionally invested in it, and affection for him in that capacity, all of which the literature mentions.[10] We include these among positive conative states. Upshot: many states fall under the rubric of a positive conative state.

Notice that, on Resilient Reliance, faith is a *role-functional psychological state*.[11] For a psychological state to be an instance of faith in someone for something is for it to take as input any of a wide variety of combinations of both positive conative and positive cognitive states toward them coming through and to give as output a disposition to rely on them to come through with resilience in the face of challenges.

So then: Christina's faith in Jesus as her Lord can make sense of her relying-on-Jesus behavior, and that's because her faith involves both positive conative

---

[9] See Alston (1996); Audi (2011); Howard-Snyder (2013; 2017b; 2019); (McKaughan 2013; 2016); Pojman (1986); Rath (2017); Schellenberg (2005).

[10] Cf. Adams (2002), Alston (1996), Audi (2011), Howard-Snyder (2013), Kvanvig (2018), McKaughan (2016; 2017).

[11] Cf. Levin (2021).

and positive cognitive states toward his coming through as her Lord. For convenience, we collect both states under the label of a *positive stance*, which appears in our theory.

Regarding *a disposition to rely*, on our view, it is a certain sort of non-basic action, one you perform by doing other things, such as relying on God by following his commands and praying regularly. But notice: you can have faith in someone for something even while you are not performing the act of relying on them for it – as when you are fast asleep – provided you have a *disposition* to perform the act of relying on them for it.[12]

As for *resilience in the face of challenges*, on our view, it is an unspecific general disposition to overcome – or to *try* to overcome – challenges to continuing to rely on those in whom we have placed our faith. It can be instantiated by many things psychologists distinguish and study, such as unperturbedness, bouncing-back, grit, fortitude, hardiness, persistence, perseverance, etc. Faith's resilience does not need to dispose us to overcome all possible challenges. We can be more or less resilient depending on the range of possible challenges to which we would respond by overcoming them. This is one way in which we can have more or less faith.[13]

We intend our theory to allow for belief of thin propositions, as well as nondoxastic states. Here we briefly call attention to one nondoxastic state by way of illustration. Consider the following case.

It's fourth down. The ball is on the two-yard line. There's one minute left. The offense needs a touchdown to stay in the game. The defensive captain considers what play the opposing quarterback will call. From his prior experience, and given the current situation, it's most plausible to him that the quarterback will call a fullback plunge. So, he assumes that's the call. Then, he acts on his assumption, aligning the defense to stop it.

We can easily imagine that the captain is in doubt about whether the quarterback will call a plunge, and so he neither believes nor disbelieves that's the call. Even so, we can easily imagine that he acts on the assumption that it is. That is, he *assumes* that a plunge was called and thereby takes a stand on the truth of that proposition, packing the line instead of aligning his men for any number of other running plays (e.g., a toss or a sweep), or for any number of passing plays (e.g., a corner or hook).

Notice that the captain does not assume that the call is a plunge in the way in which we assume something by *taking it for granted*, for example, taking it for granted that we've existed for more than five minutes: that's just belief. Nor does he assume that's the call in the way in which we assume something by *simply considering it to see what follows*, for example, simply considering

---

[12] For more on the act of relying, see Howard-Snyder and McKaughan "Relying on Another to Do Something" (unpublished).

[13] For more on faith's resilience, see Howard-Snyder and McKaughan (2022).

whether a time can be earlier than itself, for reductio: simply considering something to see what follows would not have resulted in him taking a stand on behalf of the truth of the proposition that the call is a plunge. Rather, he exhibits something different: a way of assuming something that involves neither belief nor disbelief, one that involves being in doubt, one that, nevertheless, results in taking a stand on behalf of the truth of the proposition assumed – and so acting accordingly. That is, he *belieflessly assumes* the call is a plunge.[14]

We submit that you can have faith in God for something even if you lack belief that God will come through, or belief that God exists. That's because you can have faith in God for something if you belieflessly assume that God will come through, and belieflessly assume that God exists, provided that you satisfy faith's other conditions.

7.4 Faith and Doubt

Resilient Reliance allows you to have faith in God while being in doubt about whether God will come through, and even while being in doubt about whether God exists. This is a good thing. That's because by allowing these things, Resilient Reliance can make sense of several items of secular and religious faith-data. Here we discuss four items of religious faith-data: (i) *pístis* in the Synoptics, (ii) *'emunāh* in the Hebrew scriptures, (iii) exemplars of faith in God, and (iv) the experience of people of faith today.[15]

But before we turn to these items of faith-data, we should say a brief word about doubt. We distinguish *having doubts* from *being in doubt*, and we distinguish both of them from *doubting that*. For you to have doubts about something – note the 's' – is for you to have what you regard as grounds for its negation and, as a result, for you to be at least somewhat less inclined to believe it, whereas for you to be in doubt about something is for you to regard your grounds for it as roughly on a par with your grounds for its negation and, as a result, for you neither to believe it nor disbelieve it. Having doubts about something and being in doubt about something are not to be identified with doubting that something is so. If one doubts that something is so, one disbelieves it, or is at least strongly inclined to disbelieve it; having doubts about something and being in doubt about something lack that implication. We will focus on being in doubt. One consequence of our view about doubt is that being in doubt about something is incompatible with believing it.

---

[14] To be clear, we are *not* saying the defensive captain has faith. We are saying he has a beliefless assumption. Further, we are saying that beliefless assumption is a nondoxastic positive cognitive state. Further still, we are saying that beliefless assumption could be the positive cognitive state of someone's faith. Belief is not required.

[15] On some secular data, see Howard-Snyder and McKaughan (2022).

7.4.1 *Pístis* in the Synoptic Gospels

Early in Mark's Gospel, Jesus arrives in Galilee, calling people to repentance and *faith in* (*pisteuó en*) the good news. Mark displays through his characters the nature of the faith to which Jesus calls people. In this connection, Mark has Jesus explicitly commend someone's *pístis* three times, and on each occasion their most salient feature is relying on Jesus to heal despite challenges to relying on him, sometimes including doubt. Note well: in the world of the story, it was known that Jesus was *able* to heal, but it was up for grabs whether he *would* in any specific case. With this in mind, consider the story of Jairus, the synagogue leader (Mark 5:22–24, 35–43).

After begging Jesus to come to his home to heal his sick daughter, Jesus eventually consents. As they walk together, Mark highlights counterevidence to the proposition that his daughter was alive and so a candidate for healing. First, the messengers inform him "Your daughter is dead." Second, when they arrive at his home, they are met by "people weeping and wailing loudly," a ritual mourning for the dead. Third, after Jesus says she is only sleeping, the mourners mock him. Fourth, Jairus then "went in where the child was" and saw her with his own eyes, still as stone. Perhaps his wife cradled her in her arms, gently weeping while she stroked her hair. Perhaps when Jairus met her eyes, she conveyed to him her hopelessness: it's too late, she's dead.

Mark calls our attention to this mounting counterevidence, underscoring Jairus's grounds for doubt. To nonetheless attribute to Jairus the *belief* that his daughter *is* alive seems uncharitable, especially when there is another reading available, one that ascribes no irrationality to him and one that is well within the semantic range and first-century cultural understanding of *pístis*: Jairus retains his faith in Jesus to heal his daughter from the beginning of the story to the end, even though, just prior to the vindication of his faith, he only, perhaps, belieflessly assumes Jesus will heal her, or maybe even assigns it a low credence.[16]

Or consider the story of the Canaanite woman in Matthew's Gospel (15:21–28), who is arguably "not only an exemplar of faith in Matthew, but *the* exemplar."[17] She approaches Jesus: "Have mercy on me, Lord, Son of David; my daughter is tormented by a demon." But he does not answer her, and his disciples urge him to send her away. Eventually, however, Jesus does answer: "I was sent only to the lost sheep of the house of Israel." Kneeling, she persists: "Lord, help me." He answers again: "It is not fair to take the children's food and throw it to the dogs." But she continues: "Yes, Lord, yet even the dogs eat the crumbs that fall from their

---

[16] According to Teresa Morgan (2015), in the Greco-Roman and Hellenistic-Judaic worlds from which the early churches derived their understanding of *pístis*, it centrally involves relying on others – especially, she repeatedly notes – in the face of "risk, fear, doubt, and skepticism." As such, *pístis* held people together in times of crisis.

[17] O'Donnell (2021: 21), emphasis added.

masters' table." "Then Jesus answered her, 'Woman, great is your *pístis*! Let it be done for you as you wish.' And her daughter was healed instantly."

As the Canaanite woman interacts with Jesus, Matthew underscores her mounting counterevidence to Jesus healing her daughter. First, she's a Canaanite woman, and so a target of the historical hostility between Jews and Canaanites. Second, Jesus doesn't answer her when she first speaks to him. Third, his disciples try to get rid of her. Fourth, when Jesus does answer her, he insists that God has sent him to the Jews alone, and not to her people. Fifth, when Jesus answers her the second time, he uses a racial slur to refer to her people. Sixth, Jesus further insists that it would be morally wrong for him to give to her what was intended by God to be given to the Jews.

All this counterevidence is reasonable grounds for the woman to be in belief-canceling doubt about whether Jesus will heal her daughter. To nonetheless attribute to her the irrational *belief* that Jesus *will* heal her is uncharitable, especially when the semantic range and first-century cultural understanding of *pístis* permits an alternative reading: she retains her faith in Jesus, continuing to rely on him to heal her daughter from beginning to end, even though, just before Jesus recognizes her "great faith," she only, perhaps, belieflessly assumes that Jesus will heal her daughter, or has a low degree of confidence that he will.

The narrative structure in these two stories is typical of miracle stories in the Synoptics: someone has a need, they or a proxy rely on Jesus to help, they continue to rely despite difficulty (including, sometimes, belief-canceling counterevidence), Jesus recognizes their *pístis*, he performs a miracle, and they or others respond. Several of these stories can be read in a similar way, such as Bartimaeus, the father of the demon-possessed son, and the woman with a hemorrhage.

By allowing positive cognitive states that are compatible with being in doubt, Resilient Reliance makes sense of the combination of *pístis* and doubt exhibited by these characters in the Synoptics. It also makes sense of Jesus' own disciples exhibiting "little faith," which is indicative of doubt.[18]

7.4.2 *Emunāh* in the Hebrew Scriptures

The *ʾemunāh* lexicon points to firmness in faithfulness *and* in faith, depending on how its verb form, *ʾaman*, is conjugated. The passive niphal verb form, *neʾĕmān*, is most often glossed "to be faithful" or "to endure," and when applied to persons, "stable, reliable."[19] In contrast, the active hiphil verb form,

---

[18] For more on faith and doubt in the Synoptics and other biblical material, see Howard-Snyder (2017a), McKaughan and Howard-Snyder (in press b), Morgan (2015), and Schliesser (2022).

[19] Brown et al. (1977: 52–53); Moberly (1997: 427–433); Jepsen (1977: 322–323).

he'emin, expresses action, "to be firmly set in/on something, to hold firm," and "is used especially of a person or his word: to build steadfastly on someone, or to rely on his word."[20] Interestingly, the active hiphil characterizes Abraham's exemplary response to God: "And he *he'ĕmin* the Lord; and the Lord reckoned it to him as righteousness" (Genesis 15:6). If we attend to Abraham's story, we can gain a better view of the nature of the *'emunāh* for which "the father of faith" is well known.

Abraham's story begins when God visits him and commands him to leave his family and homeland, promising to make of him a great nation that will bless the world (Genesis 12). While the narrative arc of his story has him relying on God to keep the promise, he sometimes seems not to rely on God as much as he might have, which suggests that lurking in the background lies some doubt about whether God will come through. This tension between the reliance to which God calls Abraham and the doubt Abraham experiences in relying on God arguably drives the narrative. With striking frankness, it underscores the ways Abraham falters in his relying on God, ways connected with doubt about whether God will keep the promise, through the decades of waiting for God to make good on it.[21]

Right from the start, when God calls Abraham, he – already seventy-five years old, well past his prime – hedges his bets. God says, "Go from your country *and your kindred* and your father's house to the land that I will show you," but Abraham brings some kindred along, notably his much younger nephew Lot, plausibly in the hope that Lot will produce an heir should the aging Abraham prove not up to the task (12:1, 4–5).

Moreover, both immediately before and immediately after Abraham is commended for "faithing" God (15:6), he expresses doubt. He complains, "You have given me no offspring," and seeks reassurance of the promise: "O Lord GOD, how am I to know that I shall possess [the land]?" (15:2–3, 8). The narrative explicitly ties Abraham's taking of Eliezer as his heir to his continued childlessness and his lack of confidence in God's reassurance that he will keep the promise (15:1–3). And after Abraham's faith is commended, "a deep and terrifying darkness descended upon him," prompting further reassurances from God (15:12–16). One without doubt needs no reassurance.

In addition, both Sarah and Abraham have difficulty believing that the heir will come through her womb, and difficulty relying on God to come through in this way. That's why Abraham takes Hagar as a mistress, who bears Ishmael when, as the narrative emphasizes, Abraham is eighty-six years old (16:1–4, 15). Fathering Ishmael also bespeaks doubt.

---

[20] Barton "Faith in the Hebrew Bible" (unpublished: 4), content incorporated into Barton, J. (2022), *Translating the Bible*, London: Penguin; Healey (1992: 745); Jepsen (1977: 322–323). Cf. Brown et al. (1977); Clines (1993).

[21] Cf. Stump (2012); Pace and McKaughan (2022).

Further, Abraham twice tells foreign leaders that Sarah is his sister rather than his wife, once before and once after God's specific promise (Genesis 17) that Sarah will bear a son, Isaac, and that he will be the heir (12:10–20; 20:1–18). In each case, the extent to which Abraham relies on God to protect her is compromised somewhat by his wavering; he hatches his own plan of protection (20:11). As Walter Brueggemann puts it, "even this model figure of faith was tempted to form an immediate alternative future of his own making."[22] Making his own plans likewise bespeaks doubt.

Further still, Abraham's laughter – in response to God's promise that Sarah will bear their heir – expresses serious doubt, perhaps even bordering on disbelief: "Then Abraham fell on his face and laughed, and said to himself, 'Can a child be born to a man who is a hundred years old? Can Sarah, who is ninety years old, bear a child?'" (17:17). Sarah laughs too (18:11–15). After several detours that prolong the fulfillment of the promise, the heir is given a name that commemorates that laughter: "everyone who hears will laugh with me" (21:6). Isaac's name reminds the narrative audience that nothing is "too wonderful for the LORD," but not because doubt was uncalled for (18:14). After all, as Sarah eloquently puts it, "Who would ever have said to Abraham that Sarah would nurse children? Yet I have borne him a son in his old age" (21:7). Yes, indeed; who would ever have said *that*? Again: the story displays doubt.

Finally, Abraham's relying on God to keep the promise is put to a climactic test (Genesis 22). God issues a command that will apparently destroy the basis for any fulfillment of the promise: "Take your son, your only son Isaac, whom you love, and go to the land of Moriah, and offer him there as a burnt offering on one of the mountains that I shall show you" (22:2). Whether Abraham's confidence in God at this point is maximal given their history together – or whether it isn't, and he is nonetheless resolved to obey God and to withhold nothing despite the apparent absurdity of the command – Abraham's disposition to rely on God, despite numerous occasions of doubt, has made his faith in God complete. He raises the knife.

If the story of Abraham is any indication, ʾemunāh enables people to continue to rely on God despite their doubt about whether God will come through, provided that they beliefylessly assume that he will, among many other possibilities. Bernhard Anderson sums it up well: "In the Old Testament faith is *steadfast reliance* on God amid the uncertainties and insecurities of life."[23]

Resilient Reliance makes sense of the combination of faith and doubt allowed by the ʾemunāh lexicon in the Hebrew scriptures, as illustrated by Abraham's story.[24]

---

[22] Brueggemann (1986a: 148).   [23] Anderson (1999: 3), emphasis added.
[24] For more on this item of faith-data, see McKaughan and Howard-Snyder (in press b).

7.4.3 Exemplars of Faith in God

Exemplars of faith in God sometimes struggle with doubt. In this connection, consider Jesus and Mother Teresa.

Mark's Gospel presents Jesus as a role model, and so we should expect Jesus to model something as important as faith, especially struggling with doubt, a common human experience. This we find in his relationships with the Twelve, but especially in his relationship with God, in Gethsemane and on Golgotha.[25]

In Gethsemane, Mark exhibits Jesus' disposition to rely on God as he comes to terms with how his execution will serve the new way in which God's rule will be established through him. Mark tells us that, after taking Peter, James, and John aside from the others in the garden, he became "distressed and agitated" at the prospect of the manner in which God's purposes involved him, so much so that he was "deeply grieved, even to death" (14:34). Walking a bit away from them to pray, he throws himself on the ground, begging God to find another way, saying "Abba, Father, for you all things are possible; remove this cup from me." To be sure, there is terror here but, plausibly, there is also doubt: doubt about the wisdom of God, doubt about what God's purposes require, and doubt about his own role in their fulfillment. Even so, Jesus leans into his faith in God's wisdom and purposes, thereby overcoming his terror and doubt, resolving to do God's will no matter what: "yet, not what I want, but what you want" (14:36). Notably, he finds the sleeping disciples and, after rebuffing them, he returns to pray alone where he "said the same words." Apparently, Jesus' struggle to continue relying on God despite his terror and doubt was not only intense but also recurrent.

On Golgotha, as Jesus was crucified, Mark says that, near the end, "at three o'clock," Jesus screamed, "My God, My God, why have you forsaken me?" (15:34). In the world of Mark's Gospel, Jesus has an explicit, conscious relationship of mutual faith and faithfulness with God, his "Abba, Father" (14:36). And here on the cross, Jesus expected God to be present to him in his hour of need – but his expectation is crushed. There is a sense of betrayal here, but there is also doubt, a "teetering on the edge between disillusionment and faith," as Father John Neuhaus puts it, doubt about God's care for and faithfulness to him.[26] Yet, Mark presents Jesus as an exemplar of faith. In doing so, Mark seems to say, "Look. This is what faith in God looks like in such circumstances. You rely on God – to exercise wisdom, care, faithfulness, and love – and you continue to do so, despite your inability to understand, your feelings of betrayal, and the doubt induced by your situation."

---

[25] Black (2011: 296); Rhoads (2004: 53–54). For a thorough treatment of Jesus as an exemplar of faith, see Tuggy (2017).

[26] Neuhaus (2000: 232).

Now to Mother Teresa. In 1942, after what she took to be a calling from the Lord, she made a private vow to give herself and her life completely to him, no matter what, and to serve him in the poorest of the poor. What she didn't expect at the time was that the "no matter what" clause of her vow would include five decades of relational emptiness and severe doubt. It appears from her private writings that she not only experienced the felt absence of God during that time; she also experienced doubt of a sort and degree that is incompatible with belief. "[T]here is no One to answer my prayers," she wrote: "So many unanswered questions live within me – I am afraid to uncover them – because of the blasphemy. – If there be God, please forgive me."[27] Later she wrote:

In my soul I feel just that terrible pain of loss – of God not wanting me – of God not being God – of God not really existing (Jesus, please forgive my blasphemies – I have been told to write everything). That darkness that surrounds me on all sides – I can't lift my soul to God – no light or inspiration enters my soul. – I speak of love for souls – of tender love for God – words pass through my words [*sic*, lips] – and I long with a deep longing to believe them. – What do I labour for? If there be no God – there can be no soul. – If there is no soul then Jesus – You also are not true.[28]

This was not a one-off occurrence. It was her "traveling companion" for nearly her entire adult life; nevertheless, "she carried on."[29]

How are we to understand this? In contrast with her earlier assessment of herself as having lost her faith, through sensitive, insightful spiritual direction, she later came to a different understanding, which she described with nine short words: "to live by faith and yet not to believe."[30] It is not difficult to see here someone experiencing belief-canceling doubt – quite understandable given her intimacy with pain and disease, death and suffering – and yet we plausibly also see someone resolved to rely on Jesus to come through, as her Lord, someone perhaps acting on the beliefless assumption, or perhaps even a very low credence, that the basic Christian story is true, and so keeping her vow to serve him in the poorest of the poor.[31]

Resilient Reliance makes sense of exemplars of faith in God who continue to rely on God despite belief-canceling doubt about God's love, purposes, and faithfulness – and even God's existence.

7.4.4 People of Faith Today

People of faith today struggle with doubt, among other things. Three facts suggest as much.

---

[27] Mother Teresa (2007: 187).   [28] Ibid.:192–193.   [29] Ibid.: 157, 326, 336.
[30] Ibid. (2007); contrast 187 and 193 with 248.
[31] For more on Mother Teresa as an exemplar of faith amidst doubt, see McKaughan (2018).

First, there's your own experience as a person of faith (if such you be), as well as the experience of those you know personally. Haven't you, or someone you know, experienced doubt, even belief-canceling doubt, at some point in your/their journey as people of faith? We have, as have many who have shared their stories with us. Yet here we are, continuing to rely on God in a variety of ways, despite our past and/or current doubt.

Second, there's the experience of people of faith you don't know personally but whose experience you have access to through other sources. For example, many religious leaders report that the people of faith they serve sometimes experience severe doubt. Just ask them. One pastor we know reported that, on average, throughout a twenty-year career at several churches, two people a week sought doubt-related counsel. On a 2018 trip to Jordan, we spoke about faith and doubt to sixty professors and students, wondering aloud whether people of Muslim faith experience severe doubt, as people of Christian faith sometimes do. The response was startling. The students estimated that a third of their peers experience belief-canceling doubt about the existence of Allah, among other things.[32] An orthodox rabbi recently spoke to us of many devout congregants who experience something similar.[33] Or witness the scores of easily googled self-help books that address doubting Christians, none of which would be written unless their intended audience experienced severe doubt. In an unscientific sampling, students in our recent university seminar interviewed 20 adult evangelical Protestants. Of these, 18 answered "Yes" to the question, "In the time that you have been a person of faith, have you ever been in doubt about whether God will come through with respect to what you put your faith in God for?," while 17 answered "Yes" to "In the time that you have been a person of faith, have you ever questioned the goodness or faithfulness or even the existence of God?," going on to describe their experiences in detail.

Third, beyond anecdotal evidence such as this, psychological research on religious struggle and spiritual formation reveals that people of faith sometimes struggle with doubt. Apparently, being a person of faith bears a significant positive correlation to experiencing doubt at some time – whether mild, moderate, or severe – about God's love, justice, and existence, in addition to many other religious struggles.[34] Kenneth Pargament and Julie Exline write:

If statistics are any guide, we continue to live in an age of doubt. In our large sample of adults (Exline, Pargament, & Grubbs 2014), 45.4% experienced some level of religious or spiritual doubt-related struggles over the past few weeks.... Among patients with advanced cancer, 20.0% reported some level of doubt about their faith or belief in God (Winkelman et al. 2011). A survey of Christian high

---

[32] For similar results, see Chouhoud (2018). On faith in God, and doubt, from a Muslim perspective, see Aijaz (2018).

[33] On faith in God, and doubt, from an Orthodox Jewish perspective, see Lebens (2020).

[34] Cf. Pargament and Exline (2022).

school adolescents revealed that 77.0% were currently having some doubts about religion. (Kooistra 1990)[35]

One study revealed that a staggering 90% of mothers who had given birth to a child with profound intellectual disability expressed some doubts about God's existence (Childs 1985). In an interview study of survivors of the suicide of a loved one, the majority (most of whom were religious believers at the time of the suicide) voiced deep questions about their faith. (Dransart 2018)[36]

Moreover, the most influential theory in developmental psychology of religion, James Fowler's theory of the stages of faith – which was initially based on interviews of 600 people of faith, and many more since then – recognizes continuing to rely on God in the face of challenges, including severe doubt, as a rite of passage for post-adolescent "mature" faith.[37] Further, these bodies of research continue to grow, displaying similar results.[38]

Resilient Reliance makes sense of the doubt experienced by people of faith today, including belief-canceling doubt.

In light of the faith-data adduced here, it's a good thing that our theory of faith allows for severe doubt. But what about other theories? Can they make sense of this faith-data? Here we focus on one influential theory of faith, that of Thomas Aquinas.

According to Aquinas, the object of faith is God, but since we have no immediate awareness of God, strictly speaking the object of faith is propositions about God, such as the proposition that God exists or the proposition that Jesus is God incarnate.[39] Faith, then, is an act of intellectual assent to propositions about God.[40] Many commentators call this act of intellectual assent "believing" (*credere*); we will follow suit. Notably, Aquinas says that faith shares important features with both (i) high-grade knowledge (*scientia*), such as a mathematician's knowledge of first principles and their knowledge of theorems based on demonstrations from those principles, and (ii) mere opinion, suspicion, and doubt (*opinione, suspicione et dubitatione*), such as our mere opinion that Trump's advisors colluded with conspiracy theorists and white nationalists to conduct the insurrection of January 6, 2021; our suspicion that there is extra-terrestrial sentient life; and our being in doubt about whether the number of Douglas firs in Lake Padden State Park is even. Like high-grade knowledge, faith requires believing with psychological certainty, and so no doubt, a view echoed by, among others, *The Catholic Encyclopedia*: "doubt cannot coexist with faith . . .; faith and doubt are mutually exclusive."[41] Like mere opinion, suspicion, and doubt, the evidence for faith is inadequate for

---

[35] Ibid.: 215.   [36] Ibid.: 217.   [37] Fowler (1981); Seel (2012).
[38] See works cited in Pargament and Exline (2022, ch. 10).
[39] Aquinas (1265–74/1981), II–II. q.1. a.1–2.   [40] Aquinas (1265–74/1981), II–II. q.2. a.9.
[41] Sharpe (1909).

believing with the certainty involved in high-grade knowledge, in two senses. First, it is *causally* inadequate to move someone's intellect to believe with certainty since the evidence for faith is only enough to move their intellect to mere opinion, suspicion, or doubt.[42] Second, it is *rationally* inadequate for believing with certainty since the evidence for faith is only enough to render rational mere opinion, suspicion, or doubt, and not belief. Nevertheless, someone can have faith that a proposition about God is true since they might be so attracted to its being true that their will moves their intellect to believe it is true with certainty even though their intellect alone could not be moved by the evidence to believe it.[43] And that is what faith is, says Aquinas: believing a proposition about God with certainty, on inadequate evidence, by an act of will, due to an attraction to its being true.[44]

Obviously enough, due to its certainty requirement, Aquinas's theory of faith cannot make sense of the faith-data we have adduced here: (i) *pistis* in the Synoptics, (ii) *'emunāh* in the Hebrew scriptures, (iii) exemplars of faith in God, and (iv) the experience of people of faith today.

7.5 The Revised Faith-Conflicts-with-Reason Arguments

On Resilient Reliance, the Crucial Assumption is false: faith in God does not require belief that God exists. Even so, both of the faith-conflicts-with-reason arguments can be revised to remove that defect. We treat each in turn.

Here's the first revision:

Argument 1, revised

1. Faith in God requires always, or at least sometimes, being in a positive cognitive state toward God's existence on insufficient evidence.
2. Reason requires never being in a positive cognitive state toward anything on insufficient evidence.
3. So, faith in God and reason require incompatible things – in which case they conflict.

Two observations. First, on Resilient Reliance, a wide range of positive cognitive states – both nondoxastic states as well as belief of a wide range of thinner propositions regarding God's existence – might partly constitute faith in God. Many of these require far less evidence than belief of the same content. Recognizing these possibilities gives us good reason to deny premise 1. At any rate, a proper defense of it would require decisive evidence against God's

---

[42] Aquinas (1265–74/1981), II–II. q.4. a.1
[43] Aquinas (1265–74/1981), II–II q.1 a.4; cf. Aquinas (1256–59/1951–54), q.14, a.2.
[44] For further assessment of Aquinas' view of faith, see Howard-Snyder and McKaughan (2020).

existence. Second, some epistemologists deny premise 2 since, on their theory of rationality, you can be in a rational positive cognitive state toward some proposition even if you have insufficient evidence for it.[45]

Here's the second revision:

Argument 2, revised

1. Faith in God requires being in a positive cognitive state toward God's existence.
2. Any positive cognitive state toward God's existence is irrational.
3. So, faith in God is irrational – in which case faith in God conflicts with reason.

The difficulty here is clear: it's a tall order to show that *every* positive cognitive state toward God's existence that faith in God might involve is irrational. Here's why.

Rational appraisal can apply to our thoughts, actions, and desires; epistemic, practical, and desiderative rationality, respectively. Clearly enough, epistemic rationality is at issue in these arguments. The epistemic rationality of someone's positive cognitive states can be evaluated from their own first-person perspective or from a third-person perspective. Our positive cognitive states are epistemically rational from a third-person perspective roughly when they *in fact* fit our total evidence, including our experience, and/or they are *in fact* produced by reliable cognitive capacities. They are epistemically rational from a first-person perspective roughly when they *seem* to us, on reflection, to fit our evidence and/or they *seem* to us, on reflection, to have been produced by reliable cognitive capacities. Now, notice an ambiguity in premise 2 of the revised Argument 2. It might mean

(2a)   Every positive cognitive state toward God's existence had by anyone does *not seem* to them, on reflection, to fit their evidence and/or does *not seem* to them, on reflection, to have been produced by reliable God-dedicated positive-cognitive-state-forming capacities,

or it might mean

(2b)   Every positive cognitive state toward God's existence had by anyone *in fact fails* to fit their evidence and/or *in fact has not* been produced by reliable God-dedicated positive-cognitive-state-forming capacities.

(2a) is false. Many people of faith are in a positive cognitive state toward God's existence, and it seems to them, on reflection, to fit their evidence and/or that it was produced by reliable God-dedicated positive-cognitive-state-forming capacities.

---

[45] For example, see the essays by Jason Baehr, Michael Bergmann, Keith DeRose, Alvin Goldmann, and John Greco in Dougherty (2011).

As for (2b), whether someone's positive cognitive state toward God's existence in fact fails to fit their evidence and/or in fact has not been produced by reliable God-dedicated positive-cognitive-state-forming capacities depends on (i) what the state is, (ii) whether their total evidence in fact fits the state, and/or (iii) whether that state was in fact produced by reliable God-dedicated positive-cognitive-state-forming capacities. Let's set aside (iii) for brevity's sake, although we expect that it will be no easy task to show that *in fact* no positive cognitive state of any person of faith was produced by reliable God-dedicated positive-cognitive-state-forming capacities. As for (i), let's focus initially on belieflessly assuming that God exists, for the sake of illustration. As for (ii), note that (2b) implies that the total evidence of every person of faith in fact fails to fit belieflessly assuming that God exists. But is this implication true?

In this connection, recall our defensive captain. Just as the evidence required for him to be rational in belieflessly assuming the quarterback called a plunge is much less than the evidence required for him to rationally believe that was in fact the call, so the evidence required for a person of faith to be rational in belieflessly assuming that God exists is much less than the evidence required for them to rationally believe it. That's because belieflessly assuming a proposition involves being in doubt about it, and the evidence required to rationally be in doubt about something is much less than the evidence required to rationally believe it. Therefore, those who would affirm (2b) must argue that the total evidence for God's existence is in fact *worse* than what's required for a person of faith to rationally be in doubt about it. Likewise for a person of faith believing thinner propositions; for example, Wainwright's *it seems "more reasonable to me, on the whole, than its alternatives,"* among other options. We know of no good arguments for these conclusions.

However, those who would argue for (2b) might need to argue for a more tendentious claim. For while Resilient Reliance disallows disbelief as a positive cognitive state, it allows credence. Moreover, it leaves open for discussion how low one's credence must go before it brings disbelief along with it. By general agreement, credence zero brings with it disbelief. But, arguably, any nonzero credence on proposition p that you don't regard as negligible need not bring with it disbelief, particularly if you are indisposed to assert not-p and you refuse to disavow p. *If* that's right, as Lara Buchak's, Jonathan Kvanvig's, and Richard Swinburne's theories of faith entail, then a person of faith might have faith in God while assigning a very-low-but-nonzero credence to God's existence, and so those who would affirm (2b) must argue that the total evidence for God's existence is in fact *worse* than what's required for a person of faith to be epistemically rational in assigning a very-low-but-nonzero credence that God exists.[46] No one we know of has succeeded on this score.

---

[46] Buchak (2012), Kvanvig (2018), Swinburne (2005); cf. McKaughan (2016).

As we said at the outset, faith in God conflicts with reason – or so we're told. But, so far as we can see, there's nothing about the nature of faith or reason themselves that begets any special difficulty, a difficulty beyond that of discerning what grounds you have for a positive stance toward God's existence. To speak frankly, we find it stunning how often discussions of the problem of faith and reason affirm mistaken assumptions about what faith in God requires, for example, that it requires belief that God exists on insufficient evidence, or even that it requires belief that God exists at all. Perhaps all of us will be better positioned to appreciate the challenges involved in arguing convincingly that faith in God conflicts with reason once we have a better understanding of what faith in God is, and what it is not.[47]

[47] A grant from the John Templeton Foundation supported this publication. The opinions expressed in it are those of the authors and might not reflect the views of the John Templeton Foundation. For feedback, we thank Jonathan Fuqua, John Greco, Tyler McNabb, and Michael Pace.

Part II

Religious Traditions

8 Jewish Religious Epistemology

Samuel Lebens

In this chapter, I explore three related notions that animate Jewish epistemology. Section 8.1 presents the first: knowledge by testimony. Section 8.2 presents the second: corporate knowledge. Section 8.3 presents the third: epistemic rootedness. In Section 8.4, I argue that these three notions collectively constitute a form of communitarian epistemology.

8.1 Testimony and the Kuzari Principle

The Kuzari principle has its roots in the work of Rabbi Yehuda Halevy (of the eleventh century). The principle, as articulated in contemporary times by Rabbi Dovid Gottlieb (2017), concerns the notion of a "national unforgettable." We call an event a national unforgettable if:

a)   it is remarkable, and
b)   it occurred in the presence of an entire nation (or a significant portion thereof), and
c)   its memory is widely alleged, by members of the nation in question, to have been passed down until now in an unbroken chain across the generations.

Legend has it that King Arthur ruled over a magical court in Camelot. That would have been a remarkable event. It would have been witnessed by the majority of the British nation. But the events in question were not passed down, or even alleged to have been passed down, in an unbroken chain. The first known reports of Arthur's magical court are reports of a *long-lost* tradition. Accordingly, the story of King Arthur doesn't qualify as a national unforgettable.

The story of the Blitz over London, by contrast, probably does. It was a remarkable event in the life of the British people. It was witnessed by all Londoners and was known about, at the time, by pretty much every British adult. Moreover, stories of the Blitz have certainly echoed down the generations in Great Britain in an unbroken chain.

The Kuzari principle (KP), as formulated by R. Gottlieb, can be stated as follows:

KP: Reports of a national unforgettable, when widespread within the nation in question, are reliable.

KP is an empirical generalization. There are lots of known cases of traditions of national unforgettables where the traditions are known to be true – such as the tradition about the Blitz or the Nazi occupation of France. By contrast, we know of no nation with a false tradition regarding a national unforgettable. R. Gottlieb would therefore endorse the following argument:

1. It is widely believed, among the Jewish people, that there was a revelation at Mount Sinai of God to the entire assembly of Israel, which has, according to this widespread belief, been passed down in an unbroken chain from that generation of Israelites until today.
2. If 1 is true, then there likely was a revelation at Mount Sinai, of God to the entire assembly of Israel.
3. There likely was a revelation at Mount Sinai, of God to the entire assembly of Israel.

The first premise is indisputably true. The second premise is licensed by KP. The conclusion, if both premises are true, follows at once.

   KP could be thought to embody a certain naïveté as to how national traditions emerge and evolve over time. And yet, R. Gottlieb would challenge his detractors to bring counterexamples. Are there any cases of reported national unforgettables that we know to be false? R. Gottlieb examines various candidate counterexamples and finds that they all fail to satisfy one or other of the criteria that characterize a national unforgettable.[1]

   The fact that you can *imagine* ways in which the belief in the Sinai revelation *could* have spread while being false is irrelevant to R. Gottlieb. To think that your imagination is able to undermine the soundness of his argument is, he would claim, to misunderstand how empirical generalizations work (Gottlieb 2017: 174). Empirical generalizations don't tell you how things *might have* happened; they tell you how things *tend to be*. KP tells you that, whether or not reports of national unforgettables *could be* false, in actual fact, they *tend to be true*. So, leave your imagined counterexamples to one side. If you can't find even one – or better, many (since an empirical generalization can still be a useful rule of thumb if it generally stands up but has a small number of counterexamples) – actual historical counterexamples to KP, the principle remains in good shape.

   If you're not convinced by KP, Tyron Goldschmidt (2019) offers a more compelling articulation of the principle. In doing so, he renders the principle more plausible, although his version can no longer be described as an empirical generalization. For KP to be an empirical generalization, it will need to have multiple actual historical instances (such as the Blitz and the Nazi

---

[1] A related concern might be raised that higher criticism of the Hebrew Bible renders these texts especially unreliable as witness to the events they purport to describe. I deal with such worries in §§7.3.1 and 7.3.2 of Lebens (2020b).

occupation of France). But Goldschmidt's version of KP is so gerrymandered to the specific contours of the Jewish story of the exodus from Egypt, and the revelation at Sinai, as to admit of no other examples in all of history. Nevertheless, the principle itself, even without being an empirical generalization, becomes so plausible, once Goldschmidt has amended it, that it becomes very difficult to deny. In Goldschmidt's hands, the principle becomes:

KP: A tradition is likely true if it is (1) accepted by a nation; describes (2) a national experience of a previous generation of that nation; which (3) would be expected to create a continuous national memory until the tradition is in place; is (4) insulting to that nation [e.g. it calls them stiff-necked and lists their sins];[2] and (5) makes universal, difficult and severe demands on that nation [e.g., commanding them in all sorts of arduous rituals and laws]. (2019: 233)

To test the plausibility of this amended KP, consider Goldschmidt's thought experiment about Nepal (2019: 233):

Just imagine trying to convince the Nepalese that three hundred years ago Napoleon visited their country for fifty years, and that everything he touched turned into gold. And also that: most everyone he visited tried to molest him, and so he put a curse on them – their enemies will enslave them unless they fast once a week, and tell the story to their children every day. And that they did tell the story to their children every day. It's not going to happen. The Nepalese would not believe this unless it happened.

And yet, the Jews do believe in *their* national tradition which meets all five of the criteria of Goldschmidt's amended KP. We should, therefore, conclude that the tradition is (likely) true.

My purpose isn't to assess the merits of the Kuzari argument. Instead, I wish to present the argument as an example of a general tendency within Jewish thought; a tendency that Goldschmidt summarizes as follows:

The Jewish tradition does not advertise much natural theology, though it's not averse to it. There were medieval Jewish natural theologians: Saadya, Maimonides, Crescas, et al. But . . . [the] rabbis don't care much for the business. They prefer to rely on testimony. A talkative lot. The Torah itself insists on testimony about the miracles of the exodus and revelation at Sinai. (2019: 222)

At this point, Goldschmidt cites two characteristic quotes from the Hebrew Bible:

For please ask . . . whether there has been anything like this great thing or heard like it: Has a nation heard the voice of God speaking from midst of the fire, as you

---

[2] Scholars of New Testament and Christian philosophy will recognize this fourth criterion of Goldschmidt's principle as a variation of the criterion of embarrassment. See Meier (1991: 168–171).

heard, and lived? Or has God tried to take himself a nation from the midst of a nation, with trials, with signs, and with wonders and with war, and with a strong hand, and with an outstretched arm, and with great terrors, like everything the Lord your God did for you in Egypt before your eyes? (Deuteronomy 4:32–43)

And:

Unleavened bread will be eaten throughout the seven days . . . You will tell your son on that day, saying: This is because of what the Lord did for me when I went out of Egypt. It must be a sign for you on your hand and a memorial between your eyes, so that God's law will be in your mouth, for with a strong hand the Lord brought you out of Egypt. You must observe this rule in its season forever. (Exodus 13:7–10)

As Goldschmidt concludes:

Ask about it. Tell about it. The festivals and the Sabbath are reminders of the exodus. The phylacteries and the redemption of the first born too. To say that the entirety of Jewish religious teaching and practice is about relaying and receiving the testimony would be an exaggeration. But almost all of it is. (2019: 223)

Almost every Jewish ritual is (at least in part) about reliving and relating the Jewish collective experience, and thereby (among other things) creating a chain of transmission from generation to generation. Goldschmidt is right, I think, to conclude that knowledge by testimony is, in the Jewish imagination, far more central than any knowledge that we might hope to derive from natural theology.

In the tradition of Western epistemology, testimony has often been seen as the weak link among possible sources of knowledge. Knowledge is generated by sense-experience or by *a priori* reasoning. Once knowledge has been generated, it can be transferred to others by means of testimony. In this way, testimony is parasitic on the true grounds of knowledge. Its parasitic status leads some to deny that knowledge by testimony is true knowledge. John Locke (1979 [1689]) wrote:

[W]e may as rationally hope to see with other Mens eyes, as to know by other Mens Understandings. So much as we our selves consider and comprehend of Truth and Reason, so much we possess of real and true Knowledge. The floating of other Mens Opinions in our brains, makes us not one jot the more knowing, though they happen to be true. What in them [i.e., those who testify to us] was Science [i.e., knowledge], is in us but Opiniatrety . . . . (105)

Or, in more contemporary times, Jonathan Barnes (1980) writes:

No doubt, we all do pick up beliefs in that second-hand fashion [i.e., by testimony], and I fear that we often suppose such scavengings yield knowledge. But that is only a sign of our colossal credulity: [it is] a rotten way of acquiring beliefs and it is no way at all of acquiring knowledge. (200)

But the Hebrew Bible, and the Jewish tradition, places tremendous weight upon testimony. Indeed, the key function of much of Jewish ritual, and *the* (or at least *a*) primary source of post-Biblical religious knowledge, is *testimony*. This suggests an epistemology with different priorities to the mainstream Western tradition.

8.2 Maimonides and Corporate Knowledge

Maimonides explains upon what basis the Jewish people accepted the authority of Moses. The Bible explicitly states that Moses was given certain miraculous signs to perform, such that the Israelites would believe that he had truly been sent by God (Exodus 4:5). But Maimonides declares that Israel didn't accept his prophecy, in the long term, merely because he could perform wonders. The power of a wonder to hold a people's imagination is, he claims, of limited duration. Instead:

It was the experience of Mount Sinai that made them believe in Moses, when our eyes, and no-one else's, saw, and our ears, and no-one else's, heard, and Moses drew near to the darkness, and the voice spoke to him, and we heard it saying to Moses, "Moses, Moses, go tell them such-and-such." In connection with this, it is written, "God spoke with you face to face." *Hilkhot Yesodei Hatorah*, 8:1

At Sinai, the entire people of Israel heard God speak to the prophet. This gave them a direct acquaintance, so to speak, with the fact that Moses really was a prophet. Prophets coming after Moses can claim authority on the basis that the Torah of Moses recognizes the role of a prophet. The authority of Moses, by contrast, doesn't stem from the Torah of Moses (that would be circular), but from the fact that the collected masses of Israel directly witnessed not a mere sign or wonder, but the event of God speaking to Moses.

Rabbi Yair Kahn (2017) writes:

According to the *Kuzari*, the claim of mass revelation is objective evidence, convincing even for one who was not present at Sinai. In fact, in *Sefer Ha-Kuzari*, this argument is addressed to the King of the Kuzars, who is not of Jewish descent. The Rambam [i.e., Maimonides], on the other hand, speaks of a personal, direct experience. It is meaningful only for one who witnessed the prophecy of Hashem [i.e., God] face to face.

Rabbi Kahn is sensitive to a small detail in the language used by Maimonides. The Maimonidean description of the Sinai event starts out in the third-person plural: "It was the experience of Mount Sinai that made *them* believe in Moses," before switching, surreptitiously, into the *first-person* plural, "when *our* eyes, and no-one else's, saw, and *our* ears, and no-one else's, heard . . ."

Whereas the Kuzari is interested in testimonial knowledge, which functions as objective evidence even to a third party, Maimonides is interested in first-personal sense-experience. The only problem is that everyone who had that direct experience is now dead. So, how can Maimonides speak about it as if the experience was *ours*? None of us were there.

The individuals who saw and heard the theophany at Sinai may no longer be living, but, Maimonides might say, Jews today are part of a nation – a "we" – and that nation still survives. Even to this day, *we* believe in Moses because *our* eyes saw, and *our* ears heard. The individuals have passed on – the individual eyes and ears – but the collective remains.

KP sheds light on the centrality, for the Jewish religion, of knowledge by testimony. Maimonides sheds light on something else: that knowledge is not only had by individuals but can also be had by collectives. These two insights don't conflict. They merely have a different focus.

The Biblical proof-text that Maimonides cites has Moses remind the Jewish people that:

The Lord our God made a covenant with us at Horeb [i.e. Mount Sinai]. It was not with our fathers that the Lord made this covenant, but with us, the living, every one of us who is here today. Face to face the Lord spoke to you on the mountain out of the fire. (Deuteronomy 5:2–4)

Moses spoke those words in the book of Deuteronomy, which records the final series of speeches delivered by Moses, just before he died.

Recall: in response to the sin of the people, at the time of the Ten Spies, God decreed that the Israelites would wander in the wilderness for forty years. Every adult male of the generation that left Egypt and stood at Sinai would die in the desert. A new generation would eventually take their place and enter the land of Israel. Moses would die at the end of those forty years. Accordingly, Moses is speaking to the second generation. Every adult male present at Sinai was, by that time, dead (apart from Moses, Joshua, and Caleb). Consequently, though many of his female audience were there at Sinai, and many of his male audience were there as children, a significant number of his audience were not at Sinai in person. They will only have known about the event via the testimony of their parents.

And yet, Moses tells them that the covenant at Sinai was *not* sealed between God and some past generation. "It was not with our fathers." Every one of those who are "here today" are the people to whom God spoke from out of the fire, "face to face." But that's patently untrue. In order to save the verses from absurdity, in their context, Moses must be appealing to a species of corporate knowledge. And thus, Maimonides is faithfully following a Biblical cue.

This species of corporate knowledge raises both metaphysical and epistemological questions: what it means for a collection of people to know something can be cashed out, somehow, in terms of what the individuals in that collective can be said to know. We don't need to posit the existence of some collective mind. Having said that, the cashing out is not always as straightforward as one might think.

Experiments at the Large Hadron Collider at CERN, for example, are sometimes conducted, collectively, by thousands of researchers. Very few (if any) of those researchers will be capable of understanding the finer details of the work that's done by each and every one of their collaborators, since many very specific and technical specialties will have been brought to bear upon the project. Accordingly, there might not be one person who straightforwardly *knows* what the collective has come to know through its collaboration. Whether or not the knowledge of the group can be explained without the posit of some collective mind, but purely in terms of the various mental and epistemic states of its members, which collectively constitute corporate knowledge of something not known (or, at least, not fully understood) by any one of the individuals in question, remains a matter of debate (into which we needn't venture here).[3]

I can understand how a collective can be said to have seen something, or heard something, directly – without the mediation of testimony – if the collection is comprised of people, many or some of whom had their own individual visual and aural experiences of the event, upon which the collective can draw. But it seems fair to ask (even if you believe that collective knowledge can't be straightforwardly reduced in terms of the epistemic states of the members of the collective): in what sense is that knowledge not merely knowledge by testimony once those members of the collective (the ones upon whose individual experiences the collective could draw) have died?

Maimonides might respond by having us think of a collective as an entity that's temporally extended. So long as one time-slice of that collective is comprised largely of people who had a certain sense-experience, perhaps the collective itself, at any later point, can be said to retain that empirical knowledge, so long as we're talking about the very same collective, even if its membership changes over time, such that later time-slices are not comprised of people who had the relevant sense-experience for themselves. There may be various necessary conditions for the preservation of this corporate knowledge over time, but it might still be able to survive the death of all of the original individual witnesses. If that's right, then the species of corporate knowledge in question, though not necessarily reliant upon the existence of a collective *mind*, still seems to rely upon a relatively thick social ontology and a theory of the identity of social entities over time.

---

[3] Interested readers can consult Hardwig 1985; Kitcher,1991; Thagard 1997; Tuomela 2004; List 2005; Wray 2007; Rolin 2007; Bird 2010, 2014; Fagan 2012; de Ridder 2014; Lackey 2014; Miller 2015; and Habgood-Coote 2020.

Interesting epistemological questions emerge from this metaphysical background. For instance, on this picture, it seems to follow that a person can sometimes truthfully say that, "we saw X," even though she cannot truthfully say that "I saw X." Since the seeing here is assumed to be veridical, and knowledge-generating, it would seem to follow that a person can sometimes say that "we know that p" without always being in a position to say that "I know that p" – or at least, not in a position to say that she knows that p as directly or as vividly as does the collective.[4]

Terence Cuneo (2016) comes close to a similar view in his own religious context, within Eastern Orthodox Christianity. Cuneo reveals that he isn't always comfortable saying that he *believes* in the central doctrines of the Church. This doesn't matter to him. He doesn't deny them. In fact, he finds them to be generally plausible. But such unbelief is compatible with his potentially knowing God and his being in a meaningful relationship with him. And this is, in no small part, down to the fact that a person's harboring doubts "makes no difference to his status within the church. He is not on that account a second class citizen" (2016: 217). And the Church itself, for Cuneo, can be thought of as an epistemic agent. Once again, this would license locutions that many epistemologists would resist, such as "I don't fully believe that p but we (as citizens of the Church) know that p." This thick notion of corporate knowledge is a second distinctive aspect of Jewish epistemology.

Jewish ritual is largely about relating and transmitting a national narrative. To that extent, it is about testimony. But these rituals also play a part in binding individuals together into the collective entity that, so long as its identity is sustained over time, can be the repository of empirical experience, and therefore direct empirical knowledge, had by none of its current members individually.

8.3 Conversion and Epistemic Rootedness

When the Rabbis look for a model for conversion to Judaism, they look to the book of Ruth. In the case of Naaman (in II Kings 5), the Syrian general, we see a Gentile have an epiphany that leads him to believe in Judaism. But the Rabbis can't treat him as a paradigm convert because, despite coming to believe in the truth of the religion, he doesn't join the Jewish people. Jethro-Hobab is another candidate. He comes to bless the God of Israel, but the text is ambiguous as to whether he remains with the Jewish people or returns to Midian. Accordingly, the book of Ruth becomes the default model for Jewish conversion.

---

[4] This a consequence that many (though not all) of the thinkers cited in the previous footnote would endorse.

Somewhat problematically, Ruth seems to embrace the religion more as a consequence of her commitment to Naomi than as a consequence of any theological convictions. She says that she doesn't much care what God may do to her so long as she shouldn't be parted from Naomi. One might expect, in the Rabbinic tradition, to find Midrashim that seek to accentuate (and even exaggerate) any hint that may be hiding in the text of religious conviction in Ruth's embrace of Judaism. But, as I document elsewhere (Lebens, 2021: 381–382), the central Rabbinic readings of Ruth's embrace of Judaism surprisingly seek to *undermine* any last vestige of religious conviction lurking in her words. Why did the Rabbis do this to Ruth, especially if she's supposed to function as a paradigm for future converts?

I maintain that Rabbinic readings of the book of Ruth, and their attitudes to conversion and proselytism, can only be justified in light of a certain set of assumptions about rationality and epistemic agency. On this picture, a person is rationally mandated, given the demands of practical rationality, to seek bonds of community and fraternity with others. Human flourishing requires such bonds. Furthermore, this picture recognizes that membership in a community, and other interpersonal bonds – such as friendship and family – can often make certain propositions unthinkable for an agent. A proposition is unthinkable so long as a person is unwilling (and even *unable*, in Harry Frankfurt's sense of a volitional necessity)[5] to factor the possible truth of that proposition into their practical deliberations.[6]

A good example of an unthinkable proposition is solipsism. It's very difficult to disprove the truth of solipsism, but we totally ignore its possible truth in our day-to-day practical deliberations (and rightly so).

On this conception of rationality and epistemic agency, a person isn't culpable for finding certain propositions unthinkable, so long as two conditions are met: (1) the person has to be conscientious in investigating the evidence for a wide array of beliefs, even if those beliefs are currently unthinkable to the agent in question and (2) if a person, in their investigations, finds an overwhelming amount of evidence in favor of a proposition that was previously unthinkable, that proposition has to become thinkable, and must be adopted as belief.

On this basis, even if Judaism is true, a Muslim, or a Christian, or a Hindu, may be rationally entitled not to find the truth of Judaism so much as thinkable, absent an overwhelming amount of evidence. Consequently, no just and reasonable God could condition their salvation upon the adoption

---

[5] See, for example, Frankfurt (1998)

[6] Readers might think that my appeal to epistemic roots in making some thoughts thinkable for some agents, and other thoughts thinkable for others, commits me to a doctrine of pragmatic encroachment, according to which pragmatic concerns can affect a person's epistemic climate. I dispute this claim in (Lebens 2020a), where I maintain that my appeal to epistemic roots can remain neutral on this issue.

of Judaism, hence there can be no pressing obligation to convert them.[7] Moreover, our attitude to epiphanies should be somewhat qualified, as I wrote (Lebens 2022a):

Had Ruth experienced an epiphany, Naomi might have been skeptical. One day she has a mystical vision driving her toward Judaism; perhaps the next day she'll have a different vision pushing her in a different direction. Instead, Ruth's primary commitment was to Naomi and to her people. In the long term, this made it more likely that if and when Ruth did embrace the theology of Judaism, she'd do so with a steadfast resilience. (385)

We can add that, upon becoming a member of the Jewish community, a convert is then part of a collective that has direct corporate knowledge of God, even if the convert's theological conviction is, personally, somewhat lacking.

Granted: a person can be criticized for parochialism and cultural introversion, which often leads to xenophobia and closed-mindedness. But this can be combated by the obligation we spoke of previously to investigate a wide array of competing views with an open mind, even if – in day-to-day life – we're licensed to ignore certain propositions that lack overwhelming evidence in their favor. Moreover, it is only in the context of communal and fraternal bonds that a person can realistically hope to flourish as an agent to begin with. As I wrote elsewhere (Lebens, 2020a):

[H]olding a particular identity with pride can sometimes play a role in forming a person's confidence, self-image, and conceptual and emotional landscape, allowing them to flourish and grow as moral agents, which might benefit people way beyond the confines of any particular community. (120)

Moreover, it isn't only nonepistemic goods that a person receives from membership in a community. It is often the case that communal membership will help to shape and sharpen a person's belief-forming and evidence-assessing capabilities in conversation, and sometimes in competition, with the standards of her community. Overall, and despite the risks of both peer pressure and echo chambers, we would likely think much less effectively if we were born and raised in social isolation.[8]

The third notion that I draw from the Jewish tradition is therefore the notion of epistemic rootedness according to which what we nonculpably find to be

---

[7] Tyler Mcnabb asks, in correspondence, whether this argument requires a cataphatic account of religious language such that we can infer from "justice" and "reasonableness" as applied to God what we might infer from those words when applied to some other sort of being. This is a fair question. For the purposes of this chapter, I accept that I am making that assumption. My more considered position, outlined in chapter 1 of Lebens (2020b), is that cataphatic discourse about God can at best hope for verisimilitude. And thus, my conclusion should be taken to be a central tenet of the most verisimilar theology currently known to this author.

[8] Thanks to Mark Wynn for discussion on this point.

unthinkable is a function of our social context. On this view, individual epistemic agency is not prior to social and communal affiliation.

8.4 Communitarian Epistemology

Martin Kusch (2002) defends a position that he dubs "communitarian epistemology," which he defines in terms of the following two claims:

1. "[T]he term 'knowledge' and its cognates, like 'know' and 'knower', marks a *social status* – like 'head of department'." (1)
2. "[T]he social status 'knowledge' is typically granted to, or imposed on, *groups* of people." (1)

The first claim is defended, roughly, in the following way. The word "knowledge" is a term that belongs to the English language. It is therefore an artifact of a particular linguistic community. Ultimately, it is for that community – the community of English speakers – to decide what that word means, and thus it is for that community to decide what counts as knowledge and who counts as a knower.

A distinctive feature of this epistemological program is its insistence that, in some sense or other, all knowledge depends upon testimony. The idea that testimony doesn't generate knowledge – that it's entirely parasitic – is a claim of individualistic epistemology. Communitarian epistemology thinks otherwise. Accordingly, Kusch cites the probing insight of Peter Strawson (1994):

Consider the overwhelming extent to which *what* we in fact perceive, the very nature or character of our perceptual experience itself, is determined by the instruction, the information, we have already received from the word of others. To apply . . . a phrase of Wittgenstein's, much, perhaps most, of what we see we could not see *as* what we do see it *as*, without the benefit of such instruction . . . . (26)

You see an elephant and testify to others that that's what you see. But you wouldn't see what you see *as* an elephant – in fact, you wouldn't cut your visual field up as you do into the various sorts of objects that appear to you – had you been conditioned differently. Conditioned differently, you may have just seen a moving patch of gray. This insight led Strawson to ask:

If we are to say, as we must, that the knowledge we derive from testimony depends on perception, must we equally say that the knowledge we derive from perception depends generally on testimony . . .? (1994: 26)

For Kusch, the answer is clear. There is no knowledge by perception that doesn't already depend upon testimony. Kusch is using the word "testimony" in a broad sense. The way in which our experience is culturally conditioned, so as to see certain gray patches as elephants, renders our empirical knowledge dependent upon the testimony of the community that has so shaped our experience.[9]

Moreover, every time a person uses a fragment of the English language, they are participating in a widely dispersed communal act of "performative testimony" (Kusch, 2002: 62–75). A performative utterance is one that creates the state of affairs that it describes. Performative utterances can make it the case that parliament is open (e.g., "I declare this session of parliament open") or that a couple are wed (e.g., "I declare you husband and wife"). A performative testimony would be a testimony that makes it the case that what is being testified to is true.

For instance, the English-speaking community testifies that the word "red" applies to a certain range of hues. In so testifying, they make it the case that "red" means what it means and therefore applies to the color chosen by the Royal Mail for its postboxes. If the community wanted to use that (or any other) word differently, then they could. The English-speaking community isn't an autonomous agent existing in addition to individual English speakers. Accordingly, the English-speaking community doesn't literally affirm, in a single act of testimony, that the word "red" applies to postboxes of the Royal Mail. Instead, this act of communal testimony is widely dispersed over the individual uses of the English language by members of the linguistic community. In other words, the ways in which English speakers use the word "red" is what make it the case that it means what it means.

Given this background, a person only counts as a knower if the word "knower" applies to her. That will depend, in large part, upon acts of communal performative testimony. In this way, knowledge is said to be testimonial through and through. There is no experience that isn't shaped by communal testimony – for instance, testimony as to what counts as an "elephant" rather than as a moving blob of gray – and it is, ultimately, up to the English-speaking community to testify as to what counts as "knowledge."

In Section 8.1, we saw that testimony is absolutely crucial for Jewish epistemology. In Section 8.2, we saw the extent to which the Hebrew Bible, as understood in the words of Maimonides, thinks of whole communities as epistemic agents. This makes space for Kusch's second claim, that knowledge is centrally or typically applied, not to individuals, but to groups. Or, in the more radical words of communitarian epistemologist, Lynn Hankinson Nelson (1993):

---

[9] You might be raising various objections at this point. For example, what about animal knowledge, or the knowledge of pre-linguistic human beings? As you shall see, I have great sympathy for those concerns.

[T]he knowing we do as individuals is derivative, . . . your knowing or mine depends on *our* knowing, for some "we." More to the point, . . . you or I *can* only know what *we* know (or could know), for some "we." . . . [C]ommunities that construct and acquire knowledge are not collections of independently knowing individuals; such communities are epistemologically prior to individuals who know. (124)

These words lead us directly to the notion, explored in Section 8.3, of epistemic roots: communal affiliation is prior to the epistemic agency of individuals. But, at this point, I want to make an important distinction between mainstream Jewish epistemology and the theories of Kusch and Nelson.

Communitarianism, in its original political context, was a critique of mainstream liberalism. But it was very much an in-house critique. Communitarians didn't see themselves as anti-liberal. They thought that liberalism had traditionally failed to recognize the extent to which our identities are formed in conversation with our cultural context. They wanted to remedy that failure. But they didn't want to roll back the notion of individual rights. As Rabbi Lord Jonathan Sacks (2020) wrote:

We are not mere individuals. We are social animals, embedded in a network of relationships – families, friends, colleagues, neighbors, co-workers, and co-worshippers – and some of these are constitutive of our sense of self. The "I," in and of itself, has no identity. We are who we are because of the groups to which we belong. To be sure, liberalism allows us to enter or leave such groups as we choose: that is what makes it liberal. It turns potentially coercive groups into voluntary associations. But community is essential to identity, so [some] thinkers argued, and they became known collectively as "communitarians." (136)

The idea is to recognize that we cannot make sense of ourselves without looking at the network of relationships in which we're embedded. But, of course, that shouldn't mean that we have no right to leave the groups into which we're born, or into which our choices have brought us, in certain situations, should we choose to do so. That's the liberal insight that the communitarians wanted to maintain.

Some communitarians presented their critique in metaphysical terms. They made it sound as if there could be no self in the original position of John Rawls, behind the veil of ignorance. There is, they would insist, no such entity as the antecedent chooser of ends – we are, rather, inherently socially situated beings.[10] That way of articulating the critique was unfortunate. There may well be some metaphysical substratum to a person that exists prior to any network of relations and prior to any choices that that person will one day make. The point at the heart of the communitarian critique is better articulated in epistemic

---

[10] See Mulhall & Swift (1996: 45–55; 111–113)

terms. The point is that a person behind the veil of ignorance would be seriously impaired as an epistemic agent. Accordingly, serious deliberation in the original position would be nigh on impossible. A person *can* exist without a community, but her agency would be staggeringly impoverished.

It is no part of communitarianism, as a political doctrine, for the individual, and her individual rights, to disappear altogether. But for Kusch and Nelson, truly individual knowledge is impossible. One might say: what Kusch calls "communitarian epistemology" is more aptly described as *communist epistemology*, since the individual is utterly subsumed within the community.

Kusch and Nelson assume that (1) all knowledge is mediated by language and that (2) there can be no language outside of a linguistic community. This is what gives rise to their "communism."

I have never been convinced that Wittgenstein's private language argument, or any of its descendants, is sound. Sadly, it's beyond the scope of this chapter to lay out my philosophical dissatisfaction with private language arguments.[11] This much I would concede: immersion in a linguistic community gives us the opportunity to frame much richer thoughts and thereby to acquire much more sophisticated sorts of knowledge than we could access on our own. And yet I deny that there could be no private knowledge, just as I deny that there could be no private language. Consequently, to avoid the threat of communism, the communitarian should walk back the claim that communal affiliation is wholly prior to epistemic agency. A socially isolated human *could* know things.[12] Rather, we should say that communal affiliation is prior to a human person's reaching their full epistemic potential. The communitarian should reject Kush and Nelson's second assumption.

The first assumption – that all knowledge is mediated by language – brings me to a fourth and final notion, in addition to the three main notions of this chapter, which characterizes much of mainstream Jewish epistemology. Western epistemology is fascinated with the gap between belief and knowledge. What extra ingredient must one add to belief in order to *arrive* at knowledge? Elsewhere, I've argued that the Hebrew Bible had very little interest, and no single word, for propositional belief (Lebens, in press). The nearest word it has is *emunah*, which, I argue, is more accurately translated, even when it takes propositions as an object, as *faith*. Accordingly, mainstream Jewish epistemology, from medieval times until today, has been interested in the gap, not between belief and knowledge, but between *emunah* and *da'at* (roughly, from faith to knowledge).

For Saadya Gaon in the Middle Ages,[13] as for Rabbi Meir Leibush Wisser – known as the Malbim – in the nineteenth century,[14] *emunah* can deserve to be

---

[11] Interested readers could consult McGinn (1984), Canfield (1986), and Mulhall (2007).
[12] Just as animals and pre-linguistic humans can know things.   [13] See Altmann (1946).
[14] See his commentary to the book of Hosea 2:21–22.

called knowledge. But it's a type of knowledge that is mediated by the community, either through historical chains of testimony, or through social conditioning. *Da'at*, by contrast, is a knowledge that's deeply personal. If the goal of Jewish epistemology is to take the things that we know by *emunah* and to come to know them by *da'at*,[15] then the goal is to graduate from communal to private/personal knowledge – this is an ascent that Kusch and Nelson couldn't sanction.

Moreover, one of the primary features of *da'at* is the nonpropositional content that it grasps. The first instance of *da'at* in the Hebrew Bible occurs when Adam "knew" Eve. This was an intimate second-personal knowledge. Its content wasn't in any straightforward sense linguistic – or at least not exclusively linguistic – and therefore it's a type of knowledge that doesn't necessarily depend upon the possession of any language whatsoever, private or public. Accordingly, even if there can be no private language, the Jewish tradition would insist that there can still be private or personal knowledge – the sort of knowledge whose content isn't linguistic; the sort of knowledge that one has of God in the beatific vision.

Jewish epistemology recognizes the centrality of testimony for the sustenance and also for the generation of rich, linguistically embedded forms of knowledge. It recognizes that communities can be subjects of epistemic states. Furthermore, it recognizes that a person cannot reach her full potential as an epistemic agent outside of a community. In these ways, Jewish epistemology has much in common with what Kusch would call communitarian epistemology. But, in *fact*, Jewish epistemology is *more* communitarian than so-called communitarian epistemology. So-called communitarian epistemology turns out to be, in a sense, communist. Jewish epistemology, by contrast, truly secures the delicate balance between individualism and collectivism that sat at the heart of the communitarian critique of classical liberalism.[16]

---

[15] As I argue in Lebens (in press).

[16] I extend thanks to the editors of this volume and to the members of the Joseph Butler Society at Oxford University, for discussing an earlier draft of this chapter with me.

9 Christian Religious Epistemology

Sandra Menssen and Thomas D. Sullivan

9.1 The Big Picture

Both agnostic inquirers and committed believers have a stake in the answer to a question lying at the heart of Christian epistemology: *How might Christianity be presented to display its credibility?* Superb technical work in recent analytic philosophy will, of course, contribute to the answer. And, as we'll argue in Sections 9.2, 9.3, and 9.4, the answer includes certain elements intelligible to those unschooled in technical philosophy – elements all but completely passed over in the literature, though they ground convictions of many believers, with and without formal philosophical training.

Recent analytic philosophy elaborates two basic theistic responses to the question. Evidence-based approaches look to arguments excavating *evidence* for Christianity. Non-evidence-based approaches look to something else.

Among the best, and best-known, of contemporary evidence-based accounts of Christianity's credibility is Richard Swinburne's. His magisterial series of monographs establishes general principles concerning evidence and probabilistic reasoning, then applies the principles to argue that theism is coherent and there is a strong cumulative case for God's existence, and finally feeds all this into consideration of evidence for Christianity, arguing it's highly probable Jesus was resurrected from the dead and Christianity is true. Swinburne says he modeled his project on Aquinas's because the approach of the *Summa Theologiae* seemed "one hundred percent" right, and Swinburne resolved to use the best science of our day – as Aquinas used the best (Aristotelian) science of his – to show the existence of a creator God, and more.[1] Many fine evidence-based treatises have been produced by natural theologians over the last several decades, including important investigations of underappreciated sorts of evidence: William Alston's work on religious experience as perception of God, for instance, and John Greco's on testimonial evidence.

In tandem with the labors of Swinburne and other evidence-focused Christian apologists, another prime mover in contemporary Christian philosophy, Alvin Plantinga, has developed – with fellow Reformed epistemologists such as Nicholas Wolterstorff – a sophisticated alternative approach to

---

[1] Clark (1993:186–87).

Christianity's credibility. Plantinga's multi-volume magnum opus on the subject argues that Christianity, if true, can be warranted nonevidentially.

Plantinga begins his extended argument by developing a "proper functionalist" theory of knowledge according to which beliefs may be warranted if they come into existence due to the proper functioning of cognitive faculties: evidence for the beliefs is not required. He is particularly interested in applying this general theory of knowledge in the domain of religion. It is possible, he says, that humans were built naturally to perceive religious truths – maybe we're built to do that almost automatically, if nothing interferes with our perception. However, he suggests, our cognitive-affective faculties may have become disordered through original sin, and so we are prevented from apprehending Christianity's truth. But our faculties might be restored to their proper functioning through divine aid. And in that case, we might immediately, noninferentially, take it as a "basic" belief that Christianity is true, in the way that we immediately, noninferentially, take the existence of other minds, in other people, as basic (we don't need arguments that other humans aren't robots). Some fortunate souls may possess a basic belief in Christianity throughout their thinking lives. Basic beliefs don't require evidence.

Plantinga names his account of warranted Christian belief the "Aquinas/Calvin model" (which signals complexities, given the alignment Swinburne and other evidence-focused apologists profess with Aquinas). Similar accounts of Christian religious epistemology have branched and blossomed. See, for instance, Tyler Dalton McNabb's defense of a proper functionalist approach.[2]

Plantinga can be seen as encouraging us to stand back from the question at the beginning of this essay. On his take, Reformed apologists (qua Reformed apologists) don't directly display Christianity's credibility by pointing to evidence for it; however, in explaining a possible setup in which Christianity is presented by the Holy Spirit as true, the apologists facilitate believers' recognition of Christianity's rationality.

We don't dispute Reformed epistemologists' contention that some people can rationally assent to Christianity without arguments or evidence. But the approach has limited value for outsiders who wonder whether and why they should accept Christianity. Such inquirers don't have a basic belief that it is true, or reason to think the story Plantinga offers is more than just a tale about what's possible. Further, many believers – we are among them – lack "basic" belief in Christianity and see their commitment as grounded in argument and evidence. (We view the landscape from the vantage point of former outsiders: we are adult converts to theism and Christianity.)

In the upcoming sections, we want to highlight an important but neglected type of evidence for Christianity: *the content of the Christian revelatory claim.*

---

[2] Depoe and McNabb (2020: 107–122). This volume features instructive dialectic: counterarguments are attached to each of the five positions presented.

This content consists, at its core, of scriptures and definitive statements of doctrine; these are structured, vivified, and interpreted through various media. Though evidence from the content of the Christian revelatory claim is neglected by natural theologians, Christian revelatory content has *substantial* evidential value in the minds of ordinary believers, underwriting both God's existence and Christianity itself. The role it plays for the faithful is a strong sign philosophical adepts should attend to it also.[3]

Our discussion of this professionally overlooked evidence for Christianity's credibility will target two presumptions that have shaped contemporary Christian epistemology. The first is that a convincing evidence-based case for Christianity cannot be obtained without first securing (at least) a case that the existence of a good God is more probable than not. Although the presumption is not entailed by the ordering protocol Swinburne employs for his project, philosophers following his lead often proceed as though it is entailed; indeed, respected definitions of natural theology embed it.[4] The second presumption is that a high degree of probability or certainty, perhaps even *knowledge* of Christianity's truth, is required for firm assent. Here again, the claim is not entailed by paradigmatic evidentialist projects (or nonevidentialist ones); however, it's inspired both by Swinburne's decades-long program, which argues that the evidence underwrites a high degree of probability that Christianity is true, and by Plantinga's, whose approach to the question of Christianity's credibility is geared for those already professing to *know* its truth.

While the approach we will advocate disrupts the contemporary picture by rejecting these presumptions, it comports well with the longer tradition. Our approach is drawn from . . . Aquinas! We look to him for a method to follow, but not because he explains the method: he *uses* a method he does not *characterize*.

In this chapter's remaining three sections, we'll offer beginning defenses of three theses regarding the evidential value of the Christian revelatory claim's content. We won't have room to make full cases for the theses but hope to say enough to encourage further investigation.

---

[3] Readers who'd like more detail regarding the contemporary literature than we have provided might start with DePoe and McNabb (2020): the volume's introduction overviews five positions regarding Christian religious epistemology. See also the online *Stanford Encyclopedia of Philosophy* and the *Internet Encyclopedia of Philosophy* regarding: the epistemology of religion, evidentialism, foundationalism, functionalism, externalism, reliabilism, natural theology, ramified natural theology, and connected topics. Most of the best-known authors we cite (e.g., Swinburne, Plantinga, Alston, Greco) have multiple major publications on the issues; bibliographical details can be found in this volume's references list.

[4] See Menssen and Sullivan (2007: 51–58), for discussion of the presumption's prevalence and its appearance in definitions of natural theology.

9.2 Evidence for Theism from Revelatory Content: A General Framework

Thesis: The content of a revelatory claim may provide evidence enabling an inquirer to assent simultaneously to the revelatory claim and the embedded proposition that God exists.

We take "revelatory content" to be content of a theistic revelatory claim, a claim of the form: *S asserts that G revealed that P*, where S is a subject (a person or group of persons), G is a supernatural being, and P is propositional content. Christian revelatory content, for instance, is the content of the revelatory claim made by a Christian community, including (at least) canonical scriptures and doctrines of early church councils. Revelatory content of major religions unfolds through oral narrative, poetry, and fiction; through history, biography, and legal codes; through visual arts and music – and, not least, through philosophy and theology, which systematize the content.

Arguments from revelatory content of a major religion to the truth of the associated revelatory claim (and the entailment that theism is true) can be seen as beginning with the following basic template:

- The revelatory content R, as expressed by the community that embraces it, has the recognizable characteristic of being extraordinarily F [substitute for F: unified, fitting, beautiful, sublime, resilient, fertile, original, intelligent, wise, affecting, uplifting to the hopeless and bedeviled – and the list goes on].
- If so, then the plausibility of the claim that R was revealed can rightly be enhanced for the inquirer through recognition that R is extraordinarily F.
- [So,] The plausibility that R was revealed can rightly be enhanced for an inquirer through recognition that R is extraordinarily F.

One person may, of course, grasp the characteristics that substitute for F more, or less, well than another. That does not mean there is no underlying reality to be perceived. Some religious doctrines endorse genocide; such slaughter is not just subjectively, but *objectively* abhorrent, and highly so. We may (come to) understand that religious doctrines have an objective base that is at the opposite end of the spectrum: extraordinarily unified, fitting, beautiful, and so forth.

Why would recognizing the content of a particular putative revelation as extraordinarily sublime, resilient, fertile, and so forth enhance the plausibility of the claim that the content was revealed? Because, we think, postulating a divine source (potentially) *explains* the characteristics, and when many characteristics listed in the first step of the template can reasonably be substituted for F, postulating a divine source may provide an explanation better than any other available. Our template could be extended to build in this perspective, to incorporate the methodology of "inference to the best explanation" (IBE). But having signaled that IBE would be a natural way of proceeding, we won't get into discussion of its merits or its relation to Bayesianism, likelihoodism, and so forth. Staking positions in debates over these methodologies distracts from our overarching purpose in this essay, which is to call attention to an important *sort of evidence* neglected by natural theologians for the truth of a revelatory claim: the content of the claim.

Objection: Your thesis – that the content of a revelatory claim may provide evidence enabling an inquirer to assent simultaneously to the claim and the embedded proposition that God exists – cannot be justified except by a circular argument.

The claim that "There is a God who has revealed this content [e.g., Christian doctrine]" *embeds* the claim that "There is a God." To avoid circular reasoning, doesn't the embedded claim have to be established *before* the more complex claim?

Examples show that the reasoning we recommend is not unacceptably circular. Is the same force that brings the apple down from the tree the force that makes the world go round? In other words, is gravity responsible for the orbits of the planets around the sun? That question embeds another: Does gravity exist? The embedded question may be addressed by investigating the more complex and concrete query. Einstein replaces Newtonian gravity with curved space-time. Are the trajectories of moving bodies earlier explained by Newtonian gravity due to the curvature of space-time? The embedded query (whether there's a curvature of space-time) is answered once we have an answer to the complex question. A researcher at SETI (Search for Extra-Terrestrial Intelligence) might declare: "Some alien life form sent this signal." The complex claim embeds the contention that some alien life form exists (or existed). We investigate the reality of the putative alien being through assessing the complex claim – by studying the *content* of the alleged communication.

We've said it's a common contemporary presumption that a convincing evidence-based case for the Christian revelatory claim cannot be obtained without first obtaining at least a probable case for a good God. But as these examples show, the presumption should be rejected. It's possible *simultaneously* to assent to the complex claim "God vouchsafed a revelation through Jesus Christ" and the embedded assertion "God exists."

The long conjunction that constitutes the Christian revelatory claim can't be more probable that any conjunct within it. Still, the whole Christian story may be more *believable* than embedded propositions taken in isolation.[5] If you are explaining to a colleague who gave a lecture you were expected to attend why you didn't show up, you might simply say: "Something important arose." Or you might say: "My daughter, who lives out of state, just flew in – her plane

---

[5] See Menssen and Sullivan (2021), on the apparent violation of the Kolmogorov axioms of probability.

landed at midnight – to go to the funeral of her friend's mother this morning in Minneapolis; she had only the afternoon in town before flying home tonight and needed to talk with me." The second account is more convincing, more credible, though the first is more probable (the second entails the first but the first doesn't entail the second).

The longer account is more plausible even if it's highly probable that some component in it is false. Did your daughter's plane land at *exactly* midnight? Might it have been 11:59 p.m.? You could explicitly add a rider – "or something like that" – to the relevant sentence (or the whole story); but even if you don't, it's understood that way. The same holds for the Christian revelatory claim: "That, or something like that."

For some agnostic inquirers into Christianity, everything may turn on the possibility of simultaneous assent to the revelatory claim and the embedded contention regarding God's existence, and thus of an alternative to the standard evidence-based approach to Christian religious epistemology. That's because the most daunting obstacle to belief in God is the problem of evil, and the Cross's promise of redemption and afterlife may provide the only way of recognizing that the problem can be defeated. If God is in the dock, we should review the content of putative divine revelation before pronouncing judgment. We must listen to the voice of the accused.

Examination of the content of an attractive putative revelation should, therefore, not be postponed by an agnostic inquirer until after a credible case for God's existence is in hand.

9.3 Evidence from Systematized Christian Revelatory Content: An Illustration

Thesis: Aquinas's systematic unfolding of Christian revelatory content can enhance the plausibility, both for agnostic inquirers and for believers, of the claim the content was revealed.

The explicated Christian revelatory claim constitutes a *very* large database. How does an inquirer sort through it all to identify evidential value? By using an organizing framework. Organizing structures or storylines shed new light on familiar data, helping us to draw implications from what we already know and to discover new data. Mendeleyev discovered the periodic table by organizing his knowledge of the sixty-three known chemical elements; the framework he built gave him insight into the known elements and allowed him to predict discovery of other elements.

At least three sorts of frameworks or storylines aid in investigating putative revelatory content.

The first involves *historical narratives*. The account in Deuteronomy of the Hebrews' exodus from Egypt and entry into the Promised Land provides essential structure for both Jewish and Christian revelatory claims and sets up understanding of Christian eschatology. The significance of Jesus's "I am" statements and the calling of the twelve apostles is understood through the historical narrative of the Jews.

The second sort of framework focuses our attention on *storylines that organize personal or subjective data.* These are often presented through parables. Think, for instance, of the tale the prophet Nathan tells King David (in the book of Samuel in the Hebrew Bible) about a rich man who steals and slaughters a poor man's ewe lamb. The story allows David to see in a new light his order to send Uriah to the battlefront (where Uriah was killed, allowing David to marry Uriah's wife Bathsheba), reframing events to unveil for David his wickedness.

Frameworks of the third sort provide *accounts of doctrine or theory in terms of first principles.* Aquinas organizes Christian doctrine in a way that displays its philosophical foundations: he presents causal structures that highlight *essences* of the entities under discussion. Aquinas does for Christianity something like what Euclid did for geometry. Euclid is not famous for discovering geometrical theorems – the theorems he discussed were, in the main, already familiar to the cognoscenti. Rather, he's renowned for *organizing* geometry to reveal its axioms (or most of them: later mathematicians sought to complete the task).

Here we spotlight the third sort of framework. We'll illustrate Aquinas's systematization of Christian revelation by examining a single characteristic that can substitute for F in our general template above: the characteristic of *being unified.* And we'll consider one strategy among many through which the Summa[6] displays Christian revelation's content as extraordinarily unified: the *dialectical drive toward definition and first principles.* Our discussion points to a distinctive way in which Aquinas's account unifies the reported elements of the original revelation. But, of course, these elements have their own connections, historical and existential.[7]

The Summa's systematization of Christian revelation develops through a series of articles, each with a five-part structure: first, Aquinas fixes on an inaugural question; second, he states objections to the conclusion he'll defend (the Summa includes over 10,000 such objections); third, he turns to sources he finds trustworthy to some degree, to counterbalance what was just said; fourth, he elaborates his own position; finally, he answers the original objections. Each article in the Summa (there are over 2,600) follows this dialectical pattern.

---

[6] The *Summa Theologiae* or *Summa Theologica* (ST).

[7] Our emphasis on the unity of the account could raise the question of whether this is *merely* a coherent story, but the account is replete with claims about particulars, in contrast, say, with coherentist accounts of mathematics.

Dialectic is the road (hodós) to the foundations of the sciences, Aristotle taught; and Aquinas agreed. This may strike a modern reader as absurd: our scientific methods are worlds away from Aquinas's. Still, dialectic remains a path to the foundations of science because meanings of scientific statements require clarification. We would need dialectic in science even if all we were concerned about were nominal or verbal definitions, "dictionary definitions." But dialectic *also* is a means to definition of *the thing itself*, an avenue to "real" definition, as a later tradition terms it, which identifies the most fundamental features in a substance. Think, for instance, of the *wave function*, at the heart of quantum mechanics. Pointing to a mathematical formula called the "wave function" helps clarify: it yields a nominal definition. But does the formula represent anything *real*, and if so, what? Physicists debate. The dialectical clash of opposing viewpoints forces distinctions; both nominal and real definitions are refined through distinctions. In a whole with many or disparate parts (unlike the whole that is the number *one*), the unity of the whole turns on integration of the parts. And deep explanations invoking real, fundamental definitions that account for the properties being explained exhibit that integration.

To better appreciate the role fundamental definition plays in progressive deepening of scientific explanations, consider the question: "Why doesn't gold corrode or rust?" Some answers are simply wrong: "Because it's yellow," or "Because the gods love gold." It's a huge step forward to say: "There's something about gold's atomic structure that keeps it from corroding." Research yields detail: since gold has seventy-nine protons in its nucleus, the nucleus exerts strong gravitational pull on its electrons; this causes them to move almost at the speed of light and increases the electrons' mass, which draws them closer to the nucleus so the outermost electron can't easily bond with anything else. This explanation turns on a structural or real definition of the chemical element gold – not a mere specification of necessary and sufficient conditions for something counting as gold, but rather identification of a *cause* of the fact that gold resists corrosion. The definition attempts to express the essence of the thing, where the "essence" is a fundamental feature or collection of features ontologically grounding any other properties, should there be other properties. "The sole even prime" and "2" are convertible, but "the sole even prime" doesn't express the essence of the number 2.[8]

What does the parallel situation look like with respect to the Summa's discussion of revelation? Theology is a science, for Aquinas; the Summa is a

---

[8] It's common to introduce the notion of essence by invoking the logico-semantic ideas of explanation, instantiation, definition, etc. But explanations, etc., are not properties outside our minds. The "essence" doesn't refer to the overlay; the logico-semantic ideas are overlays to get to what we're talking about at the ontological level. This sophisticated conception is elaborated in the classic theory of the predicables.

systematic exposition of that science, rooted in definition. Aquinas chains arguments throughout the Summa, with each chained argument attempting to answer a "why" question analogous to "Why doesn't gold corrode?" and reaching toward real definition, definition tied to *reality*.

For example, we get layering in God's attributes: God is eternal *because* immutable, immutable *because* simple, simple *because* all act and no potency. The argument for each attribute introduces a definition. Aquinas embraces Aristotle's understanding of an ideal syllogism as an argument whose "middle" term (the term common to the syllogism's two premises) is a definition giving the essence of the thing. Arguments of this kind yield true explanations, not mere correlations; when layered in the way we're describing, they are deeply explanatory.

The same search for definition-embedding explanations shapes Aquinas's discussion of doctrine specific to Christian revelation. What solidifies his analysis of the fittingness of the incarnation, for instance (at the beginning of ST III) is that he asks, "What *is* it to be fitting?" and gives an answer referring to natures of things.[9] God's incarnation as a human being is fitting *because* it's natural. It's natural to God *because* God's essence – goodness – is inherently diffusive. Elsewhere, Aquinas considers what diffusiveness involves. He understands God's diffusive goodness as teleological: goodness is diffusive *because* it attracts, because we are drawn to it (ST I, q.5, a.4).

The result of all this excavation is a network of arguments, from various areas, with linking definitions and explanations. Thus, *depth* of explanation of revelatory content develops together with *breadth*, just as the chemist's definition of gold, which deepens our understanding of the natural order, carries with it overarching theory – there are electrons and protons. Arguments from philosophy and from revealed theology share definitions and explanations; their intertwining is mutually supportive and contributes to the overall unity of doctrine. But the distinction between philosophy and revealed theology remains. Any argument that's philosophical will rely only on premises put forward as accessible to human reason without appeal to revelation's authority; an argument in revealed theology will have at least one premise that appeals to revelation's authority for warrant.

God, the cause of all causes, is the great unifier. But we cannot define God, cannot identify God's essence, Aquinas holds. We can get some sense of God as the referent of descriptions (God is eternal, immutable, simple), and we can investigate God as first cause, arguing from the effect; but we cannot really understand the referent itself. How does our account of Aquinas's approach so far, with its emphasis on definition, square with his position that we can't define God?

---

[9] The characteristics that substitute for F in our original template overlap: the revelation's *unity* intersects with its *fittingness*.

To begin, note that there are other circumstances where we grasp descriptions without understanding referents. A child who's been introduced to the concept of a prime number can understand the basic description of a twin prime – a pair of numbers, themselves prime, separated only by one even number – without being able to identify a twin prime. There are organisms that can feel the electrical currents of the earth, but we can't do this at all. We understand the organism's description but cannot sensorially grasp the referent.

And a point rarely noticed, which Aquinas brings out in his discussion of naming God, is that our sentences can be substantively correct though defective in mode of representation (ST I, q.13). This is evident in mathematics. When we say, "Two plus two is four," we employ the present tense. But we don't need to reassert the equation tomorrow, and the next day, and the next. "Two plus two is four" says something substantively true, but it's encased in a manner of expression that's incorrect. Mathematics is *not* temporal. All our talk about God is defective regarding the *mode* of representation, Aquinas believes; when we press on descriptions of God's characteristics, we recognize they are *at bottom* saying what God is *not*. This doesn't mean we can't make substantive affirmative statements about God. Here's one: "God is such that we can talk about God." But attempted definitions, attempts to grasp the referent, will always deny something: we can't give a perfectly affirmative definition. (Something similar occurs in mathematics and physics when we get down to the "simples"; Euclid defines a point as that which has no extension.) Since the mode of our accounts of God will be defective, though the signification may be correct, we need to add the rider (discussed in the preceding section): "Or something like that."

Recognizing the general need for this rider insulates Christian doctrine from certain criticisms. For instance: Many find religious teaching about eternal punishment a stumbling block to belief, but humans' concept of the "eternal" is taken from our concept of time, which is affected by physics (now we have space-time, and scattered simultaneity). One can say it's substantively true that the damned will never see God's face. But the claim that there will be eternal punishment isn't to be understood as asserting the punishment goes on day after day, everlastingly. That's not entailed. What *is* entailed? We don't have much of an idea. God is an infinite mystery, far transcending our cognitive capacities and language. But the system's limits contribute to its openness and robustness.

Aquinas's account of God is embedded in revelatory content that enhances our perception of its unity and plausibility. Christ, God incarnate, gives us a glimpse of incomprehensible divinity, helping us apprehend the undefinable God. Christ is a moral exemplar and a model for divinization. We are divinized by partaking in God's nature and thereby in God's actions of knowing *and loving*. Aristotle's understanding of our rationalistic, "divinized" ultimate end – limited and sterile – is transformed through Christian revelation.

The dialectic that impels Aquinas's systematizing in the Summa doesn't terminate with that text, or even with the entirety of his written corpus. There's a world out there to come to know, Aquinas held, and a world above it, and we should use any good means we can to grasp the reality. The search depends on the inquirer's participation, on examining new objections generated by contemporary science (among other things) – on clarifying, defining, and explaining. The Summa is a great monument to reason, but it's unfinished: we use it to move forward, beyond the understanding that Aquinas had, seeking to uncover new unifying patterns.

Objection: Scholastic systematization, which is far from the minds of ordinary believers, adulterates the content of revelation and misdirects assent.

This objection might be rooted in general concern about whether *any* systematized account of Christianity could enhance the revelation's plausibility. Systematizing includes much that's absent in the original revelation; therefore (the objector might suggest), there's no reason to think that what speaks for the system's content as unified, fitting, and so on, also speaks for the original.

What's to be said in response to this general worry? A reply begins with reflection on how Christian doctrine developed. Christianity's basic revelation is in Jesus Christ, in what he did and said in first-century Palestine. Not too long after that, accounts of the good news are "published." Following that, some sort of canonization occurs. A church says, for instance: to be part of our group you don't have to accept one or another differing reports of when Jesus overturned the tables in the temple, but you do need to accept that he said he was with the Father from the beginning of the world. The church makes a revelatory claim. And the process continues, with speculation, theorizing, and philosophizing: the mind tries to penetrate revelatory claims, as a mind might look at the Homeric tales and try to make sense of them. Everybody who accepts *or rejects* the Bible relies on some account of sacred doctrine. Richard Dawkins, an anti-religious biologist, has a particular target in mind – he focuses on fundamentalist Christian beliefs, thus "systematizing," though in a manner Aquinas, far from a fundamentalist, would have rejected. Rationalization, or systematization, is unavoidable in substantive discussion of the Christian revelatory claim.

And what of the specialized concern about *Scholastic* systematization, the technical philosophical organization that undergirds Aquinas's account (and the accounts of other great medieval philosopher-theologians) of the science of theology? When one reflects on the three types of organizational frameworks mentioned at the outset of this section – historical narratives, storylines that organize personal data, and philosophical accounts of first principles – it may seem that the first two are the primary vehicles through which ordinary Christian believers access revelatory content. But ordinary believers are steadied in their understanding of scripture by the work of theologians who have inherited the systematizations of medieval philosopher-theologians and of Protestant Scholastics such as Gerhard, Calov, and Turretin. The work of these philosopher-theologians comes to ordinary believers through preaching, catechizing, and publicly discussing challenging issues in Christianity. An example of the trickle-down effect in operation can be seen by thinking about what ordinary Christian believers would say if asked, "Does the doctrine of the Trinity say that there are three gods?" A common reply might be something like: "No. There's only one God. Three persons, but one God." The reply is supported by Scholastic systematization, which doesn't unshroud the entire mystery, but shows the doctrine isn't flat-out contradictory.

The third sort of organizational structure anchors and stabilizes the first two. The dialectical drive toward definition reaches for first principles, which are deeply explanatory and, hence, stabilizing. And the philosophical distinctions drawn in this process help dissolve ostensive logical paradoxes and superficial inconsistencies, thus removing worries about belief that readily occur to the philosophically minded.

The three frameworks synthesize: historical and imaginative accounts integrate with stabilizing philosophical-theological analysis. The unfolding of the wondrous whole may be just about all an inquirer needs to conclude that the associated revelatory claim is (probably) true.

9.4 Revelatory Content's Power to Obligate Belief

Thesis: An argument from revelatory content can reasonably persuade agnostic inquirers that assent to theism and Christianity is personally obligatory.

This will strike many as overreach.

Note, to start, that the explanatory framework in an argument from revelatory content can have a capaciousness we've barely hinted at. For instance, if it appears to an inquirer that *consciousness has a function*, or that *humans have libertarian freedom*, and the inquirer suspects naturalism is unable to explain how these things could be, then the non-naturalistic metaphysics of the Christian revelatory claim will feed into various of the characteristics that substitute for F in the general template and contribute to the revelatory claim's overall explanatory power. To take another example, spiritual experiences some inquirers have had or have heard about that point to a world beyond fit into the framework. And arguments independent of the explanatory power of the revelatory claim provide a reinforcing surround: a good illustration here is supplied by the classic arguments for God's existence and their intriguing contemporary variations and expansions.

So, an inquirer examines a capacious revelatory claim with a rich and attractive surround. *If it is the case* that, as we've argued, Aquinas's systematization of Christianity can enhance the plausibility of the claim it was revealed, then incremental enhancements could continually raise the revelatory claim's plausibility, as a heap of sand can, grain by grain, become a hill – and more. This process could continue, it would seem, to the point where assent is in order . . . *unless* there's reason to think a barrier will be encountered.

But a serious barrier is inevitable, it may be thought. For the Abrahamic religions – Judaism, Christianity, and Islam – insist not merely on belief, but on *wholehearted, resolute* belief. That demand generates two objections to our current thesis.

Objection 1: Wholehearted and resolute belief requires superabundant evidence, perhaps knowledge, and arguments from revelatory content can't produce that.

Although we disagree that arguments from revelatory content can't produce superabundant evidence, we won't argue the point here (beyond noting systematization may incrementally build evidence). We will instead focus on the alleged necessity of obtaining superabundant evidence, for if in fact that's not required for wholehearted, resolute belief, then the objection fails.

It can easily appear that the strong adherence Christianity demands must either require superabundant evidence *or go beyond the evidence*. And if it goes beyond the evidence, its rational appeal threatens to dissolve. We believe, with Aquinas, that the commitment goes beyond the evidence *in some sense*. There's an evidential gap *in some sense*. But (as we'll argue) the sense in which there's an evidential gap need not diminish the commitment's rational allure.

An explorer stuck in a cave thinks he sees a light from above and hears a voice, though his attempts to attract attention appear to have gone unnoticed. He believes there's a realistic possibility that attempting to climb a steep cliff will lead to a path up and out. He has multiple reasons for escaping, not least saving himself, but is particularly focused on the fact that through his fault, his companion lies beside him, badly injured. Our explorer's quick, nearly intuitive reasoning comes to this:

1. I can satisfy my obligation to help my companion, injured through my negligence, only if I can exit the cave.
2. Scaling the cliff ahead offers the best way I know of discovering and utilizing an exit.
3. Given 1 and 2, it's obligatory for me to attempt to *scale the cliff ahead* if the act is realistically possible (though I lack abundant evidence that the act can be completed).
4. Scaling the cliff is realistically possible.
5. So, it's obligatory for me to scale the cliff.[10]

---

[10] In a different setting, this analogy points in the direction of a surprising conclusion: that we can have an obligation to believe God exists. See Menssen and Sullivan (2022).

When the explorer considers whether the climb is "realistically possible," is he asking whether there's a better than a fifty-fifty chance he'll traverse the incline without falling into the chasm beneath? No. He may not attach any specific probability to the risk of falling, or his prospects of surviving a fall, or the chance that if he and his companion stay put, they'll soon be rescued. He reflects briefly but carefully on these possibilities and, *eyes on the good*, makes a considered decision – without using a formal procedure, despite (we may imagine) expertise with such procedures. Aristotle says we should not demand more precision than the subject matter admits, and Aquinas agrees.

An inquirer investigating whether there's a God, suspecting there may be light and a voice from above, reasons:

1. I can satisfy debts to some individuals I've wronged only if there is a supernatural force or being I can connect with that can help, because:
   a. The consequences of some of my wrongdoing cannot be rectified in this world, in the natural order.
2. Christianity offers the best way I know of discovering and connecting with a supernatural force or being that can help, because:
   a. Christianity claims a providential God who draws abundant good from wrongdoing and suffering, good *for the injured*, and who allows wrongdoers to collaborate in the process through prayer and sacrifice.
   b. Further, Christianity claims a savior who satisfies others' debts.
   c. I know of no other remotely plausible account of the supernatural that offers anything close to such help.
3. Given 1 and 2, it's obligatory for me to attempt to *connect with God by assenting to Christianity* if the act is realistically possible (though I lack abundant evidence the act can be completed).
4. Connecting with God by assenting to Christianity is realistically possible, because:
   a. Christianity itself is realistically possible (sufficiently plausible that I should assent to it if assent can be willed).
   b. Under these circumstances, assent to Christianity can be willed.
5. So, it's obligatory for me to assent to Christianity.

How plausible must Christianity be for 4-a to be true? As our analogy suggests, the bar is much lower than the bar for *knowing* that Christianity is true. Aquinas does not himself assert that the case for Christianity is stronger than the case against, or that Christianity is more likely than not on the natural evidence, or highly probable, or probable at all. Rather, he says the Christian does not believe for light or trifling reasons, does not believe foolishly.[11]

---

[11] Aquinas (1975a: ch. 6).

While the inquirer may hesitate to say her case for the truth of Christianity is better than her case against, she may deem the case for *acting* (assenting) better than the case against, for making a considered decision that parallels the cave explorer's decision. The splendor of Aquinas's systematization of Christianity, including its non-naturalistic metaphysics, its brilliant replies to objections, and its breathtaking explanatory power, may – in combination with other magnetic texts, including the gospels themselves – lead her to this conclusion. The injunction to believe wholeheartedly and resolutely though the evidence does not compel belief may initially be off-putting but can be embraced through awareness of an underlying rationale: the requirement of faith protects us against our frailties, steadying us in the pursuit of truth.

The argument that the cave explorer is obliged to scale the cliff doesn't contribute to the truth of the claim that scaling the cliff provides a way out of the cave. But the fact that the argument for the agnostic inquirer's assent is better than her argument against (if it's a fact) contributes to her case for the truth of the doctrine, since Christianity's explanatory power is enhanced by its ability to account for facts about obligations and their discharge, and explanatory power argues to truth. She may not be able to weigh the probabilities of the cases for and against; indeed, she may not even be able to call up all evidence, since so much of it is tacit. Nonetheless, she's obliged to assent if she accepts the argument's premises.

Are there grounds for 4-b? Resolute assent to Christianity (the type of assent required) is possible, Aquinas holds, due to the role of the *will*: assent to Christianity has evidential backing but isn't rooted in compelling evidence. Neither certainty regarding the doctrine, nor high probability, nor knowledge is required for firm assent to Christianity. The standard (contemporary) presumption that it *is* should be rejected. (Indeed, if the evidence *compelled* belief, assent could not be obligatory – it would be inescapable.) Rather, the assent, and its firmness, are grounded in an inchoate desire for the good, a desire matching the heavenly doctrine Christians say is revealed, and in the *will* to obtain that good. *The will to secure the good carries us over the evidential gap.*[12]

The will must be formed through charity, Aquinas says. Love of the good made manifest in the person and teaching of Christ perfects our will. We are held steadfast in our reach for that good by the call of Christ. Thus, the voice of Christ anchors assent to Christianity and, at the same time, conviction that a good God exists.

Objection 2: Any case for wholehearted, resolute belief would be undercut by the existence of competing revelatory claims featuring content that's extraordinarily unified, fitting, etc.

---

[12] Aquinas's fullest treatment of these ideas is in (1256–59/1951–54) *De Veritate*, q. 14, we believe. They appear also in the Summa, where they lace into foundational definitions.

Abrahamic religions other than Christianity can make their own cases for content exhibiting the characteristics substituting for F in our general template. Non-Abrahamic religions, too, have revelatory claims with arresting content, elaborated through great art, literature, and philosophy. Udayana's treatment of Vedic revelation in the *Nyāyakusumāñjali*, a marvelous late tenth-century monograph in the Nyāya-Vaiśeṣika tradition, provides a good illustration.[13] Udayana, like Aquinas, systematizes through definition and deep explanation, interweaving philosophical theology with Vedic prayer. Given competing revelatory claims, how can an inquirer who bases assent to Christianity on its revelatory content be so sure the content is true that the inquirer remains steadfast in belief, resolute in the face of challenges and attractive alternatives?

Assent to Christianity commits a believer only to those propositions that are included in revelation or are logical consequences of it. And there often is a narrow circle of what's truly entailed, particularly when the claim at issue (e.g., "Jesus is the way") is open to interpretation. The ardent Christian believer is not, strictly speaking, committed to saying there is no true religion, or partially true religion, other than Christianity. Both Hebrew and Christian scriptures declare that God speaks "at sundry times and in various ways" (Hebrews 1:1). Diverse traditions may be connected to Jesus's sacrifice in ways we do not, at present, comprehend.

Our trapped cave explorer begins his ascent, following the light he thinks he sees. Midway up, he glances to his left and perceives illumination coming from a distance. The thought passes through his mind that if he and his companion had been elsewhere in the cave, an alternative exit might have been attempted. Does he climb back down and pursue the new light source? No, not unless he's convinced the odds of escape would markedly improve. He continues his chosen direction. He needs *some* way out; he *must commit to a course of action* if he is to save himself and his friend. Perhaps, he thinks, the two potential exits converge in the end, leading to a single path from the cave. In any event, the light source, he's confident, is one: one sun, one good to be pursued, one ultimate destination.

~~~~~~~~~~~~~

How might Christianity be presented to display its credibility both to agnostic inquirers and to committed believers? Push to the front the content of the Christian revelatory claim – blow a bugle – and recognize that our best thinkers' glorious systematizations of that content light up Reality.[14]

---

[13] We thank John Kronen for discussions over the years highlighting correspondence between the Nyāya-Vaiśeṣika and Christian traditions.

[14] We thank W. Matthews Grant, Timothy Pawl, and the editors of this volume for helpful comments on an earlier draft of this chapter.

10 Islamic Religious Epistemology

Enis Doko and Jamie B. Turner

Introduction

This chapter aims to lay out a map of the diverse epistemological perspectives within the Islamic theological tradition, in the conceptual framework of contemporary analytic philosophy of religion. In order achieve that goal, it aims to consider epistemological views in light of their historic context, while at the same time seeking to "translate" those broadly medieval perspectives into contemporary philosophical language. In doing so, the chapter offers a succinct overview of the main trends within the Islamic theological tradition concerning religious epistemology. The chapter is divided into two main sections designated for discussions of differing accounts found in distinct trends of the tradition, namely the Rationalist and Traditionalist trends. The discussion concerning the Rationalist trend focuses on the philosophical-theologians of the dominant Mu'tazilite, Ash'arite, and Maturidite schools. The section on Islamic Traditionalism focuses on the Atharite scripturalism of Ibn Qudāma, and in particular the thought of Ibn Taymiyya. In order to map out these historic positions in light of contemporary religious epistemology, reference is made to a threefold typology of current views in the literature: (1) theistic evidentialism, (2) reformed epistemology, and (3) fideism.[1] As such, the remainder of the chapter will attempt to outline the different approaches toward religious epistemology in the Islamic theological tradition with this threefold typology in mind.

10.1 Islamic Rationalism

In outlining the Rationalist position, we do not mean to suggest that other positions within the tradition (i.e., Traditionalism) are *irrationalist* per se.

---

[1] Roughly, by theistic evidentialism we mean that the positive epistemic status of a given theistic belief depends on the evidence supporting the belief. We use evidence here to include nonpropositional kinds as well as propositional. Reformed epistemology is simply the thesis that theistic belief can have positive epistemic status independent from argumentation. Under the banner of fideism there are a spectrum of views, but we are thinking of it here mainly in terms of the positive epistemic status of theistic belief depending on some factor which is in some sense beyond reason, such as a spiritual disposition, or trust in God. Cf. Dougherty and Tweedt (2015).

Rather, we are aiming to pick out that segment within the tradition that laid the greatest emphasis on reason ('aql) in religious epistemology. In particular, we mean those aspects of the tradition which made the truth of Islamic belief accessible through and in some sense dependent on rational argumentation (jadal) and inference (istidlāl). Hence, in the epistemological sense, by Islamic Rationalism we are dealing broadly with forms of theistic evidentialism. In explicit terms, the Islamic Rationalist tradition here refers to the theo-philosophical schools of 'ilm al-kalām. Practitioners of kalām were known as the mutakallimūn and most famously belonged to one of the following theological schools: Mu'tazilite, Ash'arite, and Maturidite. The latter two denote the major Sunni schools of kalām, but it was at the pens of the Mu'tazilite theologians that the discipline of kalām initially began to flourish.

10.1.1 Epistemological Background

While each school of kalām takes on its own unique theological positioning, there is a common terminology drawn upon and a basic consensus with respect to fundamental concepts within their respective religious epistemologies (Mihirig 2022a: 13). First, each of the schools agreed that all forms of extreme skepticism are false. Indeed, many of the traditional books of kalām offer a refutation of skeptical and sophistical modes of thought (cf. Mihirig 2022a). Second, they divided the concept of knowledge into two rather broad kinds: eternal (qadīm) and temporal (ḥādith). Eternal knowledge is unique to God. He has eternal, unchanging knowledge (cf. al-Juwaynī 1950: 15–16). God does not need tools to gain knowledge; in fact, He does not *gain* knowledge as such. His knowledge is transcendental, timeless, and hence quite different to human knowledge. On the other hand, temporal knowledge is knowledge that has a beginning in time. It is shared by all the creatures God has created who have been given the ability to know. Human knowledge of religious, natural, as well as ethical matters is thought to belong to this category of knowledge, and since such matters have beginnings in time, knowledge of them must be acquired via some epistemic tools (cf. al-Juwaynī 1950: 16).

The schools of kalām limit their epistemological discussions primarily to temporal knowledge, and further divide it into noninferential (ḍarūrī) and inferential knowledge (iktisābī; naẓarī) (Ibrahim 2013: 102). Noninferential knowledge is available to any healthy person without any need for inference or argument, and it is also considered to be epistemically certain or indubitable (Abrahamov 1993: 21). This type of knowledge is typically divided into two main subcategories: sense perceptual knowledge (al-ma'rifa al-ḥissiyya) and rational knowledge (al-ma'rifa al-'aqliyya) (cf. Abrahamov 1993; al-Bāqillānī 2000: 14–15; al-Baghdādī 2002: 18; al-Ṣābūnī 2020: 36–38). Sense perceptual knowledge refers to one's direct sensual awareness of outward external objects (*al-ḥiss al-ẓāhir*), such as humans, plants, and animals, but also to internal states (*al-ḥiss al-bāṭin*), such as hunger, happiness, or pain. Rational knowledge – at least of the noninferential kind – on the other hand, is knowledge whose denial leads to either contradiction or absurdity. Examples include the impossibility of some object occupying two places at the same time, a part always being smaller than a whole, or other basic self-evident principles of logic (*al-badīhīyyāt*). Such knowledge is seen as the starting point of a proper noetic structure, and hence a foundationalist epistemology is broadly accepted within *kalām*. By contrast, knowledge which is *inferential* in nature is knowledge that humans acquire through reasoning. This kind of knowledge need not be gleaned from strict deduction, however, for the *mutakallimūn* did draw on inductive as well as analogical modes of inference that they deemed to be appropriate sources of knowledge (cf. Mihirig 2022b). In contrast to noninferential knowledge, inferential knowledge ranges from epistemically certain (*yaqīnī*) to probable (*ẓannī*), (al-Nasafī 2001: 1:27).

The *mutakallimūn* also agree that there are three valid sources of knowledge: reason ('*aql*), sense perception (*ḥiss*), and testimony (*khabar*) (cf. Abrahamov 1993; al-Nasafī 2001: 1:27). Reason is considered to be our ability to understand both impossible, possible, and necessary propositions and enables us to infer conclusions about the unseen (*ghayb*) when drawing on data from the five senses. They insist that one has to accept reason as a valid source of knowledge, since in order to deny it, one has to use reason to argue against its validity (cf. al-Māturīdī 2020: 29). The Qur'ān is also cited in support, as it very frequently invites both believers and nonbelievers to use reason and base their claims to knowledge on reason (cf. Qur'ān 2:44, 3:91, 6:65).

The second source of knowledge is sense perception (cf. al-Juwaynī 1950: 173; 'Abd al-Jabbār 1965a: 12:59; al-Māturīdī 2020: 46). The different schools of *kalām* are broadly empiricist of sorts, for they considered most of our knowledge to come directly from the senses, or via reason gleaned from our sense experience. The *mutakallimūn* do acknowledge that our senses can sometimes mislead us, but that nevertheless all of our knowledge about the physical world initially comes via our five senses, and hence sense perception is considered to be an indispensable source of knowledge.

The third source of knowledge is testimony (cf. 'Abd al-Jabbār 1965a: 15: 317; al-Baghdādī 2002: 25; al-Māturīdī 2020: 27–28). Testimonial knowledge refers to the knowledge that we gain from other people. Our knowledge of the events in the places and times in which we are not present, for instance, is gained via testimony. In general, testimony is considered to be less epistemically reliable relative to reason and sense experience because people can be more easily deceived in this case. Testimony is taken to be an essential source of religious knowledge, however, for we do not receive knowledge of divine revelation directly; rather, we gain it through testimony. Similarly, the life and

deeds of Prophet Muḥammad (*al-Sunna*),[2] which hold great religious significance, also come from testimonial reports. There are two types of testimonies:
multiple or mass-testimonial reports (*khabar mutawātir*) and singular testimonial reports (*khabar āḥad*) (cf. Abrahamov 1993; al-Māturīdī 2020: 28).
Multiple or mass testimony is given by narrators so numerous that it is highly
unlikely that the report is false. Hence, such testimony is taken as a very
reliable source of knowledge (*qaṭi'ī*). Usually, it is expected that the report
comes from at least three independent witnesses. Witnesses should also be
known to be honest or trusted by society. Moreover, the content of the
testimonial report should not be in conflict with well-known facts and self-
evident dictates of reason. The Qur'ān and parts of the *Sunna* are considered
by the *mutakallimūn* to belong to this category of testimony.

10.1.2 Religious Epistemology

A central issue discussed by the *mutakallimūn* concerns the relationship
between knowledge and religious belief or faith (*īmān*). In the Qur'ān, God
asks Muslims to have faith and declare their belief in Him (cf. Qur'ān 29:46,
4:171), and so it is taken as a matter of upmost importance to understand what
it means to have faith in God. The schools of *kalām* typically insisted that faith
is achieved through a certain methodical fashion. Crucial to this methodical
process is the way in which religious belief *ought* to be formed. Roughly, the
mutkallimūn considered there to be two primary ways that one can form a
religious belief: on the basis of independent investigation, or by accepting the
beliefs of some person or society. The latter kind of belief formation is known
as belief by imitation (*taqlīd*) (al-Nasafī 2001: 1:39–40). *Taqlīd* refers to blind
imitation or following (Mustafa 2013: 6). A person who believes by imitation
is known as a *muqallid*. *Taqlīd* has been understood as involving two things:
belief without evidence and accepting someone as an authority on religious
matters besides God. This is typically taken to be epistemically *and* morally
unacceptable in the formation of religious belief. If one does not base his
beliefs on evidence and investigation, then the thought is that he will get to
the truth simply by a matter of luck. As such, none of the schools of *kalām*
hold that belief by *taqlīd* is desirable, and they encourage believers to form
their religious beliefs based upon evidence (*dalīl*). Nonetheless, the schools of
kalām did develop some interesting nuance on this issue.

The majority of Mu'tazilite thinkers insisted that religious belief grounded in
taqlīd cannot be sufficiently appraised to be considered knowledge. One of the
foremost representatives of Mu'tazilite theology was Qāḍī 'Abd al-Jabbār
(d. 1025 CE). According to 'Abd al-Jabbār, the first duty of the religious

---

[2] Upon whom be God's peace and blessings.

believer is "discursive reasoning (*al-naẓar*) which leads to knowledge of God, because He is not known noninferentially (*ḍarūratan*) nor by the senses (*bi'l-mushāhada*). Thus, He must be known by reflection and speculation" (1965b: 39). Moreover, if we were to blindly follow some person, group or society as a means to belief in any given religion, then getting the right belief will be matter of luck because "it is impossible that all these [differing] systems of thought should be right – for each contradicts the other." ('Abd al-Jabbār 1988: 201). But then, if someone sees this to be the case, one must also recognize that if one adopts the method of *taqlīd*, then it will just be a matter of epistemic luck if one arrives at the true religion, and knowledge precludes such epistemic luck (cf. Adamson 2022: 7–8). Therefore, one could not be said to *know* one's religion to be true in this case. Hence, 'Abd al-Jabbār asks, "Why is the *taqlīd* of the believer in God's oneness any better than the *taqlīd* of the unbeliever?" (1988, 199). At an epistemic level, he concludes that neither is any more justified than the other.

The Maturidite position, is somewhat more nuanced. In his famous work *Kitāb al-Tawḥīd*, the eponym of the Maturidite school Abū Manṣūr al-Māturīdī (d. 944 CE) opened the first chapter of his magnum opus with a thorough rejection of *taqlīd* in matters of faith:

> We find that all people, with all their different religious opinions and sects, agree on one statement, namely, that whatever one holds to be true, is valid, and, as a result, that whatever others than him hold, is invalid . . .. Therefore, it is taken for granted that *taqlīd* excuses its embracer from holding the opposite view on the same question. This, however, only accounts for the multiplicity of number. The only way out of this is if one of them has his ultimate argument based on intellect (*'aql*) by way of which his truth can be known and if he has proof by way of which he can persuade fair-minded people to accept his truth. (Quoted in Cerić 1995: 67–68)

The first thing to note about this passage is that al-Māturīdī embraces the position that Muslims have a "duty to reason in matters of faith" (*wujūb al-naẓar*), and he posits the intellect as the source of religious knowledge. Second, al-Māturīdī cites the problem of "religious disagreement" as being at the heart of the necessity to arrive at knowledge of God by use of the intellect. Thus, as J. Meric Pessagno explains in commenting on the above passage, according to al-Māturīdī, "what is needed for a true knowledge of religion is, first, an intellectual argument (*al-ḥujja al-'aqliyya*) that will convince the hearer of the personal trustworthiness (*ṣidq*) of the teacher, and, second, a proof (*burhān*) of the objective truth (*ḥaqq*) of what is taught. Only when both aspects are thus known is religion *known*" (1979: 21–22). If the person does not settle the problem of "religious disagreement" without recourse to some form of intellectual proof or argument, then each claim, al-Māturīdī thinks, would be equally invalid, and the *muqallid* in his grasping of religious truths would be in no significantly better epistemic state than one who grasps religious falsities. Thus, Maturidites believe that, ideally, we all ought to base our religious belief on *propositional* evidence. However, some Maturidites did take *nonpropositional evidence* to be epistemically valid as well. For example, Abū'l Mu'īn al-Nasafī (d. 1142 CE) thought a religious faith is valid if based on miracles or even reports of miracles, or due to religious experience through reading the Qur'ān (cf. al-Nasafī 2001: 1:38–42).

Turning to the Ash'arite school. According to its eponym, Abū'l Ḥasan al-Ash'arī (d. 936 CE), religious faith is fundamentally a question of *taṣdīq* (assent). That is, to assent to what another proposes and what one henceforth holds to be true (Uslu 2007: 167–168). Indeed, as the Ash'arite theologian al-Juwaynī writes, "the true sense of faith is assent to God (*al-taṣdīq bi'llāh*) . . . the assent, strictly speaking, is interior speaking, but it exists only along with knowledge" (quoted in Frank 1989: 40). Some Ash'arite theologians, however, recognized a distinction between individual and communal obligations with respect to grounding one's religious faith on rational argument. In this regard, the Ash'arite theologian Abū al-Qāsim al-Anṣārī (d. 1118 CE) offers a succinct account of the positions among the early Ash'arites on this matter. He writes:

Since it is a fact that rational inquiry is in principle obligatory, it is obligatory for *the community as a whole*. Whether it is, however, an obligation of *every individual* is something based on a principle that explains how one achieves adequate knowledge of God and of His attributes and His Apostles and the particular teaching of Islam. The followers of our school disagree on this: [1] Some of them hold that what is required is belief that is founded in a definitive, rational proof of what one is obliged to believe and accordingly his belief in what he believes is thus a true knowing . . . [2] Some of them hold that belief must be based on proof (*dalīl*), but that the proof may be one given in revelation (*sam'ī*), either in the text of the Scripture and the Sunna or from the consensus of the community; and it may be purely rational (*'aqlī*) . . . [3] Some of them say that what is required is a belief that apperceives its object as it really is and as such; accordingly, belief in it, so characterized, is knowledge. (Quoted in Frank 1989: 46–47)

Al-Anṣārī explains that those who adopt the first position divide the reasoning and speculation concerning the fundamental religious principles, such as belief in God and the Prophet, into those aspects which are "an individual obligation" and those that consist in "things which are a communal obligation." As for the former, they hold that an individual obligation is upon each responsible sane person (*al-mukallaf*) to have proper knowledge of God, and by extension the veracity of the Prophet's claims, on the basis of propositional evidence. In the case of the latter, what is said to be a communal rather than individual duty is attending to those matters such that if the community of the faithful neglected them, then they would be thereby committing collective sin. Al-Anṣārī states that these pertain to matters such as, "the drawing out of multiple proofs," "defending the core of Islam," "refuting opponents" of the religion and "to dispose of the false reasoning of those who teach error and of heretics" (quoted in Frank 1989: 47). As such, rational argument is essential to the positive epistemic status of one's Islamic belief, but the acquisition of evidence may be satisfied communally, as opposed to individually.

10.1.3 Kalāmic Evidentialism

In light of the following discussion concerning *kalām*, a synopsis of its religious epistemology can be drawn out by the recognition of it as typically a combination of "strong foundationalism" and "theistic evidentialism." The version of foundationalism upheld within the epistemology of paradigmatic *kalām* is perhaps best rendered – following Dewey Hoitenga – "medieval foundationalism." This premodern form of classical foundationalism holds that only those beliefs which are "self-evident truths of reason," "evident to the senses," and "incorrigible" are among those beliefs which may be known in a noninferential fashion (Hoitenga 1991: 181–182).

This sort of foundationalist epistemology can be found in all of the major strands of the *kalām* tradition. First, by upholding the notion of *'ilm ḍarūrī* they admitted the basic foundationalist thesis that there can be noninferential knowledge. Second, what was stipulated as comprising *'ilm ḍarūrī* was generally considered to be epistemically certain. Third, the sorts of beliefs that were restricted within the category of *'ilm ḍarūrī* closely parallels the classical foundationalist models of proper noninferential beliefs in Western thought. The consequence of this foundationalist epistemology – in so far as it relates to knowledge and theistic belief – is neatly summed up by Nicholas Heer in the following terms:

Knowledge of all these matters [i.e., God's existence and the truth of scripture] can be gained *only* through reasoning (*naẓar*). This is because such knowledge is *not* necessary knowledge (*ḍarūrī*), but is, on the contrary, acquired knowledge (*muktasab*). God's existence, for example, is not known through sense perception, nor is it self-evident (*badīhī*) as are the axioms of logic and mathematics. Nor can knowledge of these matters be gained through illumination (*ilhām*) . . . or through purification of the inner self (*taṣfiyat al-bāṭin*) . . . or by instruction (*ta'līm*) of an infallible *imam*. (1993: 187–188)

As Heer accurately observes, given that theistic beliefs are not considered to be among our properly noninferential beliefs according to the *mutakallimūn*, they must be conceived as being part of our properly inferential beliefs. Consequently, for religious beliefs to receive the epistemic appraisal of knowledge, they must be based upon some evidence (*dalīl*) or set of evidences (*adilla*). Thus, it is the epistemological foundationalism of paradigmatic *kalām*, which results in its subsequent "theistic evidentialism," encapsulated by the supposition that such forms of knowledge do not comprise part of *'ilm ḍarūrī*.

This perspective is epitomized by the traditional *kalām* insistence on the epistemic (and moral) duty to engage in rational inquiry concerning religious belief: *wujūb al-naẓar* (cf. Spevack 2020: 237–242; Adamson 2022: 7–11). As suggested in the previous section, this doctrine essentially seeks to condemn blind imitation of one's community (*taqlīd*) in matters of faith. The idea transfigures into the notion that: (a) the first duty incumbent on humans is the fulfillment of the obligation to *know* God and (b) that this duty is to be fulfilled through reflection over the proofs for God's existence and broader attributes (cf. al-Rāzī 1991: 130). Reflection on the above would suggest that a *kalām*-based evidentialism on the nature of religious belief entails a sort of *strong theistic evidentialism*. This is because for religious belief to be classed as knowledge for a believer, they must engage in and formulate an argument for their religious beliefs in propositional terms. It is not sufficient that it be based upon seemings, intuitions, or experience. As suggested above, however, some Maturidites had a broader conception of the sort of theistic evidence necessary to fulfill one's epistemic duty to reason to God (cf. al-Ṣābūnī 2020: 347). This might suggest that a more *moderate* form of theistic evidentialism could be upheld. Recently, Tobias Andersson (2022) has also argued that a "phenomenal conservatist" (PC) conception of (*moderate*) theistic evidentialism may be worked into the religious epistemology of Ash'arite theologian Muḥammad b. Yūsuf al-Sanūsī (d. 1490 CE).[3] Andersson notes that although as a *mutakallim* al-Sanūsī upholds the principle of *wujūb al-naẓar*, he also recognizes that the sort of evidence required to fulfill that duty may depend on one's circumstances. As such, al-Sanūsī draws a distinction between "'detailed' or 'specific' evidence (*dalīl tafṣīlī*)" and "'general' evidence (*dalīl jumlī*)" (2022: 134). Whereas the former kind of evidence is necessary for theologians, the latter may be sufficient for the layman to acquire epistemic justification, and a *dalīl jumlī* may comprise the sort of evidence recognized by PC (i.e., *seemings*).

At the same time, we have also seen that some of the Ash'arites distinguished between an individual obligation (*farḍ 'ayn*) and a communal obligation (*farḍ kifāya*) in satisfying the duty of *wujūb al-naẓar*. This might allow us to consider a different form of theistic evidentialism within *kalām*, namely what Stephen Wykstra coined "sensible evidentialism" (cf. Wykstra 1998).[4] In this case, propositional evidence is necessary for the positive epistemic status of one's theistic belief and for the epistemic health of the community.

---

[3] Phenomenal conservatism is roughly the view that a subject S is prima facie justified in believing that p if it seems to S that p, in the absence of defeaters S may have for p. Thus, in the absence of defeaters, if it seems to S that God exists through reflection over aspects of nature, say, then their seeming counts as prima facie evidence that God exists, and prima facie grounds of justification for believing that God exists (cf. Tucker 2011).

[4] By sensible evidentialism we mean the idea that for a belief to be sufficiently epistemically appraised as knowledge, some propositional evidence is essential, not necessarily due to the individual, but at least it must be had within the broader epistemic community.

However, it is not a requirement that each individual acquire this evidence themselves, providing that it is secured by some within the community. Interestingly, in his recent work on Maturidite theology, Ramon Harvey suggests that al-Māturīdī's religious epistemology may be understood in a similar way to that of Wykstra's "sensible evidentialism," (Harvey 2021: 222).

Thus, even if *strong* theistic evidentialism is the paradigmatic view within *kalām*, its Rationalist approach to religious epistemology is perhaps at least compatible with weaker forms of the evidentialist requirement (i.e., *moderate* theistic evidentialism and *sensible* evidentialism).

10.2 Islamic Traditionalism

Traditionalist Islamic theology is sometimes referred to as Hanbalism or Atharism. Hanbalism takes its name from its eponym, the famous Muslim jurist and champion of Sunni orthodoxy, Aḥmad ibn Ḥanbal (d. 855 CE). This theological orientation is also sometimes called Atharism – coming from the term *āthār*, roughly meaning "tradition" – because of the general emphasis and focus it lends to *āthār*, that is, Ḥadīth and Qur'ānic scripture. In turning to Muslim Traditionalist theology, we are turning toward a theological approach that appears prima facie to gravitate toward a fideistic religious epistemological outlook. By fideism, here, we do not mean irrationalism or an outright rejection of reason per se, but rather a position that denotes the general view that theistic belief is *in some sense* supra-rational. The particular *sense* in which religious belief is supra-rational, however, depends on how exactly it is exemplified. Thus, there is a spectrum of fideistic views, some of which may even be compatible with theistic evidentialism (Dougherty and Tweedt 2015: 554).

10.2.1 Qadāmite Traditionalism

In his article "Orthodoxy and Ḥanbalite Fideism," Aziz al-Azmeh defines Hanbalite fideism as, "the affirmation of dogmatic articles without a qualification that would discursively carry them beyond the bounds of their given textuality" (1988: 256). Roughly, al-Azmeh's idea seems to be that in the Hanbalite view, scripture (*naql*) ought to be given precedence to reason ('*aql*) and that the latter must conform to the dictates of the former. He also goes on to suggest that religious belief and affiliation is construed in terms of *taqlīd*, consisting of a testimonial passing from one generation of believers to the next, which is "a purely affirmative form of expression, and belongs properly to an act of devotion more than to one of intellection" (al-Azmeh 1988: 266). The positive epistemic status of religious belief, then, would somehow have to be ultimately grounded in and through religious scripture, even if its dictates *appear* contrary to the deliverances of reason.

Perhaps a good example of this particular brand of fideism can be found in the writings of the staunch Hanbalite theological apologist, Muwaffaq al-Dīn Ibn Qudāma (d. 1223 CE). Ibn Qudāma was a loyal defender of Traditionalist Hanbalite theology who sought to preserve and transmit religious knowledge as understood by the earliest generation of Muslims (*al-salaf al-ṣāliḥ*). In that vein, Ibn Qudāma rejected any form of *kalām* and chastised its practitioners. In his famous *Taḥrīm al-naẓar fī kutub ahl al-kalām*, Ibn Qudāma argued that *kalām* was religiously abominable on a number of grounds. The most important in the context of the present discussion being his argument against *ijtihād* in religious matters. By *ijtihād* we roughly mean independent critical thought or reasoning. In the *kalām* sense, we can see this, for instance, in the "duty to reason" (*wujūb al-naẓar*) discussed in the previous section. According to Ibn Qudāma, to impose the duty of *ijtihād* upon all Muslims is wrongheaded for at least two reasons: (a) because it imposes an obligation upon Muslims who are unable to carry out the duty, and (b) that it is contrary to the Prophet's teaching because he never imposed such an obligation upon the Muslim community (cf. Ibn Qudāma 1962: 17–18). With that said, Ibn Qudāma asserts the following:

> To profess the obligation of *ijtihād* upon all would entail a condemnation of the broad masses to error, by reason of their neglect of that which is incumbent upon them. The only thing in respect of which the use of *taqlīd* has been said to be unlawful for them are those conspicuous matters, which they know by virtue of them being so conspicuous, without requiring special pains, thought, or examination; namely, the profession of the unity of God, the mission of Muhammad, the knowledge of the obligation of the five daily prayers, the fasting of Ramadan, and the rest of the pillars whose religious obligation is of common knowledge. These obligations, having become known by way of *ijmā'*, require no study or examination. Therefore, with regard to these obligations, it is unlawful for them to make use of *taqlid*. (Ibn Qudāma 1962: 18–19)

In this passage, Ibn Qudāma attempts to outline the proper place for *ijtihād* and that of *taqlīd*. However, he does so in a way that appears somewhat problematic. On the one hand, Ibn Qudāma argues that it is unlawful for a religious believer to accept the most essential religious doctrines via means of *taqlīd*. The reasoning is that such knowledge has been made obvious and manifest through scholarly consensus (*ijmā'*); it is not among the "minutiae of religious beliefs" that it is the job of scholarly experts to explicate. Thus, it would imply that such knowledge is to be attained through means of *ijtihād*. Yet, on the other hand, if knowledge of central Islamic doctrines is made manifest and hence known in and through *ijmā'*, that implies that such knowledge actually depends upon a form of *taqlīd* (i.e., adhering to the dictates of the scholarly community).[5]

---

[5] For further discussion of Qadāmite Traditionalism with respect to the issues just raised, cf. Aijaz (2018).

Perhaps one might argue in response that, in fact, this knowledge does not depend on *taqlīd* nor *ijtihād*, but rather *ittibā'*, that is, adherence to religious dogma through means of evidence from religious scripture. The idea then would be that one's knowledge of God, for instance, was derived from one's own independent study of basic scriptural texts. Nonetheless, from an epistemological point of view, this would not ultimately salvage Ibn Qudāma's view from appearing strongly fideistic or even presuppositionalist, because *ittibā'* presupposes the truth of religious scripture. Thus, George Makdisi concludes his analysis of Ibn Qudāma's religious epistemological approach by stating that the religious knowledge required for salvation, "may be known only through the traditions [i.e., Qur'ān & Ḥadīth], of which the depositaries and legitimate transmitters are obviously the traditionalists – certainly not the speculative theologians" (Ibn Qudāma 1962: xix).

Nevertheless, we suspect that Ibn Qudāma himself would deny that knowledge of God and scripture is something known by faith alone, or something that in some sense stands above or against reason. In fact, Muslim traditionalists did draw on different kinds of rational argumentation in proving their doctrinal commitments, and "they also believed in the harmony of scripture and reason" (Mustafa 2013: 46). As Binyamin Abrahamov notes, "the proofs that many traditionalists brought were not only proofs from the Qur'an and the Sunna but also rational proofs, sometimes even kalam arguments" (2016: 273). As such, perhaps there is an alternative conception of Islamic Traditionalism that makes better sense of its impetus for the place of "reason" in religious epistemology.

10.2.2 Taymiyyan Traditionalism

Sherman Jackson rightly points out that "the Traditionalists invoked 'reason' almost as readily as did the Rationalists; they simply rejected the notion that 'reason' was limited to the composite Islamicized Hellenistic-Late Antiquity version of it that the Rationalists embraced" (2009: 132). This latter idea on the nature of reason comes out most clearly in the thought of the Traditionalist theologian Taqī al-Dīn Ibn Taymiyya (d. 1328 CE). In his seminal work on the relationship between reason ('*aql*) and revelation (*naql*), Ibn Taymiyya attempts to refute "claims to rationality made by Muslim theologians and philosophers, and sets forth his own vision of true rationality that accords with divine revelation" (Hoover 2019: 32).

Central to Ibn Taymiyya's conception of reason is the notion of '*aql ṣarīḥ*, that is, pure or clear reason (cf. 1979: 1:376). For Ibn Taymiyya, '*aql ṣarīḥ* is always congruent with *naql ṣaḥīḥ*, that is, authentic religious tradition (cf. 1995: 12:217). As such, any apparent conflict between the two can be explained in reference to either *bid'ī 'aqlī* (innovated/contaminated rationality) or *bid'ī naqlī* (innovated/contaminated revelation) (El-Tobgui 2020: 165). In critiquing the general claim of certain theologians and philosophers concerning the alleged conflict between reason and revelation, Ibn Taymiyya seeks not to reject reason outright, but perhaps something closer to what C. Stephen Evans has termed elsewhere "*concrete reason*," as opposed to "*ideal reason*" (Evans 1998: 94). That is to say, Ibn Taymiyya rejects the conception of reason or of what is "reasonable" as concretely conceived in the intellectual strata of society in his time. In his case, this refers to an "Islamicized Hellenistic-Late Antiquity" conception of reason. For Ibn Taymiyya, this is not "*ideal reason*" or *ʿaql ṣarīḥ*, as he would put it, but rather *bidʿī ʿaqlī*, an example of the ways in which human reason is limited and often flawed. For ideal or sound reason could never be at odds with true revelation, even if that appears to be the case when reason is construed through the lens of Islamicized Hellenism. A crucial component of a Taymiyyan conception of ideal reason that is highly relevant for the present discussion is his notion of *fiṭra*.

For Ibn Taymiyya, *ʿaql ṣarīḥ* is predicated on *fiṭra*: "the foundation of reason is grounded in the soundness and health of the *fiṭra*" (2005: 369). Interestingly, al-Azmeh points out that "Ḥanbalite writers often use the notion of innate natural knowledge (*fiṭra*) to express what they see as the self-evidence of their position" (1988: 257). So, perhaps the notion of *fiṭra* could better explain the supposed self-evidence of those very clear or "conspicuous matters" of Islamic dogma alluded to by Ibn Qudāma, in such a way that salvages the apparent superfluity with which his fideistic religious epistemology regards the place of reason.

According to Ibn Taymiyya, "*fiṭra* is the original nature of human beings, uncorrupted by later beliefs and practices, ready to accept the true notions of Islam" (1995: 4:245–246). Jon Hoover suggests that it may be viewed "in Ibn Taymiyya's thought as an *innate* faculty" (2007: 39). However, it would not be quite right to think of *fiṭra* as a distinct cognitive faculty per se. Rather, at least from an epistemological perspective, it is perhaps best thought of as our human cognitive constitution. Ibn Taymiyya puts it that

[God] made the *fiṭra* of His servants disposed to the apprehension and understanding of the realities [of things] and to know them. And if it were not for this readiness (i.e., *fiṭra*) within the hearts/minds (*qalb*) to know the truth, neither speculative reasoning would be possible, nor demonstration, discourse or language. (1979: 5:62)

In a sense, then – looked at from a purely epistemological angle – this quote suggests that *fiṭra* is the natural constitution of our cognitive capacities. Significantly, from the epistemic point of view, Ibn Taymiyya conceives of "the proper functioning of *all* our epistemic faculties ... [as] predicated in *all* cases on the health and proper functioning of the *fiṭra*" (El-Tobgui 2020: 271). Accordingly, it is due to *fiṭra* that a human's "knowledge of truth ... and the recognition of falsehood" is grounded (Ibn Taymiyya 2014: 49). Consequently, on the Taymiyyan epistemic scheme, the positive epistemic status of one's belief is achieved through the reliable workings of the natural cognitive capacities God has created us with, when they're sufficiently tied to *fiṭra* (i.e., working naturally or properly).

Significantly, *fiṭra* in a crucial (albeit partial) sense resembles the sort of *sensus divinitatis* to which Alvin Plantinga refers in his work on reformed epistemology (cf. Plantinga 2000b; El-Tobgui 2020: 275; Turner 2021).[6] Indeed, Ibn Taymiyya declares that "the affirmation of the Creator and His perfection is natural (*fiṭrīyya*) and noninferential (*ḍarūrīyya*) with respect to one whose *fiṭra* remains intact" (1995: 6:73). According to Ibn Taymiyya, this knowledge of God is actualized through a recognition of theistic signs present in the natural world and in scripture (Ibn Taymiyya 1979: 7:302; 2005: 401). Indeed, Ibn Taymiyya holds that, "everything else other than He is evidence of His Self and signs of His existence . . . no contingent existent can be actualized without His very self being actual. All contingent existents are entailed by Him; they are evidence and a sign of Him" (2005: 197).[7] Ibn Taymiyya also argues on theological grounds that "it was the method of the prophets – may God bless them – in proving the existence of God to [make] mention of His signs (*āyāt*) . . . [and] God's method of proof through signs are plentiful in the Qur'ān" (2005: 193–194). However, crucially, this "inference through signs" (*istidlāl bi'l-āyāt*) is not to be conceived as an inference of any traditional kind. It does not appear to work on the basis of premises from which a conclusion is inferred. This is what Ibn Taymiyya suggests when he writes that, "affirming one's knowledge of the Creator and prophecy does not depend on any syllogisms (*al-aqyisa*). Rather, this knowledge is attained from the signs (*āyāt*) that prove a specific matter that is not shared by others. These matters are known by means of noninferential knowledge (*bi'l-ʿilm al-ḍarūrī*), which does not require discursive reasoning (*naẓar*)" (2005: 401). Therefore, the epistemic and cognitive process does not involve argumentation, and the religious beliefs that are a consequence of such a process are duly noninferential.

One way of construing how this cognitive process may proceed is in terms of a kind of quasi-perceptual model. For according to Ibn Taymiyya, "the signs of God are always known through sense perception" (1995: 2:48), which as Wael Hallaq notes, includes both its "internal" and "external" dimensions (*al-bāṭin wa'l-ẓāhir*), (1991: 63). With this in mind, we might think that Ibn Taymiyya's thesis runs something close to what Del Ratzsch has argued for on the basis of Thomas Reid's epistemology: that belief in a designer from the

---

[6] Although it must be pointed out that *fiṭra* and a *sensus divinitatis* are different, the latter being a faculty and the former our natural constitution that includes that kind of faculty. In other words, *fiṭra* has within it a divine spark that inclines human beings to the knowledge and worship of God.

[7] Whether those signs be what he refers to as "*āyāt al-anfus*" – signs within oneself – or "*āyāt al-āfāq*" – signs within the cosmos (Ibn Taymiyya 1979: 3:108).

apparent design in nature can be formed *noninferentially*, akin to the way in which we form our ordinary perceptual beliefs (cf. Ratzsch 2003). In following Ratzsch, we might think that Ibn Taymiyya holds a similar position concerning the connection between our disposition (*fiṭra*) to form theistic beliefs – upon an apprehension of theistic signs in nature – and our sense perceptual faculties. That is, given our *fiṭrī* theistic disposition, our sense perceptual faculties may be geared up to form noninferential beliefs about God from perceiving His signs in nature. Although this process centers on our perceptual faculties, this is not to say that it does not also involve reason or rational reflection. Indeed, for Ibn Taymiyya recognizing God through His signs is to be conceived as "rational" (Ibn Taymiyya 1995: 1:49), and hence in a sense grounded in reason. Providing our *fiṭrī* theistic disposition is working naturally and properly we can know that God exists noninferentially through a perception of theistic signs.

That being said, Ibn Taymiyya recognized that *fiṭra* is susceptible to cognitive impediment; it can become corrupted in some sense (cf. Ibn Taymiyya 1979: 7:72). Impediments may arise due to certain desires (*hawā*) or personal motives (*gharaḍ*) which hinders one from accepting the truth (cf. 1979: 6:271). They could also be due to doubts or spurious objections (*shubuhāt*), blind imitation of one's socio-environment (*taqlīd*), or engagement in sheer conjecture (*ẓann*), (cf. 1979: 3:317). Consequently, it is possible that one may need propositional evidence to revive *fiṭra* and acquire knowledge of God (Ibn Taymiyya 1995: 16:458). That said, *fiṭra* may also be kept intact through spiritual practice (Ibn Taymiyya 1972: 2:341).

Ibn Taymiyya's emphasis on the congruence of reason and revelation sees him affirming that, in some sense, reason (*'aql*) is the epistemic ground for accepting revelation (*naql*) (cf. El-Tobgui 2020: 149–155). As we have seen, he also admits that propositional evidence, and therefore argument, may be epistemically required for knowledge of God. Yet, at the same time, his acknowledgment of being able to know God via *fiṭra* noninferentially, coupled with the notion that *fiṭra* is nurtured spiritually, means that it is possible to see Ibn Taymiyya simultaneously embracing all three religious epistemological positions: reformed epistemology, theistic evidentialism, and fideism. First, it is evident that his position maps onto reformed epistemology in the fullest sense because he holds to the thesis that God can be known in the absence of argument. Second, he can also be seen as a *moderate* theistic evidentialist, and third, a weak (or *responsible*) fideist (cf. Evans 1998; Dougherty and Tweedt 2015: 547).[8] His *moderate* evidentialism can be gleaned from the fact that he has a broad evidential scope when it comes to evidence drawn upon to know

---

[8] Roughly, we take *weak* fideism to be the view that evidence for God (at least for the most part) cannot be properly noticed without a certain prior disposition or affective-cum-spiritual character.

God, that is, a sign (*āyā*), propositional evidence (*dalīl*), testimony (*khabar*), and spiritual inspiration or religious experience (*kashf*) (cf. 1995: 20:202). He also appears to suggest that all forms of theistic knowledge will involve evidence, broadly construed. Finally, his weak fideism can be gleaned from his understanding that religious knowledge grounded on *fiṭra* rests on religious and spiritual practice such as meditative remembrance of God (*ẓikr*), without which the mind/heart (*qalb*) is unable to properly grasp the evidence for God (cf. 1995: 9:312-314).

Conclusion

This chapter has surveyed the main theological trends within the Islamic theological tradition concerning religious epistemology and has considered ways in which those approaches might be understood in contemporary philosophical terms. In summary, the broadly Rationalist trend within the tradition has been thought to embrace versions of theistic evidentialism. By contrast, the Traditionalist trend has been understood to adopt positions closer to fideism and reformed epistemology, yet without at the same time entirely doing away with demands for evidence.

11 Hindu Religious Epistemology

Thomas A. Forsthoefel

In certain versions of Hindu philosophy, we learn of the three "qualities (*gunas*)" or elemental characteristics – *sattva* (lucidity), *rajas* (activity), and *tamas* (torpor) – that constitute the one material reality (*prakriti*). This is sometimes likened to three strands that constitute a single rope. Each are qualitatively different, but together – that is, invariably bound together – they produce a tight, unified whole and a way of understanding the diverse phenomena of a single material matrix. Similarly, South Asian philosophical systems typically weave three strands of philosophical reasoning into a unified vision (*darshana*) of reality. First, Indian schools index knowledge to salvation, carefully weaving together epistemology and soteriology, with saving knowledge typically preceded by careful review of how we know anything at all. At the same time, Indian epistemological and soteriological reflections are also invariably linked to metaphysics, for to advance a saving knowledge of the Ultimate requires also addressing what that Ultimate is and how we can come to know it.

This chapter will first illustrate the triple weave of epistemology, metaphysics, and soteriology in Advaita Vedanta, focusing on ideas advanced by the master exponent of Advaita, Shankara (c. 750 CE). Drawing from contemporary Anglophone epistemological reflection, particularly that of Alvin Plantinga and William Alston, the chapter will show that Shankara's soteriological and metaphysical reflection is supported by externalist and internalist epistemologies, with the most important, in my view, being internalist, owing to Shankara's metaphysical presuppositions. These two epistemological heuristics are deployed to gain insight into Shankara's religious epistemology and then stimulate an extended discussion of – and argument for – the epistemic merit of religious testimony and religious experience. Successfully doing all this will illuminate the epistemic value of those two mechanisms but also illustrate the triple weave of philosophical reflection in India, a single intellectual rope, as it were, now constituted by the strands of metaphysics, epistemology, and soteriology. While the focus and stimulus of this chapter is Shankara's thought and the epistemic merit of religious testimony, I will first briefly point to other thinkers and systems that similarly – and, arguably, invariably – also employ this threefold strand of reasoned reflection to establish and advance their fundamental philosophical positions (*darshana*).

11.1 Philosophy of Religion in India

Among Indian schools – Jainism and Buddhism included – gaining an ultimate knowledge of the true nature of reality assumed and required gaining a proper understanding of mundane reality; this, in turn, required careful understanding of the cognitive processes that allow us to know anything at all. Thus, philosophical schools in these traditions typically addressed and assessed *pramana*s, cognitive mechanisms that produce valid knowledge, the most universal of which is perception (*pratyaksha*). Cognitive outputs are therefore properly called valid (*prama*) when they are the product of properly functioning perceptual and reasoning equipment. For example, as the fourteenth-century systematizer Madhava tersely registers, "Right knowledge always accompanies the mechanism of right knowledge (Cowell and Gough 1989: 228; translation slightly modified)." The Nyaya Sutra (c. second century BCE) is the foundational text of the Nyaya school, among whose chief concerns is the proper operation of logic. The reason for this focus is clear: saving knowledge first requires thinking properly. The Sutra (1.1.3) cites and defines its set of mechanisms that produce valid knowledge: perception (*pratyaksha*), inference (*anumana*), comparison (*upamana*), and testimony (*sabda*); its strategy appears to follow the maxim "to know the thing to be measured, you must first know the measure" (Cowell and Gough 1989: 228).

Emphases on knowledge-producing mechanisms in Indian philosophical traditions are typically indexed to underlying metaphysical presuppositions and soteriological goals. For example, Samkhya and Yoga emphasize the importance of inference as a mechanism of valid knowledge, and for very good reason. Both schools are dualistic: reality is fundamentally constituted by two reals, spirit and matter. The former denotes an infinite number of separate souls (*purusha/atman*) and the latter – the physical, material "stuff" of the universe (*prakriti*) – originally emerges from a primordial, subtle, unmanifest (*avyakta*) state. But perception, the most common and self-evident *pramana*, has as its scope material, observable, physical reality and thus cannot yield knowledge either of the immaterial Self or of the primordial unmanifest material reality. Hence, inference is required to demonstrate – or at least supply reasonable theories of – the truth of the soul.

Similarly, the related schools of Nyaya and Vaisheshika both stressed the importance of perception and inference, in part to establish their own versions of realistic pluralism. Such efforts never were "mere" philosophizing as both schools, along with most Indian philosophical traditions, clearly hold right knowledge to be the *sine qua non* for saving liberation. Indeed, Nyaya Sutra 1.1.1 stipulates that the "supreme felicity" is attained by knowledge of sixteen epistemological and logical categories, beginning, above all, with the mechanisms of right knowledge (*pramana*) (Vidyabhusana 1975: 1).

11.2 Externalism and Internalism

Before moving on to Shankara's thought, a brief discussion of externalist and internalist epistemologies is in order. Although different thinkers do not use the terms univocally, useful characterizations can be made that help us gain insight into the processes of knowing.

Externalism and internalism attempt to answer how we know and how we know that we know, and the latter query segues into theories of epistemic justification; such theories consider or evaluate the epistemic merit or status of a belief. Internalism holds that the method for arriving at a "justified true belief" is, in a relevant sense, internal to the subject. According to some versions of internalism, what gives positive epistemic status to a belief – the notion that the belief is warranted or justified – is the mechanism of introspection; through introspection, the knower has some sort of privileged access to a standard or state that, in turn, confers justification. Although he does not use the term "internalism" here, John Hick's words aptly capture key instincts of this theory:

There can therefore be no question of a criterion of knowledge external to the act of knowing; knowing is a self-contained process. The claim to know requires no endorsement from outside; knowledge shines in its own light with sufficient and self-certifying authority. (Hick 1966: 202)

Externalism is sometimes defined in opposition to internalism; it holds that at least some of the mechanisms that confer justification are not limited to internal states or inward processes of the subject. Some may be external to the believer's cognitive perspective. An important version of externalism is reliabilism; in this case, the subject is engaged with (external) belief-forming processes that should be evaluated in terms of their reliability in producing true beliefs; justification of the belief is largely the result of an "appropriate causal ancestry" of the belief and its relationship to reliable belief-forming mechanisms (Swain 1988: 461). The main requirement for justification in this version of externalism is roughly "that the belief be produced in a way or via a process that makes it objectively likely that the belief is true" (BonJour 1992: 133). Plantinga (1993a) adds a crucial component to justification (he prefers the term warrant), namely, proper function. Humans are equipped with a "design plan" – by God or evolution or both – with cognitive faculties to be utilized in an appropriate cognitive environment properly suited to them. When the faculties function properly, and in an appropriate cognitive environment, the outputs of such processes enjoy warrant. Examples of such mechanisms are perception, testimony, and memory. William Alston (1991) has added his own nuances to externalism by arguing that direct experiential awareness of God – what he calls mystical perception – enjoys prima facie justification much in the same way we take it for granted in sensory perception. Just as sensory perceptual beliefs, produced by established doxastic practices and free of negating "overriders" – information or evidence that defeats the belief – are granted prima facie justification, so mystical perceptual beliefs, produced by socially established practices and free of overriders, are granted prima facie justification. While I prefer to speak of religious experience – not the fraught term "mysticism" – it is precisely the epistemic merit of the beliefs emerging from such experience that shapes the reflections of the latter part of this chapter. There, I will explore the epistemic status of religious testimony in two modes: the witness of a tradition's scriptures and the witness of religious *virtuosi* in the world's religious traditions.

11.3 Religious Epistemology, Metaphysics and Soteriology in Shankara

When we come to the Advaita of Shankara, we run into some challenges concerning "knowledge" owing to its foundational metaphysic: nondualism.[1] Epistemology naturally involves reasoning on the cognizer (*pramatr*), the cognition (*prama*), and the object of cognition (*prameya*). To keep true to its ultimate premise and goal while also recognizing the real-world importance of proper cognitive functioning in an appropriate cognitive environment, Advaita introduces the epistemological framework of the two standpoints (*avastha*). Hence, Advaita creates intellectual space for conventional philosophical and ethical discourse, the "relative standpoint" (*vyavaharika avastha*), while nonetheless always "pointing to," as it were, the Ultimate. From the relative standpoint, nondualism notwithstanding, Advaita is decidedly realistic and pluralistic, admitting any number of metaphysical, epistemological, and ethical distinctions – subject, object, categories, whole-part relations, the means of producing knowledge, merit, demerit, dharma (duty, law), etc. This relative standpoint is critical, for it allows Advaita to enter the philosophical playing field to engage and debate rival schools. Without the *vyavaharika*, Advaita is reduced to silence, since the Ultimate is beyond words and distinctions; it's no wonder that the premier spiritual archetype in some Hindu traditions is the *muni*, the silent sage. That said, with the "relative standpoint" or *vyavaharika*, Advaita Vedanta can – as has been amply demonstrated over centuries – debate, attempt to persuade or evoke a commitment to nondual truth. Admittedly, the standpoint of the absolute (*paramarthika avastha*) is a kind of trump card, for at this level, no discourse is possible, "and philosophy, which begins with *pramana-prameya vyavahara* comes to an end in respect of the *paramarthika*" (Balasubramanian

---

[1] The discussion of Shankara's thought and its philosophical contexts draws from Forsthoefel (2002).

1990: 22). The *paramarthika avastha*, the ultimate standpoint, is, by definition, transpersonal, transphenomenal, and absolute, thus apparently having
nothing to do with pedestrian reality. Indeed, for Shankara, Brahman – the
"imperishable Real" (*aksharam satyam*) – is entirely beyond the scope of
perception. Thus, perception, appropriate as a conventional *pramana*, appears
to offer no purchase on saving knowledge.

The knowledge that saves or *is salvation*, according to Shankara, is not
constricted by time or space; it is transcendent. Therefore, perception, whose
function and scope are limited to mundane reality, cannot by itself reveal the
Unconditioned or Ultimate Real, and another device is needed. For Shankara,
the mechanism *par excellence* for realizing saving knowledge is revelation
or sacred *testimony*, scripture (*shruti*), i.e., the Vedas, and above all the
Upanishads. And while the Vedas may be traditionally understood as eternal
and primordial sound forms "heard" by ancient seers, we might also consider
them as socially established doxastic mechanisms, following Alston; scripture,
therefore, is central to the externalist elements in Shankara's religious epistemology. This mechanism is supported by others – such as the function and role
of the guru and traditional Vedic training – and is complemented or finally
enhanced by an internalist religious epistemology, owing to Advaita's metaphysical premises. If Brahman is the Self of all or if there is, in some relevant
sense, nothing but Brahman, then we are already equipped to realize it. How?
By internally accessing this Ultimate Real, or in the words of the extraordinary
twentieth-century South Indian mystic nondualist Ramana Maharshi, "to dive
within." "One should know one's Self with one's own eye of wisdom," and, for
Ramana, "it is futile to search for it in books" (Maharshi 1995: 14). Instead, by
processes internal to the subject – including discrimination (between Self and
not-self) driven by the question "Who am I?" – one realizes the limitless Self.

This internalist sensibility squares well with the universalism implicit in
Advaita's nondualism; this, in turn, has allowed Advaitin thought to migrate
well, as it were, and to flourish cross-culturally. Based on its metaphysic,
Advaita underscores a supreme nondualism while recognizing empirical,
though ultimately illusory, conventional reality. This means cultural structures
and patterns are ontologically inferior, as is everything under the relative
standpoint; thus, they may be minimized, no matter how important they
may be. The externalist structures of Advaita are indeed significant, but not
absolutely, owing to its nondualism. Indeed, as much as the Vedas are essential, even they must be transcended. In that nondual state, "the Vedas are not
the Vedas" (Brhadaranyaka Upanishad 4.3.22, in Radhakrishnan 1992: 263).
Before addressing these two modalities further, a few additional comments are
in order concerning Shankara's metaphysic and religious epistemology.

That metaphysic is, of course, nondualism, and Shankara's religious epistemology begins with the two standpoints. Although the ultimate standpoint
decisively reveals the nondual Real (Brahman [the Supreme] or Atman [the

true Self]), getting there, as it were, involves a division by dichotomy: Self and not-self, whose fundamental differences, says Shankara, are as opposed as the light and the dark. In short, any object of empirical perception is not-the-Self or not-self (*anatman*). Anything known *by* the Self thus cannot *be* the Self. This means that the Self itself *cannot be known*, for what is known is an object of knowledge. This may be confusing since one often encounters in Advaitin teaching the supreme importance of "Self-knowledge." Nevertheless, Shankara insists that the Self is the supreme subject, not an object. Therefore, the Self cannot "know" itself because such would imply parts, thereby undermining nondual truth. Instead, the Self is pure, unalloyed knowledge. Thus, "Self-knowledge," the presumed goal of Advaita, cannot be taken literally – or, perhaps better, conventionally – but should be understood as a term of courtesy, driven more by soteriological concerns than conventional epistemology. Indeed, owing to the ultimate standpoint (*paramarthika avastha*) of nonduality, it seems we lose hold of the term "knowledge" in any usual way of construing it. Some thinkers prefer to use words such as "awareness" or "consciousness," and these can be helpful in noting any relevant difference between the terms "knowledge" and "consciousness." For some thinkers, however, even the term consciousness is not particularly helpful. A. B. Keith, for example, suggested that the ultimate state, owing to its radical absence of subject and object, "differs so entirely from the very nature of consciousness as not in our view to deserve the name at all" (Keith 1989: 507).

But this seems extreme to me. While from the standpoint of the Supreme, all distinctions for the Advaitin dissolve and the true Self shines in all its effulgent glory, there must be some degree of continuity between what we normally call consciousness and what is held to be this nondual supreme consciousness. While conventional cognitive protocols may well indeed be negated or canceled by realization, there must be some sort of base or residuum on the relative plane of experience that provides a window to the Supreme. Otherwise, an unbridgeable gap obtains between the phenomenal and the real, rendering impossible its connection to lived experience and, by extension, its "connection" to saving experience.

Shankara is typically understood as – and sometimes criticized for –operating from a cognitive distinction that creates that epistemic chasm. Closely related to the two standpoints, and following the Mundaka Upanishad, he appeals to two kinds of knowledge, higher and lower (*para, apara vidya*), the former being knowledge of the supreme Brahman, the Unconditioned, Ultimate Real, and the latter everything else. Eliot Deutsch holds that these two must be incommensurable, for higher knowledge (*para vidya*) is entirely *sui generis* (Deutsch 1969: 82). Yet, the fact of being incommensurable has the undesirable consequence, in my view, of having absolutely no relevance to lived experience whatsoever. It is hard to imagine even broaching the subject if it is utterly incommensurable with any ordinary conscious processes. And, in fact, closer analysis of Shankara's metaphysics of experience allows for important subtleties that make room for a measure of continuity between the relative and the ultimate standpoints.

One of the most revealing passages concerning Shankara's consideration of experience is his discussion of the second sutra in the Brahma Sutra, the core text of Advaita ascribed to Badarayana (c. fourth century CE). That sutra establishes Brahman as the source and of the origin and dissolution of the world, and Shankara's gloss on it is illuminating. In his discussion, he surveys the various means for gaining knowledge of the supreme, affirming, above all, reflective appropriation of the import of sacred texts (*shruti*), particularly the Upanishads. Thus, Shankara clearly privileges sacred *testimony*, that is, scripture (*shruti*), in his religious epistemology; we therefore see a potent externalist feature to it. I will say more about the epistemic value of sacred testimony in the next section. Here, we see that Shankara, while privileging scripture as the most critical apparatus in his religious epistemology *and* soteriology, nonetheless still accords significant value for inference and other reasoning practices as ancillary helps in the process of realization: the correct interpretation of scripture requires argumentation, and human understanding assists scripture (Gambhirananda 1993: 15). But Shankara adds something else that allows us to explore the soteriological potential in everyday experience. He first notes that *sruti* and various supportive hermeneutical strategies are the only mechanisms that produce valid knowledge of *dharma* (eternal law, sacred duty), another transcendent category that was the particular focus of the Mimamsaka school. The same narrow set of tools applies to knowledge of Brahman, but Shankara includes personal experience (*anubhava*) as well (Gambhirananda 1993: 16). There is no doubt that Shankara affirms the singular importance of sacred testimony (*shruti*; i.e., Upanishads) in the path of salvation; however, he does appear to grant a measured probative status to experience in that path. But, as Karl Potter shrewdly notes, while experience may constitute a "proof," it is one that may never be used. He explains, "When one has Self-knowledge one no longer has doubts or needs proof, and when one needs proof, one is not in a position to have Self-knowledge, since one is under the sway of ignorance" (Potter 1981: 98).

Still, as Wilhelm Halbfass helpfully explains, Shankara uses the term *anubhava* in accordance with his own hierarchy of conventional and absolute truth: "there is wrong and right, provisional and absolute experience (Halbfass 1990: 390)." But, he explains, there is a common denominator.

Even false *anubhava*, which implies the superimposition and false identification of the self, is still *anubhava*, containing the element of immediate presence, in which being and knowing, subject and object coincide. Insofar as any act of perception or awareness can remind us of, and help us to approach, that absolute and ultimate experience which according to the Upanishads, coincides with the being of *Brahman* itself (Halbfass 1990).

This suggests that mundane experience itself can be a window to the Supreme, a kind of "soft" *pramana*. Let me clarify. Shankara never engages in a systematic analysis of the *pramana*s, and so to conflate "experience" with full "pramanic" status would indeed be misguided. Not only are there limited intimations of the knowledge-producing power of experience (*anubhava*) in Shankara's writings – there are also limited concessions to the value and significance of the traditional *pramana*s since they fall under the domain of the relative standpoint (*vyavaharika avastha*). The standard expectation of a *pramana* was that it operated only within its particular and specific boundaries and produced new knowledge (i.e., knowledge not already available through the proper functioning of other *pramana*s). Under this model, *anubhava* would apparently fall under perception (*pratyaksa*) for whatever is perceived is experienced.

But this constricts experience (*anubhava*) to the scope of the relative standpoint, which is not the force of Shankara's appeal to *anubhava* as a kind of *pramana*, "for the knowledge of Brahman culminates in experience" (Gambhirananda 1993: 16). This cannot mean mundane experience here, and, indeed, he emphasizes elsewhere that "immediate experience . . . is the Supreme Self" (Alston 1990: 116). *Pramana*s, by definition, involve duality, which is the opposing position rejected by Shankara's metaphysic, *a-dvaita* (nondualism). So, *anubhava* here must be read as a *pramana* in a soft or weak sense as a "*valid means of knowledge*" rather than "*a means of valid knowledge*." Still, a soft sense of the probative value of experience suggests that *anubhava* is an appropriate mechanism for producing *jnana*, knowledge, a broad term that can range from cognition or mental episode to varying degrees of truth or certainty. *Prama*, a more precise and limited term, is, by definition, valid knowledge. Shankara clearly says that *anubhava* generates knowledge (*jnana*), a broader term than *prama*; "knowledge," in this case, transcends the limitations of subject–object dichotomies. This state or plane is a "knowing beyond knowledge," a cognitive state – one is not insensible or catatonic – freed of parts, distinctions, or pluralities. In such "religious experience" (a fraught locution since it typically implies subject–object dualism, precisely what Advaita rejects), we arrive at a particular cognitive event, but one that doesn't imply duality, as does *prama*. In this sense, *anubhava*/experience, is an independent means of knowledge, drawing from but extending beyond the scope of mundane perception. By shifting the qualifier in the terms "valid knowledge" (*prama*) to valid means of knowledge (*pramana*), we avoid the duality in the former expression and gain the advantage of affirming Shankara's value of experience (*anubhava*) as an instrument of saving knowledge.

To sum up, Shankara keenly weaves the three central strands of Indian philosophy into an integrated unit, a single philosophical rope, as it were. The metaphysic is classic Indian nondualism, the knowledge of which is liberation. That knowledge, while clearly something rather different from quotidian knowledge, nevertheless relies on a host of socially established doxastic processes – traditional learning, standard reasoning practices, the training that obtains in the guru–disciple relationship, and culturally embedded scriptures and their exposition and commentary. These externalist structures serve as the mechanisms that ultimately reveal a transcendent, saving knowledge. The soteriological process only removes congenital ignorance and reveals what already is there, the nondual Supreme, Brahman. The externalist structures are complemented by an internalist process, a reflective inwardness or introversion. Indeed, the traditional training suggests both soteriological epistemologies: *shravana, manana, nididhyasana* – "hearing" (*shravana*), that is, the words of a teacher, reflecting upon them critically (*manana*), and contemplation (*nididhyasana*), internalizing the teaching into an integrated awareness, an experiential knowing whose epistemic substance, value, and merit is directly proportional to the experience itself. That experiential knowledge carries substantive epistemic weight. It becomes another kind religious testimony in addition to scripture, both of whose epistemic merits are worthy of exploration, a subject to which I shall now turn.

11.4 Epistemic Value of Sacred Testimony in Two Modes

As noted earlier, Shankara decisively privileges sacred *testimony* in his religious epistemology, above all the Upanishads and their proper exposition. Here, I wish to engage a broader consideration of the epistemic potential and value of sacred testimony. *Verbal* testimony (*shabda*), of course, was one of the classic knowledge-producing mechanisms (*pramanas*) in Indian – and Western – thought; this makes good sense, since probably most of what we count on as reliable knowledge comes from persons equipped with substantive training in particular fields or from firsthand eyewitnesses to or experiencers of events. While testimony, as inference, can be wrong – as misdiagnoses by doctors and car mechanics can sadly illustrate – it nevertheless holds high epistemic merit, at least minimally by way of prima facie justification. Indeed, another Sanskrit term for testimony is *apta vakya*, the word (*vakya*) of an expert or reliable (*apta*) person. In this case, the word of one exquisitely skilled or one with direct, immediate experience of a phenomenon enjoys high epistemic value. For example, I am not trained in hematology, but when routine blood tests reveal elevated cholesterol counts and my doctor advises me to take Lipitor to reduce the risk of a cardiac event, that counsel, given my doctor's training and clinical experience, carries much epistemic weight. Similarly, I have never walked on the moon, nor have I borne children, but I trust the testimony of astronauts and mothers as exquisitely informative of such experiences. In the end, much – perhaps most – of our bank of knowledge comes from testimony or the report of experts; even if such testimony carries "mere" prima facie justification, it carries weight.

Therefore, it makes good epistemic sense to take seriously and consider carefully sacred or religious *testimony* in two modes, the first being a historical textual (literary or oral) witness – that is, a tradition's sacred scriptures – which emerge and unfold over time in a profound historical and social context of faith and practice, interpretation and commentary, and analysis and debate. All of this creates a cohesive and coherent system – with concomitant socially established belief-producing practices – whose enduring witness becomes compelling and merits at least prima facie justification of the claims emerging from that system and sets of practices. The claims, passing the test of time, and undergoing repeated intellectual and moral scrutinies, carry epistemic merit. But they can be overridden; for example, Jain scriptures hold that the earth is flat. While that claim is defeated by physics, satellites, and rocket ships, it doesn't mean that all the claims of Jainism are therefore overridden, and, as many Christians have come to accept after decades of Biblical scholarship, scriptures are not, after all, scientific textbooks. They concern metaphysical truths – understandings of reality in its most complex context – not the physical truths delivered by the scientific method.

Recognizing the potential epistemic merit of religious claims, however warily and tentatively, shows respect for what the tradition purports to be doing with those claims, namely, communicating a cohesive understanding – knowledge – about reality. Doing so avoids an arrogance that summarily dismisses any cognitive dimension to religious claims.

But not any claim will do. The enduring testimony of the Jewish tradition, for example, seems to me to be a virtual argument for the existence of God. How? By its astonishing, long, rich, and storied history, its equally long record of spiritual, intellectual, and moral excellence, its rather small numbers that nevertheless have endured generation after generation, and its undaunted ability to overcome catastrophic trauma. Such a context provides greater epistemic weight to its doxastic claims, more so than, say, those of emerging from the Church of the Flying Spaghetti Monster or even the Church of Scientology. This intends no disrespect to the latter Churches, since other important values are clearly operative in them as well, including meeting needs for meaning, purpose, and community and, in the case of the first, satirizing traditional religion and religious claims. Instead, making this distinction simply recognizes that the historical arc of a tradition – replete with a long and complex formation of sacred texts – literary or oral – and the social processes which render them authoritative, as well as with communities of practice and interpretation and much more – lends greater epistemic value to that tradition's doxastic claims. On the other hand, the epistemic merit in the religious claims emerging from Scientology's mythos – which features an overlord, Xenu, a Galactic Confederacy that he ruled, and nuclear bombs dropped in volcanos on earth in which the surplus population of the Confederacy were trapped (Urban 2015: 143) – appears to be weak. First,

Scientology's origin myths had originally been housed as esoterica reserved for an elite endowed with the financial means to access them. The absence of transparency, at least originally, was part of a strategy to generate income. Indeed, the myths – as well as the creation of Scientology itself – appear not only to have emerged from its founder L. Ron Hubbard's boundless imagination as a science fiction writer; doing so, in part, was fueled by an underlying financial motivation. Hubbard is reported to have said on repeated occasions, "I'd like to start a religion. That's where the money is" (Wright 2013: 100).

This is not the place to discuss what constitutes religion and whether Scientology fits those criteria; here, we are considering the epistemic status of religious testimonies. Context is everything, even as prosecuting attorneys understand when evaluating the testimony of witnesses in criminal cases. The testimony of those motivated by self-interest will not immediately be taken at face value; witnesses lie on occasion to protect themselves. The lack of any checks or balances in the development of Scientology's scripture or the development of critical hermeneutical strategies or traditions of interpretation, along with the financial motivation to establish Scientology as a religion in the first place, undermines or vitiates the epistemic value of its religious testimony. However, it does not mean other legitimate values are necessarily absent in the Church.

Sacred or religious testimony is not limited to authoritative texts of a tradition but includes the witness of religious *virtuosi* in those traditions as well. In this case, such individuals appear to *know* something; they appear to have arrived at a particular kind of knowledge gained by training and experience. In turn, they often communicate, teach, or transmit that knowledge in multiple ways, including, perhaps most importantly, by example. And, just as I trust the expert witness of my doctor and auto mechanic – and act on their insight and counsel – so it seems reasonable and even salutary to consider the epistemic merit of the testimony of saints, sages, prophets, seers, and gurus in our religious traditions – and perhaps act on their counsel as well. The objective content of such testimony may be quite different – Buddhist teachings on emptiness, for example, are rather different from the passionate devotionalism seen in some theistic traditions. In that case, it becomes a creative project of thinkers to scrutinize contrasting testimonies for their reasonableness, coherence, significant differences, relevant similarities, and finally, their epistemic merit. While such projects are complicated and fraught with challenges, there may be something even more basic at play: a discovery of a common ground that reveals a certain kinship on the diverse paths to the divine. Extraordinary religious exemplars appear to bear witness, along with the scriptures of their traditions, to some sort of transcendent state, an ultimate state or plane that decisively surpasses limited, conventional reality. What that ultimate state *is* will be up for debate, discussion, and analysis and constitutes the work of philosophers of religion. Still, that great saints and their religious traditions offer testimony or bear witness to an Ultimate – however it is construed – suggests that a cumulative, cross-cultural testimony to it may at least enjoy prima facie justification.

I wish to add that while cross-cultural religious testimonies – personal and scriptural – are culturally inflected, they also appear to be typically joined to ethics. This ethical dimension enhances the epistemic potential of religious claims. To offer an extended argument for assigning ethical criteria in evaluating the epistemic merit of religious claims goes beyond the scope of this chapter, but I will at least offer a few initial, relevant observations. Again, I am underscoring a critical, moral criterion as part of evaluating the epistemic merit of the testimony of religious *virtuosi*. Doing so may be controverted; some thinkers may argue that the Transcendent is wholly beyond pedestrian categories of good and evil, or that moral flaws fall on the relative plane of reality and are therefore somewhat beside the point. Indeed, one heterodox school in ancient India precisely held such a position – the soul was untouched by any moral imprint, evil or good, a position roundly condemned by the Buddha on philosophical and ethical grounds. Antinomianism has a fascinating, episodic occurrence in the history of religions, emerging with enough regularity to be viewed, perhaps, as a nihilistic alter ego to the so-called perennial philosophy.

Nevertheless, ethics provides an important evaluative element to epistemic claims of religion. This amounts to a "you will know them by their fruits" position, one that has considerable practical and theoretical value. In the face of egregious or hypocritical offenses, the epistemic merit of any claims from such a subject become attenuated. Ethical behavior is thus an important criterion that lends weight to the claims of religious *virtuosi*. The lived example of teachers becomes probative, at least partly so, and thus religions typically emphasize high ethical standards for teachers. Indeed, the Buddha was held to be the very embodiment of wisdom and compassion, collectively understood as "Dhamma": "whoever sees Dhamma, sees me; whoever sees me, sees Dhamma" (Harvey 1996: 28). The Buddha is one who has Dhamma as his body (*Dhamma-kaya*), one who has *become* Dhamma (*Dhamma-bhuta*) (Harvey 1996). And Shankara, writing in the prose section of the *Upadeshasahasri*, unambiguously establishes a pedagogy in which the ethics of the teacher are paramount:

And the teacher is able to consider the pros and cons [of an argument], is endowed with understanding, memory, tranquility, self-control, compassion, favor, and the like; he is versed in the traditional doctrine; not attached to any enjoyments, visible or invisible, he has abandoned all the rituals and their requisites; a knower of Brahman, he is established in Brahman; he leads a blameless life, free from faults such as deceit, pride, trickery, wickedness, fraud, jealousy, falsehood, egotism, self-interest, and so forth; with the only purpose of helping others he wishes to make use of knowledge. (Mayeda 1992: 212)

The teacher's moral excellence thus becomes a key criterion for authentic teaching, and, consequently, the teacher's words carry weight; they enjoy epistemic merit. To take another example from India, one of the four cardinal offenses in early Buddhist monasticism – violations of conduct that are grounds for expulsion from the monastery – is lying about one's spiritual attainments. The reason for this is clear: doing so not only reveals an attachment to ego (betraying the core Buddhist truth of selflessness), but any associated or subsequent teaching therefore lacks value and credibility; the consequence of such ethical violation is the spiritual jeopardy of disciples. We can easily understand why. Just as the epistemic merit or prima facie justification of a doctor's testimony or counsel may be immediately vitiated if one discovers lies about his/her/their training or experience, so the epistemic merit of the testimony of religious leaders can reasonably and properly be called into question in the face of egregious ethical lapses; these include not just lying about one's spiritual training or experience, but other offenses, such as sexual violation and theft (two additional "defeaters"' of monastic life in Buddhism, incidentally).

These ethical lapses I consider to be "overriders," the term Alston uses to suggest information or evidence that vitiates or defeats an original epistemic claim. The claim "the stick in the pond is bent"' – granted prima facie justification in virtue of perception – is overridden or defeated upon closer inspection. Prima facie justification of socially established doxastic claims, produced in a coherent, cohesive, and, I would add, ethical system, is undeniably eroded, and with good reason, by egregious moral flaws (i.e., moral failings that far surpass the imperfections to which all humans are subject). This partly explains why many Roman Catholics have abandoned the institutional Church upon the revelations of systematic and universal sexual abuse *and its coverup* by the hierarchy. And the proper response to those who left the Church is empathy. But the Church itself has otherwise keenly understood the social and epistemic problems of scandal because scandal undermines the faith and cohesion of the community. To put it another way, scandal severely erodes the epistemic merit of socially produced doxastic claims. They lose credibility; they generate doubt; they carry less weight.

The Catholic Church, however, has a many-centuries-long record of demonstrating a host of extraordinary virtues – generosity, holiness, self-sacrifice, service, intellectual vigor, and much more, which contextualizes (but does not excuse) its historical incongruities and moral failures; in other words, while the epistemic merit of doxastic claims may be threatened or weakened, it might not be absolutely defeated. This may not be the case for certain newer religious communities, such as Scientology. Critical values may be genuinely operative in newer religions – community and connection, a shared vision and ethos, the powerful need for meaning, etc. – but the epistemic merit of certain doxastic claims may be minimal or absent in certain contexts.

Scholars of religion typically bracket biases and judgments – properly so – in order to better understand religions and religious phenomena. However, the philosopher of religion can – and should – evaluate the epistemic merit of claims produced in any particular social and ethical system. My brief argument here is that ethical excellence – virtue – gives epistemic weight to the testimony of religious experts and leaders, the holy ones of our traditions. Their witness – in different religious contexts and cultures – becomes compelling and commands attention; it signals, along with the sacred testimony found in the scriptures of their traditions, something of supreme or ultimate value. Such testimony carries epistemic weight; it thus behooves us to consider it carefully.

11.5 Conclusion: In Praise of Prima Facie

This chapter has accomplished multiple objectives. First, with its focus on Shankara's thought, it illustrates the triple weave of metaphysics, epistemology, and soteriology that is characteristic of Indian religions and perhaps all religious traditions. This makes sense, since, if the teachings of a tradition bear witness to an ultimate reality, then reasoned discourse naturally engages discussion of the proper understanding of that reality and the mechanisms to realize it. Thus, metaphysics, epistemology, and soteriology become a single intellectual rope, as it were, constituted by distinct but connected strands of reflection.

The soteriological goal in Shankara is, of course, liberation (*moksha*), the realization of the nondual Ultimate, Brahman. That soteriological goal instantly implicates – and requires discussion of – metaphysics and religious epistemology. That metaphysic is nondualism. However, the ultimate nondual Real is not *empirically* evident, so this requires discussion of how we come to discover, realize, or in some sense *know* it, and this involves religious epistemology. For Shankara, that epistemology draws heavily from externalist structures – sets of socially established belief-producing mechanisms – that are properly functioning, as well as their traditions of reflection, debate, and practice. The most important externalist structure is sacred testimony, *shruti* – and its subsequent traditions of interpretation, commentary, and debate.

There is a powerful companion to the externalist dimension in Shankara's religious epistemology. That is the internalist dynamic of "diving within" to access that which we are already. The external structures of Vedas and other supports are helpful, even crucial, but they are not absolute given the premises of the Advaitin metaphysic. Internally accessing this ultimate state balances – and arguably outweighs – the externalist structures in traditional Advaita, a point of view evident in the teaching of Ramana Maharshi, as well as Western nondualists such as Master Nome, a contemporary interpreter and exponent of Ramana's teachings.

Recognizing the importance of sacred testimony in Shankara's thought leads to broader meditation on its epistemic value cross-culturally. Just as we grant epistemic merit to the claims of professional experts – and withdraw it in the face of overriding or undermining evidence – so also, in my view, the testimony of saints and scriptures, borne of systems and processes with sets of self-critiques, self-checks, and ethical contexts, also merits prima facie justification. While arriving at such a standing may seem minimalist, we do well to remember that the history of science demonstrates that hosts of accepted assumptions and conclusions are sometimes overridden by new information and investigation. This is the natural process of refining what we know in the empirical world, and the laboratory and field are the sites to engage and cultivate that process. The cumulative and enduring testimony of the world's religions over millennia bear witness, in multiple and diverse contexts, to an Ultimate, however construed. Rather than immediately dismiss the epistemic merit of claims about that reality – or, worse, reducing them to psychological or social processes – those claims, emerging in a great spiritual laboratory and operating under the critical contexts and conditions addressed earlier, also merit prima facie justification. What does that get us? Insofar as such religions testify to an Ultimate – that is, to something unsurpassably real and valuable – it therefore behooves us to take seriously and consider the claims of those traditions. We may learn something deeply constructive about the nature of things and the nature of humanity, both of which outcomes having the potential to transform our insights, actions, and relationships. If there is an Ultimate, it is worthy of knowing. Investigating the testimony of saints and scriptures begins that quest.

12 Buddhist Religious Epistemology

Victoria S. Harrison and John Zhao

Introduction

Buddhism contains a rich variety of epistemological perspectives. This chapter surveys three of these perspectives: that of early Buddhism, that of the Pramāṇavāda school, and that of the Madhyamaka school.[1] These epistemologies have been selected because they are representative of the variety and sophistication of Buddhist epistemological traditions. Early Buddhist epistemology is often regarded as a form of empiricism because of its focus and reliance on personal sensory and supersensory knowledge. The more systematic Pramāṇavāda school regards particulars (*svalakṣaṇa*) and universals (*sāmānyalakṣaṇa*) as the only two objects of knowledge, corresponding with perception (*pratyakṣa*) and inference (*anumāna*) as their respective means of being known (*pramāṇa*).[2] The distinctiveness of the Madhyamaka school is its critical examination of the interdependence of objects of knowledge and their means of being known, and its focus on two truths (conventional and ultimate truth, *saṃvṛti-satya* and *paramārtha-satya*) as two modes in which things can be known, which are jointly necessary for full understanding. Although the epistemologies of these three Buddhist schools have different emphases, and there has been vigorous debate between their proponents, they share the aim of assisting human beings in their journey toward spiritual liberation.

The quest for knowledge has played a central role in Indian religion and philosophy from the earliest times. Early Buddhist epistemology developed in conversation with the ancient cosmological speculations found in the Brahmanical Vedic tradition, which were concerned with knowledge of the spiritual forces that were thought to lie behind mundane appearances. By "early Buddhism" we mean the teachings of the historical Buddha (who is thought to have lived from 485 to 405 BCE) and his close disciples as these are recorded in Buddhism's core text, the Pāli canon (Pāli Nikāyas). Early Buddhism, in keeping with the Brahmanical Vedic tradition, teaches that knowledge is philosophically and spiritually important. Nonetheless, knowledge in early Buddhism is not

---

[1] The term "school" is a translation of the Sanskrit word *darśana,* which means philosophical perspective.

[2] Buddhist thought has been expressed in many languages. In this chapter, we give technical terms in Sanskrit unless the context demands Pāli, Tibetan, or Chinese.

Table 12.1 *Objects of knowledge*

Traditions	Early Buddhism	Pramāṇavāda School	Madhyamaka School
Objects of Knowledge	Whatever is known through the senses	Particulars	Conventional truths
	Whatever is known through the supersensory faculties	Universals	Ultimate Truth

conceived of as a salvific insight into a transcendent, metaphysical reality. Instead, the content of soteriologically relevant knowledge is held to be the origin and cessation of human suffering (*dukkha*), for it is this that is held by Buddhists to lead to spiritual liberation. Spiritual liberation is thought to require knowledge of the causal factors that shape human experience, and understanding of what eventually coalesced into Buddhism's two core philosophical commitments: that all things are impermanent and that all phenomena are interdependent (see Harrison 2022). Early Buddhist texts provide a detailed account of the way human beings perceive and grasp the sensory world. This account underlies all later philosophical developments within Buddhism. Although the epistemological reflections of early Buddhism are nascent, the later, more systematic and sophisticated epistemic theories developed by the Pramāṇavāda and Madhyamaka schools were largely based on the insights of early Buddhism.

To engage Buddhism with contemporary epistemological debates, modern philosophers of religion often characterize early Buddhism as a form of empiricism, the Pramāṇavāda school as foundationalist, and the Madhyamaka school as coherentist. We will employ this characterization here, while noting that caution is needed when applying modern philosophical labels to ancient schools of thought (see Holder 2013: 224). This chapter will review the most important claims and arguments made by the three Buddhist schools, suggesting that their key differences can largely be explained by attending to how they characterize the object of knowledge (see Table 12.1).

12.1 The Empiricism of Early Buddhism

As we stated earlier, the Buddha is often regarded as an empiricist because his religious philosophy was grounded on experience (see Jayatilleke 1963; Kalupahana 1992; Harvey 2009; and Holder 2013). John Holder explains that

experience figures prominently in the Buddha's teaching in at least three ways: first, he taught that experience is the proper way to justify claims to knowledge – this is the heart of modern empiricism; second, the experience of suffering is the motivation for seeking a religious path in life; and, third, he provided a highly sophisticated psychological account of experience as a way of explaining how suffering arises, and how one might gain control over the causes of suffering so as to bring about the cessation of suffering. (Holder 2013: 224)

The Buddha's empiricism is also evident in his handling of metaphysically speculative questions and claims about religious authority (see for example, MN.II.63, Ñāṇamoli and Bodhi 1995: 533–5).[3] Whereas most Indian religious traditions are largely based on metaphysically speculative beliefs, the Buddha taught his followers that one should believe only those doctrines that can be verified through personal experience. This is underlined in the story of the Buddha's meeting with a group known as the Kālāmas, who approached the Buddha for help because they were confused by greatly differing claims professed by the various religious teachers who were active during the Buddha's lifetime. The Kālāmas asked, "How does one know which is the right view? What criteria can one use to determine who is telling the truth? Whom should one believe?" The Buddha instructed the Kālāmas:

It is fitting for you to be perplexed, Kālāmas, fitting for you to be in doubt. Doubt has arisen in you about a perplexing matter. Come, Kālāmas, do not go by oral tradition, by lineage of teaching, by hearsay, by a collection of scriptures, by logical reasoning, by inferential reasoning, by reasoned cogitation, by the acceptance of a view after pondering it, by the seeming competence [of a speaker], or because you think: 'The ascetic is our guru.' But when, Kālāmas, you know for yourselves: 'These things are unwholesome; these things are blameworthy; these things are censured by the wise; these things, if accepted and undertaken, lead to harm and suffering,' then you should abandon them. (AN.I.189, Bodhi 2012: 280)[4]

The Buddha highlights that there should be proper reasons for accepting any religious or philosophical doctrine and that what counts as a proper reason must be grounded in one's own personal experience. The Buddha disagreed with traditions that require unquestioning faith in scriptures or spiritual leaders. He was critical of dogmatism of any sort: it is not proper for an intelligent person, safeguarding the truth, to come categorically to the conclusion in a given matter that such alone is true and whatever else is false (MN.II.170–1, Ñāṇamoli and Bodhi 1995: 779). According to the Buddha, the intelligent person remains open to new facts and never considers any belief as final and unrevisable.

Because of the close connection he saw between knowledge and experience, and in the service of the goal of spiritual liberation, the Buddha offered a detailed analysis of human experience. This analysis provided a framework for thinking about the processes that lead to suffering and a pathway to the

---

[3] MN stands for *Majjhima Nikāya* (*The Middle Length Discourses of the Buddha*).
[4] AN stands for *Aṅguttara Nikāya* (*The Numerical Discourses of the Buddha*).

transformation of experience so that suffering no longer arises. Being grounded in spiritual practice, the Buddha's empiricist epistemology focuses not only on the justification of knowledge claims but on the psychological processes that comprise human experience.

The Buddha's view of experience is intimately connected to his distinctive understanding of the human person. In his account, a human being is composed of five changing factors or processes (*khandhas*): the body (*rūpa*), feeling (*vedanā*), interpretive perception (*saññā*), mental formation (*saṅkhārā*), and consciousness (*viññāna*) (see Harrison 2019: 105–13). None of these factors is static or permanent. A person, then, is a complex arrangement of mental and physical processes. It should be noted, however, that the Buddha was not a mind–body dualist, for he did not claim that the mind and the body were metaphysically distinct parts of the person. The Buddha spoke of the human person as an integrated, psycho-physical complex (*nāmarūpa*) and he never discussed the psychological or the physical aspects of a person in isolation (Gowans 2003: 63–116).

Given his account of human persons, the Buddha had to explain how experience and consciousness arose without reference to a permanent self. In the "Discourse of the Honeyball," the arising of visual consciousness and experience is explained as the result of a naturally emergent process:[5]

Dependent on the eye and forms, eye-consciousness arises. The meeting of the three is contact. With contact as condition there is feeling. What one feels, that one perceives. What one perceives, that one thinks about. What one thinks about, that one mentally proliferates. With what one has mentally proliferated as the source, perceptions and notions [born of] mental proliferation beset a man with respect to past, future, and present forms cognizable through the eye. (MN.I.111–12, Ñāṇamoli and Bodhi 1995: 203)

The Buddha took the same pattern to hold for the other five modes of consciousness (auditory consciousness, olfactory consciousness, tactile consciousness, gustatory consciousness, and mental consciousness). He taught that each mode of consciousness arises from the interactions of a sensory organ and sensory objects. Conscious experience, then, in his view, is an integrated process that can be analyzed by scrutinizing the coordination of sensory organs and sensory objects.

Although the Buddha claimed that all knowledge is based on sense experience, he did not hold such experience to yield infallible knowledge. The Buddha realized that the data given by the senses can lead to errors of judgment. He did not take this to be due to a defect in perception, per se, but to the way that a corrupted mind processes the data given by the senses.

---

[5] Consciousness was held to exist in six modes, which corresponded to the six sensory modalities recognized within Indian philosophical traditions.

The Buddha recognized that affective dimensions of experience such as likes and dislikes, attachments, aversions, confusion, and fears can prevent one from perceiving things as they are. The fact that all experience is mediated by affective factors in the human mind makes it extremely unlikely that human experience could provide us with a completely objective and unbiased view of reality. The Buddha taught that it is precisely because of the way the mind distorts experience in unwholesome ways that we need radically to transform our minds through meditation and the development of insight (see Holder 2013 for an extended discussion).

According to early Buddhist texts, one who meditates can extend the range of the normal six sensory modalities (in addition to hearing, olfaction, sight, touch, and taste, mind is regarded as a sensory modality). Along with the six sensory modes, the Buddha recognized six supersensory modes of perception (*abhiññā*):[6] psychokinesis, clairaudience, telepathy, retrocognition, clairvoyance, and the knowledge that leads to the destruction of the defilements. He did not hold these supersensory powers to be supernatural powers, for he took them to be available to anyone who becomes adept at meditation.

The supersensory modes of attaining knowledge were used by the Buddha to probe deeper into the causes of human suffering. In particular, he claimed to have used them to develop direct knowledge about the universality of dependent arising, impermanence, and the lack of a permanent essence in all things. The Buddha also held that knowledge acquired through supersensory modes leads to the purification of the defilements (*āsavas*). The defilements are the psychological factors of greed, aversion, and delusion that pervade the unenlightened mind, like sin damaging the "Sensus Divinitatis" in Plantingian terms (Plantinga 2000b: 113). The Buddha taught that these defilements distort our perceptions in unwholesome ways that lead ultimately to suffering and that eliminating them thus has a positive, purifying effect on the mind, allowing it to become supple, flexible, steady, and undisturbed (DN.I.76, Walshe 1995: 1034; see Holder 2013).[7]

In early Buddhist thought, knowledge derived from the supersenses does not contradict knowledge derived from the normal senses but rather builds on it. When one sees things as they truly are, as processes and not as permanent entities, one realizes the futility of attachment to personal possessions, sensual pleasures, and the fiction of a permanent self. This is how knowledge leads to spiritual liberation, *nibbāna*. The elimination of the unwholesome affective factors of greed and hatred gives rise to compassion, while eliminating the unwholesome cognitive factor of delusion gives rise to wisdom. Compassion and wisdom, according to early Buddhist teaching, are the two key components

---

[6] In Buddhist contexts, *abhiññā* is generally translated as "direct knowledge," "higher knowledge," or "supersensory knowledge."

[7] DN stands for *Digha Nikāya* (*The Long Discourse of the Buddha*).

of the *nibbanic* experience (Karunadasa 2017: 120). Given this, one thing is abundantly clear in the early Buddhist texts: *nibbāna* is not knowledge of a transcendent or highest reality but a transformed way of living in this world. Even the highest kind of knowledge in early Buddhism is not an end in itself but a key factor and instrument for spiritual transformation (Holder 2013).

As we have shown, in early Buddhism, sensory and supersensory perception are regarded as two valid means of acquiring knowledge. The Pramāṇavāda school inherited this standpoint but altered it significantly by giving a foundational role to perception.[8] The Pramāṇavāda school also advanced Buddhist epistemological reflection by turning attention to the nature of inference, which it held to be based on perception, as another means of acquiring knowledge. This development is mirrored by the school's characterization of the objects of knowledge as either particulars or universals. We now turn to take a closer look at this school.

12.2 The Foundationalism of the Pramāṇavāda School

Dignāga (c. 480–540 CE) and Dharmakīrti (c. 550–650 CE) were the first to explicitly formulate a complete Buddhist logico-epistemological system.[9] They are regarded as the key figures of what became known as the Pramāṇavāda school. Much of the most sophisticated elaboration of Buddhist epistemological theory is developed in the commentarial literature on their works. Until modern times this school had no official or widely used name in Sanskrit. The convenient Sanskrit term *Pramāṇavāda* is in fact a modern coinage. The root meaning of the term *pramāṇa* derives from *māṇa*, to measure, and it "conveys justification or warrant, and instrumentality as well as that which is delivered by instruments that confer warrant" (Garfield 2015: 215). Indian Buddhist epistemology revolves most centrally around the notion of *pramāṇa* (see Ganeri 2018; and Harrison 2019). The Tibetan expression *tshad ma* and the Chinese *liang xue* (量学) capture the meaning of the term nicely. (For comprehensive modern discussions of this school, see Stcherbatsky 1930, 1932; Matilal 1986; Hayes 1988; Dreyfus 1997; Tillemans 1999, 2021; Bhatt and Mehrotra 2000; Dunne 2004; Yao 2004; Arnold 2005; and Stoltz 2009, 2021.)

Both Dignāga and Dharmakīrti were active at the time when Indian philosophy, propelled by the influence of philosophers associated with the Nyāya school, was turning toward logic and epistemology to defend existing religious doctrines.[10] This new concern motivated thinkers to elaborate systematic

---

[8] The Pramāṇavāda school is also known as "the school of Dignāga," "the Epistemological school," "the Yogācāra-Sautrāntika school," and "the Buddhist Logic school."

[9] Dignāga is commonly regarded as the father of Buddhist epistemology and logic.

[10] The Nyāya school was one of the six philosophical schools in the Vedic tradition. It was known for its emphases on logic and reasoning (see Harrison 2019: 36–50).

theories about the sources and types of knowledge and proper methods of reasoning (see Dreyfus 1997).

According to the Pramāṇavāda school, just as there are only two kinds of objects of knowledge – real particulars and fictional universals – there are only two means of coming to know (*pramāṇa*), namely, perception (*pratyakṣa*) and inference (*anumāna*). Each means of knowledge was held to cognize its own distinctive object. What we perceive are particulars, and what we know through inference are universals. Although both perception and inference are *pramāṇas*, there is a hierarchy between these two means of knowledge. Perception, according to the school, is always purely nonconceptual and nonlinguistic, whereas inference is conceptual, linguistic thinking that proceeds on the basis of good reasons. Perception was accorded the special status of giving direct access to the real, whereas conceptual thought was held to be in an important way distorted (*bhrānta*) because it "superimposes" universals that are not actually there in the particulars themselves.

Given the above claims, Siderits (2007), Thakchöe (2012), Garfield (2015), and Westerhoff (2018) regard the Pramāṇavāda school as pursuing a reductionist project of epistemological foundationalism. Westerhoff remarks that "such projects consider particular parts of our knowledge as immune to skeptical doubt, and they proceed to reconstruct the rest of our knowledge on the basis of such an unshakeable foundation" (Westerhoff 2018: 223).[11] According to the Pramāṇavāda school, perception engages directly and causally with particulars and corresponds to the particular itself. It is for that reason that perception is the fundamental "contact" with the world upon which the superstructure of conceptual cognition rests. Inference, on the other hand, is always engaged with the universal, and it is never free from the mediation of language, conception, and deception. However, as critics of the school have noted, the radical split between perception and inference can seem counterintuitive. Moreover, it raises the following two questions:

1) Why are particulars regarded as the only real things?
2) If universals are fictional, how can inference give us knowledge of the world?

In the following two sections, we will see how the school answered these questions.

12.2.1 Real Particulars

According to the Pramāṇavāda school, if something is to count as real, it must possess two characteristics: causal efficacy (*arthakriyāsamartha*) and

---

[11] The form of Indian foundationalism being discussed here is akin to a version of classical foundationalism in the Western tradition.

momentariness (*kṣaṇikatva*). Regarding the first characteristic, for Dharmakīrti what is real must have the power to actually affect things and bring about change. More exactly, one criterion for something being real is that it must have causal powers and perform causal roles. Dharmakīrti pointed out that particulars but not universals have causal efficacy, and so, according to this criterion, particulars but not universals are real (see Tillemans 2011). We can see this argument clearly in Dharmakīrti's most influential work, the *Pramāṇavārttika* (Commentary on Epistemology) III.3 (with Manorathanandin's additions in brackets):

Whatever has causal powers, that really exists (*paramārthasat*) in this context [i.e., when we examine reality]. Anything else is declared to be [just] customarily existent (*saṃvṛtisat*) [because it is practically accepted through mere conceptual fictions]. These two [i.e., the real and the customary] are [respectively] particulars and universals. (Pandeya 1989: 64)

As Tom Tillemans (2021) remarks, the key step in Dharmakīrti's argument is that "nothing causes new effects while itself remaining the same." This explains the significance of the second characteristic of whatever is real: momentariness, which turns out to coincide with causal efficacy. The Pramāṇavāda school's two criteria for judging whether something is real – causal efficacy and momentariness – explain why they regard particulars as the only real things.

12.2.2 Fictional Universals

Dharmakīrti, in the opening passages of the *Vādanyāya* (Logic of Argumentation), argues that if something were permanent (*nitya*), it would be causally inert as it would neither produce its effects all at once (*yaugapadyena*) nor serially (*kramena*). He further argues that things, properties, and powers, if real and causally efficient, must occupy just one location in time (*kāla*) and space (*deśa*) and have only a singular nature, by which he means that nothing real can span, or be present in, several distinct objects over different times and places and possess the many natures of the various particulars. As Tillemans (2021) notes,

this not only rules out 'horizontal universals' (*tiryaglakṣaṇa*), like blueness, which would have to be present in several blue particulars at one time, but it also rules out 'vertical universals' (*ūrdhvatālakṣaṇa*), or substances persisting throughout time, the numerically identical individual that would be present in each time-slice of a thing. It is only series of qualitatively similar moments that constitute what we customarily take to be enduring objects, but there is actually nothing that remains numerically the same for more than one instant.

Consequently, causally inert and permanent universals are regarded as conceptual projections and held to be entirely unreal. This analysis is what generates the second question listed above. If universals are fictional, how can inference give us knowledge of the world?

Dignāga and Dharmakīrti developed the theory of exclusion (*apoha*) as a conceptual tool to explain the connection between perception and inference (see Siderits, Tillemans, and Chakrabarti 2011 for detailed discussions), and thereby explain the ability of inference to generate knowledge. The term *apoha* literally means exclusion of that which is other. Jay Garfield regards *apoha* theory as a distinctive Buddhist contribution to epistemology and illustrates it as follows: "To be a cow would seem to be to possess the property of bovinity, and this is indeed how all non-Buddhist Indian traditions see the matter. But on *apoha* theory, it is not. It is to be excluded from being a non-cow" (Garfield 2015: 218). This understanding of the meaning of kind terms is intended to avoid commitment to the real existence of universals and is thus considered to be a form of nominalism. If everything is unique, then the nature of a particular is just its difference from everything else. Its nature is to exclude all other particulars.

Still, certain particulars might be grouped together under a kind term if we could overlook their mutual differences and focus instead on their shared exclusion of some group that is "other" (see Siderits 2007: 220–1). This shared exclusion, according to Dharmakīrti, is based on the judgment of similarity that is grounded in linguistic and cognitive practice and its efficacy in fulfilling specific human purposes (see Guerrero 2013). Responding to his critics, then, Dharmakīrti further argues that judgments of similarity do not entail commitment to the real existence of universal properties that make particulars similar. Instead, he argues that we create properties to encode our habitual cognitive tendencies to regard certain things as similar. As Garfield notes, when we reformulate the realist assertion that "X is a cow" into the nominalist *apoha* form that "X is not a non-cow," we regard X as both different from all of the things to which the label "cow" is not applied and similar to all of the things to which the label "not a non-cow" is being applied. Garfield remarks that this form of negation is attractive to Buddhist philosophers, for it is a way of "eschewing ontological commitment" (Garfield 2015: 219).

After the sixth century, it was impossible for philosophers in India to ignore the epistemological developments of thinkers in the Pramāṇavāda school. The Madhyamaka school, for instance, was in constant debate with the philosophers associated with the Pramāṇavāda school. As we will next explain, Mādhyamikas (that is, philosophers associated with the Madhyamaka school) often diverged from the teaching of the Pramāṇavāda school regarding the nature and number of *pramāṇas* (see Garfield 2015).

12.3 The Coherentism of the Madhyamaka School

Nāgārjuna (c. 150–250 CE), who is widely regarded as the founding philosopher of the Madhyamaka school, in his *Vaidalyaprakarana* (Treatise on Pulverization) and *Vigrahavyāvartanī* (Dispeller of Objections) sketched out his view on epistemology and related metaphysical issues to establish that all things were empty of "own being" or intrinsic nature (*svabhava*). Nāgārjuna lists four means of knowledge: perception, inference, recognition of likeness (*upamāna*), and testimony (*āgama*). His epistemological project, as Jan Westerhoff points out, is to investigate whether any of these epistemic procedures are "intrinsically and essentially [a] means of knowledge" (2009: 180). Westerhoff elaborates: "Means of knowledge and their objects are notionally interdependent: without its ability to give us epistemic access to some thing, we would not label a cognitive procedure a means of knowledge" (2009: 180). This is the meaning of Nāgārjuna's claim that epistemic means cannot have "own being" (see Harrison 2022: 24–42). By denying that any epistemic means could have "own being," Nāgārjuna does not undermine the utility of epistemic means; rather, according to Jay Garfield, he defends the first explicit argument for "epistemological coherentism" in the history of world philosophy (Garfield 2015: 235).

Nāgārjuna often wrote in different voices, so careful exegesis is required to distinguish his own view from that of the philosophers he is intellectually sparring with. In *Dispeller of Objections*, Nāgārjuna explicitly rejects the Nyāya view that any means of knowledge could be self-established, arguing that if any means of knowledge were self-established, it should be able to exist independently of its object. He argues as follows:

> If pramāṇas were self-established,
> They would be independent of prameyas.
> These pramāṇas you [Nyāya] would establish,
> Being self-established, would depend on nothing else. (verse 40)

> If, as you would have it, the pramāṇas
> Are independent of their objects, the prameyas
> Then these pramāṇas
> Would pertain to nothing at all. (verse 41) (Westerhoff 2010, 32)

Nāgārjuna's argument can be illustrated by taking visual perception as an example. If visual perception could be established from its own side, then it should be independent of visual objects. However, if visual perception were independent of visual objects, how could we perceive anything? Pointing out the problem of the independence of means of knowledge from their objects, the Madhyamaka school argues that the epistemic means and its object are mutually established. Developing Nāgārjuna's argument further, Candrakīrti

(c. 600–c. 650) provides us with the following characterization of the epistemological instruments and their objects:

> Thus, in this way it is established that mundane objects are known by the means of the fourfold epistemic instruments. Now, these are themselves established through the force of mutual interdependence – by virtue of the presence of epistemic instruments (*pramāṇa*) there come to be epistemic objects (*prameya*), and by virtue of the presence of epistemic objects there come to be epistemic instruments. But there is no intrinsic establishment (*svābhāvikī siddhi*) of either the epistemic instruments or the epistemic objects. (Thakchöe 2011: 54)

Mādhyamikas thus argue that a proper account of knowledge rejects metaphysical and epistemological foundationalism. Both Nāgārjuna and Candrakīrti claim that only because all epistemic instruments and objects are empty of intrinsic nature can cognitions be epistemically possible in the context of the mutual dependence of epistemic means and objects (see Westerhoff 2009, 2010, 2018; Thakchöe 2011, 2012; and Garfield 2015). Given this claim, Candrakīrti is critical of the Pramāṇavāda school's perception-based foundationalism.[12] Like Nāgārjuna, Candrakīrti follows the Nyāya system of *pramāṇas* (perception, inference, analogy and testimony); thus, he holds that the Pramāṇavāda school does not have good reasons to rule out analogy and testimony as epistemic instruments.

Candrakīrti points out that the knowledge we get from the *pramāṇas* is in the category of conventional truth, for it depends upon our language and the biological structure underlying our conceptual apparatus. He argues, however, that besides the conventional perspective, there is an equally important ultimate perspective. This aspect of Candrakīrti's thought was taken up and developed by the later Tibetan philosopher Tsongkhapa (1357–1419), who argues that these two perspectives represent two aspects of reality and two natures of phenomena. This is known as the theory of two truths (conventional and ultimate truth), which many now regard as at the core of Buddhist philosophy. Prior to Tsongkhapa, Nāgārjuna had already regarded the two truths teaching as the Buddha's deepest insight, and later Mādhyamikas did not regard it as a departure from the original teaching of the Buddha. The Sanskrit term for conventional truth is *saṃvṛti-satya*, which denotes conventional and concealing, while *paramartha-satya*, or ultimate truth, refers to the way things really are. In the context of Madhyamaka philosophy, conventional truth often refers to phenomena as they are dependently arising, while ultimate truth often refers to phenomena from the perspective of the Madhyamaka account of emptiness (see Garfield 2015 for extended discussions).

---

[12] For extended discussions of Candrakīrti's critical response to foundationalism, see Arnold (2005), Siderits (1980, 1981), and Thakchöe (2011, 2012, 2013).

Both Candrakīrti and Tsongkhapa hold that the distinction between conventional and ultimate truth is epistemological. Conventional truth is delivered by unimpaired cognitive faculties when they are used properly. All persons are thought to be equipped with reliable, conventionally nondeceptive epistemic instruments that enable them to follow mundane epistemic conventions. According to the later Madhyamaka tradition, however, conventional knowledge cannot withstand analysis. Conventional truths are metaphysically deceptive and unstable, for they change along with developments of human civilization and enhancements of our epistemic instruments (consider, spectacles and microscopes for example). In contrast, coming to know the ultimate truth requires employing one's analytical and critical reasoning to go beyond the conventionality of things. According to Sonam Thakchöe's interpretation, Candrakīrti holds knowledge of both conventional and ultimate truths to be jointly necessary for understanding. Thakchöe illustrates this claim as follows:

Reflection on the selflessness of the person, for example, requires both nonanalytically seeing the five aggregates using conventional cognition and critically establishing them to be selfless by rational insight. If rational insight is excluded, the nonanalytical perspective on the person would remain, but from this perspective one would not be able to establish the person to be selfless, as this requires critical analysis. Similarly, if the role of conventional cognition is excluded, one would not be able to see the conventionally real person, and without this conventional basis, there would be no basis of the knowledge of the ultimate truth. (Thakchöe 2011: 46)

Although the two truths (and two modes of cognition) are epistemologically distinct, according to both Candrakīrti and Tsongkhapa, what is known is the same reality, a reality that lacks intrinsic nature (see Thakchöe 2007, 2012; and Garfield 2015).

12.4 Spiritual Liberation

Most world religious traditions offer an account of what they consider to be the human spiritual predicament. Buddhism is no exception. Buddhism is about solving the problem of suffering, and its central intuition is that the solution to this problem is the extirpation of ignorance (*avidyā*). Buddhism is thus intensely engaged with eradicating the ignorance that, the Buddha taught, lies at the heart of our spiritual malady. Despite great disagreement about what it is that we are ignorant of, each Indian philosophical school responded to the problem of ignorance, and its philosophers sought to provide theoretical accounts of what we need to know (Harrison 2019: 34–5). Buddhism was no exception. For Buddhists, ignorance of "how things really are" is thought to produce craving and hence lead to suffering. Knowledge is, therefore, regarded by Buddhists as the antidote to the ignorance that causes suffering; this is why Buddhist texts often describe the Buddha metaphorically as the "Great Physician."

The epistemologies of the three forms of Buddhist philosophy introduced above each emphasize what they regard as the objects of knowledge. Early Buddhist epistemology holds that objects of knowledge can be both sensory and supersensory. Focusing on the knowledge of ordinary cognitive agents and its relation to their progress toward liberation, the Pramāṇavāda school believes that only momentary particulars are real and foundational for genuine knowledge. Denying the foundational status and self-establishment of any means of coming to know an object of knowledge, the Madhyamaka school proposes a coherentist epistemology and emphasizes that conventional and ultimate truth are two modes in which things can be known.

Jonathan Stoltz remarks that within Buddhism "the study of epistemology – and the development of one's reasoning – is a necessary, but not sufficient, condition for spiritual realization" (2009: 547). For the Buddha, the route to liberating knowledge is a path that invites empirical investigation and leads to a personal realization of the truth of his teaching (Harvey 2009: 175). The quest for spiritual liberation also motivated the epistemological developments of the Pramāṇavāda school. Hayes remarks that both Dignāga and Dharmakīrti are, first and foremost, Buddhist apologists "with a strong interest in demonstrating the truth of the Buddhist position through rational argument" (1988: 33). The Madhyamaka school highlights that nuanced understanding of conventional and ultimate truth, and the relationship between them lies at the heart of Buddhist epistemology and soteriology.

Although each tradition has specific concerns, and between them there are sharp disagreements over some issues, each makes a distinctive contribution to our understanding of the nature of knowledge. Early Buddhism is concerned to explain human experience, the Pramāṇavāda school is more focused on logic and argumentation, and the Madhyamaka school is oriented toward clarifying the relationship between conventional and ultimate truth. These schools each provide us with different tools, skills, and perspectives to understand the human cognitive condition with its possibilities and limitations. The range of perspectives found within Buddhist epistemology offers us a comprehensive and illuminating view of things as they are, which, according to the Buddha, may serve to liberate us.

Part III

New Directions

13 Trust, Testimony, and Religious Belief

Laura Frances Callahan

Introduction

Descartes was disturbed by disagreement, especially across different places and cultures. He felt this disagreement undermined the trustworthiness of the prevailing thought of his own time, including Christian thought. So, he shut himself up in a house "alone" (presumably there were servants keeping him fed and making this possible) and thought very carefully and methodically about what, if anything, he could know for certain, abstracting as far as possible from everything he had merely been led to believe by others. Descartes's subsequent religiosity and belief in God was, by his own (psychologically implausible) account, based upon this independent investigation and his own version of the ontological argument.[1]

To understate: this is not a common way of becoming religious, acquiring faith, or coming to believe in God. Most religious people do not independently reason their way to their creeds. Even where there is some process of independent evaluation or monitoring of our beliefs, we are heavily influenced by the claims of our communities, as well as the claims of scholars, eyewitnesses to miracles, and institutions. Religious beliefs are in fact largely formed via *social* epistemological processes. Indeed, they are largely necessarily so, given the putatively transcendent nature of some claims and the historical nature of others.

Is this social epistemic dependence when it comes to religion regrettable? Would it be better if we could rely instead (or rely more heavily) on perception and reason – if we could be a bit more Cartesian? There seem to be epistemological and theological reasons to answer negatively. On the former, the current epistemological consensus, as evidenced by much of the discussion in social epistemology over the last thirty years, is that testimony is a perfectly good and fabulously useful, not to mention necessary, source of beliefs about the world.[2] We may suspect the Cartesian (or indeed Lockean) preference for individual

---

[1] This brief paragraph necessarily caricatures Descartes and is not meant to do his views justice. Caricature Descartes is a useful stalking horse for my purposes.

[2] Contemporary conversation has been shaped and progressed by, for example, Audi (1997); Coady (1992); Burge (1993); E Fricker (1994); M Fricker (2007); Foley (2001); Goldberg (2007); Goldman (1999); Graham (1997); Hardwig (1985; 1991); Hinchman (2005); Lackey (2008); Moran (2005); McMyler (2011); and Zagzebski (2012).

reasoning as just that – a *preference* for individual achievements and disdain for communal reliance, based on a dubious glorification of the individual.

On the latter, according to some theological traditions God *wants* us to form religious beliefs on the basis of testimony and trust. I'll focus in this chapter on the Christian tradition, for a manageable scope and to avoid ignorant mistakes about traditions less familiar to me. But I invite those familiar with other traditions to consider whether analogous remarks might apply.

In the Christian case, consider that Jesus didn't tell his disciples to stay home and pray that everyone else would be given personal mystical experiences or reason their way to certainty in God's existence and his own divinity. He sent his disciples out to "all nations," enjoining them to witness to others.[3] And while philosophers' concept of "testimony" is distinct from the traditions of "testimony" in various churches, wherein congregants are encouraged to present their personal faith stories and experiences to the group and to outsiders, the two are certainly related; if God exists and is roughly as the Christian tradition has it, God seems to want us to tell each other about what we know and have experienced of God.[4] Finally, while there is certainly a variety of interesting religious language for good (pseudo- or semi-)cognitive ways of relating to God ("believing," "having faith," "knowing," "following," etc.), "*trusting*" is a central term in many traditions – whether trusting one's religious community/leaders or trusting God. "Trust in the Lord with all your heart and lean not on your own understanding," enjoins Proverbs 3:5. Not exactly Descartes's favorite verse, I imagine.

So, we do get our religious views largely via testimony and trust, and – at least if these views are *true* or *known* – these social epistemological means are far from regrettable.[5] They are sanctioned by many contemporary epistemologists, and in many traditions they are specifically religiously encouraged.

In the next two sections of this chapter, I survey some of what contemporary epistemologists have had to say about trust and testimony – what it means to trust or believe on testimony and when this is appropriate or valuable. I will focus on implications for religious epistemology.

In the final section of the chapter, I turn briefly to a novel question connecting contemporary literature on trust with the philosophy of religion. I'll suggest that those who trust God are necessarily ready to feel *betrayed* by God – to feel angry, disappointed, etc. – in some (perhaps counterpossible)

---

[3] Matthew 28:19–20.
[4] Crummett (2015) expounds this theme in developing a "responsibility" response to the problem of divine hiddenness.
[5] One might think common means of acquiring religious views would be nonregrettable even where the resulting religious views are false – perhaps if those religious views are nonetheless justified/rational or if they constitute (nonfactive) understanding. In the text I simply stick to the weaker claim that true or known religious beliefs are not flawed due to social acquisition.

situations in which God seems to have testified falsely. This thesis connects with recent literature on the propriety of anger and lament in religious life.

13.1 Testimony

Recent literature on testimony has taken up a variety of questions, most of which we won't have space to consider here. I will not be directly concerned with the conditions under which testimony can transmit or generate knowledge.[6] Nor will I be concerned with certain aspects of the reductionism/antireductionism debate – in particular I won't discuss whether we have a default entitlement to believe what others say.[7]

The aspect of that debate that *will* concern me is the question whether testimonial justification reduces to other kinds of justification, or whether it is a *sui generis* epistemic source.[8] Say you witness a car crash. Your justification for your beliefs about this car crash is largely perceptual; your justification shortly after the event is perceptual/memorial. Say you then tell me about the crash. Might I get some special, distinctly testimonial justification for believing the details you share? Or am I simply justified in believing – by virtue of your perception/memory, together with my reasoned, inductive assessment – that you are reliably testifying? Reductionists take the eponymous, reducing line; antireductionists go for a *sui generis* story.

Anscombe foreshadowed and partly inspired contemporary antireductionism in her paper, originally published in 1979, "What Is It to Believe Someone?" There, she makes a strong case that believing someone is different from believing what they say, since "[W]hat someone's saying a thing may bring about, is that one forms one's *own* judgment that the thing is true. In teaching philosophy we do not hope that our pupils will *believe us,* but rather, that they will *come to see* that what we say is true – if it is" (2008: 4). Moreover, believing someone is different even from believing what they say on the strength of their saying so.

For suppose I were convinced that B wished to deceive me and would tell the opposite of what he believed, but that on the matter in hand B would be believing the opposite of the truth. By calculation on this, then, I believe what B says, on the strength of his saying it – but only in a comical sense can I be said to believe *him.* (Anscombe 2008: 4)

---

[6] For thorough, recent treatments of these questions, see for example, Lackey (2008) or Greco (2021).

[7] The idea is that if you assert that p, I have a *prima facie* reason to believe that p, unless there are indications that you are unreliable or insincere. See, for example, Foley (2001) and Zagzebski (2012) for thoughtful defenses; see Fricker (1994) for dissent.

[8] Or a *sui generis* epistemic means of transmission. See Greco (2021), who argues for this distinction.

For Anscombe, there is a form of testimonial belief – believing someone – that is not so calculating and that is essentially personal. She suggests in particular that "believing someone (in the particular case) is *trusting him for the truth* – in the particular case" (Anscombe 2008: 9, emphasis mine).

Anscombe thus connects antireductionism about testimony with the phenomenon of trust, to which I'll turn directly in the next section. More recent antireductionists include, for example, McMyler (2011) and Moran (2005), who develop related views in which the speaker in a testimonial exchange invites the hearer to rest her justification for belief with the speaker. Should the hearer be asked why she believes that *p*, she might appropriately say that the speaker told her that *p* – any questions should be referred to *them*. McMyler terms this "second-personal" justification; in Moran's terminology, a testifier as such gives her assurance that *p* and invites the hearer to trust *her* that *p*.

Notice that antireductionism may make justified religious belief easier to come by. This is not to say personal relationships wherein we give each other assurances or take each other's word are easy! But antireductionists posit these personal exchanges as an additional basic source justification, over and above the agreed-upon sources like perception and reasoning. And this suggests that proper trust in a person, an institution, or indeed God could – in principle anyway – ground proper (justified, knowledgeable) belief on the basis of religious testimony. An antireductionist can think that when I trust my mother's religious instruction, my justification for beliefs held thereby needn't reduce to the non-testimonial evidence I have for her trustworthiness on religious matters. Indeed, I may *not* have strong evidence of her reliability on religious matters. But – at least, assuming I don't have egregious evidence against her reliability – my basic trust of her could still give me some reason for believing what she tells me.

On the other hand, a reductionist will insist that belief in religious testimony is only justified insofar as it is justified by some combination of, for example, perception and reasoning. Reductionists generally have a harder time explaining how we could be justified in our wide breadth of testimonially dependent beliefs. (Do little children have adequate track-record evidence to trust their parents for the meanings of words, for example?[9]) But even if we suppose that the reductionist can somehow explain the justification of many of our ordinary, garden-variety beliefs,[10] we might worry that religious beliefs in particular will look difficult to explain on a reductionist picture.

Consider what it would take to arrive at particular, justified religious beliefs if testimonial evidence must be cashed out as reasoning and perception. While

---

[9] This is a fairly standard criticism of reductionism in the literature; see especially Coady (1992) and Greco (2021).

[10] Goldman (2001: 87–8) tentatively suggests that children might really acquire good "track-record" evidence for trusting speakers by seeing people talk about objects the child herself also sees (and sees the speaker seeing).

some of us have powerful, individual religious experiences that could inform our views, others of us are faced only with conflicting reports spanning centuries and subject to a dizzying array of interpretations and historical influences – the adjudication of which calls out for expertise in philosophy as well as biblical studies, ancient Near Eastern history, human psychology, political science, literature, etc. If what we get from the scriptures, church tradition, and religious authorities in our communities is simply additional evidence or justification of the standard, nontestimonial sort, it seems we are not generally in a good position to interpret that evidence and not justified in firm, positive views.

Regardless of one's position on reductionism/antireductionism, one may be interested in the contemporary conversation about trust. Antireductionists may be especially interested in trust as the "special ingredient" in distinctly testimonial justification. But even reductionists, though they will think any *epistemic* value of trust ultimately reduces to other sources of justification, may be interested in the practical value of trust and the conditions under which trust may be appropriate.

13.2 Trust

In this section, then, I will review the – rather surprisingly separate – contemporary literature on trust. Annette Baier's "Trust and Antitrust" (1986) ignited this conversation, and particularly influential was her distinction between trust and mere "reliance." I'll start (Section 13.2.1) with this distinction and the connection between trust and certain reactive attitudes (in a Strawsonian sense). In Section 13.2.2 I turn to questions of value, asking what's valuable about (robust) trust, as opposed to mere reliance, and in Section 13.2.3 I begin to consider upshots for religious epistemology in particular.

13.2.1 Trust and Reactive Attitudes

Trust, observes Baier (1986), involves something more than merely building in someone's doing something to one's plans or assumptions. A con artist carefully observing you could come to do that – could rely on your behaving predictably. Or, to borrow a less sinister example from Nguyen (in press), if you usually walk past my office door around noon on your way to class, I might start relying on you to time my lunch break. But I certainly wouldn't *trust* you to walk by at noon, not in any robust way. Trust's distinctive character, contemporary philosophers tend to agree, involves a *participant stance,* in Strawson's sense.[11] We do not regard trusted people merely as

---

[11] Strawson (1974: 9).

predictable objects; they are not like car clocks or thermometers in our eyes.[12] We regard them as responsible agents whose attitudes toward us – as displayed in their actions and words – are the proper occasion of reactions such as gratitude and resentment.[13] And this shows up most clearly in the difference in our reactions when someone doesn't behave as we trust them to do versus merely as we rely on them to do; trust is vulnerable to *betrayal*.

If a con artist was relying on your going into the office this morning, but you happened to decide to work from home, the con artist might feel surprised, disappointed, frustrated, etc. But it would not be reasonable for the con artist to feel betrayed by or resentful of you. As Holton (1994: 67) puts it:

> When you trust someone to do something, you rely on them to do it, and you regard that reliance in a certain way: you have a readiness to feel betrayal should it be disappointed, and gratitude should it be upheld. In short, you take a stance of trust towards the person on whom you rely. It is the stance that makes the difference between reliance and trust. When the car breaks down, we might be angry, but when a friend lets us down, we feel betrayed.

There are various ways of diagnosing the underlying cause of this difference in our reactive attitudes when people do not behave as we trust/rely on them to do. Baier herself proposes that when we trust A to φ, we depend not just on A's φ-ing but also on A's having *good will* toward us.[14] We feel betrayed when they reveal a lack of good will. Other recent proposals highlight the presumed *responsiveness* involved in trust. Perhaps: when we trust A to φ, we believe A will be motivated to φ in part *by* our trust.[15] We feel betrayed when they seem not to have seen our trust as a reason to "come through." Alternatively, Hawley (2014) suggests that when we trust, we take the trusted to have made a *commitment*. We feel betrayed if they renege on that commitment to us.[16]

Regardless of its precise cause, readiness to feel betrayed should one's trust (seem to) be let down is generally agreed to be an essential feature of trust.[17]

---

[12] Cf. Hieronymi (2008: 222). I here bracket the possibility Nguyen (in press) highlights, of robustly trusting objects.

[13] Nguyen (in press) would dispute this as a truth about *all* objects of trust, but he does allow for distinct interpersonal forms.

[14] This resonates with Strawson's own diagnosis of the reactive attitudes (Cf. 1974: 10).

[15] Cf. Faulkner (2007) and Jones (2012).

[16] Nguyen (in press) points out that we can trust – and feel betrayed by – not only people but objects and even body parts (think climbing ropes, car engines, knee joints, and smartphones). He proposes that trust is an "unquestioning attitude" by which we attempt to integrate other people and objects into our own functioning or agency; we feel betrayed when those things we are disposed not to question, on which we premise all our agency, fail us. Still, Nguyen thinks there may be distinct, interpersonal forms of trust as well. These are my primary concerns here.

[17] Despite the philosophical consensus, one could of course object here. Perhaps readiness to *feel* betrayed rather than simply regard oneself as betrayed is psychologically contingent. Certainly, dispositions to feel betrayed can be masked or perhaps shaped by one's

When we trust A to φ, we are disposed to feel betrayed should we conclude that A did not in fact φ.[18]

What about the special, testimonial case when we trust A *that* p? Consistency pressures us to say that in this case, too, we would be ready to feel betrayed should p turn out to be false or should A's belief turn out to be unjustified. This squares with certain antireductionist themes of resting one's justification with a speaker or taking their assurance. Perhaps when we trust A that p, we trust A to "hold" or to have the justification for our belief that p. And if we should find out that A does not know that p (or that A is not justified in believing that p, or that p is not true – which is in turn often evidence that A is not justified in believing p), we feel betrayed.[19] We allow the possibility for people to let us down when we trust them, whether to water our plants or to be responsible for the justification of our beliefs.[20]

Just as in more active cases of trusting versus relying on A to *do* something, we may contrast trusting A that p with merely relying on A for the information that p, or even merely relying on A's testimony that p. Suppose a colleague says that the faculty meeting starts at 3:00, but they do not know this and in fact the meeting starts at 2:00. Version 1: this colleague tells you the meeting starts at 3:00, perhaps implicitly or explicitly inviting your trust, and you do just trust them. ("No, you don't need to look it up – I know it's at 3:00. You can trust me.") Version 2: this colleague tells you the meeting starts at 3:00 and you believe their testimony, but you merely rely on it and do not trust them. You inductively calculate their likely truthfulness and judge that they are likely to be speaking reliably on this issue. Version 3: you merely overhear your colleague saying that the faculty meeting starts at 3:00 to a stranger in the hallway.

---

circumstances and personality quirks. Perhaps a better account of trust would have it that trust is sufficient for a disposition to some range of reactive attitudes, where "feeling betrayed" is paradigmatic but not strictly necessary. Thanks to Michael Rea for discussion on this point.

[18] It is common to talk more simply of a disposition to feel betrayed when A does not φ, and I take it that such talk is generally harmless. But strictly, a trusting spouse, for example, is not disposed to feel betrayed in the moment that their partner cheats. They will be disposed to feel betrayed should they come to *believe* their spouse is cheating/has cheated. Thanks to Justus Hibshman for discussion on this point.

[19] I don't mean to take any stand on exactly what a speaker commits to or invites a hearer to trust them for, in asserting that p. This may be knowledge or justification.

[20] Of course, in cases of relatively trivial beliefs we might say we trust someone without (much of) a disposition to feel betrayed. Say you're idly wondering what's the capital of Kentucky, I tell you it's Lexington, and you trust me. Actually, the capital is Frankfort. When you find this out, we might think, surely you needn't feel *betrayed*. (Thanks to Stephen Ogden for a very similar case.) Still, I'm inclined to reject this admittedly natural thought and maintain the consensus view of trust. It's *also* pretty plausible to understand the case as involving (i) trivial or weak feelings of betrayal (or offense, or other reactive attitudes) and/or (ii) no "real" trust, as opposed to a less involved reliance, in the first place.

The going accounts of trust predict that in version 1 of the case you would feel (to some degree, however slight) betrayed upon learning the real time of the faculty meeting – at least until you heard a good excuse from your colleague! They also predict you would not feel so betrayed in either of version 2 or – perhaps especially – version 3, where trust is not present. This seems intuitive. Trust in testimony, like more practical cases of trust, involves vulnerability to betrayal.

13.2.2 The Value of Trust

Vulnerability might seem like a generally bad thing. We might wonder what's nonetheless valuable about trust and, relatedly, when we should or may trust.

One might think that one ought to trust only if one ought to believe that the relevant party is trustworthy (in the relevant way). And indeed, some "cognitivists" about trust will say that trusting A to φ requires believing that A will in fact φ.[21] This in turn suggests that the conditions for appropriate trust may inherit conditions for the appropriateness of the relevant beliefs about trustworthiness. If I have to believe you are trustworthy in order to trust you, then – arguably – in order for it to be appropriate for me to trust you, it must be appropriate for me to believe you are trustworthy.[22]

But even on cognitivist views, trust needn't be *equivalent* to belief in trustworthiness; such belief is necessary but not sufficient for trust on these views. For one thing, real trust involves the participant stance and vulnerability to betrayal. Thus, it makes sense even for cognitivists to ask: even if one has reason to believe the relevant party trustworthy, why go ahead and *trust* them? What's valuable about trust *per se*?

I'll focus here just on trust in testimony, rather than practical cases (trusting someone to fix your car, be faithful to you in a relationship, etc.).[23] Trust can seem valuable either as something necessary for epistemic flourishing or (also/ instead) as a strictly optional but valuable aspect of said flourishing. This reference to flourishing alerts us to one possible view of trust, on which it is an intellectual virtue, although we lack space to explore this further here.

Let's start with the necessity of trust. Some basic *reliance* on one another seems epistemically inescapable, totally necessary for any significant

---

[21] See McMyler and Ogungbure (2018) for extended discussion of the cognitivism/ noncognitivism debate. For an intriguing defense of cognitivism, see, e.g., Hieronymi (2008).

[22] One *could* claim that some trust is fully appropriate despite necessarily involving inappropriate trustworthiness beliefs. But I take it there is a tension here; thanks to Ted Warfield for discussion.

[23] In passing, it is not clear to me these can or need to be cleanly separated. When I trust someone to do something practical for me, I typically believe that they will (and premise all sorts of further reasoning on that belief). And when I trust someone's testimony, it may directly inform my practical actions.

epistemic achievement. I say "basic" reliance because, like many epistemologists, I am skeptical of the reductionist project, at least in its full generality. The justification we have for believing our early teachers, parents, and community members for information about our own identities, word meanings, etc. is surely not reducible to the evidence we have that they are knowledgeable and sincere. Relying on one another is a necessary component of our acquiring any large, interesting, and (hopefully largely) true set of beliefs.

If such reliance is necessary, then plausibly, as a matter of human psychology, trust is also necessary. *In general,* humans are mind readers; we do, in general, naturally relate to one another as subjects or agents and not merely as objects; we take up participant stances.

Now it is one thing to claim that trust is a necessary ingredient in epistemic flourishing. It is another to claim that we may have epistemic reasons to trust *beyond* what is necessary. One might think that trust is valuable for getting our epistemic projects off the ground, as it were, but that trust only introduces unnecessary epistemic risk or heteronomy thereafter and should be eschewed.

On the contrary, it seems to me, there is no limit to the extent that trust could extend a person's individual epistemic capacities in valuable ways. I don't merely trust my parents for my name – I trust the local paper for important recent developments in my community; I trust my doctor for accurate diagnoses and the recommendations of current medical science; I often trust individuals when they report their own experiences. By being willing to trust, I acquire knowledge about events I didn't witness, about advanced scientific research I did not perform and do not understand, and about what it's like to walk in other people's shoes. And this is a tiny sample! Trust seems not only epistemically necessary but fabulously epistemically useful.

Finally, trust in testimony – like trust generally – seems also to have significant social, nonepistemic value. Recall the participant stance we take in trust, the genuine vulnerability we invite, in relying specifically on the will, commitments, and intentions of other people as agents. By these means trust binds us together socially. Vulnerability is a risk, but in making us vulnerable, trust also has the potential to make us close, intimate. Trusting what people say is integral to healthy friendships, romantic partnerships, and broader community belonging.

There is of course much more that could be said about the value of trust – and much more still that could be said about its risks and the dangers of inappropriate trust, a topic I regretfully omit. But I wish to turn now more specifically to trust and its value in religious contexts.

13.2.3 Trust in Religious Contexts

The contemporary philosophical discussion of trust does not typically include discussion of implications for religion. In Baier's seminal article (1986), she is uneasy about the propriety of trusting God and decries using such religious trust as a model for morally appropriate human trust.[24] Be that as it may – in Section 13.3 I want to explore an instance of modeling in the opposite direction: what could our theories of human trust imply for trust in God?

Here, I'll make one additional observation about the discussion thus far as relates to religious epistemology. Much of what deserves to be called "religious trust" is in fact trust in other humans and human institutions, rather than strictly in supernatural or divine entities.[25] Christians trust the eyewitnesses and disciples to (relatively) faithfully record the events of Jesus's life. We trust the early church for faithfully interpreting and codifying, under divine guidance, basic Christian theology. We trust the countless scribes and scholars who have given us the Bible as it is today. We trust our pastors, mentors, and friends; we trust (some of) those who claim to have had mystical or religious experiences. All of this describes trust that is arguably essential to belief or faith.

If this is right – if the religious life is shot through and partly constituted by trust in fellow humans – then our theories of when trust is appropriate would seem to have a direct bearing on the propriety of various religious lives and belief systems. And our understanding of the value of trust should also inform (and perhaps be informed by!) our understanding of what's good about those lives and beliefs. Again, according to many traditions, God wants us to believe *together,* in community, on the basis of each other's testimony.

13.3 Trusting God and Dispositions to Feel Betrayed

In this final section I want to raise a novel question about trust in religious contexts. Does trusting God involve the disposition to feel angry at, frustrated with, resentful toward, or disappointed in God should our trust be disappointed?[26]

This question arises from considering the seeming philosophical consensus we've just reviewed – that trust involves vulnerability to betrayal and the disposition to take up various reactive attitudes should one's trust be

---

[24] "The persistent human adult tendency to profess trust in a creator-God can also be seen as an infantile residue of this crucial innate readiness of infants to initially impute goodwill to the powerful persons on whom they depend. So we should perhaps welcome, or at least tolerate, religious trust, if we value any form of trust. Nevertheless the theological literature on trust in God is of very limited help to us if we want to understand trust in human persons" (Baier 1986: 242). This comment may remind the reader of the "Freud and Marx complaint" Plantinga addresses in *Warranted Christian Belief* (2000b).

[25] Of course, even humans and human institutions may have the benefit of divine inspiration or guidance. It is not clear that there is any clear boundary here.

[26] We could also, of course, ask whether trusting a religious leader or institution involves parallel dispositions, but I will set these questions aside, since the possibility of trustful dispositions to feel angry with God may seem more surprising and problematic.

disappointed. If I trust you, I will feel betrayed by you should I come to believe that you have let me down. I may resent you; I may feel angry, frustrated, or disappointed with you as an agent. Such claims are by now familiar. But they seem to imply something rather surprising about trusting God; must those who trust God also be disposed to feel betrayed, etc.?

Exploring this question requires asking further questions about the proper role of *lament* and *anger* in religious life. For example, is it *ever* appropriate to feel or express anger toward God?[27] Second, isn't it impossible for proper trust in God to be disappointed – hence, shouldn't what appears to be disappointed trust be immediately reinterpreted as misplaced, uninvited trust? Relatedly – what are we really invited to trust God *for*?

Let's focus on epistemic, testimonial trust – cases of trusting God *that p*. Of course, such testimony is typically mediated by scriptures, prophets, mystics, or institutions. And it is often vague, or at least subject to multiple interpretations. (E.g., What does it mean that "all shall be well"?[28] Are we invited to trust God that the world was literally created in six days, as per Genesis 1, or what exactly are we invited to believe on the basis of that chapter?) But such messiness is not unique to the divine case. Human speech, too, can be filtered through institutions and can be vague or subject to multiple interpretations. ("Was she being sarcastic? I couldn't tell" is an extreme example.) Though God's testimony is messier in these ways than I would personally like, it does appear to be out there as a candidate for trust. If God exists, God makes promises and tells us things.

So, suppose one takes oneself to be invited to trust God that *p* and does trust God that *p*. And suppose one receives overwhelming evidence that ~*p* and comes to believe that ~*p*. Which reactions are consistent with "real" trust? I'll consider three sorts of answers here.

One might think that those who really trusted God will always feel betrayed by God (or other reactive attitudes, perhaps including anger or frustration with God) in such cases. This sort of answer could be directly inspired by reflections on human, interpersonal trust and the seeming necessity of trust's vulnerability to betrayal.

On the other hand, reflection on the religious case makes salient a certain possibility that is often overlooked in discussions of interpersonal trust. Namely, the failure of a trusted party to "come through" may, in some situations, give us evidence that our trust was misplaced or uninvited in the first place. Perhaps we misinterpreted or were otherwise mistaken about what God was trying to tell us; perhaps God never really testified that *p* in the first place. And a general, trusting disposition to feel betrayed seems compatible with the disposition *not* to feel betrayal, but rather to revoke or revise trust, in

---

[27] Cf., for example, Brueggemann (1986b); Rea (2018, 2021); and Timpe (2022).
[28] This communication was reported by Julian of Norwich after a mystical experience of Jesus.

the specific circumstances where one's trust is disappointed in a way that provides evidence that one's trust was uninvited or misplaced all along.

Returning to an earlier example: I may indeed be generally disposed to feel betrayed (or angry, disappointed, etc.) if I trusted you that the meeting started at 3:00 and I come to believe that in fact it started at 2:00. Such a general disposition is compatible, however, with the more fine-grained disposition *not* to feel betrayed if I come to believe both that the meeting started at 2:00 and that I simply misheard or misunderstood you.

And especially in the divine case, there may be occasions when a trusted party's very failure to "come through" – to have spoken truly, or to have promised what in fact comes about – ought to be interpreted as providing evidence that one's specific trust was uninvited or based on a misunderstanding. Finding out that the meeting really started at 2:00 might raise to salience the possibility that I misheard you as well as the possibility that you let me down.

This brings me to the second sort of answer to the question of what real trust in God requires. One might think that *all* putative failures of God's trustworthiness should be so interpreted by the "real" truster, without any sense of betrayal. After all, if it seems that God invited you to trust that God that *p*, and it becomes obvious that ~*p*, then there are two possible conclusions to draw. Either you misunderstood the invitation, or God – *God* – lied or was mistaken or otherwise let you down.[29] One might think the first possibility is always more likely; and, indeed, one might think specifically that the *trusting* conclusion to draw is the first rather than the second. As I'm conceiving of this position, it would entail that feelings of betrayal, etc. are never appropriate when it turns out that ~*p* despite one's having trusted God that *p*.

This second sort of answer may seem more attractive, but ultimately, I think it too is problematic. Notice that there is yet a third possibility – that those who trust God will *often* assume they misunderstood any invitations to trust that turn out to be disappointed, though they will still be disposed to feel betrayed in a rather narrow set of circumstances.

Such an answer may sound less principled, but in fact I think it is not. Some reluctance to conclude that invited trust has been disappointed seems to be possibly another quite general feature of trust, at least where close personal relationships are involved.[30] The person who really trusts – whether God or a friend/partner/parent – might quite generally be reluctant to accept that the trusted party led them astray, looking instead to the possibility that testimony was misunderstood. Such dispositions to suspect misunderstanding are clearly

---

[29] Thanks to Shlomo Zuckier for this framing.

[30] Perhaps the disposition to evaluate evidence relevant to one's trust being disappointed may bear similarities to our evidential dispositions vis-à-vis matters that reflect on our *friends*. Cf., for example, Stroud (2006). Thanks to Justin Brittain for discussion on this point.

compatible with the disposition to feel betrayed if one does (reluctantly) conclude that (trusted party said that p) $^\wedge$ ($\sim p$). And a special reluctance to conclude this in the divine case could be explained both by belief in God's impeccable character and the messy, easily misunderstood nature of divine testimony.

This third answer seems preferable to the view that real trusters would *never* feel betrayed by God for two reasons. (i) The view that real trusters could never feel betrayed by God requires a deep disanalogy between trust in God (invulnerable to betrayal, on this view) and trust in humans (necessarily vulnerable), and, moreover, (ii) there seem to be limitations on the flexibility of real, robust trust.

Just a brief comment on (i). Those with certain theological convictions may find deep disanalogies between trust in God and trust in other humans easier to swallow than others. But for those who emphasize the *personal* nature of God and hence the *interpersonal* nature of our relationship with God, it does seem a cost to admit a stark difference between divine and human forms of interpersonal trust.[31]

On (ii), a human example may help make the point. Suppose you and I explicitly agreed you'd come by my office daily during the week to remind me to eat lunch. (Perhaps I often forget, which leaves me cranky and woozy during afternoon classes.) Suppose that one day, with no explanation, you just don't show up. Indeed, you don't show up the next day either, or the next. And suppose that I am not bothered; I do not feel betrayal. Rather, I simply and dispassionately conclude that I must have misunderstood the agreement.

In this case, you *clearly* invited my trust. I'd have to radically doubt my own memory or social and perceptual skills to doubt our agreement. And – crucially – my quickness so to doubt them without even passing through any experience of betrayal seems to indicate a lack of real trust in the first place. If I had really been counting on you to come by my office, I would not be so unbothered about your failure to show up.

Returning to the religious case, there are *some* things God clearly invites us to trust God for, according to different religious traditions. (At a minimum, perhaps, the aforementioned, admittedly vague promise that "all will be well.")[32] While it's certainly possible for us to make mistakes about the precise nature of those invitations, and while perhaps sometimes we ought to infer such a mistake from disappointed trust, it seems to me there are limits on the extent to which real trusters can be willing to make such inferences – at least *without also experiencing betrayal*.

---

[31] Thanks to Alli Thornton for discussion on this point.
[32] Thanks to John Schwenkler for discussion on this point.

Now some will be deeply uncomfortable with this. How could it be right to have even counterfactual (or counterpossible)[33] dispositions to be angry with God or feel betrayed by God? Isn't God always simply to be thanked and praised?[34]

We've returned to the question whether feeling or expressing anger toward God could ever be appropriate. I'm inclined to think it sometimes is. For one thing, unbroken fawning certainly *isn't* what's universally modeled by faithful people in the Bible. Brueggeman (1986) calls our attention to the many psalms of lament, where the psalmist variously berates God, accuses God of injustice and unfair absence, and pleads with God to "come through" in various ways (usually involving the crushing of enemies). More recently, Rea (2018: chapter 8; 2021) calls our attention to the biblical books of Job and Lamentations as examples of protestation and lament apparently "validated" by God. Both these contemporary authors have argued in different ways that lament has an important function in developing relationships between God and God's people; moreover, God is clearly presented in scripture as tolerating, if not inviting or validating, such lament. Consider, too, that Jesus himself seems to experience something like betrayal by God on the cross. Quoting Psalm 22, he cries "My God, my God, why have you forsaken me?" just before his death.[35]

Second, we can separate the question of how it is *right* to feel toward God from the question of what feelings (dispositions to) *trust* involves. If we really believed that it is never appropriate to feel anger toward God or even to be counterfactually (or counterpossibly) disposed to such feelings, it seems to me the right thing to say would be that it is also never appropriate to trust God. Again, really trusting a human person's testimony involves not only assessing them to be reliable or accepting what they say but counting on them as an agent – counting on their commitments to hold justification for their claims, their good will toward us, or their responsiveness to our trust. Why would really trusting a personal God be different, and why wouldn't this necessarily involve vulnerability to feelings of disappointment, betrayal, and anger?[36] If, instead, we are *always* ready, should our trusting expectations of God not be

---

[33] One may be disposed to feel betrayed by God only in circumstances that never in fact arise (counterfactual dispositions), or one may be disposed to feel betrayed by God only in circumstances that never *could* arise, which are not metaphysically possible (counterpossible dispositions). Because I believe that in fact *all will be well,* I think I will never see the state of affairs in which all is never well – indeed, I'm inclined to think this state of affairs strictly impossible. But I still may have certain dispositions to feel and act that would be triggered by this state of affairs.

[34] From Eucharistic Prayer II from the Book of Common Prayer: "It is truly right and just, our duty and our salvation, always and everywhere to give you thanks..."

[35] Cf., for example, Mark 15:34. Thanks to Jane Heath for this example.

[36] Again, one's particular theological commitments may affect the plausibility that trust in God would be radically different.

met, to simply revise our own expectations without any sense of having been let down or betrayed by God, then it seems to me we merely fear and admire God rather than trust God.

One could argue that fear and admiration are more appropriate than trust for this reason. This is a position to be taken seriously. However, as I've hinted in the introduction and discussed again in the present section, the propriety of trust in religious life does seem to have strong biblical support. It seems to me there is pressure to say both:

If Christianity is true, then people should trust God (and some human testifiers about religion),

and

Trusting God (and some human testifiers about religion) requires a readiness or disposition to feel betrayed.

Thus, contemporary work on trust, together with the importance of trust in the Christian tradition, pressures us to say: if Christianity is true, people should be ready/disposed to feel betrayed by, angry with, or disappointed in God (and some human testifiers about religion) – at least in some rather narrow range of circumstances. This is rather surprising and seems to me to deserve far greater discussion.

My aim here has largely been to raise this question and, over the earlier sections, to connect more general contemporary discussions of trust and testimony with issues specific to religious epistemology. If we want to be antireductionists about testimony and fans of robust trust as a basic source of justification for belief, we may also need to accept the propriety of certain dispositions to feel angry with God.[37]

---

[37] Special thanks to participants in the discussion group for the Center for Philosophy of Religion at Notre Dame, October 2021, as well as Jonathan Fuqua and John Greco for comments that vastly improved this chapter.

14 Religious Disagreement

Katherine Dormandy

Introduction

Religious belief systems provide orientation, and they contain information about what their adherents think is true and important. But they come in massive variety, and many are logically incompatible with others. They cannot all simultaneously be perfectly accurate. Even within religions there is significant disagreement, and atheist beliefs say that few if any religious beliefs are accurate. We may call this situation *religious disagreement*.

Many philosophers regard religious disagreement as a problem. For having beliefs usually means taking reality to be as they describe. But how do you know *your* belief system is accurate, instead of one of the many others? Other philosophers regard religious disagreement as an opportunity, for engaging thoughtfully with alternative beliefs may help improve your own. I'll discuss both mindsets in turn: the threat mindset (Section 14.1) and the opportunity mindset (Section 14.2).

A few clarifications. Beliefs about religious matters, as construed here, have at least one of the following features. They pertain to ontology, either affirming or denying something about a transcendent reality (such as God). Or they pertain to practical matters, specifically the consequences of the ontological beliefs on our lives, for example what (not) to eat, or whether certain people may become religious leaders.

Although the following concerns religious disagreement, many of the ideas apply equally to disagreement over other complex belief systems, such as ethical or political ones. Where an argument is unique to religious disagreement should be clear.

14.1 Religious Disagreement as an Epistemic Threat

Many people with mutually incompatible beliefs about religious matters seem highly intelligent and personally admirable. Yet most of their belief systems (there being so many) must be inaccurate. How can this be? And can you be sure yours is not among the mistaken ones? This is the *epistemic problem of religious disagreement*.

It can be expressed as the following argument.

The Argument from Religious Disagreement

1. There are many people whose beliefs about religious matters are incompatible with mine, yet whose epistemic qualifications are on a par with mine (RD-evidence).
2. RD-evidence, against the backdrop of my other total evidence, speaks against my own beliefs about religious matters.
3. If premises 1 and 2 are true, then I (epistemically) should weaken or even abandon my own beliefs about religious matters.
4. Therefore, I (epistemically) should weaken or even abandon my own beliefs about religious matters.

Consider premise 1. A person's *epistemic qualifications* are factors that are relevant for forming true beliefs or knowledge, particularly evidence and epistemic competences. Two people's epistemic qualifications can be on a par without being identical: Each person may have excellent but different evidence, for example religious experience versus philosophical argumentation. And each person may be equally but differently competent, for example in emotional perception versus logical argumentation. Religious matters are multifaceted, generating highly varied evidence (tradition, experiences, arguments, etc.), and one can form beliefs about them through different evidence or competences. If a person's epistemic qualifications are on a par with yours, then even if they are different, her chances at obtaining truth and knowledge on religious matters would, without further information, seem as high as yours.

Some authors endorse a narrower understanding of epistemic parity, or peerhood, on which two people possess *exactly the same* evidence and competences (Feldman and Warfield 2010: 2). This would imply that, in the highly complex area of religion, there are virtually no epistemic peers (King 2012). Defining epistemic parity this way is one strategy for rejecting premise 1. But it fails to take the problem of religious disagreement seriously (Lackey 2014), for a major aspect of this problem is that you may be missing something, be it certain evidence or competences. Articulating the problem of religious disagreement requires the broad notion of parity outlined here.

Much speaks for premise 1. Religious matters are complex, and nobody can have all the relevant evidence about them – not least because there is some evidence that you can only get by *practicing* a religion (Cottingham 2005, chapter 5). Nor can a single person develop all the relevant competences in one lifetime. And we likely know and respect people with incompatible beliefs about religion to ours. Even if not, we have sufficient evidence that they exist. It would be the height of intellectual arrogance, the thought goes, to suppose that our evidence and competences are superior to everyone else's.

Now consider premises 2 and 3. Taken together, they form the view known as *conciliationism*: that religious peer disagreement requires both parties to weaken their confidence or even abandon their beliefs (Christensen 2007; Elga 2007; Feldman 2007). This view stands opposed to the *steadfast view*, which holds that peers can legitimately maintain their beliefs at their original levels of confidence despite RD-evidence (Plantinga 2000a; Kelly 2005; Conee 2010; Bergmann 2015, 2017). We'll see how these general epistemological views play out in the case of religious disagreement.

Zoom in on premise 2, the claim that RD-evidence, against the backdrop of your other evidence, speaks against your beliefs. I am thinking of *evidence* broadly, as a person's representational experiences and (internally) justified beliefs (Conee and Feldman 2004).[1] Premise 2 says that RD-evidence makes your beliefs less likely to be true than otherwise, given your other evidence. For a piece of evidence does not speak alone, but only against the backdrop of one's other evidence. For example, even the experiential evidence of the shining sun, supporting your belief that the sun is shining, works alongside your implicit belief that your eyes are functioning. Because of this, the extent to which RD-evidence speaks against your beliefs depends partly on your other evidence. Premise 2 assumes that most everyone has the sort of background evidence, for example about the complexity of the world, that makes RD-evidence speak against their beliefs at least somewhat.

There are two ways in which RD-evidence might speak against your beliefs about religious matters. One is direct: The sheer number of belief systems incompatible with yours, adhered to by admirable people, makes it statistically unlikely that *yours* is the accurate one. The second is indirect. Rather than impugning your beliefs themselves, it impugns the way you formed them. Compare: If you believe that 436 + 387 = 816 because you added in your head, and an epistemic peer insists instead that the answer is 823, you have reason to second-guess your calculation. Similarly, religious disagreement by epistemic peers gives you reason to suspect that your evidence or competences misled you.

Premise 3 makes a claim about the epistemic consequence of premises 1 and 2, supposing they are true: that you should weaken your own beliefs about religious matters, that is, hold them less confidently than before (Gutting 1982; Quinn 2000; McKim 2001), or completely abandon them in favor of belief suspension (Feldman 2007; Schellenberg 2007).

Why endorse premise 3? Because you think that a person's total evidence exerts a legitimate epistemic influence on his beliefs, which he (epistemically) ought to abide by. After all, from our internal perspective, evidence is our biggest clue to the way things are. And the fact that an epistemic peer forms a belief that is incompatible with yours indicates that something has gone wrong somewhere. At most, one of two incompatible beliefs can be true, and

---

[1] Those who construe evidence as knowledge or as externally justified beliefs can substitute for "evidence" "the considerations internal to one's perspective that one has to go on in forming beliefs."

because we cannot take a God's-eye view of the situation, we are not in a position to conclude that it is definitely ours.

Thus the Argument from Religious Disagreement threatens your beliefs about religious matters. At least, it does if you care about evidence. Otherwise you might adopt a *strong fideist* response: You might agree with the premises and conclude that you epistemically ought to adjust your beliefs, but deny that epistemic oughts matter most. For example, an atheist may prefer to maintain her strong atheist beliefs despite RD-evidence because of peer pressure. Or a religious person might prefer to maintain his strong religious beliefs because he thinks this is what faith requires.

But if you do care about evidence, you must respond in another way.

14.1.1 Denying the Evidence (Denying Premise 1)

One strategy for resisting this argument is to deny premise 1 – to deny that RD-evidence obtains.

Religious pluralists deny the first conjunct of premise 1. They hold that belief systems pertaining at least to the major world religions are simultaneously accurate at a general level (Hick 1989; Harrison 2006). But even supposing this is true, it cannot dissolve the problem of religious disagreement. First, there are other less common religious belief systems beside the major religions. Second, there are disagreeing atheists. Third, many people disagree with religious pluralism itself. Fourth, there is still intrareligious disagreement.

A more promising route is to deny the second conjunct of premise 1, that those who disagree with you about religious matters are on an epistemic par with you. This *denial-of-parity* strategy takes on many forms. When it comes to large worldview questions, it typically has a negative and a positive component. The negative component maintains that *disagreeing interlocutors are epistemically disadvantaged*; the positive one says that *you (or your community) are epistemically advantaged*. These components can be offered separately, but typically they form a package.

One such package is intended for religious believers. It is part of a more general religious epistemology that we may call *divine-help epistemology* (Plantinga 2000b; Moser 2010; Bergmann 2015). It claims that the world suffers from a theologically significant form of imperfection, typically called "sin," which manifests itself in our behavior, but also in our cognition. People cannot obtain knowledge about God unless God helps us overcome sin's effects. The *negative* part of this package says that those who disagree with you about religion do so because God has not (yet) helped their cognition, making them epistemically disadvantaged on religious matters. The *positive* part says that God has specially inspired the cognition of your belief community, making you epistemically advantaged on religious matters.

A similar package is available to the nonreligious (Rini 2017). It claims that your epistemic community shares your values. Naturally, you take these to be good values, so they should influence your beliefs. *Negatively*, this package says that you may regard community outsiders, because they do not share your values, as epistemically disadvantaged. *Positively*, it lets you regard your community as epistemically advantaged.

Either package, if true, falsifies premise 1. For they say that those who disagree with you about religious matters are not on a par with you epistemically – they are worse off, and you are better off.

The starting premises of these packages are not inherently problematic. The theological story about sin has been developed with nuance. And the idea that group values can promote epistemic aims is familiar in science, the epistemic success of which can be explained by values such as self-criticism and respect for evidence (Anderson 1995).

But the denial-of-parity strategy as a whole is epistemically problematic. It separates people into epistemic in-groups and out-groups: the epistemically privileged and the rest. It is a "discrediting mechanism" (McKim 2001: 136), epistemically demoting outsiders a priori, without evaluating the merits of their particular views. Discrediting mechanisms are problematic. Often people reject community beliefs not just due to epistemic shortcomings, but for reasons the community could learn from (Dormandy 2018a; Lougheed 2018). For example, outsiders may be uncomfortable with the way an accurate doctrine is communicated, with the way it is misused to hide wrongdoing, or with supposed implications that it may in fact not have. (Think of how religious texts were misused to justify slavery and eugenics.) Dialoguing with dissenters may epistemically benefit the community – in many religions, epistemically valuable dissent is provided by prophets. This does not obligate communities to heed all dissenters (think of neo-Nazis); but they should not be demoted en masse.

One might object that demoting people from parity a priori does not commit you to ignoring insights they do have – you can learn from them when the occasion warrants. But matters are not so simple. Once an insider/outsider division has been established, it encourages in-group members to perceive out-group members through the lens of implicit, epistemically demoting stereotypes (Fricker 2007). The result is twofold. First, insiders are less apt to judge outsiders as having worthwhile insights at all. Second, even if an insider does deem an outsider's views worth engaging with, she is disposed to evaluate them more negatively than if they were given by an in-group member (Saul 2013). Because this psychological process is implicit, she will mistakenly take herself to be evaluating the out-group member's view on its merits (Saul 2013). This disposition is very hard to uproot without eliminating the in-group/out-group mentality that creates the stereotypes to begin with. But the denial-of-parity strategy does the opposite – in sanctioning the epistemic in-group/out-group distinction, it promotes such stereotypes.

One might object that some claims to epistemic privilege are true. For example, scientists legitimately claim epistemic superiority when nonscientists disagree with well-established scientific claims, such as that the earth is round. The denial-of-parity claim about religious matters, says the objection, is epistemically no different from the claim that Flat Earthers are not on a par with scientists.

But there is an important epistemic difference between scientific communities and communities defined by religious or secular adherence. Science builds dissent among scientists into its belief-forming practices, and these practices enjoy broad acceptance outside the scientific community – Flat Earthers and the like being rare exceptions. In contrast, communities defined by religious or secular adherence do not typically have belief-forming methods about religious matters that are broadly accepted outside their community. When on top of this they epistemically demote outsiders a priori, they take on the character of *echo chambers,* deliberately and systematically excluding outside evidence and viewpoints (Nguyen 2018).

Echo chambers are epistemically problematic. First, they desensitize their members against nuanced thinking and perceiving, for the cognitive categories they use to make sense of new information become, for lack of challenge, oversimplified. To see how, note that a healthy way to respond to challenging new information is to find an equilibrium between adjusting one's cognitive categories in light of it and interpreting it in light of one's categories. Echo chambers do only the latter.

Second, epistemic "insiders" in an echo chamber, who demote anyone who disagrees with them, thereby threaten their own epistemic reliability. They risk becoming more self-assured than they deserve and may be lulled into overlooking their epistemic shortcomings (Medina 2013). And to the extent that their community is an echo chamber, they face little accountability. This is so even if their beliefs are generally accurate. Think of epistemic communities, which for argument's sake we may suppose have largely accurate beliefs, whose members cannot bring themselves to believe (truly) that their leaders have committed abuse.

Of course, this does not mean that religious or secular communities do not enjoy any epistemic privilege. On the contrary, whichever communities (if any) are aided by God, or employ the most truth-conducive values, are in better shape than others. But the way to stay in epistemic shape, I'll argue, is not to demote outsiders a priori from epistemic parity. It is to engage with them hoping to learn something (Section 14.2).

In summary, a community that applies the denial-of-parity strategy risks overlooking important insights from community outsiders and becoming an echo chamber.

14.1.2 Denying that the Evidence Is a Big Deal (Denying Premises 2 or 3)

Even if you accept premise 1 and thus acknowledge the existence of RD-evidence, you might deny that it is a big deal. This makes you a proponent of the steadfast view. Depending on which version you adopt, you might deny premise 2 or 3.

Consider premise 3, the claim that, if there is RD-evidence and this speaks against your beliefs, you should adjust or even abandon your beliefs. One might deny this by claiming that respecting your evidence is not the most important thing, epistemically speaking. But what else would make beliefs epistemically good? A frequent answer points to some externalist factor, such as the reliability (Goldman 1979), competence (Greco 2010), or proper functioning (Plantinga 2000b) of the way you formed your beliefs, or whether your beliefs are reasonable, apart from the evidence of disagreement, from a God's-eye view (Kelly 2005). Some steadfasters who deny premise 3 argue that, because your beliefs have one of these qualities, you are epistemically permitted to maintain them even though RD-evidence speaks against them (e.g., Kelly 2005; Bergmann 2015, 2017).

But even if epistemic goodness does hinge mainly on external qualities, evidence is part of your internal perspective. And many externalists regard a coherent internal perspective as a minimum epistemic constraint (Goldman 1979; Plantinga 2000b). Because of this, even they typically claim that you must reconcile RD-evidence, as well as other counterevidence, with your original beliefs (e.g., Plantinga 2000b). One might think that this is doable. After all, your beliefs have a good chance of being true given their externalist merits, making RD-evidence likely misleading. For example, suppose God exists. In this case, the existence of atheist epistemic peers is just misleading evidence against his existence that arises from a fallen world. Or suppose there is no God. In this case, evidence *for* God's existence may come from perceptions and arguments laden with cultural baggage.

But RD-evidence, even if it is misleading, is particularly hard to counter. After all, by hypothesis your disagreeing interlocutor is your epistemic peer: He has evidence or competences that you lack. Addressing the RD-evidence so that it no longer speaks against your beliefs may be a tall order.

For this reason, some steadfasters deny premise 3 in a different way. Rather than rely on an external source of epistemic goodness for your beliefs, they agree that evidence is important – but they claim that it is *permissive*: it can be interpreted variously. This means that any given body of total evidence – including RD-evidence – can support a range of incompatible doxastic attitudes (i.e., levels of confidence, beliefs) toward a given proposition (Kelly 2014b). For example, it might support strong or weak belief in some religious doctrine, or weak belief and suspension of judgment. Just as science is not always clear about which hypothesis scientific findings support, evidence about religious matters can be similarly ambiguous. So RD-evidence, together with your other evidence, might on one interpretation speak against your beliefs, whereas on another interpretation it might not. One interpretation might make conciliation inevitable, but another might legitimate keeping your beliefs. Premise 3, the claim that RD-evidence *requires* conciliating, would be falsified.

However, even if evidence is permissive, not anything goes. Any body of evidence will support a *limited range* of doxastic attitudes toward a given proposition. Which doxastic attitudes fall within that range depends on what is reasonable given your total evidence – of which RD-evidence is only one part. So if epistemic permissiveness is to support the steadfast view, we must say more about a person's total evidence about religious matters.

This brings us to premise 2, the claim that RD-evidence, against the backdrop of your other evidence, speaks against your beliefs about religious matters. One version of the steadfast view denies this premise. This view tends to be limited to the special case of *religious* disagreement, although variations could be applied to moral or political disagreement too. This view divides evidence about religious matters into two mutually exclusive categories, where one category tends to support your own beliefs about religion more than the other does. It then argues that evidence in the former category can be weighted more heavily than evidence in the latter. In this case, supposing you have the right background evidence, RD-evidence need not speak against your beliefs at all, making premise 2 false.

The two categories of evidence may be called *impartialist* and *partialist* (Dormandy 2018b). Impartialist evidence includes beliefs that even those who disagree with you can affirm, and experiences that they too could predictably undergo in the right circumstances. Examples include philosophical arguments, empirical investigations meeting standards of intersubjectivity, and common experiences such as mundane sense perception or suffering. Partialist evidence includes all other evidence: beliefs that those who disagree with you would *not* affirm, and experiences that – for example because of the different cognitive framework through which other people perceive reality – others would not predictably undergo in certain circumstances. Examples include religious experiences (Alston 1991), community doctrines, and the testimony of community authorities on religious matters (Zagzebski 2012). In addition, van Inwagen posits "incommunicable evidence" that supports your view even though you cannot articulate it to others (2009); and Plantinga and Bergmann posit a feeling of veridicality that you have in entertaining your beliefs, which Plantinga calls "doxastic experience" and Bergmann calls "epistemic intuitions" (Plantinga 2000b: 203–204; Bergmann 2017). Every person tends to have a mixture of impartialist and partialist evidence in their total evidence.

Partialist evidence is more likely to support your beliefs, since it is colored by them – all the more so if it legitimately includes incommunicable evidence, doxastic experiences, and the like. Impartialist evidence, though it can support your beliefs, is more likely to include considerations speaking against them. For impartialist evidence is *not* particularly colored by your own belief system.

RD-evidence is impartialist. To have it, you need only recognize that there are various incompatible belief systems concerning religious matters, and adopt a notion of epistemic parity that does not exclude others a priori simply because of their disagreement with your community-specific beliefs.

This brings us to the steadfast strategy for denying premise 2. It starts with the claim that beliefs about religious matters should reflect your total evidence. This is a common evidentialist claim; the steadfast strategy adds a further claim. It says that you are entitled to assign partialist evidence a good deal of evidential weight, whereas you typically need not assign much weight to impartialist evidence (Alston 1991; Gellman 1993; Plantinga 2000b; Moser 2010). Thus, your partialist evidence, when weighed against your impartialist evidence (including RD-evidence), can count for more. As a result, your total evidence is apt, to a greater or lesser extent depending on what precise partialist and impartialist evidence you have, to lend greater support to your original beliefs. If you are an atheist, your total evidence is prone to support atheist-friendly beliefs; if you are a religious believer, it is prone to support your religious beliefs.

Why should partialist evidence receive greater weight? For religious believers, for whom this view was developed, the idea is that God communicates in a more detailed and direct way through partialist evidence. Think of divinely gifted community tradition, scripture, and religious experiences. Impartialist evidence, in contrast, is less tradition-centered and more ambiguous. Moreover, much evidence *against* religious beliefs tends to draw on impartialist considerations. For example, everyone can agree that there is suffering (impartialist evidence), but nonbelievers use this to argue for God's nonexistence. And everyone can agree that scientific methods are applicable to the natural world (the results of science amounting to impartialist evidence), but nonbelievers use this to argue against the supernatural. Supposing, as religious communities do, that there is a God and that their partialist evidence reliably points to him, weighting it more heavily promotes accurate beliefs about religious matters.

This strategy might seem promising for those whose beliefs *are* reliably formed and thus largely accurate. But what if your beliefs are not accurate? In this case, privileging your partialist evidence, colored by a largely inaccurate belief system, will likely make your beliefs more inaccurate yet. For example, permitting Flat Earthers to privilege their partialist evidence will entrench their flat-earth beliefs. So this strategy carries great costs for those starting off with inaccurate beliefs (Dormandy 2018b).

But perhaps surprisingly, this strategy is epistemically problematic for those with accurate beliefs too. Privileging partialist evidence over impartialist evidence (including RD-evidence) risks complacency or even dogmatism. The risk of echo chambers (Section 14.1.1), with their desensitizing of people against nuanced thinking and perceiving, arises here too. Even when you start with accurate beliefs, if you rely too heavily on partialist as opposed to impartialist evidence, you risk perceiving more things as fitting neatly with your beliefs than they really do. For example, even if you are right that there is a God, you may incline too much toward interpreting events as divine intervention. Thus, allowing people to systematically give greater weight to partialist evidence is likely to gradually corrode the accuracy even of belief systems that start off accurate.

One might think that being aware of this risk can position you to avoid it. Certainly, being aware of it is better than not. But even if you are aware of the general risk, a partialist evidence-weighting policy will make it hard for you to recognize specific instances where this risk plays out. For your partialist evidence will typically support your already existing beliefs.

In summary, denying any of the premises of the Argument from Religious Disagreement – at least in the ways canvassed here – comes with epistemological problems. Is our only option to accept the conclusion that you should weaken or even abandon your beliefs about religious matters? This is epistemically problematic too. For it would result in no one's having beliefs, at least confident ones, about religious matters at all – to say nothing of morality, politics, and philosophy. Widespread agnosticism about complex and important matters would result. This would significantly *reduce* knowledge about them – all the more so given that certain knowledge, especially about religion, is only available through the lens of committed belief (Cottingham 2005, chapter 5).

I have two proposals in response. The first is an alternative epistemology to the steadfast strategies just discussed. To see what it is, note that I criticized the privileging of partialist evidence over impartialist. But one can take this criticism too far, and instead weight *impartialist* evidence more heavily than partialist (e.g., Locke 1979 [1689]; Schellenberg 2005; Philipse 2012). This impartialist epistemology may be right for science, which examines aspects of the world that are accessible to anyone with the requisite tools and expertise. But there are other aspects of reality to which it does not apply. One is knowledge of other people, which draws on individual – partialist – experiences of a person that come from a special relationship. Another is religious matters. For transcendent reality, if there is one, cannot be assumed – being transcendent – to answer to empirical science.

Privileging impartialist evidence is one error made by conciliationists, who endorse the Argument from Disagreement. Specifically, conciliationists privilege a specific type of impartialist evidence – RD-evidence. In so doing, they undervalue a person's other evidence, especially but not limited to partialist evidence, that provides a backdrop for assessing the import of RD-evidence (Kelly 2010). I suggest that, instead of privileging one kind of evidence (or worse, a single instance of one kind of evidence, such as RD-evidence), we should give both types of evidence approximately equal weight,[2] a view I call *egalitarianism* (Dormandy 2018b; Pittard 2019).

Both partialist and impartialist evidence are important. Partialist evidence reflects important insights from individual and community perspectives. Impartialist evidence reflects a common reality to which any belief system must do justice. Privileging one over the other yields the problems just discussed. Giving both types approximately equal weight allows us to take seriously the unique insights of partialist evidence, while using impartialist evidence to restrain dogmatic excess. When RD-evidence is part of our total evidence, egalitarianism is apt to yield more belief adjustment than the steadfast responses discussed above. But it will not typically yield as much as impartialist epistemology might, and certainly not as much as the conciliationism, which only takes account of RD-evidence. Exactly how much adjustment, if any, egalitarianism calls for depends on your total evidence, including but not limited to RD-evidence – so we may think of egalitarianism as issuing in a version of Kelly's Total Evidence View (2010). If you wind up conciliating to a greater or lesser extent, the reason will be because your total evidence guides you this way. If you wind up steadfastly maintaining your view, the reason will *not* be because you have succumbed to an echo chamber, but because this is what your total evidence recommends.

My second proposal is a shift of frame. Until now we have construed religious disagreement as a *threat* to your beliefs. But what if we changed the frame to one of *opportunity*? Religious disagreement could then be something we might learn from – about our own beliefs, about others' beliefs, or about ultimate reality.

The opportunity mindset moves away from the question of how to respond to the bare fact of RD-evidence. It asks a different question entirely: how can you make the most, epistemically, of the remarkable fact that there are people on an epistemic par with you who nonetheless think dramatically different things about religious matters?

---

[2] Egalitarianism is not to be confused with the Equal-Weight View, a form of conciliationism about peer disagreement (Elga 2007). Egalitarianism says you should ascribe equal evidential weight to partialist and impartialist evidence generally. Elga's Equal-Weight View is limited to RD-evidence, and says that each disagreeing interlocutor should respond to it by moving their degree of belief equally toward the other person's.

14.2 Religious Disagreement as an Epistemic Opportunity

The threat mindset is more psychologically natural. Our minds seek coherent beliefs, especially on worldview matters, and religious disagreement presents claims that upset coherence. The opportunity mindset is more psychologically challenging. It requires a tolerance of ambiguity and cognitive dissonance, for example between the comfort of one's familiar beliefs and the acceptance that they may not tell the whole story (Festinger 1957; Solomon, Greenberg, and Pyszczynski 1991).

I'll argue that the opportunity mindset is epistemically preferable to the threat mindset. But first, why must we choose one over the other? The reason is that the two mindsets have diametrically opposed affective profiles. The threat mindset is characterized by negative emotions such as anxiety or defensiveness, the opportunity mindset by positive emotions such as excitement or curiosity. These affective profiles activate incompatible neurological and physiological circuits. As a result, they have different, incompatible, effects on our belief-formation.

Why is the opportunity mindset epistemically preferable? Because it is apt to reduce the psychological stress of the ambiguity and cognitive dissonance associated with religious disagreement. And so it can help disagreeing interlocutors engage with each other less defensively than otherwise. This matters, because when we are feeling defensive, we are more prone to cognitive distortions such as confirmation biases and stereotyping (Kahneman 2011). Transitioning from the threat mindset to the opportunity mindset can help excise dogmatic tendencies, helping us appreciate insights in interlocutors' views and weaknesses in our own. This claim is subject to empirical confirmation, but it stands to reason given the psychological power of positive reframes.

I'd like to highlight one epistemically advantageous behavior that the opportunity mindset facilitates: engaging respectfully in religious disagreement. My claim is this (Dormandy 2020):

The Epistemic-Potential Claim: Engaging respectfully in religious disagreement for the sake of learning new things about ultimate reality has the strong potential to promote epistemic aims concerning religious matters, to a greater extent than avoiding it does.

The idea is that you and disagreeing interlocutors discuss your respective beliefs charitably and open-endedly – not to persuade, but to appreciate how the world appears from the other perspective. You might pursue various epistemic aims, such as knowledge, evidence, or understanding.

The Epistemic-Potential Claim is analogous to a claim about science: that engaging in respectful disagreement helps you hone hypotheses by yielding evidence, objections, and alternative perspectives (Longino 1990). But the analogy is not complete. One difference is that scientists ideally regard their hypotheses with neutral detachment, whereas people are often *committed* to many of their beliefs about religious matters. But this is not the hindrance that one might think. Recall that we are dealing not with isolated beliefs but with belief *systems*. So even if you cordon off certain core beliefs you are unwilling to revise, there is likely an outer layer of beliefs that are revisable without significant disruption.

The Epistemic-Potential Claim does not state an epistemic requirement. It is thus unlike Basinger's rule, which posits an epistemic duty in the face of RD-evidence to reexamine your beliefs (Basinger 2002). Rather, the Epistemic-Potential Claim – in the spirit of the opportunity mindset – issues an invitation. For those interested in improving their epistemic situation vis-à-vis religious matters, engaging in religious disagreement is a promising way.

I'll discuss two epistemic advantages of the opportunity mindset – specifically of engaging in religious disagreement.

First, engaging in religious disagreement can provide constructive external criticism of your beliefs, which you could not easily generate alone (Dormandy 2020). To see how, note that belief systems are held together by a network of background beliefs, many of which remain implicit unless attention is called to them – and many of which can be mistaken (Longino 1990). Take for example the belief, long operative in the Christian church, that scripture is authoritative on scientific matters. This proved false, at least as the church understood it, when scientific disagreement produced overwhelming evidence for heliocentrism. Recognizing this helped the church better understand how authority is best ascribed to religious texts. Moreover, belief systems about religious matters rely on beliefs *not* directly pertaining to religion, but that serve as *auxiliary beliefs*. Some auxiliary beliefs concern metaphysics: Assumptions about God's relation to time, for instance, may affect our understanding of how God relates to us. Other beliefs, as in the heliocentrism case, are empirical. Yet others are epistemological. For example, many of the arguments presented in this chapter do not draw on religion but are highly relevant to it. It often takes a disagreeing interlocutor to notice implicit auxiliary beliefs that you are unaware of, and that may or may not be essential to your core beliefs.

Second, engaging in religious disagreement can expand your evidential basis (Dormandy 2020). It provides you not just with bare RD-evidence but also, more interestingly, with information about your interlocutor's evidence. This matters, because evidence is not "out there" in the world; it consists of experiences and beliefs filtered through another's perspective. Your evidence is just as filtered as your interlocutor's, just differently. So learning about the evidence of someone with radically different filters to you can significantly expand your evidential basis, providing a more representative sample of the kinds of evidence one can have. This will challenge your belief system – in the positive sense of the opportunity mindset – to accommodate this radically different evidence.

The Epistemic-Potential Claim faces objections from religious nonbelievers and believers alike. A nonbeliever might endorse the *not-worth-taking-ser-iously* objection. Surely, this says, engaging seriously with people who believe in a transcendent reality is like a scientist engaging seriously with a Flat Earther. Some views are just too outlandish to learn from. In response, flat-earth disagreement differs significantly from religious disagreement. Scientists and Flat Earthers, ostensibly both working from an impartialist epistemology, are answerable to publicly available evidence – which heavily favors the scientists. But nonbelievers and believers operate (or should operate, I've argued) with an egalitarian epistemology, which recognizes the importance of personal experiences and community testimony. Atheists no less than religious believers should, and do, incorporate these in their total evidence for atheism, and by parity of reasoning are not in a position to dismiss the partialist evidence of religious believers.

Many objections against the Epistemic-Potential Claim come from religious believers. The *divine-help* objection says that God has already graced you or your community with reliable belief-forming processes (Plantinga 2000b). Because of this, engaging in religious disagreement would merely provide *misleading* evidence – so you shouldn't do it if you want epistemic benefits. In response, suppose for argument's sake that the believer or her community does receive divine epistemic help. Nonetheless, if she is to deny the Epistemic-Potential Claim, she must construe divine help very strictly (Dormandy 2020). First, it must make her or her community *impervious* to error – on nonreligious as well as religious matters. For as we saw, religious beliefs hang together with nonreligious auxiliary beliefs; and it would be a highly micromanaging God – not portrayed in any major traditions – who would *guarantee* true beliefs on politics, science, and so forth. Second, the believer must deny that God would use religious disagreement to provide insight. This requires construing the history of most religious belief systems – which drew on massive religious disagreement with outsiders, as well as with heretics or marginalized prophets inside religious communities – as aberrations not to be repeated.

The *objection from risk* says that even if the Epistemic-Potential Claim is true, it is still epistemically better to avoid religious disagreement. For dis-agreement may yield evidence against one's religious beliefs – and the pro-spect of a few epistemic improvements is not worth the risk of compromising the (true) beliefs you already have.

In response, engaging in religious disagreement does involve risk. But whether this risk is prohibitive for religious believers depends on how it weighs against the risks you take with the alternative course of action, avoiding religious disagreement (Dormandy 2021). For this courts substantial risks too. First are those discussed above, associated with the threat mindset in response to the Argument from Disagreement. The most extreme risks include cultivating echo chambers or foregoing important discoveries – for example, that certain moral or political beliefs that you think your religious beliefs imply are in fact extraneous add-ons. (Again, think of the idea that Christian scriptures legitimated slavery.)

Second, deliberately avoiding disagreement might create the impression that your religious beliefs *could not* withstand scrutiny – which could be more epistemically and psychologically troubling than disagreement itself.

Third, deliberately avoiding religious disagreement in a community may generate the impression that acceptance in the community is linked to epistemic conformity. And this is epistemically dangerous. It risks promoting a warped view of God (or whatever you call ultimate reality) as valuing strict doxastic obedience over understanding powered by love.

Finally, the *loyalty objection* comes from religious traditions positing a personal God. It says that, because religious beliefs are a gift from God for knowing and relating to him, treating them like any other hypothesis by engaging in religious disagreement is disloyal.

In response, engaging in disagreement does not entail treating your religious beliefs like a hypothesis. First, we saw that this is compatible with maintaining core beliefs while being open to adjusting others, including beliefs that turn out to be human add-ons. Second, engaging in religious disagreement might be motivated not by disloyalty but by fascination to learn how God operates outside your immediate experiences. This could actually be loyal: Rather than expecting God to speak through the filter of your concepts, beliefs, and community, you trust him to be who he is and to reveal aspects of himself in other contexts too. For if God really is ultimate, he (or she, or they) will explode our categories anyway. A loyal fascination with knowing God better may include hunger to experience how God does so (Dormandy 2021).

In summary, the opportunity mindset, and with it the Epistemic-Potential Claim, presents an epistemically richer and more promising alternative to the threat mindset.

14.3 Conclusion

Religious disagreement can be troubling. There are strategies for blocking any epistemic significance it may have. You can deny the epistemic parity of most or all people who disagree with you, or you can insist on according their disagreement very little epistemic weight. But I argued that these strategies create more epistemic problems than they solve – even if the belief system that you are defending is largely accurate. Religious disagreement should only be evaluated alongside your other evidence, where partialist and impartialist evidence are weighted equally – with more varied results than conciliationist or steadfast views. But rather than frame religious disagreement as a threat to be defended against, I advocate embracing it as an opportunity. Whatever the truth about religious matters, it is better served not by defensiveness, which hampers our rational capacity, but by curiosity, which expands it.[3]

---

[3] Many thanks to Jonathan Fuqua, John Greco, and Tyler McNabb for very helpful comments on this chapter.

15 Franciscan Knowledge

Lorraine Juliano Keller

Introduction

In "Francis and Dominic: Persons, Patterns, and the Trinity," Eleonore Stump (2000) introduces the term "Franciscan knowledge" for a type of nonpropositional knowledge that includes, but is not limited to, knowledge by acquaintance. Examples include certain sorts of self-knowledge, knowing music (without being able to identify it), and knowledge of other persons through second-person experience and narratives. Perhaps most importantly, Stump claims that we can have Franciscan knowledge of God. Although Stump admits that she cannot give a classical definition of Franciscan knowledge in terms of necessary and sufficient conditions, what unifies all the examples she cites is their being instances of "knowledge which cannot be reduced to knowledge *that*" (2010: 52). In her influential monograph, *Wandering in Darkness: Narrative and The Problem of Suffering*, Stump appeals to Franciscan knowledge in her response to the problem of evil, and a number of other philosophers appeal to Stump's account, or to some version of it, in their accounts of nonpropositional knowledge, interpersonal knowledge, and knowledge of God (e.g., Benton 2018, Duncan 2020; Efird and Worsley 2017; Keller 2018a; Wolterstorff 2016).

The main purpose of this chapter is to explain what Franciscan knowledge is and to discuss some of the ways it has influenced recent work in the philosophy of religion. However, the overwhelming tendency in contemporary epistemology is to either ignore or reject nonpropositional knowledge (with the occasional exception of knowledge-how). Because nonpropositional knowledge is so controversial, an important task for the defender of Franciscan knowledge is to explain why it's plausible that this category of nonpropositional knowledge exists. Hence, another task of this chapter will be to offer a modest defense of the very existence of Franciscan knowledge.

This chapter will proceed as follows. In Section 15.1, I explain Stump's account of Franciscan knowledge. I first give a general overview and then focus on Franciscan knowledge of persons through second-person experience and narratives. In this section, I also defend the existence of Franciscan knowledge from an objection targeting its nonpropositional status. I argue that Franciscan knowledge deserves a place in our noetic taxonomy.

Section 15.1 has three subsections in which I briefly canvas three different ways that Stump's account of Franciscan knowledge of God has influenced recent philosophical work. In Section 15.1.1, I explore Stump's own appeal to Franciscan knowledge in her response to the problem of evil. As part of her defense, Stump appeals to Franciscan knowledge gained through narratives that describe "a world in which God exists and has morally sufficient reason for allowing human beings to suffer" (2010: 61).

In Section 15.1.2, I discuss the use of Franciscan knowledge to defend apophaticism in the work of David Efird and David Worsley (2017). Efird and Worsley appeal to Franciscan knowledge of God to resolve a tension in apophatic theology between the claims that God is ineffable and that we will know God fully in the beatific vision.

Finally, in Section 15.1.3, I discuss Matthew Benton's development of an account of second-personal knowledge that he contrasts with Stump's account of Franciscan knowledge (2018). Benton defends the existence of *interpersonal knowledge*, a kind of nonpropositional knowledge that one person can have of another, and applies this account to knowledge of God. While Benton acknowledges the similarity between his own account and Stump's, he thinks it is a shortcoming of Stump's account that we can have Franciscan knowledge of the nonexistent (e.g., fictional characters). I defend Stump's view from Benton's criticism by pointing out that there are degrees of Franciscan knowledge: Stump can use this aspect of her account to distinguish a kind of Franciscan knowledge of persons that is existence-entailing from lesser degrees of Franciscan knowledge that are not.

15.1 Stump on Franciscan Knowledge

Stump introduces the distinction between Dominican and Franciscan knowledge in her paper, "Francis and Dominic: Persons, Patterns, and the Trinity" (2000). The basic distinction is between knowledge of truths, that is, knowledge that can, in principle, be linguistically expressed and put in propositional form, and the multifarious kinds of knowledge that evade such characterization. Following the Medieval practice of typology, Stump associates the former with St. Dominic and the latter with St. Francis of Assisi. Though both were founders of mendicant religious orders, Dominic evangelized primarily with the force of argument, while Francis evangelized primarily with the force of his personality. Likewise, Dominican knowledge is characteristic of discursive reasoning, while Franciscan knowledge is the sort of direct, immediate, and intuitive knowledge we gain from personal experiences and narratives.

In *Wandering in Darkness*, her monumental work on the problem of suffering, Stump utilizes Franciscan knowledge to address what she views as a significant shortcoming in analytic epistemology that has had a negative influence on philosophy of religion: its obsession with propositional (i.e., Dominican) knowledge (2010: chapter 3). This is the sort of knowledge that we express with "that"-clauses (i.e., sentences of the form 'S knows that p'), and it is standard to construe the relata of this knowledge relation as a (typically human) subject and a proposition – hence the label *propositional* knowledge. Part of the reason for analytic epistemology's focus on propositional knowledge is that knowledge is standardly defined as true belief plus the satisfaction of some normative condition (e.g., justification, warrant, safety, or being the outcome of a reliable or virtuous process), where belief itself is assumed to be a relation between a subject and a proposition. If knowledge entails true belief and belief is propositional, then knowledge must be propositional.

With the exception of some accounts of knowledge-how – on which there's a lively debate between intellectualists, who hold that knowledge-how is a species of knowledge-that, and anti-intellectualists, who hold that knowledge-how is a distinct species of knowledge – nonpropositional knowledge has been virtually ignored in the mainstream analytic epistemology literature. When it is not ignored, it is usually greeted with skepticism: there's close to a consensus that any putative example of nonpropositional knowledge can ultimately be reduced to, or analyzed in terms of, propositional knowledge.

But ignoring or denying the possibility of nonpropositional forms of knowledge leads analytic philosophy to stumble when it approaches persons and interpersonal relationships. As Stump explains, "In case the thing being characterized is not amenable to crisp definition and precision, then, paradoxically, the vague but intuitive Franciscan approach will be more accurate than the Dominican approach, whose search for an unavailable accuracy will result in carefully patterned mischaracterization" (2010: 42). Furthermore, since God is personal, this also hampers the analytic approach to understanding God. Stump sums up the centrality and importance of Franciscan knowledge thus:

For Francis, God is personal, and the personal nature of God is most fully revealed by Christ. The ultimate foundation of reality for Francis . . . is thus also personal, and for that reason knowledge of it will be a knowledge of persons. (2010: 47)

Historically, when analytic philosophers have acknowledged a type of nonpropositional knowledge, it's typically been knowledge by acquaintance or knowledge-how. Bertrand Russell (in)famously argued for the distinction between knowledge by description and knowledge by acquaintance in *The Problems of Philosophy* (1912), and Gilbert Ryle argued for the distinction between knowledge-that and knowledge-how in *The Concept of Mind* (1949). Though it encompasses knowledge by acquaintance, which is primarily a knowledge of one's own first-person, conscious experiences, the most important example of Franciscan knowledge is knowledge of persons gained through second-person experience and narratives. Stump argues that Franciscan knowledge of persons is distinct from, and cannot be reduced to, knowledge by acquaintance.

The primary way we gain knowledge of another person is through second-person experiences. Second-person experience comes in degrees, and Stump cites the following set of necessary conditions that are also sufficient for a *minimal* degree of second-person experience:

A person A has second-person experience of another person B only if:

(1) A is aware of B as a person,
(2) A's personal interaction with B is of a direct and immediate sort, and
(3) B is conscious (Stump 2010: 76–7).

Second-person experience requires that one be conscious of another person as a person and as *other*. By contrast, first-person experience involves direct and immediate awareness of a person, but not as other (since it's simply experience of oneself), and third-person experience can give one knowledge of another person, but not in virtue of being conscious of them *as* a person. As Stump explains, "[I]t is necessary for a second-person experience, as it is not for a first- or third-person experience, that you interact consciously and directly with another person who is conscious and present to you as a person, in one way or another" (78).

To be clear, Stump does not deny the obvious truth that we can have third-personal knowledge of other persons. For example, a doctor can learn a lot of facts about a patient before meeting them by consulting their chart and medical history. But the type of knowledge the doctor gains in this way is *propositional* knowledge. Stump's contention is that there's an important way that we gain knowledge of other persons that cannot be conveyed propositionally. For example, the sort of knowledge the doctor gains when she meets her patient for the first time is knowledge she could not have gained by reading a list of facts about her patient.

To make this point, Stump introduces a twist on Frank Jackson's famous thought experiment about Mary, the neuroscientist imprisoned in a black and white room (Jackson 1982). Stump asks us to imagine that Mary, instead of being deprived of all color experience for her entire life, is deprived of all personal interaction as well as the experience of watching movies, reading plays and novels, or having any experience that could convey second-person knowledge in narrative form. Yet Mary has complete scientific knowledge of people, knowing all of the theoretical information that can be expressed in propositional form. Imagine, then, that Mary is finally released from her confinement and meets her mother for the first time:

When Mary is first united with her mother, it seems indisputable that Mary will know things she did not know before, even if she knew everything about her mother that could be made available to her in non-narrative propositional form, including her mother's psychological states. (2012: 53)

Given that the knowledge Mary gained when she personally interacted with her mother for the first time cannot be expressed in propositional form, it seems that this sort of second-person knowledge is incommunicable. Stump, however, does not take this extreme position, and instead presents a nuanced view according to which Franciscan knowledge of persons can be communicated. Stump acknowledges that though the knowledge gained through second-person experience cannot be expressed in propositional form, it can find limited expression in narrative form, which can function as a sort of simulacrum of second-person experience. As Stump explains,

A story takes a real or imagined set of second-person experiences of one sort or another and makes it available to a wider audience to share. It does so by making possible, to one degree or another, for a person to experience some of what she would have experienced if she had been an onlooker in the second-person experience represented in the story. That is, a story gives a person some of what she would have had if she had had unmediated personal interaction with the characters in the story while they were conscious and interacting with each other, without actually making her part of the story itself. (2010: 79)

This is why it was important to her thought experiment that Mary was not only deprived of second-person experience, but also of the sort of narrative forms that convey second-person experience. If Mary had had access to stories about her mother before she met her, or if the doctor had had letters from her patient before they met, then Mary and the doctor would have been in a position to gain (some) Franciscan knowledge of the persons they had not yet interacted with. However, the knowledge of other persons gained through narratives is not equivalent to second-person experience – engagement with a narrative about a person does not give you second-person experience of that person (2010).

My primary focus here is on Stump's account of Franciscan knowledge of persons, but it will help to understand the nature of Franciscan knowledge in general to look briefly at some of its other forms. Another example of Franciscan knowledge that Stump cites is the ability to know (or, as we might put it, recognize) music that one hears without knowing the title of the piece, who is performing it, and who composed it (2010: 52). Imagine, for example, that my daughter comes into the kitchen while I'm playing music on a speaker and exclaims, "I *know* this song!" but she cannot name the song and does not know who is performing it, etc. This is a sort of immediate, direct, perception-based knowledge that seems distinct from propositional knowledge. What my daughter knows cannot be put into words.[1]

---

[1] Note that it will not suffice to say that what my daughter knows in this case is *that* she knows this song, for that is knowledge of her own mental state, which is distinct from her knowledge *of* the song.

Stump also cites Dominic Lopes' work on knowledge mediated by pictures (what Lopes calls "knowledge-in") that is not equivalent to knowledge *about* pictures. Lopes claims that we gain a certain sort of knowledge by perceiving a picture that is not reducible to knowledge of facts *about* the picture (the medium, the artist, etc.): "A still life by Chardin depicts a collection of objects as appearing in a certain way, and grasp of the picture requires only that its viewer see the objects in it; but seeing-in is arguably non-propositional" (Lopes 2005: 37).

To summarize, Franciscan knowledge encompasses the variety of forms of knowledge that cannot be reduced to propositional knowledge, including knowledge of oneself and one's first-person experiences, knowledge of other persons, and certain sorts of knowledge of music and pictures (Stump 2010: chapter 4). Franciscan knowledge of *persons* can only be acquired through second-person experiences and narratives.

According to one standard objection, putative cases of nonpropositional knowledge are either (i) ultimately reducible to propositional knowledge or (ii) not knowledge after all. In a recent paper, Katalin Farkas presents this objection to accounts of irreducibly nonpropositional knowledge of persons (Farkas 2019). Farkas does not discuss Stump's account of Franciscan knowledge of persons, but she discusses a somewhat similar account of interpersonal knowledge defended by Matthew Benton (2017). I will discuss Benton's view below; for now, the important point of similarity between Stump's and Benton's accounts to keep in mind is that both claim that there is a sort of knowledge of persons that can be acquired through personal interaction and that is irreducible to propositional knowledge. I will present Farkas' objection and show how it can be modified to apply to Stump's account.

Farkas first objects that interpersonal knowledge is really a form of propositional knowledge. She then considers a response on behalf of the defender of interpersonal knowledge and modifies her objection, claiming that any nonpropositional aspects of the relevant states are noncognitive and, hence, do not qualify as knowledge.

Farkas first objects that interpersonal knowledge is ultimately reducible to propositional knowledge: it is best understood as a type of propositional knowledge that requires a special sort of causal interaction. By analogy, she considers perceptual and testimonial knowledge, which are arguably cases of propositional knowledge that require causal interaction with an object or another subject. It's plausible, she argues, that interpersonal knowledge is like perceptual or testimonial knowledge: it essentially involves a certain sort of experience of another person *not* because it is nonpropositional, but because its justification or production requires that sort of experience.

Farkas concedes that, *prima facie,* this objection misses something important: as she puts it, "interactions are important because they produce and sustain not only propositional knowledge in each of the participants, but also an interpersonal relationship between them" (2019: 270). The worry is that, insofar as this objection treats interpersonal knowledge as being analogous to testimonial or perceptual knowledge, it misses the importance of "considering another subject as a subject" or, as Stump puts it, being aware of them as a person (Stump 2010). Interpersonal knowledge seems to essentially involve this element of relationship or being aware of the other as a person, and *not* mere causal interaction. In this way, it differs from forms of knowledge that merely require causal interaction with a person for their production or justification.

Farkas goes on to dismiss this worry because she thinks that the distinctive features of interpersonal knowledge (viz., an interpersonal relationship or the attitude of considering another as a subject) are noncognitive. Since the distinctive features of interpersonal knowledge are not cognitive features, but rather the holding of certain social and emotional attitudes toward another person, she argues that these features do not amount to knowledge: to be included in the genus of *knowledge* requires being a sort of *cognitive* achievement. Because what makes interpersonal knowledge *seem* irreducibly nonpropositional is its basis in interactions with salient social and emotional overtones (which are noncognitive features), Farkas concludes that there does not seem to be a distinctive, irreducibly nonpropositional *knowledge* of persons.

But there is a problem with Farkas' objection for the purposes of our discussion: because it is concerned with a theory of interpersonal knowledge that *requires* what Stump would call "second-person experience," it misses the mark where Franciscan knowledge is concerned, since Franciscan knowledge (as we saw) can also be gained through narratives. On Stump's view, Franciscan knowledge of persons can be gained without *any* relationship or second-person experience of the other, even in cases where the other is a fictional character. So, it cannot be said that, on Stump's view, personal interactions or relationships are *required* for the production or justification of Franciscan knowledge of persons.

However, I think that Farkas' objection can still be pressed against Stump's account of Franciscan knowledge. Although Stump does allow for narratives as a vehicle for Franciscan knowledge of persons, recall that this is *because* they simulate second-person experiences. It seems fair to say that, for Stump, the fundamental way of gaining Franciscan knowledge of persons is *via* second-person experience, and that the sort of knowledge gained through narratives is a lesser degree of knowledge that is based on the ability of the subject to have second-person experiences. Narratives could then be seen as making certain propositions available to the subject by simulating second-person experiences. The reader imagines herself to be having second-person experiences that then make the relevant propositions about the persons she is "interacting" with accessible to her. Again, reiterating the contours of Farkas' objection stated above, the emotions that the reader experiences while engaging with the text are certainly rich and important aspects of her experience, but they are not cognitive achievements and so do not change the nature of her knowledge state – it remains propositional knowledge.

The upshot of Farkas' objection, as modified to apply to Stump's account, is that second-person experiences and narratives do not give subjects nonpropositional knowledge of other persons; rather, they are required for the production or justification of Franciscan knowledge. Just as perceptual knowledge is distinctively perceptual and testimonial knowledge is distinctively testimonial because they are produced (or justified) by perceptual or testimonial experiences, so Franciscan knowledge is distinctively second-personal because it is produced (or justified) by second-person experiences (either directly or in a mediated form, through narratives). And just as perceptual and testimonial knowledge do not fail to be propositional because of the way they are produced (or justified), so with Franciscan knowledge of persons.

To set up my response to Farkas' objection, it will be helpful to consider the nature of *propositional* knowledge in more detail in order to draw attention to its limitations. On a currently widely accepted way of thinking about propositions, they are abstract, mind- and language-independent bearers of truth-value that are the potential referents of "that"-clauses and are expressible (in principle) by declarative sentences (in contexts of utterance). Propositional knowledge consists in believing true propositions (and fulfilling the relevant normative conditions), which would seem to require grasping the relevant propositions. Grasping a proposition can come about in many ways: David reads a book and comes to learn that lizards lack eyelids by grasping a sentence in the book that expresses the proposition *lizards lack eyelids*; Izzy learns that the cucumber plants have sprouted by observing the sprouts emerging from the soil and forming the belief that has the proposition *the cucumbers have sprouted* as its content; etc. One can come to grasp a proposition in a linguistically mediated way (reading) or in a nonlinguistic, experiential way (observing), among other ways. However, propositional knowledge can, in principle, be linguistically communicated as the literal content of declarative sentences. If David and Izzy met the requisite normative conditions and, so, had knowledge in the cases we considered, then David's knowledge would be testimonial and Izzy's would be perceptual. Notice that because their knowledge is propositional, it is readily communicable to others. Izzy can utter the sentence, "The cucumber plants have sprouted" and pass along this information to her sister, Maggie. Since David's knowledge was transmitted to him linguistically, it's obvious that he can pass along the information that he learned too.

Now recall Stump's thought experiment involving Mary and what she learns when she meets her mother for the first time. The point of that thought experiment was that what Mary learned could *not* have been transmitted to her as the literal propositional contents of declarative sentences. What Mary knew, when she met her mother for the first time, was not something that could be linguistically transmitted through fact-stating discourse – her second-person experience of her mother did not merely put Mary into a position of being able to grasp some new propositions *about* her mother. By interacting with her mother, Mary comes to know *her*, not just a list of facts about her (which she could have had access to in her confinement).

But perhaps putting things in this way makes it seem like I'm just asserting that Mary's knowledge of her mother isn't propositional, or saying, "Can't you just see that what she learns is not propositional?" I want to try to give some more positive, substantive reasons for thinking that what Mary knows is not only *not* propositional but deserves to count as knowledge. For Farkas acknowledges the importance of interpersonal interactions but does not think that what they "add" amounts to a cognitive achievement; hence, they do not produce a *sui generis* form of knowledge.

One reason for thinking that Franciscan knowledge is not propositional is that propositional representation is digital, whereas states like acquaintance and second-person experience involve analog representation (cf. Camp 2007; Dretske 1981; Duncan 2020). For example, the proposition *Maggie's shirt is red* represents Maggie's shirt as being red, but not any particular shade of red. Contrast this with David's visual experience of Maggie's shirt, which represents it as having a particular shade (or perhaps multiple shades) of red, having a subtle round oil stain just above the chest, and being slightly torn on the left side of the collar, etc. Propositions simply cannot capture the richness of David's experience. When David is acquainted with the redness of Maggie's shirt, what he knows cannot be captured in propositional form. Similarly, propositions cannot capture Mary's second-person experiences of her mother in all of their richness. In a frequently quoted passage, Fred Dretske vividly illustrates the difference between digital and analog representation:

> If I simply *tell* you, "This cup has coffee in it," this . . . carries the information that the cup has coffee in it in digital form. No more specific information is supplied about the cup (or the coffee) than that there is some coffee in the cup. You are not told *how much* coffee there is in the cup, how large the cup is, *how dark* the coffee is . . .. If, on the other hand, I photograph the scene and show you the picture, the information that the cup has coffee in it is conveyed in analog form. The picture tells you that there is some coffee in the cup by telling you, roughly, how much coffee is in the cup, the shape, the size, and the color of the cup, and so on. (1981: 137, quoted in Camp 2007 and Duncan 2020)

I would add that actual experience of the coffee supplies even more rich detail that is left out by the photograph, such as the coffee's aroma, for example. It does not seem fair to deny that this sort of multifaceted, analog representation is a *cognitive* achievement.[2] Thus, the resulting state, which cannot be captured or conveyed propositionally, is (arguably) *knowledge*.[3]

One important complication to address here is Stump's claim that Franciscan knowledge of persons can be conveyed through narratives. How can narratives, which are linguistic items, convey knowledge of persons, if *not* propositionally? I understand Stump to be claiming that narratives, though expressed linguistically, do not convey Franciscan knowledge by expressing propositions as the literal contents of the sentences that constitute them. Rather, narratives are linguistic vehicles that allow readers to imaginatively enter into simulated second-person experiences. It is those simulated *experiences* that convey Franciscan knowledge of persons, though in an attenuated way.

My defense of Stump's claim that Franciscan knowledge is irreducibly nonpropositional is unlikely to satisfy those who are thoroughly convinced that all knowledge is propositional. However, I hope to have at least provided further reason for giving this claim serious consideration.

15.1.1 Franciscan Knowledge and the Problem of Evil

One of Stump's main reasons for invoking Franciscan knowledge in *Wandering in Darkness* is to construct a novel response to the problem of evil. In this subsection, I'll present the basic elements of Stump's defense, focusing on the important role Franciscan knowledge plays in it.

Stump's aim is to describe "a world in which God exists and has morally sufficient reason for allowing human beings to suffer" (2010: 61).[4] According to Stump, God's reason for permitting us to suffer is God's love for us: God wants our ultimate and unending flourishing, which can only come about through union with God. Central to Stump's defense is her embrace of Thomas Aquinas' scale of value, according to which the greatest good for human beings is an unending union of love with God and the greatest evil is unending separation from God, with its accompanying mental fragmentation and self-alienation (388). Stump's general explanation of God's permission of

---

[2] This is not to say that Mary's Franciscan knowledge of her mother consists merely of a very rich phenomenal experience – it's not just Mary's first-person experience of her mother but her *second*-personal experience of her mother that contributes to her non-propositional knowledge when she meets her mother for the first time. As Stump is at pains to point out, however, it's not possible to describe (propositionally) what Mary knows, and to suppose one could do so would be incoherent (2010: 52–3).

[3] See Duncan 2020 (especially 2.1) for further arguments defending the claim that non-propositional knowledge of things is genuine knowledge. Duncan's arguments could also be applied *mutatis mutandis* in defense of Franciscan knowledge.

[4] According to a standard way of distinguishing a defense from a theodicy, if her description is taken as merely possibly true, then it is being taken as a defense; if it is taken as actually true, then it is being taken as a theodicy. For simplicity, I will just refer to it as a "defense."

human suffering is its contribution to attaining the greatest good and warding off the greatest evil for human beings (372). In essence, our experience of suffering helps us to attain a union of love with God and to avoid eternal separation from God. God is morally justified in permitting our suffering because we are the primary beneficiaries of the suffering God permits, and the good that results from our suffering outweighs the badness of the suffering itself (14).

The crucial question for Stump to address is why suffering would be required for our attainment of union with, or avoidance of separation from, God. Stump's answer to this question draws heavily on Aquinas' moral psychology. To do justice to all of the nuances of Stump's implementation of Aquinas' moral psychology is beyond the scope of this chapter, so I will settle for presenting the basic contours of the account; I direct the interested reader to Part 2 of *Wandering in Darkness* for the details.

One important claim about human moral psychology that Stump adopts from Aquinas is that a human being can only be fully integrated around the good. Any desire for evil will thus always cause internal fragmentation in a human person. However, because of the fall "all human beings have a latent disease in the will" that inevitably leads to our choosing to do evil: "people not only will what is morally wrong; they cling tenaciously to the moral wrong they will. They not only fail to will the good; they also fail to will to will it" (155, 153). Thus, we all "lack internal integration to some degree" (156).[5] This internal fragmentation makes us incapable of a true union of love not only with God, but with other persons as well.

In order to overcome this condition of "willed loneliness," it's not enough to simply decide we don't want to be in this state anymore (156). As Stump explains, a person's

> lack of internal integration is just her unwillingness to unify herself in will. She is not internally integrated in will because she does not *want* to be . . . . So the defect in the will is such that it could be fixed by the person who has it only if she did not have the defect. (159)

Not even God can miraculously fix a person's defective will: "Mutual closeness of the sort required for union depends on an agreement between two different wills. But, if God determines [a person's] will, then the only will operative in [that person] is God's will" (159). Hence, the union of a person's will with God's can only be achieved by the cooperation of that person with God.

---

[5] Stump acknowledges that many of her readers do not accept the doctrine of original sin. All that's needed for the purposes of her defense is to accept the fairly obvious fact of the human propensity to moral wrongdoing, and that this propensity does not impugn God in any way (2010: 156).

The problem is that post-fall human beings have no desire for their own internal integration and no desire to cooperate with God's grace. This is where the necessity of suffering comes in: through suffering, our hardened hearts begin to crack, and even a tiny opening is enough for God's grace to enter and start to work. Our experience of suffering, while not initially having the effect of making us cooperative with God's grace, at least helps us to lower our resistance to it. Once our resistance is lowered, we are able to experience God's love and to start to *desire* the union of love with God that is our ultimate happiness.

Stump follows Aquinas in claiming that the remedies for the human propensity to evil-doing and its concomitant willed loneliness are the processes of justification and sanctification (152). However, she understands these processes as being essentially second-personal (172). As she puts it, "A second-person connection of love between God and a human person is... what justification and sanctification aim at and effect" (172). Justification is the process whereby a person stops resisting God and is able to receive the grace of justifying faith (168). This grace, freely given by God and able to be received when the person finally stops actively preventing it, grants the person the higher-order volition to will union with God (which is consistent with her still having first-order volitions that are not compatible with this union). Sanctification, which follows justification, is the process whereby God strengthens the justified person so that her first-order volitions are in accord with her higher-order will to be united to God. Both justification and sanctification "unite [a person], in increasing degree, with God in love" (166).

Both justification and sanctification, insofar as they essentially involve surrender to and cooperation with God, not only aim at a particular second-personal state (viz., union with God) but are second-personal processes. They can be described from a third-person perspective but are more easily grasped when presented in narrative form, which allows them to be understood from a second-person perspective. It's instructive in this regard also to notice that some of the most compelling narratives that portray the processes of justification and sanctification are written largely in the second person, being addressed to God – think, for example, of Augustine's *Confessions* or St. Teresa of Avila's *Life*.

Justification and sanctification are processes by which people attain Franciscan knowledge of God, either through narratives or through second-person experience of God. So, Franciscan knowledge plays a role within Stump's defense as characterizing the process by which God uses suffering to regenerate fallen human beings and draw them into relationship with God. Franciscan knowledge also plays a role in Stump's presentation of her defense, as she uses the Biblical narratives of Job, Abraham and Isaac, Samson, and Mary of Bethany to illustrate how God permits suffering to bring about the ultimate good for human beings.

15.1.2 Franciscan Knowledge and Apophaticism

In their paper, "What An Apophaticist Can Know: Divine Ineffability and the Beatific Vision" (2017), David Efird and David Worsley invoke Stump's distinction between Dominican and Franciscan knowledge to help resolve a tension between the apophaticist claims of divine ineffability and the promise of knowing God fully, as we are known, in the beatific vision. They explain the tension between these two doctrines as follows:

> If God is beyond description and comprehension, if He is in some sense unknowable, how on earth (or in heaven) can we come to have *full* knowledge of Him? Conversely, if it turns out that we can know Him even as He knows us, in what sense can God be considered ineffable at all? (2017: 208)

The doctrine of divine ineffability is central to apophatic theology. Efird and Worsley characterize it, roughly, as the claim that God is "beyond description, or beyond human concepts" (208). As they point out, apophaticism was ubiquitous among the theologians of the church in the first few hundred years. Yet so also was adherence to the claim that we will know God fully in the beatific vision (call this "beatific knowledge"). It seems highly unlikely that so many church fathers accepted a blatant contradiction. Efird and Worsley argue that the claims of divine ineffability and beatific knowledge can be shown to be consistent if we distinguish between two different kinds of ineffability. They show that the doctrine of divine ineffability can be understood in two different ways by invoking Stump's account of Dominican and Franciscan knowledge.

Efird and Worsley first point out that Franciscan knowledge itself is, in some sense, ineffable, since it cannot be propositionally expressed. They call this type of ineffability "propositional ineffability" (211). They go on to argue:

> If knowledge of other persons can be propositionally ineffable, (in Stump's modified thought experiment, the knowledge Mary gains as she learns what it is like for her mother to love her would be propositionally ineffable), it is easy to see how God, too, could be, in some comparable sense, propositionally ineffable (simply replace Mary's mother with God in Stump's modified thought experiment). (211)

Efird and Worsley highlight a significant difference between the propositional ineffability involved in Franciscan knowledge of persons and the propositional ineffability of God. They claim that it is consistent with Stump's account to say that when Mary met her mother for the first time, she could have been learning something old in a new way; that is, Mary's Franciscan knowledge of her mother "is in some sense captured by what was previously known, namely, pertinent propositional knowledge" (216, fn. 10). But, they claim, this is not a possibility for Franciscan knowledge of God – this cannot consist of learning something old in a new way, since we can know nothing of what God is like intrinsically or fundamentally in propositional form.

I disagree with Efird and Worsley's interpretation of Stump on this point: I think it is inconsistent with Stump's stated position to claim that Mary's Franciscan knowledge of her mother could be captured propositionally. Stump is adamant that Franciscan knowledge is irreducibly nonpropositional. So, it seems to me that the crucial difference between other persons and God with respect to propositional ineffability is that nothing about what God is like intrinsically can be perspicuously propositionally expressed, but we *can* make true intrinsic predications of other persons. Efird and Worsley are right to claim that God is propositionally ineffable. But I don't think that the fact that we can express facts about the intrinsic natures of other persons propositionally means that Franciscan knowledge of them can in some sense be expressed propositionally. What we learn through Franciscan knowledge are not facts about a person's intrinsic nature – we don't (only) come to know new facts about them (even facts that could only be known through direct experience), we come to know *them.*

Efird and Worsley claim that God is propositionally ineffable: "God remains both beyond (fundamental) description and beyond (fundamental) human concepts, in that knowledge of him can never be fully comprehended by or captured in (fundamental) descriptions or concepts" (214). This is how they interpret the apophaticist doctrine of divine ineffability. They reconcile the doctrine of divine ineffability with beatific knowledge by claiming that beatific knowledge of God is Franciscan knowledge. As they put it, God is "propositionally ineffable but personally effable" (205).

To allay worries that claiming that God is personally effable weakens the doctrine of divine ineffability too much, Efird and Worsley point out this claim supports the doctrine that God has revealed Godself to humankind through creation, the incarnation, and scripture.

If Franciscan knowledge can be transmitted through second-personal experience and narrative as Stump maintains, and if God has indeed revealed something, indeed anything, of Himself in a creation we can experience through second-personal interaction in the incarnation or through the narratives in scripture, it looks like God cannot be personally ineffable (214).

Thus, Efird and Worsley make use of Stump's account of Franciscan knowledge in a creative way to reconcile the doctrines of divine ineffability and beatific knowledge.

15.1.3 Franciscan Knowledge or Interpersonal Knowledge?

In "Epistemology Personalized" (2017) and "God and Interpersonal Knowledge" (2018), Matthew Benton develops an account of interpersonal knowledge, which is a state not of an individual mind, but of two individuals who "know each other personally, as subjects, from the second-person perspective" (2018: 421).

To differentiate interpersonal knowledge from other sorts of knowledge of persons, Benton distinguishes three grades of personal involvement: the first grade consists of propositional knowledge of facts about a person gained without direct causal interaction with them; the second grade consists of propositional knowledge gained through perceptual access to a person (including mediated access through screens or images), though the causal direction of knowledge goes in one direction (from the person known to the knower); the third grade of personal involvement requires treating the other person as a subject and two-way interactions between the two persons (423–4). Though the first two grades of personal involvement result in knowledge-*who* (i.e., the ability to distinguish someone from other people), neither suffices for knowing someone personally. Only the third grade of involvement results in interpersonal knowledge.

Like Franciscan knowledge, interpersonal knowledge is nonpropositional. Benton writes:

Interpersonal knowledge ... is not the kind of thing that can be built up out of knowing more and more propositions about someone, or by gaining more qualitative knowledge of them. And interpersonal knowledge is autonomous relative to any particular propositions known about a person, in this sense: for any set of propositions one knows about someone, one could in principle know that someone personally without knowing those particular propositions about them. (423)

According to Benton, interpersonal knowledge requires two-way, personal encounters in which each person treats the other second-personally (424). The requirement of personal encounters leaves open the possibility that, for example, I could be said to have interpersonal knowledge of my grandfather, who died when I was 11, given that we causally interacted with each other and treated each other second-personally in the past. However, Benton thinks it's plausible that interpersonal knowledge should fulfill a stronger condition of symmetry: a person A interpersonally knows a person B only if B interpersonally knows A (425). If this stronger condition holds, then when my grandfather died, my interpersonal knowledge of him was lost. This is an important point of contention between Benton's account and Stump's: Benton holds that interpersonal knowledge requires the existence of the two subjects involved.

Benton discusses several applications of his account of interpersonal knowledge, but most importantly for our purposes, Benton claims that there can be interpersonal knowledge between us and God. He cites several authors who argue that God is properly known in a personal way, not as an object. Benton also discusses recent accounts of liturgical knowledge that seem to claim we can attain knowledge of God through liturgical practices and rituals in which we address God second-personally.

Benton then turns to Stump's account of Franciscan knowledge. He acknowledges important similarities between his account and Stump's, but then criticizes Stump's account for allowing Franciscan knowledge of the nonexistent (e.g., dead people and fictional characters). Benton traces this defect in Stump's account to her claim that Franciscan knowledge of persons can be gained, not only through second-person experience, but through narratives. Puzzlingly, he says that Franciscan knowledge of persons "primarily comes through by way of narratives," but I cannot find any support for that claim in Stump's work (430). On the contrary, it seems to me that Stump very clearly makes second-person experience the primary way of gaining Franciscan knowledge. She first introduces the concept with the story of Mary, who finally comes to know her mother when she *meets* and *interacts* with her, and none of her five examples of Franciscan knowledge of persons involve narratives (Stump 2010: 54–5). Also, the way Stump describes how narratives impart Franciscan knowledge (by providing a sort of simulacrum of second-person experience) conveys that second-person experience is the fundamental way of gaining such knowledge, while narratives only do so in a sort of derivative way.

Benton argues that the possibility of having Franciscan knowledge of someone who does not exist is a highly counterintuitive consequence of Stump's account. In defense of Stump, I would argue, first, that it seems plausible that we have knowledge (of some sort) of fictional characters. For example, if you take a class on Tolstoy, you might be tested on your knowledge of the characters in *Anna Karenina* by being asked questions like, "Why did Anna leave her husband? How did her decision affect her son, Seryozha? How did Levin's attitude toward his wife change after the death of his brother?" Note that these are all factual questions that one could find the answers to on a SparksNotes page. However, it's very plausible that we gain a different sort of knowledge when we actually read the book, and this includes the sort of knowledge we gain of the characters. We come to know *them*, and not merely a list of facts about them: this is plausibly Franciscan knowledge of fictional characters.

Benton goes on to argue that the fact that Franciscan knowledge is not existence-entailing generates problems for Stump's response to the problem of evil. For on Stump's view, we could have Franciscan knowledge of God even if there were no God. Benton asks, "How does it help with the problem of evil to urge that we might know God (personally), in the Franciscan sense, if one could have such knowledge without there being a God?" (431). I think this criticism misunderstands the role that Franciscan knowledge plays in Stump's defense. Stump does not invoke Franciscan knowledge in any sort of evidential way or to make the claim that God exists more plausible. Rather, as we saw, Franciscan knowledge characterizes the processes of justification and sanctification by which God draws our ultimate good from suffering. Stump's account is presented as a possible world in which God exists and the relevant claims about suffering, etc., hold. The Biblical narratives she uses help facilitate our understanding of why God would permit human suffering. In any case, if interpersonal knowledge in Benton's sense is fallible, it will be subject to the same sort of problem: we might *think* we have interpersonal knowledge of God but be mistaken.

Finally, Stump claims that there are degrees of Franciscan knowledge. I think she could elaborate on this aspect of her view by claiming that the highest degrees of Franciscan knowledge are gained through second-person experiences of a particularly intimate sort. She could claim that this degree of Franciscan knowledge is existence-entailing, while lower degrees attained through narratives are not existence-entailing.

15.2 Conclusion

Eleonore Stump has started an important conversation in philosophy of religion with her introduction of Franciscan knowledge and her use of narratives to address the problem of evil. She has opened up new avenues for addressing topics of the utmost importance, such as the nature of personal relationships and our ability to know God. In this chapter, I've tried to give a basic introduction to Stump's account of Franciscan knowledge, answer some objections to it, and discuss some of the recent ways it has been applied and interacted with. I've had to leave out other intriguing responses to and interactions with Stump's work: for example, Nicholas Wolterstorff (2016) finds points of connection with Stump's account of Franciscan knowledge in his work on liturgical knowledge, and Matt Duncan (2020) acknowledges connections between Stump's account and his account of knowledge of things. But I hope to have given enough of a sense of the excitement of this topic and the intriguing conversations that have opened up to induce the reader to explore further.

16 Liturgically Infused Practical Understanding

Terence Cuneo

In this chapter, I grapple with a long-standing concern about corporate ritualized religious activity ('liturgical activity,' for short).

The worry stems from a trio of observations. The first is that the major monotheistic traditions enjoin having attitudes such as faith, hope, and love, as well as performing actions that express these attitudes. The second is that these traditions call for their practitioners regularly to engage in liturgical activity, participating in rites of corporate worship. There is, however, a condition on whether such activity has religious worth, fittingly relating the community and its members to God: it must align in the right ways with core religious attitudes—in the ideal case, expressing them. The third observation is that liturgical activity systematically fails to align in this way, often being rote, mechanical, insincere, or focused on whether it is being performed correctly.[1] Hence the long-standing worry that liturgical activity systematically fails to have religious worth – or at least its worth is severely diminished or defeated by the lack of alignment. The problem is only exacerbated by the fact that some religious traditions place great emphasis on participating in liturgical activity. This emphasis can seem misplaced, since the conditions under which such activity has religious worth systematically fail to be satisfied.

Several strategies of response present themselves. One is to insist that the lack of alignment just mentioned is either exaggerated or unproblematic. Another is to acknowledge that the lack of alignment between core religious attitudes and liturgical activity is real and problematic but that there are ready ways in practice to remedy it. A third response is to hold that the lack of alignment is genuine and problematic but probably less significant than the worry voiced above alleges. Using the Eastern Orthodox Christian liturgies as my focal case, I develop a variant of this third response to what I'll refer to as the 'alignment worry.'

---

[1] After studying large-scale fire rituals in India, the Dutch linguist and anthropologist Frits Staal concluded that when people perform rituals, they "concentrate on correctness of act, recitation, and chant. Their primary concern, if not obsession, is with rules. There are no symbolic meanings going through their minds when they are engaged in performing ritual" (1979: 3).

The response proceeds on the assumption that liturgy is practical in orientation, being constituted by actions that function to shape us and the world in various ways. The first stage of the discussion sketches an account of practical understanding that could underwrite such action, albeit one that emphasizes the epistemic dimensions of such understanding. How exactly do the church's liturgies function to shape their participants? The second stage of the response lays out a multifaceted vision of the world, human beings, and God that animates and finds expression in the Orthodox liturgies. It is practical understanding of this vision, I suggest, that the church's liturgies function to instill in us. This is the 'liturgically infused' understanding to which the title of this chapter adverts. With these materials in hand, I contend that we have reason to hold that liturgical activity has significant religious worth, even if it has other worrisome features.

I believe the response just sketched blunts the force of the alignment worry. I doubt, however, that it represents a complete reply. For one thing, the reply draws upon the resources of the Eastern Orthodox tradition. But there is a legitimate question of whether anything like those resources is available to other religious traditions. For another, one might wonder whether traditions like Orthodoxy are themselves well situated to draw upon these resources. At the close of this chapter, I revisit these concerns, gesturing toward where further work needs to be done.

16.1 Practical Understanding

Some of us have had the experience of being coerced into taking piano lessons when children. If things went well enough, this experience instilled practical knowledge of how to play the instrument. We learned how to move our fingers to play the correct notes, how to play in time, and how to use dynamics when playing, emphasizing some passages but not others. In addition, we learned when to apply our knowledge-how – when to use the piano's pedals to deaden the sound, play with increased emphasis, or pause for effect. This knowledge-how and knowledge-when coalesced into practical musical knowledge.

The process of learning piano didn't advance much further than this for many of us. But for some the process continued. They learned how not only to perform musical works, but also how to listen to music, appreciating its compositional properties and nuances. Some even learned how to perform musical works with others, learning how and what to pay attention to in these joint performances. Indeed, some have had the experience of progressing to the point at which they developed not just practical musical knowledge, but also musical sensibilities of certain kinds.

By musical "sensibilities," I mean sub-doxastic abilities of a certain range, which involve being sensitive to subtle cues for what a composition or a performance of it calls for, being able to discern whether a composition or performance meets certain levels of adequacy and excellence, and the capacity to experience the performance of a musical work as expressing musical influences of certain kinds. So understood, sensibilities are interpretive and evaluative abilities of a given range. Like many such abilities, articulating their deliverances, let alone the exact features of a composition or performance that they key into, is often extraordinarily difficult. Still, with time, repetition, and training, musical sensibilities can be inculcated, developed, refined, and evaluated, delivering verdicts and responses that are more or less fitting. When developed to a high degree, these sensibilities can be very finely attuned to the nuances of compositions and performances. Although, it should also be said that musical sensibilities can be highly idiosyncratic: it is not as if they simply track extant norms of adequacy and excellence. They can also yield highly novel ways of approaching or engaging in composition, performance, listening, and the like.

I have presented a sketch of musical cognition according to which agents progress from gaining rudimentary practical musical knowledge to acquiring musical sensibilities of certain kinds. I have, however, refrained from calling these musical abilities *skills*. My thinking is simply that practical knowledge can be rote or highly circumscribed, failing to be guided by a grasp of the activity one is performing. Similarly, sensibilities can be developed only to a low degree and exercised indiscriminately. Skills are different. To be skilled in an activity involves being able not only to engage competently in that activity, but also to be guided by one's grasp of that activity in such a way that one can competently engage in it in a wide range of circumstances.

John Campbell draws attention to these features of skills when he writes of tools:

[I]f you understand how a tool works, there will be a certain systematicity in your understanding of it. You will know how to use this tool in a wide variety of contexts, under various permutations of its intrinsic characteristics . . .. The modulation of the pattern of use is systemic, in that the pattern of use covaries with the variation in the standing properties of target and tool. And the modulation of the pattern of use is general, in that the same underlying sets of connections can be exercised in connection with endlessly many different tools. (2011: 174–5; 179)[2]

Campbell's observations about tools extend to the realm of music. You may know how to perform the piano part of a score composed for an ensemble. But if you lack the ability to attend to and coordinate your actions with the other instrumentalists, then you lack a relevant performance skill: your practical

---

[2] Quoted in Bengson (2020: 219). My treatment of practical understanding is indebted to Bengson's essay.

knowledge is too parochial. To possess the requisite performance skills, you must be able to perform your part competently with other instrumentalists in a variety of contexts. Similarly, you may know how to listen to performances of a particular work of music. But if you do not know how to listen to novel interpretations and adaptations of it, then you lack crucial listening skills: your practical knowledge is too narrow. To have the requisite listening skills, your knowledge of how to listen to performances of a piece of music must generalize to unusual adaptations and interpretations of it. Let me reemphasize that more is required than this. For you to manifest the requisite skills, it is not enough that you can exercise your musical abilities in a variety of contexts. In the cases of performance and listening, your abilities must flow from your grasp of what it takes to competently perform or listen to works of music; it can't be merely rote or haphazard.

These observations about practical skills suggest that we need a category of practical cognition that goes beyond practical knowledge. In keeping with recent developments in epistemology, I propose that the relevant category is that of *practical understanding* (see Bengson 2020). It won't be necessary for my purposes to present anything like a full characterization of practical understanding. It is enough to note that having such understanding incorporates elements central to having skill: it involves an agent's grasping a type of activity (and any means used to perform it) in such a way that that grasp both guides and explains that agent's performance of that type of activity in a wide variety of conditions. To have practical understanding of how to listen to a work of music, for example, involves having a grasp of this activity that guides how one listens to performances of that work, including ones that are rather different from those to which one might be accustomed to hearing.

Achieving the type of grasp involved is demanding in some senses, but not in another. It is demanding insofar as it is incompatible with deep or systematic confusion regarding the type of activity in question. Imagine that you know how to play a score for a work of music and, indeed, regularly perform it competently. Your grasp of how to play this piece would not constitute practical understanding if you were deeply confused about its time signature. For in that case, your ability to perform the piece would not flow from and be guided by a correct and stable grasp of some of its most important features. (I should emphasize that this last condition is compatible with an agent's having a variety of misconceptions regarding a work of music, such as who composed it.) Likewise, your grasp would not be of the requisite sort if it failed to cohere with other things one understands about music, such as that a work of music can shift time signatures multiple times. The sense in which practical understanding is not demanding is that agents can understand how to perform an activity without grasping why that activity has certain relevant features. Someone may understand how to improvise over complex chord changes without grasping what accounts for why the use of certain note patterns over certain chord progressions is fitting. In this regard, there is probably a significant difference between practical and theoretical understanding. While the latter typically involves resolving explanatory questions as to why things have certain properties or certain events have occurred, the same is not true of the former. The types of questions that practical understanding resolves are not why-questions but practical ones regarding how to perform a given activity well.

In characterizing practical understanding this way, I have taken a stand on some fairly contentious issues. I've rejected so-called anti-intellectualist views, which minimize the cognitive dimensions of practical understanding, as well as 'explanationist' views, which hold that understanding (of any sort) must incorporate the resolution of why-questions. These maneuvers have advantages. For one thing, they help to make sense of what strikes me as an independently plausible thesis, namely, that gaining practical understanding is a bona fide epistemic achievement. Think of agents who enjoy the types of musical skills mentioned above. These people are admirable not simply because of their musical prowess but also due to their understanding of how to engage with music. Their practical understanding incorporates a grasp of how to perform and listen to music that is stable (it doesn't wax and wane), robust (applies to a wide variety of circumstances), coherent (it fits with their grasp of other core musical activities), and free of deep and systematic confusion. The enjoyment of these features explains why practical understanding is epistemically meritorious.

16.2 The Maximian Vision

Liturgical activity is many things, but worship lies at its core. Worship of God, in turn, is adoration – to use Nicholas Wolterstorff's characterization, it is awed, reverential, and grateful adoration of God (2015: 26). Given the centrality of worship to liturgy, it is a striking and puzzling feature of the Eastern Orthodox liturgies that they so often involve their participants directing their attention to not God but a wide variety of material objects, such as water, oil, bread, wine, chalices, icons, crosses, copies of the Gospels, vestments, and the like. These items elicit a wide range of bodily responses. They range from approaching, viewing, touching, kissing, bowing, and prostrating to eating, drinking, and readying one's body to receive. For example, in the small parishes where I've celebrated Great Lent, at the end of the service of Holy Wednesday, a copy of the Gospels is taken from the altar and placed in the middle of the room on a stand beside an icon of Christ. The people individually file forward, each fully prostrating themselves to the wood floor three times before the copy of the Gospel and the icon. They kiss both, and then proceed to where the Priest stands; he anoints the forehead of each with oil and they kiss a wooden cross held in his hand. The question I'd like to pursue is: Why would the church's liturgies regularly prescribe the performance of actions such as these?

In broad outline, the answer I'll propose is that the liturgies present a multifaceted vision of the natural world, human beings, and God, and how they are and should be related. What the vision endeavors to disclose about the natural world, us, and God is not apparent to the untrained eye; it is obscure in the sense of being largely veiled or hidden. Nonetheless, I want to suggest that this vision informs and helps to make sense of liturgical activities of the sort to which I've called attention. Given that this vision incorporates themes central to the work of the Orthodox theologian Maximos the Confesssor, I'll refer to it as the 'Maximian vision.' The overarching proposal I will develop is that liturgy functions so as to develop in its participants practical understanding of how to view, treat, and experience the world in accordance with the Maximian vision. This proposal will form the core of my response to the concern, which has framed our discussion, about the religious worth of liturgical activity.

Let me identify some themes central to this vision. The first is that God bears a very intimate relation to the natural world. As the tradition tends to characterize it, that relation is not simply that of *being the creator of*. Instead, it involves God being intimately present in the creation in a way (say) that an artist is ordinarily not present in an artifact. The theme of *God being present in* the creation is impossible to miss in the liturgical texts of the church. The Trisagion Prayers, which are probably the most commonly used prayers in the Orthodox tradition, begin with the invocation:

O Heavenly King, the Paraclete, the Spirit of Truth, who is present everywhere, and fills all things, Treasury of Good and Giver of Life, come and dwell in us, cleanse us of every stain, and save our souls, O good One. (McGuckin 2011)[3]

The prayer at once acknowledges the Holy Spirit's omnipresence while also inviting it to inhabit and act in particular ways in those who pray.

The flipside of the relation *God being present in* – namely, *being present in God* – is also widely affirmed in the tradition. In her fine book, *Living in God's Creation*, Elizabeth Theokritoff notes that, when responding to Gregory the Theologian's description of each human being as "a particle of God," Maximos writes:

The one Creator of all enters into all things . . . and the many things that differ from one another by nature come into one, converging around the one nature of man. And God himself becomes all things in all, encompassing all things and giving them real existence in himself. (2009: 61)[4]

---

[3] I lightly modify the translation from the Greek.

[4] Maximos is echoing Gregory of Nyssa: "That God should have clothed himself with our nature is a fact that should not seem strange or extravagant to minds that do not form too paltry an idea of reality. Who, looking at the universe, would be so feeble-minded as not to believe that God is all in all; that he clothes himself with the universe, and at the same time

It is because of claims of the sort made in this last sentence that Bishop Kalistos (Ware) of Diokleia writes that he finds "no difficulty in endorsing panentheism," according to which God is present in the creation and the creation in God (2013: 90).[5] Ware goes on to note that the tradition has endeavored to find ways of speaking that could make sense of this mutual *being present in*. Most famously, Gregory of Palamas invoked the essence/energy distinction to do so: "God is in the universe and the universe in God, the one sustaining, the other being sustained by him. Thus all things participate in God's sustaining energy but not his essence."[6] To be clear: in highlighting these ideas, my claim is not that the Orthodox liturgies presuppose a form of panentheism. It is rather that the tradition has affirmed a relation between the creator and creation of sufficient intimacy that some of its most prominent voices have seen fit to describe it in panentheistic terms.

The liturgical texts emphasize that God is not simply present in creation, but also active in it. In the Great Blessing of Waters, performed on Theophany, the text likens God's activity in the world to a rescue mission:

For you, being God uncircumscribed, without beginning and inexpressible, came upon earth, taking the form of a servant, being found in the likeness of mortals. For you could not bear, Master, in the compassion of your mercy to watch the human race being tyrannized by the devil, but you came and saved us. We acknowledge your grace, we proclaim your mercy, we do not conceal your benevolence. You freed the generations of our race.

The text does not stop here, however. It voices a second Maximian theme, which is that the activity of redemption extends not just to human beings but to all of creation. In highly poetic language, the text speaks of the significance of Christ's baptism in the Jordan:

Today the grace of the Holy Spirit in the form of a dove dwelt upon the waters. Today the Sun that never sets has dawned and the world is made radiant with the light of the Lord. Today the Moon with its radiant beams sheds light on the world. Today the stars formed of light make the inhabited world lovely with the brightness of their splendor . . .. Today the streams of Jordan are changed into healing by the presence of the Lord. Today all creation is watered by mystical streams . . ... Today all creation shines with light from on high . . ... Today earth and sea share the joy of the world, and the world has been filled with gladness.

---

contains it and dwells in it? What exists depends on Him who exists, and nothing can exist except in the bosom of Him who is." Quoted in Clément (1993: 41).

[5] *Cp.* Theokritoff (2009: 245). One is put in mind of St. Paul's affirmation of "For in him, we live, and move, and have our being" (Acts 17:28).

[6] Quoted by Theokritoff (2009: 64).

The language here does not suggest that the moon, sun, stars, and streams have been emancipated in the way that human beings have. Rather, it suggests that the natural world is being transformed or renewed: "Today the streams of Jordan are changed into healing by the presence of the Lord." The text, then, suggests that human beings are being redeemed in the sense of being rescued, while the natural world is being redeemed in the sense of being renewed – each transformed in its own way. In his extensive work on liturgy, the eminent Orthodox theologian Alexander Schmemann emphasizes that the contrast with which these texts operate is not between the *sacred* and *profane*, or the *natural* and *supernatural*, but rather the *old* and the *new*. Somehow, through divine action, the world is being made new (1973: 120–1).

The upshot – and this is a third Maximian theme – is that, insofar as it is being renewed, the natural world can function as a bridge to God. The sentence just quoted gestures at this idea, but it comes into even sharper focus in the text read during the blessing of the water itself. Echoing the baptismal rite, the blessing calls upon God to act so that

> this water might be hallowed by the might, operation, and descent of the Holy Spirit . . . That [it] may become the gift of sanctification, redemption from sins, for the healing of soul and body, and for every suitable purpose . . . That it may be for the purification of soul and body to all who with faith take and drink of it; let us pray to the Lord.

The point of this passage is not to invoke God's power in order to change the nature of water; there is no transubstantiation. Nor is it to endow the water with special powers of redemption or purification. Rather – or so the dominant interpretation runs – it is to impose on the water a new function. Theokritoff characterizes the imposition as one in which water is "'promoted' to doing the Holy Spirit's work of sanctifying and giving life," extending the ordinary life-giving work that water already does in our daily lives (2009: 185). Schmemann affirms a yet stronger claim. The renewal of the material world not only enables it to function as a conduit to God, but worship also reveals otherwise obscure aspects of the material world's nature. The imposition of a sacramental function on material objects enables us to recognize that the world is "an *epiphany* of God, a means of His revelation, presence, and power." Indeed, "worship is based on an . . . experience of the world as" an epiphany: "the world – in worship – is revealed in its true nature and vocation as 'sacrament'" (1973: 120). As Schmemann understands things, that is more or less what it is for a material object to be a sacrament: it is for it to function as an epiphany of God (1973: 15).

Which leads us to the fourth Maximian theme: our role as human agents lies, in part, in orienting ourselves properly to the creation. Again, Schmemann's work is especially relevant here. His thinking is that this orientation consists in offering thanksgiving or *eucharistia* for the creation and its various elements. In emphasizing this theme, Schmemann is not claiming that offering thanks is the only apt response to the creation; cherishing, loving, revering, and the like are also fitting responses. The thought, rather, is that thanksgiving is the fundamental orientation for human beings to take toward the creation, especially in the context of worship.

The leading idea here echoes the passage quoted above from Maximos: when fulfilling their vocation, human beings play a unifying function in the created order, acting as that which brings the created order into communion with God. That, in turn, consists in their both blessing elements of the created order, such as water and oil, and offering them back to God as a sacrifice. In the remarkable first chapter of his book *For the Life of the World*, Schmemann states the idea as follows:

Human beings stand in the center of the world and unify it in their act of blessing God, of both receiving the world from God and offering it to God – and by filling the world with this eucharist, they transform their life, the one that they receive from the world, into life in God, into communion with God. (1973: 15)[7]

When we combine this passage with the one quoted just above, all four Maximian themes emerge. God is intimately related to the creation (the first theme); worship is founded, in part, on an epiphany that this is so. Human beings are called to bless the creation in worship, offering elements of it back to God as sacrifice (the fourth theme). Such blessing consists in imposing functions of certain kinds on elements of the created order, whereby they can play the role of contributing to the flourishing of human beings and communion with God (the second and third themes).

My primary concern in this section has been to present (a compressed version of) the Maximian vision. I've merely begun to sketch a case for the claim that this vision animates and makes sense of central elements of the church's liturgies. A fully developed case would involve examining the church's liturgies in finer detail, eliciting elements of the vision, while also considering competing explanations of why these liturgies take their particular shape. No liturgical scholar, to my knowledge, has developed such a case. Still, as the quotations from thinkers such as Schmemann, Ware, and Theokritoff indicate, the way has been paved. So, I'll proceed on the assumption that, while a fuller case awaits development, we have powerful reason to hold that the Maximian vision animates and explains puzzling but important elements of the church's liturgies. Or to approach the matter from the opposite direction, I'll assume that the church's liturgies give expression to the Maximian vision. So expressed, the vision is there for participants in the liturgy to understand. Understanding how to treat, view, and experience the

---

[7] This is an ungendered "quotation."

world and God in accordance with this vision is what I have called 'liturgically infused' understanding of the world and God.

16.3 Liturgically Infused Understanding

At the beginning of this discussion, I noted that while many of us took piano lessons as children, rather few of us emerged with anything more than rudimentary practical musical knowledge. Something similar is true of ritualized religious activity. Although our younger selves were frequently inculcated into religious traditions, the result was often nothing more than rudimentary knowledge of how to engage in these services. To progress further, much more was needed than what we experienced.

In the musical case, the way to progress would typically involve immersion in social practices of certain kinds. Specifically, making such progress would require immersion in practices of performing, composing, and listening, which would facilitate developing the skill-like activities constitutive of practical musical understanding. This, in turn, would ordinarily involve gaining facility with musical traditions of performing, composing, and listening, and the musical visions that animate them. The parallel to religion is close. The route to gaining practical religious understanding (broadly construed) also goes through immersion in social practices, such as religious instruction, study of the scriptures, prayer, fasting, almsgiving, and so forth. I've suggested that achieving liturgically infused understanding would involve immersion in the liturgies of the church wherein the Maximian vision finds expression. But merely absorbing the Maximian vision to some degree through such immersion would not be enough. The grasp of this vision and the ways it is expressed in these liturgies would also need to shape agents' participation in these liturgies.

For example, such a grasp would guide how they listen to, focus on, and interpret texts such as those used during Epiphany. These texts are not just evocative poetry; they express the idea that somehow God is renewing the creation, and that we have a part to play in this. The grasp would also guide the performance of bodily actions such as receiving anointing of oil, viewing it as a rite by which both God and human beings can be active in healing, extending the healing powers already possessed by oil. Moreover, such a grasp would guide how agents view their own performance of these very actions and their subsequent reflections on them. In this case, agents might strive to perform these actions so that they conform to the liturgical scripts but resist making correct performance their focus, as if omissions and mistakes somehow invalidate the ways in which their actions express elements of the Maximian vision. And so forth. At a minimum, a satisfactory practical grasp of the vision that animates the liturgies would guarantee that agents could not view venerating an icon, blessing water, or kissing a copy of the Gospels as simply something that one does in church. Instead, such a grasp would involve grasping that these activities are ones by which God reaches out to human beings and they reach out to God.

Yet making progress to this extent wouldn't be enough to achieve the type of understanding I have in mind. In addition to stably guiding one's activities, grasp of the Maximian vision and how it is expressed would need to cohere with one's convictions about the material world, human beings, and God. Imagine, for example, you were to endorse the Manichean claim that the material world is an obstacle to divine presence, or that the point of liturgical action is to curry God's favor. It is very difficult to see how such views could fit with a practical understanding of the liturgy that is in accordance with the Maximian vision. Or, to emphasize so-called practical coherence, there would be considerable tension between treating the Eucharistic elements with great reverence during enactments of the Divine Liturgy but, say, throwing them in the garbage after the completion of the service. Even if coherence of either sort could be achieved, this would be insufficient for enjoying the type of practical understanding in question. For views such as Manicheanism and what Kant calls religious "fetishism" are seriously mistaken (2018 [1793]). They could not be aspects of a liturgically infused practical understanding of the world and God.

It may be worth acknowledging that I've employed this last phrase deliberately. The phrase suggests that the understanding in question does not pertain solely to what transpires in liturgical settings. The understanding pertains to the world, which includes a good deal more than things liturgical. This point is a natural application of the earlier observation that skill-like activities must generalize in appropriate ways. Understanding how to use a tool, or how to listen to the performance of a work of music, cannot be highly circumscribed; they must be applicable to a wide range of circumstances, even novel ones. The same is true of practical understanding of the type under discussion here.

In making this observation, my concern is not with cases in which agents faithfully participate in the church's liturgies but view such participation as having only very limited implications regarding how they conduct their lives. Rather, my concern is with cases in which agents grasp important elements of the Maximian vision as it is expressed in the liturgies, but this understanding fails to extend to how they treat, view, or experience the world at large. Think of agents who view the liturgies as expressing the Maximian vision but, outside of a liturgical context, treat, view, or experience the material world as devoid of the divine presence, merely there to be used and enjoyed. They do not treat, view, or experience it as a locus of the divine energies or as that which is being renewed by the work of the Holy Spirit. They do not view themselves as playing any sort of unifying function. In short, their understanding of how to view, treat, and experience the world in accordance with the vision fails to generalize. To be clear, the claim is not that a person's liturgically infused practical understanding would be overly restricted were that person to fail (say) to treat all water as if it were holy (blessed) water. That would be no more plausible than maintaining that a person's love of neighbor would be overly restricted were she to fail to treat all fellow human beings as if they are family, friends, or loved ones. In the case of neighbor-love, achieving the relevant ideal consists in recognizing that there are clear limits on how to treat one's neighbors, that there are ends that we should desire for them and often pursue on their behalf, and that we should be prepared to make significant sacrifices to realize these things. These things are true because one's neighbors are fellow bearers of the *imago dei*. Similarly, achieving the ideal of adequately grasping the Maximian vision consists in recognizing that there are evident limits on how to treat the creation, that there are ends we should desire for it and often pursue, and that we should be prepared to make significant sacrifices to realize these things. The creation is, after all, intimately related to God in the ways specified by the vision. The person who has liturgically infused understanding of the world recognizes this and, so, extends their grasp of the Maximian vision beyond the confines of the liturgy to the world at large.

Like Ware, Theokritoff, and others, I believe that these points have substantive ethical implications. But given my present aim of exploring the character of liturgically infused practical understanding, I want to emphasize three points about it.

First, such understanding is distinct from what I earlier called the core religious attitudes, such as faith, hope, and love, and actions that express them. Their intentional objects are different: practical understanding concerns *ways of doing things* (broadly construed), while the core religious attitudes concern persons or propositions. In addition, the type of grasp that constitutes practical understanding is not a species of belief, trust, desire, or the like, which I take to be the primary candidates for the types of attitudes that constitute the core religious attitudes. Indeed, if what I've said is correct, liturgically infused practical understanding involves the possession of religious sensibilities, which are broadly sub-doxastic interpretive and evaluative abilities, and whose deliverances needn't be beliefs, credences, or the like.

To spell this out just a bit: having liturgically infused practical understanding involves grasping *ways of viewing* the world and how God is related to it, *ways of treating* the creation in light of how human beings and God are related to it, and *ways of experiencing* the world in light of how human beings and God are related to it. The implementation of such understanding lies, in considerable measure, in the exercise of these sensibilities. Implementing a way of doing something, such as viewing the world in a certain way, needn't involve believing that things are as that way characterizes the world. I should also emphasize that, while I understand *ways of doing things* broadly so that they needn't involve intentional doings, it may be that grasping ways of viewing, treating, and experiencing the world and God requires intentional agential activity. Just as one may try to hear a work of music in a certain way – say, by intently focusing on some of its features or suspending one's expectations of how it should proceed – so also one may try to view, treat, and experience the world in accord with the Maximian vision.

In distinguishing the cognitive constituents of liturgically infused practical understanding from the core religious attitudes, I do not mean to suggest that they float free from each other. Having this type of practical understanding can be the product of an individual's faith, love, or hope, or an effort to implement or acquire it. It is certainly the product of the community's faith, love, and hope. But I wish to underscore the point that the liturgies appear to do more than generate in their practitioners the core religious attitudes or be activities whereby these attitudes are expressed. Instead, they appear to function so as to get their participants to see, treat, and experience the world and God differently.

The second point I want to make is that having and exercising the type of practical understanding described appears to have considerable religious worth. Grant, for argument's sake, that the Maximian vision is largely accurate. Having practical understanding of the type under discussion is exactly the sort of thing that helps to bring one, and one's community, into fitting relationship with God. My own view is that this worth is not merely instrumental; having and exercising practical understanding of the world, human beings, and God in accordance with the Maximian vision looks like it is not a mere means to something else that has religious worth, such as faith. Instead, having and exercising such understanding appear to be ways of doing things that themselves have religious worth (all else being equal). If that were true, it would make sense of why the liturgy functions to instill such understanding in its participants.

The third point is that having this type of understanding is an epistemic achievement. For it involves an accurate grasp of how to view, treat, and experience the world and God that stably guides action, is free from deep misunderstanding, coheres with one's other views and practical commitments, and generalizes in the way that skills do. What is more, the epistemic achievement in question is not an add-on to the religious worth that such understanding enjoys: instead, there is considerable overlap between what grounds the religious worth of practical understanding and what grounds its epistemic meritoriousness. Think, for example, of the generalizability of such understanding. That is something that both grounds the religious worth of such understanding and its epistemic meritoriousness. The agent who has this ability grasps how to see, treat, or experience the world and God in ways that do not suffer from defects such as being provincial, shortsighted, or arbitrary. (Indeed, it may be that liturgically infused understanding owes its religious worth, in part, to its epistemic meritoriousness.) In this regard, the epistemic status of such understanding looks rather different from other epistemic merits to which epistemologists of religion have devoted extended attention. That one's belief in the existence of God is supported by evidence or reliably formed may have little or no religious worth. But that cannot be fairly said, I believe, of ways of viewing, treating, and experiencing the world and God in accordance with the Maximian vision.

16.4 The Alignment Worry, Again

We are now ready to return to the worry that has framed our discussion. Recall that it runs as follows: the major monotheistic traditions enjoin having core religious attitudes such as faith, hope, and love, as well as performing actions that express them. These traditions also call for their practitioners regularly to engage in liturgical activity. But such activity systematically fails to align in the appropriate ways with the core religious attitudes and actions. Hence the worry that liturgical activity systematically fails to have religious worth, or that its worth is seriously diminished or defeated by the lack of alignment. I said that the response I would offer, which focuses on the Eastern Orthodox liturgies, acknowledges that the worry is genuine but that it is less significant than it might seem. Let me close by explaining why.

The justification for thinking the alignment worry is real hinges on a pair of convictions. The first is based on the empirical observation that liturgical activity is often rote, mechanical, insincere, or primarily focused on satisfying certain correctness conditions of performance. This is the curse of ancient religious traditions. They tend to ossify, being more concerned with self-preservation than anything else. The second is that these deficiencies jeopardize the religious worth that the enactments of liturgies may have due to other factors. For example, enactments of the liturgies may have some religious worth because they are *expressive of* apt attitudes – where, roughly, this is a matter of those liturgies incorporating activities that are fitting ways to express these attitudes (even if their enactments fail to actually express them). But this worth can be severely diminished or neutralized by an enactment's being rote, mechanical, insincere, performed in bad faith, and so forth.

As for why the lack of alignment is probably less significant than it might seem, the following exercise may help to explain why. Imagine that there is a complex property F such that understanding how to view, treat, and experience the world as being F has religious worth. Assume, further, the world's being F is obscure: it is not manifest to most and, even when it is apparent, there are a variety of dynamics that would occlude its presence. Add now that there is an activity that instantiates some aspects of F and, when performed well enough, would position agents to gain the requisite sort of understanding of how to view, treat, and experience the world as being *F*. With these assumptions in place, we can ask whether that activity would thereby have religious worth as well.

I believe it would, as that activity bears a very intimate relation to realizing the religious worth at issue. Think of practices of character formation as a comparison. Having character traits such as kindnesss and wisdom is of moral and prudential worth, yet their worth isn't always apparent; we often need practices that reorient our thinking in order for us to appreciate their value. And we will not acquire these traits on our own; we need to be immersed in practices that are suited to form them in us. These practices, I would say, have moral and prudential worth insofar as they are intimately related to the goal of inculcating admirable traits, playing indispensable roles in achieving it. This is true even when these practices are infrequently successful in this endeavor. In a similar way, the liturgies of the church have religious worth insofar as they are intimately related to the end of achieving liturgically infused understanding, playing indispensable roles in contributing to achieving this good. This is so even when they are frequently unsuccessful in producing such understanding, as they often are.

To spell this out a bit more, consider the complex property specified by the Maximian vision, whose components include *being the locus of divine presence and activity* and *being renewed by God*. That the material world has these properties is hardly manifest; in fact, there are powerful dynamics at work that would occlude recognition that the world has these qualities. Furthermore, the church's liturgies instantiate components of the Maximian vision. The Eucharistic liturgies, in particular, involve acts wherein the church expresses its thanks to God's gift of the world and offers elements of it back to God in sacrifice. Finally, these liturgies appear uniquely calibrated to position agents to gain practical understanding of how to view, treat, and experience the world in accordance with the Maximian vision – viewing, treating, and experiencing the world as one in which God is present and active in particular ways. If all this is correct, then we have reason to hold that enactments of the liturgies have significant religious worth even when they exhibit the lack of alignment described above. For they are uniquely poised to provide agents with liturgically infused practical understanding.

The claim here is not that the 'Maximian property' (as we might call it) uniquely possesses the profile of property *F*. Other properties may as well. Nor is the claim that *F*'s profile is the only thing whose possession would confer religious worth on the church's liturgies. There might be others. The claim is simply that the liturgies have religious worth in virtue of poising their participants to gain practical understanding of the Maximian vision.

I believe the response just offered helps to address the alignment worry. But for reasons canvassed at the outset of this chapter, it is probably not fully adequate.

One limitation is that the alignment worry pertains to not just Eastern Christianity, but also to many other theistic traditions. The response I've developed, however, draws upon resources specific to Eastern Christianity. But a commitment to the Maximian vision is largely alien to other theistic traditions, even other Christian ones; so it is hardly evident that they can feasibly draw upon the resources assembled here. This raises the question of whether the type of strategy I've employed can generalize, being available to other religious traditions in responding to the alignment worry. The honest answer is: I am not sure. I suspect that it can in some cases, but the details would need to be worked out.

A further limitation of the response is that, even if correct, it may gesture toward a deeper concern. The "worry behind the worry" is that Eastern Christianity tends to proceed as if its adherents will absorb the Maximian vision by osmosis. Other theistic traditions appear to proceed similarly. But this looks naive. As the response above concedes, these traditions are infrequently successful in forming agents who enjoy liturgically infused understanding. And so, in a way, the response highlights the limits of what could reasonably be expected from immersion in the church's liturgies. Arguably, for the liturgies to play their formative roles effectively, they must work in concert with other influences. These might include widely accepted interpretations of the functions of liturgy and how to view one's own experience of ritual. As recent empirical work on teaching people how to experience awe illustrates, agents often need to be "primed" in the right way. When agents have firmly in mind that they are looking for what inspires awe, and attend to their own responses of feeling awe, they tend to experience it more frequently in a wider range of conditions (Weger and Wagemann 2021). Something similar may be true of liturgically infused understanding. When an agent firmly grasps the Maximian vision and attends to their own attempts to view, treat, and experience the world and God in accordance with it, they may deepen their understanding of how to do these things.[8]

---

[8] Thanks to John Greco, Tyler McNabb, Kenny Pearce, and Nick Wolterstorff for comments on earlier versions of this chapter.

17 Knowledge-First Epistemology and Religious Belief

Christina H. Dietz and John Hawthorne

The approach to epistemology known as "knowledge-first epistemology" puts knowledge at the explanatory center of things as far as epistemology is concerned.[1] It is pointless to try to carefully investigate which doctrines do and don't belong to knowledge-first epistemology – that would be to confuse a somewhat vague slogan with something it is not. But one can nevertheless identify some important themes that are often found in the work of those theorists that give knowledge explanatory primacy within epistemology. In this chapter we shall present two such themes. In each case, knowledge-first ideas have interesting implications for philosophy of religion.

17.1 Two Themes of Knowledge-First Epistemology

17.1.1 Evidence

The concept of evidence plays some important theoretical roles. It is used to explain why some theories are better supported than others. It is used to explain why it is appropriate to be more confident in some outcomes than others. And it is used to explain why certain choices of action are better than others. One way of giving knowledge center stage is to argue that these theoretical roles for evidence are best served by knowledge. It is worth distinguishing two versions of this idea.

The most radical version takes the form of Williamson's "E=K" equation, which "identifies the total evidence available with the total knowledge available" (Williamson 2000: 189).[2] This thesis is best not advanced as capturing all ordinary uses of the expression "evidence." (As Williamson notes, we may speak of a "bloodied knife" as evidence [2000: 194], but a bloodied knife is not a proposition, and thus this is not an instance of propositional knowledge.) Rather, the idea is that the "central theoretical functions" (2000:194) of

---

[1] The idea of writing about how religious belief connects with knowledge-first epistemology was suggested to us by John Greco. It struck us as a good idea.

The knowledge-first approach is associated above all with Timothy Williamson (2000). This introductory section will draw heavily from that book.

[2] Of course, it is a further matter to explain what makes one's total evidence count as evidence *for* some given proposition.

evidence are best served by an identification of the total body of someone's evidence at a time with the total body of propositions that they know at the time.

It is not hard to muster some prima facie sympathy for the E=K equation. Suppose we ask which hypothesis about whodunnit is best supported by a particular detective's evidence at a particular time. If they know the murder happened at noon and that Jones was asleep at noon, that is surely part of their evidence – in this case exculpatory evidence regarding Jones. And if they don't know that Jones was asleep when the murder happened, then that fact is surely not part of their evidence. If we proceed as if, despite being known, the fact that Jones was asleep at noon was not part of the detective's evidence, we would seem to be ignoring something that is fairly obvious, namely that the detective's evidence is incompatible with the hypothesis that Jones committed the murder at noon. And inclusion of such facts as evidence in the situation when they are unknown would lead us to overestimate what the detective's evidence rules out. Considerations like this make the identification of what one has to go on (i.e., one's total body of evidence) with what's known seem quite natural.

A more guarded idea than E=K is to adopt a conception of evidence according to which one's evidence is a proper subset of one's knowledge (call this the "E to K thesis"). There is one kind of theoretical role for evidence for which the more guarded conception might seem more appropriate, namely explanations of knowledge in terms of evidence. Evidence-based explanations of knowledge are hard to pull off in an E=K framework, since in any setting where one knows p, p will automatically be part of one's evidence. In an E=K framework, explaining the fact that you know something by appealing to the fact that you have good evidence for it is like trying to explain the fact that you know something by appealing to the fact that you know it. For the purpose of modeling knowledge in a way in which evidence plays a distinctively explanatory role for less "direct" kinds of knowledge, it may be helpful to identify one's body of evidence with a subset of one's knowledge. Models of this kind will thus distinguish what we might call "evidential knowledge" – knowledge that is part of one's evidence, from nonevidential knowledge, knowledge that is not part of one's evidence but which is explained, at least in part, by one's evidential knowledge.[3]

---

[3] We find this kind of model, for example, in Goodman and Salow (2018).

We mention in passing an idea that has some affinity with the thesis that any piece of evidence is a piece of knowledge, namely the doctrine that any motivating reason (or what Grice 2001 called "personal reasons") is a known proposition. The idea here is that, at least on the primary use of "one's reason" (the possessive is notoriously context-sensitive so the "primary use" qualification is important here), if one's reason (or one of one's reasons) for doing such and such/believing such and such/feeling such and such is that p, then one knows p. For further discussion see Hyman (1999), Dietz (2018), and Hawthorne and Magidor (2018). We shall not explore the religious ramifications of this idea in this chapter. (For a brief discussion, see Hawthorne and Dunaway 2017).

Of course, one need not be monolithic here. It may be that certain theoretical roles for evidence are best served by models in which one's total evidence is identified with the totality of known propositions, while others are best served by identifying one's total evidence with a suitably chosen subset. If the name of the game is to precisify the concept of evidence in a way suitable for this or that theoretical role, different roles might cry out for different precisifications.

Returning to the bolder E=K thesis, it is worth noting three upshots of that conception that will be particularly relevant to the discussion below.

First, it will tend in many settings to make questions about an individual's total evidence very tendentious. Insofar as one what one knows is a matter of dispute, the nature and limits of one's body of evidence will be up for dispute too. Thus, as Williamson emphasizes, the principle of "Evidence Neutrality," according to which "whether a proposition constitutes evidence is in principle uncontentiously decidable" (Williamson 2007: 210), will fail dramatically.

Second, there will be limits on one's access to one's own evidence from the inside. Assuming that sometimes one knows without being in a position to know that one knows (what are sometimes called failures of "positive introspection"), there will be cases where one has p as part of one's evidence but is unable to access the fact that p is part of one's evidence; and assuming that sometimes one is in no position to know that one lacks a certain piece of knowledge (what are sometimes called failures of "negative introspection"), there will be cases where p is not part of one's evidence but one is unable to access the fact that p is not part of one's evidence.

Third, the phenomenon of "knowledge defeat" will be somewhat problematized. What we have in mind by knowledge defeat is the alleged phenomenon where a person's knowledge is present at one time but blocked at a later time by the acquisition of information of which the person is unaware at the earlier time.[4] The natural way to account for defeat is to appeal to the fact that a body

---

Note that the E=K proponent might stick to their guns and insist that it is a mistake to think that certain kinds of knowledge can be explained by anything like the fact of a proposition's being well supported by some restricted subset of one's knowledge. For example, a safety-style E=K theorist might insist that what explains knowledge even in cases of "indirect knowledge" (like inductive knowledge) is not the quality of the evidence but the fact that at no close world does the method generate false belief. The explanatory role of the "more direct" evidence is not nothing – it will presumably show up as part of the method whereby the inductive knowledge is acquired – but there still may be no real need to impose a distinction between evidential and nonevidential knowledge.

[4] Sometimes the idea of defeat is introduced using much broader brushstrokes. Michael Sudduth's overview in *The Internet Encyclopedia of Philosophy* (n.d.) is representative here: "The generic idea is that a person S knows p only if there is no true proposition, d, such that if S were to believe d (or d were added to S's evidence for p), S would no longer be justified in believing p." This kind of idea is extraordinarily hard to keep under control. Suppose, for example, that Jones' father is dead at t but Jones does not know about it. It is natural to think that Jones can still know that his car has not been stolen. But if he learned the disjunction "Either my father is dead or my car has been stolen" he would arguably not be justified in

of evidence may support p and yet an enrichment of that body may not. But this fact cannot explain defeat in cases where the body of evidence entails p, since this entailment will be preserved under enrichment. And once this simple model of defeat is precluded, it is much more challenging to make room for the phenomenon. Indeed, at least some philosophers working in a knowledge-first orbit have raised considerable skepticism about whether standard cases of defeat should be described as such, at least in those versions of the case where the person who knows soldiers on dogmatically and on the same basis as before. (See, notably, Lasonen-Aarnio 2010.[5] A central idea of that paper is that cases that many classify as defeated knowledge should instead be classified as "unreasonable knowledge" – the person knows, but is manifesting dispositions that render them unreasonable.)

These considerations will carry over to some extent to the E to K thesis. Restricting evidence to a proper subset of one's knowledge may reduce tendentiousness but is unlikely to take one all the way to Evidence Neutrality.[6] Moreover, assuming that no kind of knowledge is immune from both failures of positive and negative introspection, some limits on access to one's own evidence will remain. Finally, while the phenomenon of knowledge defeat may not be problematized in general, there may remain a particular challenge to making sense of defeat to *evidential knowledge*. For in that special case, the fact known is entailed by one's evidence, and so the kind of challenge to making sense of knowledge defeat that is faced by the E=K enthusiast will apply in that special case. (And here, in partial analogy with Lasonen-Aarnio's stance, the E to K proponent might argue that there is no such phenomenon as evidential knowledge defeat, at least for certain kinds of dogmatic believers.)

To conclude this subsection, we turn to the connection between knowledge and action. Like the ideas above, this will also have interesting application to religious belief. The bolder E=K thesis allows for a substantial reconciliation between decision theory and a highly intuitive norm connecting knowledge and action. The norm we have in mind is this: if you face a choice between x and y and you know that you would do better by doing x than y, then you ought to do x. Decision theory, meanwhile, recommends that one acts to maximize expected utility. Even assuming that "betterness" is calibrated

---

thinking that his car had not been stolen. A literature emerged in the 1970s that tried to put constraints on which true propositions can count as genuine defeaters – refining the generic idea by delimiting "true proposition" to "true proposition that meets the constraints." But it is challenging to say the least to find constraints that will do the job in a satisfactory way.

[5] One consideration that is moving Lasonen-Aarnio is a safety model of knowledge according to which one knows just in case there are no close worlds where one is in error. If one starts off knowing and is thus in a situation where there are no close worlds where one is in error, how is the confrontation with misleading evidence supposed to somehow make it that there are now close worlds where one is in error?

[6] Indeed, it is hard to imagine any conception of evidence that fully vindicates Evidence Neutrality, though some views will yield a closer approximation than others.

according to the relevant utility function, there is a potential clash here in a setting where not everything known is part of one's total body of evidence. Suppose, for example, one can open box A or box B, that one gets the contents of the box one opens, and that all one cares about in the context is short-term monetary gain. Suppose further that the utility of a billion dollars is more than a thousand times the utility of a dollar.[7] One knows that box A has a dollar. One knows box B is empty (and would remain empty if one opened it), but the fact that it is empty is not part of one's evidence (a combination that is presumably possible if one denies that all of one's knowledge is part of one's evidence). In fact, it is 999/1000 on one's evidence that were you to open B it would be empty and 1/1000 on one's evidence that it would contain a billion dollars. On the assumption that the evidential and knowledge-theoretic facts break this way, then it seems that the knowledge norm and decision theory would offer competing recommendations. The knowledge norm recommends opening box A – after all, one knows that one would get a dollar by opening A and nothing by opening B, and a dollar is better than nothing. On the other hand, decision theory recommends opening box B – a one in a thousand shot at a billion dollars has greater expected utility than a certain gain of merely a dollar. The E=K proposal precludes this kind of situation ever arising and thus offers an interesting reconciliation between decision theory and intuitive connections between knowledge and action.

17.1.2 Justification

Another trend in knowledge-first epistemology is to reverse the order of explanation between knowledge and justified belief. Gettier (1963) refuted the idea of analyzing knowledge as a combination of truth and a nonfactive relation of justifiedly believing (i.e., a relation that one can have to a falsehood). Subsequent attempts to analyze knowledge in terms of a nonfactive relation of this sort – in combination with a more complicated combination of conditions – have also seemed to many of us to be unpromising. An alternative approach turns the tables by attempting to illuminate justification and various related positive epistemic statuses in terms of knowledge. There are various ways that one might try to do this. Let us mention two kinds of idea, both of which one can find versions of in the Williamson corpus.[8]

---

[7] We can imagine the utility of dollars dropping off as one gets more and more – and so dollars needn't be linear with utilities. The assumption is merely that it does not drop off too quickly.

[8] Here is Williamson (2000: 185–186): "That order of explanation has been reversed in this book. The concept *knows* is fundamental, the primary implement of epistemological inquiry . . . That frees us to try the experiment of understanding the justification of belief in terms of knowledge." The evidence chapter of Williamson (2000) deploys a support-theoretic notion of justification, where it is knowledge that provides the support. Elsewhere, disposition theoretic accounts of nonfactive positive statuses get attention (see especially

One approach appeals to evidential support: A belief is justified just in case the proposition believed is strongly supported by what the person knows.[9] (One natural way to develop this is probabilistically – assuming some suitable background set of priors, a person's belief in p is justified just in case, relative to the priors, p has a suitably high probability conditional on the proposition q that is a conjunction of what one knows.[10])

A different approach is dispositional. The general idea is that one can get a nonfactive positive epistemic status by having some kind of general dispositions to know. Someone with a general disposition to know may nevertheless not know in unusually unfavorable circumstances.[11] To fix ideas, we'll present a few versions of this approach. One version: a belief that p is justified just in case, in believing p, one manifests dispositions that under all normal circumstances would yield knowledge. Another version: a belief that p is justified just in case one manifests dispositions that under some normal circumstances would yield knowledge.[12]

The dispositional idea will tend to come apart from the support-theoretic one. First, supposing the threshold of "sufficient support" is short of entailment, there will obviously be cases where one has the support-theoretic status but lacks the dispositional one. After all, there may be cases where one has a belief that passes the threshold but where one knows it isn't knowledge and so,

Williamson (in press) and Williamson (2017)), though Williamson (in press) also suggests that it is best to think of justification as of a piece of knowledge, with various dispositional ideas used to codify excusability rather than justification. Williamson (2017) suggests that philosophical theorizing about rationality tends to rely on the problematic conflation of the property of having evidential support for p and the property of being in circumstances where a person who was disposed to conform their beliefs to what the evidence supports would believe p. The implication is that ordinary philosophical theorizing about rationality is somewhat broken.

[9] A slightly different idea: a belief that p is justified just so long as the proposition that one knows p is supported by one's evidence. We will not explore this idea here.

[10] Williamson's (2000) concept of evidential probability is cashed out along these lines: the evidential probability of a proposition p is its conditional probability on the conjunction of what one knows relative to some assumed background set of primitive ur-priors (which are thought of as something like objective levels of plausibility in the absence of evidence, not as subjective credences).

[11] And if you are like Lasonen-Aarnio (2010), you might wish to make room for someone who knows but lacks a suitably general disposition to know and so is still unreasonable.

[12] One might instead use the ideology of relative normality: there is the status of manifesting dispositions that in the most normal situations would produce knowledge. One might instead explicitly deploy the ideology of processes or methods rather than dispositions: one generates the belief by a process or method that in normal circumstances/the most normal circumstances produce knowledge. How any of these conceptions play out will depend (as discussions of the so-called generality problem make clear) on how one individuates methods/processes/dispositions for the purposes of epistemological theorizing.

Another kind of knowledge-dependent status is one that attaches to a belief that p if one has a possible internal duplicate that knows p. Related statuses can be generated using various notions of partial duplication. For more discussion, see Hawthorne, Isaacs, and Lasonen-Aarnio (2021).

plausibly, is not manifesting a disposition to know under normal circumstances when forming the belief. (For example, a belief that the next card drawn will not be the king of spades might have high probability given what one knows but, assuming no special insider knowledge, is something that has no shot at being knowledge.) Second, there may be cases where one forms a belief in a way that would normally produce knowledge but where, assuming one's evidence is limited to what one knows, one's belief lacks evidential support. Suppose, for example, creatures of a certain species are born knowing there are predators not too far away. If a creature of that species is born in very strange circumstances – on a rocket ship, for example – its belief that there are predators nearby may be false and may not have much evidential support either; and yet that belief may be formed in such a way that in normal circumstances it would count as knowledge.[13] Of course, the details of how particular implementations of the support and dispositional ideas come apart will depend on both the details of the implementations and other aspects of the nature of knowledge. But even these schematic thoughts should make us very hesitant about the idea that they harmonize.

Insofar as one is looking for some nonfactive positive epistemic status that is explanatorily interesting, which kind of idea should one run with? That may depend on what one is trying to do with that status, as well as upon other epistemic decision points. For example, insofar as one thought of knowledge as the aim of belief and one wanted a positive epistemic status that was at the very least exculpatory, one might place more normative weight on some version of the dispositional idea than on the support-theoretic idea on the grounds that high support is compatible with knowably failing to attain the aim of belief. On the other hand, if one were dealing with a kind of belief for which knowledge was not the aim of the game (a suspicion, perhaps), then it might be more apt to lean on a support-theoretic parameter of assessment. This is not the place to look at various detailed implementations of these ideas – even the rough and ready versions will allow us to make some suggestive remarks in connection with religious belief.

17.2 Knowledge-First Epistemology

Let us now look at how the ideas presented in the last section might be important to religious epistemology.

---

[13] One model for this is a safety theoretic approach to knowledge: a belief in normal circumstances by a member of this special may be such that it could not easily have been false. Various normality theoretic glosses on knowledge might deliver a similar result.

17.2.1 Evidence and Reformed Epistemology

Both the E=K and E to K approaches suggest tweaks to the influential reformed epistemology made popular by Plantinga and Wolterstorff.[14] Standard presentations take a central idea of reformed epistemology to be that rationally acceptable belief in God does not require any significant evidence for theism. As Plantinga describes things, the fundamental turn was to question whether a "belief in God, if it is to be rationally acceptable, must be such that there is *good evidence* for it" (2000b: 70).

From an E=K perspective, this may not be quite the right way to put things, even if one has a religious orientation that is very much like Plantinga's. As a theist, one may instead want to say that one has, in one natural sense, the best possible evidence for theism, since it is part of one's evidence that there is a God. Of course, one's evidence may not be easily shareable with nonbelievers, since one's claim to possess that evidence will be understandably regarded with suspicion. But the fact of theism is part of one's body of evidence nonetheless. When one is in pain, the fact that one is in pain is part of what one has to go on. The reformed epistemologist who espouses theism should think that part of what they have to go on – in exactly the same sense – is that there is a God. Someone who thinks of inner sensations rather than known propositions as evidence might try to draw a significant evidential wedge between theism and pain and suggest: "In the case of pain, there are sensations that constitute powerful evidence, but in the case of at least most theists there is no analogous evidence." For the E=K proponent this is misconceived. Facts become part of one's body of evidence – in the theoretically interesting sense – when they become known. That a fact concerns the goings-on inside one's head does not make an important difference here. If not known, the fact that one has a sensation of type S is not part of one's evidence. Once known, it is. If not known, the fact that there is a God is not part of one's evidence. Once known, it is.

Granted, if a theist were to be asked "What is your evidence for theism?", it will sound a little strange to say "The fact that there is a God!" But it is clear enough why such a response is going to be strange. It is clear in context that one's interlocutor is not going to treat the fact that there is a God as common ground. Nor are they going to take that proposition on board on your say-so. And so, if one hopes to make any dialectical progress, it will be completely pointless to rely on one's possession of that fact as evidence. As Williamson notes, "what is wrong with citing e in answer to the question 'What is the evidence for e?' may be conversational inappropriateness rather than untruth" (1997: 735).

---

[14] See, for example, Wolterstorff (1976, 1983a) and Plantinga (1991, 2000b).

Now, the way Plantinga actually tends to proceed is this: he notes that objectors to theism claim that there is insufficient evidence for it. He responds by claiming that the objector relies on evidentialism. Plantinga (1991) puts it this way: "On this view, one who accepts belief in God but has no evidence for that belief is not, intellectually speaking, up to snuff." And against this concern, Plantinga claims that the presumption that rational belief in God requires evidence is inappropriate. From an E=K perspective, what is most saliently wrong about the objector from the perspective of the theist is their assumption that they, the theist, lack evidence. By the lights of the kind of newfangled reformed epistemologist we have in mind, the situation is akin to someone S who has a headache but has interlocutors that strongly suspect that S is a zombie. It's not that S lacks evidence that they have a headache. Their only problem is that despite decisive evidence, they may be able to do little to bring their interlocutor around. Their predicament is thus dialectical, not epistemological.

Now one might think that all of this misses the point. One might think it is crucial to reformed epistemology that *even if there is no God*, the typical theist's belief is rationally acceptable. But it is not so clear that this is an important part of Plantinga's worldview. His emphasis tends not to be that a claim of rational defectiveness for theism is out of the question. Rather, his thought is that it is tendentious, since it is hard to defend without presuming the falsity of theism. Plantinga (1991) put it this way: "So the dispute as to who is healthy and who diseased has ontological or theological roots, and is finally to be settled, if at all at that level." In effect, there is the germ of a concession here – if an atheist worldview is correct, then there may well be a strong case that theism is rationally defective. This concession then becomes absolutely explicit in Plantinga (2000b).[15] (Of course, such a concession may well not trouble those who take themselves to know that there is a God, since they will take themselves to know the falsity of the antecedent of the relevant conditional.[16]) We shall return to this issue shortly.

Within an E=K framework one might try to reformulate the evidentialist concern. One might, for example, insist that a commitment to theism be "based" on *other* evidence apart from the fact of theism. But once the demand is put this way, it rings especially hollow. There is no requirement in general that a belief that p be based on other evidence apart from p. Why the special demand for theism? It may also bear emphasis how little of our knowledge is properly explained by supposed basing on other evidence. Suppose a child sees

---

[15] See especially the discussion in Plantinga (2000: 186–188, beginning with "Here (despite the appearance of carelessness) perhaps Freud's instincts are right: I shall argue that if theistic belief is false, but taken in the basic way, it probably has no warrant."

[16] Of course, Plantinga also famously thinks there is an internal problem to naturalism, in that on the assumption of naturalism there should be no expectation that our faculties are oriented toward the truth. We shall not engage with that critique here.

a zebra, notes it has stripes, and this triggers acceptance of the generic proposition that zebras have stripes.[17] Another person sees a beautiful sunset and this triggers acceptance of theism. It would be tendentious to deny that the child acquires knowledge of the generic proposition in the first case. But it would also be unhelpful to suppose that this knowledge is somehow explained by the fact that the single case provides powerful evidence for the generic proposition. At least from the perspective of mainstream externalist epistemology, knowledge of the generic proposition will have to do with the reliability, safety, or such of the belief-forming process in the environmental niche in which the child is embedded. From the theist perspective, the second case may have a very similar epistemological structure.

Note that the E to K framework may have a slightly different spin on reformed epistemology. That view, as we noted, makes a distinction between evidential knowledge and nonevidential knowledge, where the distinction is not between which knowledge one has evidence for and which knowledge not, but instead between which pieces of knowledge are pieces of evidence and which not. From that perspective we suggest that the most natural reconstruction of the spirit of reformed epistemology is the thesis that theism is evidential knowledge: while various things that one knows inductively, abductively, and so on, are not part of one's body of evidence, theism *is* part of one's (i.e., the relevant theist's) body of evidence. This view shares with "E=K reformed epistemology" the view that theism is part of the relevant theist's body of evidence. It differs by claiming that this sets it apart from a good deal of other knowledge (and in that way conforms even more closely to the original outlook of reformed epistemology).

17.2.2 Theism, Counterevidence and Defeat

Supposing theism is part of a certain theist's body of evidence – something that will not be surprising from either the point of view of E=K reformed epistemology or E to K reformed epistemology. What bearing will supposed arguments against theism have on the epistemic status of the theist's belief?

One thing is clear: if a theist is presented with such arguments, their theism is not going to get into trouble merely by adding new evidence – say, facts about horrendous evil – to the evidence already possessed. There is a simple reason for this, one already alluded to: if theism is part of their evidence, then any enrichment of their evidence will entail theism. If the conjunction of a set of propositions entails p, then the conjunction of any superset of that set will also entail p. Thus, if theism were to attain poor epistemic standing by the

---

[17] Acceptance of generics on the basis of very limited exposure to instances is commonplace. See Abelson and Kanouse (1966).

introduction of arguments and evidence, it is not going to be by a process of enrichment. It seems clear that if we are going to try to model a shift from knowledge of theism to an endpoint where theism has poor epistemic standing, it will be by appeal to some other mechanism of defeat.

But here we wish to return to a theme that we adverted to earlier. The alleged phenomenon of defeat is problematized within knowledge-first epistemology. Within an E=K version, all knowledge defeat is problematized. And within an E to K version, knowledge defeat is problematized for those pieces of knowledge that are pieces of evidence. To drive this point home, let us focus on some pieces of knowledge that are plausibly going to be treated as evidential whether or not one goes for E=K or E to K. Our examples are (a) Someone is aware that they have a headache and (b) Someone remembers that they had a bagel for breakfast. Let us try to imagine cases where someone starts being aware that they are in pain or remembers that they had a bagel for breakfast, and then encounters misleading counterevidence. Perhaps a person of superior intellect provides all sorts of sophisticated arguments that pain is an illusion, or that there are no bagels in reality, or else a panel of experts provides all sorts of (sophistical) data suggesting that the person's pain detection or memory system is going radically awry. And suppose they are the kind of person who says at the end of it: "That's all very well, but I'm telling you I have a headache!" or "That's all very well, but I'm telling you I had a bagel for breakfast!" How should we describe such people? Should we say that they are no longer aware that they are in pain or no longer remember that they had a bagel for breakfast? This is, intuitively, a very uncomfortable concession. Should we instead say that while they are aware they are in pain, they do not know they are in pain or that while they remember that they had a bagel for breakfast, they do not know that they had a bagel for breakfast? This seems very uncomfortable too. Being aware that and remembering that seem to entail knowing that.[18] It is thus very challenging, when it comes to paradigmatic kinds of evidential knowledge, to produce a compelling case that knowledge is really destroyed in such cases. (We don't want to be too doctrinaire here: we merely want to emphasize that when a piece of knowledge is part of one's evidence, the putative mechanisms of defeat are significantly problematized.) And importantly, the reformed epistemologist wants to think of knowledge of theism very much on the model of these paradigms. In that case too, the idea that exposure to new evidence and arguments will inevitably induce knowledge defeat are at best problematic, even without getting into the details of those arguments.

---

[18] For more on this see Williamson (2000, chapter 1).

17.2.3 Unfriendly Atheism?

William Rowe made a well-known distinction between friendly atheism and unfriendly atheism. The friendly atheist concedes that "some theists are rationally justified in believing that God exists" (Rowe 1979: 340), while the unfriendly atheist argues that none are. Of course, allowing for just a few rational theists is hardly very friendly. If we said that certain theists with an unusually sheltered existence were rationally justified but that pretty much every other theist was not rationally justified, we would pass the stated test for friendly atheism but would hardly come across as very friendly. For our purposes it's perhaps better to think of friendly atheism as the view that lots of ordinary people in modern society are rationally justified in believing theism and the unfriendly atheist as one who denies this.[19]

Should the knowledge-firster who is an atheist veer in the direction of friendly or unfriendly atheism, taken in this sense? Now of course, there is nothing in principle incoherent about the friendly position. One might think that one has extra evidence that supports atheism, but that theism is rationally justified for many theists, given where they find themselves in the world. Yet we think there are reasons to hesitate about moving in a friendly direction, at least given the knowledge-first conceptions of justification adumbrated earlier.

One reason for thinking this is that, assuming the atheistic worldview, the theist does not manifest dispositions to know of the sort adverted to earlier. Contrast a theist with a brain in a vat. A brain in a vat makes myriad errors. Yet the externalist epistemologist can contrive various positive epistemological statuses that are disposition-theoretic along the lines alluded to earlier – the brain in a vat manifests dispositions that in normal circumstances generate knowledge.[20] But if the naturalistic worldview is correct, the standard theist gets no such consolation prize. For assuming that naturalistic worldview, the theist is not manifesting dispositions that normally tend toward truth. From the perspective of a standard atheist worldview, the typical theist is putting their eggs in a basket that reliably has no resemblance whatsoever to the

---

[19] Rowe himself refines the question of interest to whether "some people in modern society, people who are aware of the usual grounds for belief and disbelief and are acquainted to some degree with modern science, are yet rationally justified in accepting theism" (1979: 340). We have two reasons for resisting this precisification. First, the question of grounds may be quite tendentious (in the way that the question of what evidence is available is). Second, one way of being acquainted with modern science to some degree is to be acquainted with an enormous degree. We don't want to get into whether a deep understanding of fine-tuning might justify theism via lines of thought that are unavailable to most ordinary people.

[20] The so-called new evil demon problem for externalist epistemology is the challenge of accounting for the apparently positive epistemic status of brain-in-a-vat beliefs. Note that we are here setting aside the worry that Boltzmann brains are pretty normal (arguably more normal than embodied brains) and thus that our own dispositions have a pretty poor success rate across normal circumstances.

structure of reality. (Of course, the theist may feel from the inside that they are on the right track. And they will not know that they do not know. Does this get them epistemological points? The stock in trade of internalist epistemology – seemings and such – will not count for much when the focus is on dispositions to know. And it is in any case worth recalling that most paradigms of abject irrationality – someone that thinks they are Julius Caesar, for example – may feel from the inside that they are on the right track and do not know that they fail to know.) Thus, if one's go-to nonfactive positive epistemic statuses are crafted in terms of dispositions to know, then if one is an atheist, one may very well end up an unfriendly atheist.

How about the evidence-based conception? Here, things are more complicated, since different theists may have different bodies of evidence. Assuming atheism, no theist will have the fact that there is a God as part of their body of evidence. But their bodies of evidence may differ in all sorts of other ways that make a difference to the evidential probability of theism for them.[21] Yet the atheist may be tempted to veer in an unfriendly direction, at least when it comes to typical theists. Start with an extreme case. Someone sees the beauty of a sunset, is moved to theism, reads a bunch of Plantinga and Wolterstorff, and talks the talk of their theism being a "properly basic belief." If atheism is correct, the person does not have the fact that there is a God as their evidence. And it would take a rather perverse conception of the priors to suppose that the evidential probability of theism conditional on a beautiful sunset is decently high. If there is a God, the sunset may be playing the role of triggering knowledge, where the person ends up with overwhelmingly strong evidence that there is a God. But if there is not, the sunset may well be triggering a belief that has very low probability conditional on the person's actual body of evidence. That is an extreme sort of case, of course. Many ordinary people have many friends and family who believe in theism and have read books that many people seem to trust that advocate theism, and so on. The question as to the conditional evidential probability of theism on that body of evidence may be less obvious. Nevertheless, it seems to us to be a fairly respectable position for the atheist to suppose that the prior of theism is very low and that the body of evidence possessed by most people – especially when one throws in what they know about evil into the mix – does not get theism very high.

One thing that bears emphasis here is that the ideology of evidential probability in play requires some ideology of objective prior probabilities, and that if there are such probabilities, their distribution will be, like many other things, a contentious matter. The atheist may know that theism has a low prior but, since

---

[21] Note that the metaphysical impossibility of theism – if it is impossible – may not in itself be that telling. It may be metaphysically impossible that water lacks hydrogen, and yet we want a conception of evidential probability according to which it might be quite likely on a person's evidence that water lacks hydrogen.

the issue is tendentious, may not succeed in bringing certain theists around to that point of view. (Of course, some theists may be willing to concede theism has a low prior – after all, if one knows that there is God, then a low prior for God will not stand in the way of theism's ending up with a glowing evidential probability.) While tendentious, the view that theism has quite low evidential probability given the body of knowledge most ordinary theists actually have is one that may be a quite respectable one for atheists to adopt (and even something that is among those tendentious things that are nevertheless knowable). Even on an evidence-based conception of positive evidential status, the atheist may be tempted toward a rather unfriendly posture.

We will not pursue the matter further here.

17.2.4 Knowledge, Action, and Public Reason Liberalism

When there are radical disagreements about who knows what, it is difficult to find compromises about what to do, at least if knowledge connects to action in the way that knowledge-firsters often tend to presume. A good illustration of these difficulties can be seen by looking at the aspirations of what is known as "Public Reason Liberalism" in the political sphere. The key idea of Public Reason Liberalism is that for a law to be justified, it must be acceptable to all reasonable citizens. This proposal is offered as a path forward in a setting where modern societies are confronted by, as Rawls puts it, "profound and irreconcilable differences in citizens' reasonable and philosophical conceptions of the world" (Rawls 2001: 3).[22] But supposing knowledge can justify action in the way we typically suppose, the expectation that reasonable people conform to that norm seems at best tendentious. To present a dramatic but by no means far-fetched example, suppose a society contains a large segment of the population whose religious worldview includes beliefs to the effect that abortion is murder, that any murder is a horrendous evil, and thus that the legalization of abortion is tantamount to allowing murder on an enormous scale. The Public Reason Liberal tends to want to be nonpartisan. That view is typically presented as something that does not presume the falsity of perspectives such as these but rather as a way forward when society manifests a diversity of perspectives that include perspectives such as these. But is it really coherent for the Public Liberal to be neutral on whether those who have that perspective know that what they are saying is true? Suppose someone did know that the legalization of abortion is tantamount to murder on an enormous scale and that any murder has enormous disvalue. And suppose there are reasonable people who don't know these things and for whom any attempt to

---

[22] For relevant and well-known work on Public Reason Liberalism, see Rawls (1996, 2001), Quong (2011), and Gaus (2015, chapter 5).

justify making abortion illegal would rely on claims so tendentious that they are unwilling to accept them.[23] In this setting a public justification will be unavailable. And yet if the emboldened group really did know those things, one can hardly expect them to conform to the public justification norm. If one knew that pushing through a law would prevent egregious evil, a violation of the public justification norm would be well worth it.

Now of course, if these people were under an illusion and did not in fact know what they think they know, the situation would be radically different. They then would possess a far more impoverished body of evidence and would certainly not know that pushing through the relevant law would prevent egregious evil.[24] The challenge to the Public Reason Liberal is to make a case against pushing through policies that lack public justification that avoids taking sides as to whether the relevant worldview is correct. The fundamental problem in this case can be made vivid by considering the following speech: "Even if you do know that allowing abortion involves the murder of millions and even if you do know that any murder is a horrendous evil, you shouldn't be trying to make abortion illegal." That speech sounds very strained. And once one thinks of one's body of evidence as including all of one's body of knowledge, the speech sounds even odder, since there is then far less wiggle room for arguing that the evidence fails to justify the actions despite the presence of knowledge.[25]

It is unclear what the best path forward is here for the Public Reason Liberal. Perhaps they will reject the identification of evidence with what one knows and, on that basis, reject intuitive connections between knowledge and action. Or perhaps they will reject the possibility of knowing such propositions as that all abortions are murder. (One version of this approach might rely on a contextualism about "know" that militates for a relatively sparse extension within the political theater.) But either way, the view will turn out to be rather more tendentious than it may first seem (though that does not immediately imply that the view is false). The main point that we wish to emphasize is that

---

[23] Note that it would hardly further the cause of Public Reason Liberalism to say that if the religious worldview is correct, then agnostics are unreasonable. (Such a view would save the letter of Public Reason Liberalism – which only requires rules being justified to *reasonable* people – at the cost of departing entirely from the spirit of that view.)

[24] And if they are under an illusion, they may not even count as reasonable – perhaps an unfriendly view is correct in that case – and it would thus not be necessary to satisfy them to pass the public justification standard. Of course, the Public Reason Liberal is free to treat "reasonable" as a theoretical term to be taken in the context of their theory, and it may serve their purposes to distribute it in a more friendly way. But we do not see any precisification of "reasonable" that makes the kind of challenge under consideration go away.

[25] Remember that if one's evidence is something other than one's body of knowledge, then one might learn to live with the idea that an action has lower expected utility than another action even if one knows that one would be better off by performing it.

There are obvious points of contact between these brief remarks and David Enoch's (2017) more developed case against Public Reason Liberalism.

irreconcilable differences about who knows what on foundational issues of the sort presented by religious worldviews will make the task of negotiating what to do as a society extremely challenging. If one side knows what they think they know, certain actions will be expected to be vastly superior in comparison with various alternatives, at least if evidential probabilities are calibrated to knowledge. And in many cases, if that side knows what they think they know, the preferred actions will be known to be better than the alternatives. But if those people do not know what they think they know, those actions may not be superior by those people's own lights – that is, given what those very people in fact have to go on (at least if "what one has to go on" is given a knowledge-theoretic construal). When people can be radically mistaken about what they and others have to go on, there may be no compromise to be had. Religious worldviews are particularly liable to have a destabilizing effect; it may be hoping too much for a nonpartisan political philosophy that can keep things in check. Certain theists will understandably argue that no political philosophy ought to stop one doing what one knows to be best. On the other hand, this may all be more grist for the unfriendly atheist's mill, where now the unfriendliness may have a more practical aspect.[26]

[26] We are grateful to John Greco for valuable comments on an earlier draft of this chapter, and to Charity Anderson, Jeremy Goodman, Yoaav Isaacs, Clayton Littlejohn, Jeff Russell, and Collis Tahzib for helpful conversations.

18 Epistemic Disjunctivism and Religious Knowledge

Kegan J. Shaw

Introduction

Epistemological disjunctivism defends the following view: in ideal cases, when you know that p through visual perception, your reason for believing that p consists in your seeing p to be the case. It's important to point out straightaway what exactly the view entails. First, it entails that in ordinary cases perception provides one with grounds that *logically guarantee* the truth of the target belief. That is because seeing that p, like knowing that p, is *factive*. Like knowing that p, you cannot see that p unless p is true. Second, the fact that one has such grounds is supposed to reveal why adopting the target belief is intellectually respectable from the subject's point of view. It is usually claimed in this connection that such grounds need to be *reflectively accessible* to the subject herself. Altogether then, the commonsense view entails that in ideal cases when you know that p through visual perception, you have rational grounds for believing that p that are both factive and reflectively accessible to the subject.[1]

While epistemological disjunctivism is usually invoked in connection with visual perception, we might wonder whether we can adopt it to defend interesting theses with regard to the reflectively accessible grounds arising in connection with knowledge from other sources. That question has only recently started receiving attention (cf. Doyle, Millburn, and Pritchard 2019). In this chapter I explore the connection between epistemological disjunctivism and knowledge from religious sources, focusing exclusively on *religious perception*. I'll argue that so long as there is perception of God, there is no obvious reason to think that this doesn't give rise to relevant beliefs about God that enjoy rational support that is both factive and reflectively accessible.[2] The result is a novel view for which I'll outline several key benefits.

[1] Epistemological disjunctivism originates with McDowell (1982, 1994, 1995) and has been recently popularized by Pritchard (2012).
[2] This chapter offers a fresh defense of the view I defend in Shaw (2016).

18.1 Religious Epistemological Disjunctivism

18.1.1 Epistemological Disjunctivism in Its Original Context

Before moving to consider the religious question, I should first present epistemological disjunctivism in its original context:

Empirical Epistemological Disjunctivism (EED). In ideal cases of visual-perceptual knowledge that p, one has grounds for believing that p that are both factive and reflectively accessible to the subject.

By an "ideal case" I have in mind situations that Duncan Pritchard (2012: 29) describes as both "objectively" and "subjectively" epistemically good. Suppose you open the fridge and see what are in fact ripe tomatoes. You would not be in an objectively good situation if, unbeknownst to you, your partner enjoys swapping pieces of fruit around the house for artificial lookalikes. For then, too easily might you be wrong that you are seeing actual tomatoes in the fridge. And you would not be in a subjectively good situation if you had *good evidence* for thinking that your partner plays pranks of this kind. Then, once again, you would not be ideally epistemically situated with respect to the proposition that the things you see in the fridge are tomatoes. EED, then, is a theory of the nature of the grounds available in cases where no such funny business obtains.

Now, why the view has such an obscure name will become clear in due course. But it's safe to say that this view is not currently in vogue. This is best seen by noting the very different verdicts it issues about the information that is reflectively accessible to one in cases that are exactly similar from the subject's point of view. I'll explain.

Let "the good case" refer to the ordinary situation mentioned above, in which you know that there are tomatoes in the fridge because you have looked into the fridge and seen them. Philosophers are famous for thinking up corresponding "bad cases." These include cases that while *introspectively indistinguishable* from the good case are cases in which one is wildly deceived. Imagine, for example, that your entire visual experience, including its appearing to you as if there are tomatoes in the fridge, is being artificially induced by some evil genius/mad scientist who, for some time now, has had your brain removed from your skull and placed in a vat in a high-security lab somewhere. While in the bad case it certainly still *seems* to you that you see tomatoes (and much else besides), you don't – this is a perfect hallucination.

Now EED entails that in the good case you have grounds for believing that there are tomatoes in the fridge that are both factive and reflectively accessible to you. Such grounds consist in your *seeing that* there are tomatoes in the fridge. Importantly, however, you have no such reflectively accessible grounds in the bad case. Since one cannot see that p unless p is true, you cannot see that there are tomatoes in the fridge so long as you're a brain in a vat being artificially induced to hallucinate tomatoes that aren't there. At best, you only *seem to see* that you have tomatoes. So then, while in the good case you have reflective access to factive grounds for adopting the target belief, in the bad case you have reflective access only to nonfactive grounds, such as facts about what you only seem to see. This, of course, entails that you have reflectively accessible grounds in the good case that are *far superior* to what you have in the corresponding bad case, *despite* these cases being introspectively indistinguishable from each other.

Now, this tends to shock mainstream sensibilities in epistemology. On what can fairly be called the orthodox view, any reasons you have for thinking there are tomatoes in the fridge in the good case *are reasons you would have anyway* if you were in the bad case. But since in the bad case you have no better than nonfactive grounds, it follows that you have no better than nonfactive grounds in the good case too. Call this the No Factive Reasons Thesis:

No Factive Reasons Thesis. Even in ideal cases involving visual-perceptual knowledge that p, one cannot have better than nonfactive reflectively accessible grounds for believing that p.

So, for example, if this thesis is true, then even in the good case your reflectively accessible grounds for thinking that there are tomatoes in the fridge *cannot* depend on your seeing that there are, but rather on your merely *seeming to see* that there are. Such grounds are of the same nonfactive kind that you have in the corresponding bad case, so that there is no handing out of different verdicts between the two cases here.

Why accept the No Factive Reasons thesis? Proponents will point out that the good case is, after all, introspectively indistinguishable from the bad case: Even in the good case one cannot tell on the basis of introspection alone that one is not in the bad case. It can seem to follow without further ado that even in the good case one cannot know *on the basis of reflection alone* anything that would presuppose that one is not in the bad case. Given that seeing that p entails that one is not in a bad case, it follows that no such factive states are reflectively accessible to the subject. Mainstream epistemology accepts, then, the following inference:

The Mainstream Inference

1. The good case is introspectively indistinguishable from the bad case.
2. Therefore, in the good case one cannot know anything on the basis of reflection alone that would presuppose that one is not in the bad case.

Of course, EED maintains that in the good case one has reflective access to the fact that one sees that p. Because the view is therefore inconsistent with claim 2 above, EED flat out rejects the mainstream inference. Notice this inference from 1 to 2 assumes, in effect, that for any case that is introspectively indistinguishable from the good case, one's reflectively accessible grounds are of the same *nonfactive* kind. EED rejects this assumption, thereby earning its name: for any case that is introspectively indistinguishable from the good case, one's reflectively accessible grounds are *either* of the nonfactive *or* the factive kind (depending upon which case one is actually in).

Proponents of EED claim for their view important advantages over the rival orthodox view. I won't take the time to spell those out in detail, since the central aim of the chapter is elsewhere: to articulate and defend the prospects of a *religious* epistemological disjunctivism. I move on to this next.[3]

18.1.2 Religious Epistemological Disjunctivism

If epistemological disjunctivism is true, then in ideal cases of visual-perceptual knowledge, one is put in possession of factive grounds for accepting target empirical beliefs. If so, then *religious* epistemological disjunctivism would entail that in ideal cases of knowledge from religious sources, one is likewise put in possession of factive grounds for accepting target religious beliefs. In what follows I'll spell out such a view in connection with what I will call *theistic perception.*

When you look to see tomatoes in the fridge, the tomatoes themselves are "given" or "presented" to your conscious awareness. This involves the tomatoes presenting themselves to you in various way – as red and round, for example – and we thus speak of your visually perceiving the tomatoes (and some of their properties). Well, suppose God himself can be given or presented to one's conscious awareness. Suppose God himself can appear in consciousness as, for example, loving, or wholly good, or as encouraging one. If so, then there exists what William Alston called "mystical" or what I'll call *theistic* perception. Alston (1991) argued at length that there is no good reason to think that theistic perception is not metaphysically on all fours with, for example, visual perception; and I'm going to simply take that for granted here. Suppose, then, theistic perception sometimes occurs, affording opportunities for knowledge about God. If so, this naturally invites us to consider the following view:

Religious Epistemological Disjunctivism (RED). In ideal cases of theistic-perceptual knowledge that *p*, one has grounds for believing that *p* that are both factive and reflectively accessible to the subject.

---

[3] These are mostly in connection with staving off radical skeptical problems. See, for example, McDowell (1995) and Pritchard (2016).

Three quick comments are in order.

First, which religious beliefs are suitable items of knowledge in cases of theistic perception? Here I'll simply follow Alston. These are what he calls "manifestation beliefs" (or M-beliefs): "beliefs, based on mystical perception, to the effect that God has some perceivable property or is engaging in some perceivable activity" (1991: 77). So, for example, if God really is now presenting (or manifesting) himself to one's conscious awareness as loving, then the proposition <God is loving> would be a suitable content for an M-belief.

Second, the view holds that one has reflective access to factive grounds for claims about God *in ideal cases* of theistic-perceptual knowledge. An ideal case here involves legitimate perception of God where, again, epistemic conditions are both objectively and subjectively good. For example, one's epistemic environment has to be favorable: it can't be that one has just been slipped a pill that makes one now prone to delusory religious experiences. Furthermore, one must not be presently in the grips of a defeater for the target M-belief: it can't be that one is presently battling doubt that God exists because, for example, one is very impressed by the problem of evil. Do such ideal cases ever occur? Well, I certainly cannot argue for that here. That would involve a full-on defense of the existence of God. Rather, I am arguing that *if they do occur*, then there is no good reason to think that they don't involve having grounds for suitable M-beliefs that are both factive and reflectively accessible.

Third, what form do these factive grounds take? I'll simply say that theistic perception can make available to one factive grounds in the form of one's *perceiving that God is thus and so* where, in the present context, we'll understand this to signify the kind of perceiving that goes on in the religious context. Let's now have an example to illustrate the view.

James is a devout Christian, often taking himself to be in personal communion with God. After investing many years and financial resources into his education, James is now struggling mightily in a terrible academic job market. After submitting countless job applications, James is invited to interview for only a single position, which he's now learned has not been successful. Taking this all in, James finds himself incredibly discouraged. But just then James has an experience that, if asked, he'd describe in terms of his being aware of God's gentle encouragement through this difficulty.

Suppose, now, in light of this theistic-perceptual experience, James forms the M-belief that God is encouraging him. Suppose this is an ideal case, so that James comes to know, as a result, that God is encouraging him. If RED is true, then James here has reflective access to factive grounds for believing this. Specifically, James' reason for thinking that God is encouraging him in this moment is that he perceives that God is encouraging him. As with EED, this is meant to be consistent with the fact that there exists a bad case that is introspectively indistinguishable from James' actual case, in which James is not perceiving God at all but is undergoing a delusory religious experience in a naturalistic world. In this bad case James doesn't have reflective access to the fact that he perceives that God is encouraging him, despite his views to the contrary, because he isn't perceiving God at all.

The next thing to note is that RED is clearly opposed to a suitably modified version of the No Factive Reasons Thesis highlighted above. Call it the Religious No Factive Reasons Thesis (Religious NFR Thesis).

Religious No Factive Reasons Thesis. Even in ideal cases involving theistic-perceptual knowledge that *p*, one cannot have better than nonfactive reflectively accessible grounds for believing that *p*.

So, even in the ideal situation this thesis would represent James as believing that God is encouraging him on the basis of reasons he'd have anyway even if he were having a delusory religious experience. We are to imagine, for example, that James, even in the ideal case, deems it entirely appropriate to accept that God is encouraging him because it *seems* to him that he is.

This thesis will seem attractive to anyone prone to accept the mainstream inference highlighted above. After all, on the basis of introspection alone James can't tell his present case apart from the bad case in which he's suffering a delusory religious experience. And it can seem to follow straightaway that he therefore cannot have reflective access to information that would privilege his being in the good versus the bad case. Again, the underlying assumption here is that for any case that is introspectively indistinguishable from the ideal case, one cannot have better than nonfactive reflectively accessible grounds for accepting a suitable M-belief. RED takes exception: for any case that is introspectively indistinguishable from the ideal case, one has *either* reflectively accessible grounds of the factive kind *or* the nonfactive kind, depending upon the actual case one is in.

That is RED now on the table. It next requires some defense. In what follows I consider and address some objections to the view before turning to highlight some of its key advantages.

18.2 Problems: More on Reflective Accessibility and Rational Support

18.2.1 The Distinguishability Problem

If RED is true, then the fact that one perceives that God is thus and so can be reflectively accessible to the subject. But now *what exactly* does such reflective access consist in? There is a worry that any clear answer to this question will spell problems, making it more reasonable to retain the Religious NFR thesis and reject disjunctivism.[4] Consider first what Duncan Pritchard says about reflective access:

What it means for a fact to be reflectively accessible is that the agent can come to know that fact simply by reflecting on the matter, and thus without having to make any further empirical inquiries. Note that 'reflection' here will usually involve introspection, *a priori* reasoning and memory of knowledge gained via either of these two sources. (Pritchard 2016: 78)

Now, if relevant access to the fact that one perceives that God is thus and so involves one of the modes of reflective access that Pritchard identifies here as "usual," then it must involve introspective access. This is the kind of access that one has to the nature and content of one's own conscious mental states, for example. On the other hand, relevant access might involve a mode of reflective access that doesn't neatly fit into the traditional categories. From here, one can press the following dilemma:

The Reflective Access Dilemma

1. Either relevant access to factive grounds consists in having introspective access or it consists in having some novel kind of access that is neither via introspection nor *a priori* reasoning, nor memory of knowledge acquired in these ways.
2. If having relevant access consists in having introspective access, then we lose the idea that the good case can be introspectively indistinguishable from the bad case.
3. If having relevant access consists in having some novel kind of access then the proposal is *ad hoc* (i.e., insufficiently well motivated).
   ————————
   Therefore, religious epistemological disjunctivism is either fundamentally *ad hoc* or else must abandon the idea that the good case can be introspectively indistinguishable from the bad case.

Space constraints limit how thorough our treatment of this dilemma can be. For that reason, I'll consider only premise 2. I'll assume that we should want to retain the idea that the good case can be introspectively indistinguishable from the bad case. What we mean is that if James is in the good case and so has grounds for accepting the target M-belief that are both factive and reflectively accessible, he still cannot tell *on the basis of introspection alone* that he is not suffering a delusory religious experience. Premise 2 suggests that this position cannot be made compatible with the idea that relevant access in the good case

---

[4] Neither of the two following objections are unique to religious epistemological disjunctivism. Versions of these objections can be pressed into service against empirical epistemological disjunctivism as well. For discussion of the distinguishability problem in connection with empirical epistemological disjunctivism, see Pritchard (2012, part 2).

consists of introspective access. In another context Pritchard calls this *The Distinguishability Problem* for disjunctivism. I think this objection misfires. In showing why, I'll articulate in my own way a version of the strategy offered in Pritchard (2012) for defending empirical epistemological disjunctivism against a similar charge.

Suppose that introspection alone can reveal that one is perceiving that God is thus and so. Does it follow that introspection alone can reveal that one is *not* suffering a delusory religious experience (and/or *is not* in the bad case)? Not at all. To explain why, it will be helpful to avail ourselves of the common distinction between *immediate* and *inferential* justification.

If a source gives one immediate justification to accept a claim, then such justification does not depend upon one's having justification to accept anything else. In this way the target belief can be said to be justified by the source alone. By contrast, if a source gives one inferential justification to accept a claim, then such justification *does* depend upon one's justification to accept other claims. In this way the target belief is not properly conceived as being justified by the source *alone*, but only in conjunction with this justification to believe some different claim(s). So, for example, in ordinary circumstances someone's telling you that they are thirsty might give you immediate justification to believe that they are. Whereas someone's telling you this in the context of a murder mystery dinner party might give you justification to believe this *only* in conjunction with justification to believe that your informant has broken character. Such is inferential justification.

Now premise 2 above overlooks the possibility that while introspection *immediately justifies* the belief that one is perceiving that God is thus and so, it does not immediately justify the belief that one is *not* suffering a delusory religious experience. It's not implausible to think this latter belief is justified inferentially: in part through the availability of a deductive inference from the belief, justified immediately by introspection, that one is perceiving that God is thus and so. It's open to religious epistemological disjunctivism to maintain that, in this way, introspection alone cannot reveal that one is not suffering a delusory religious experience even if introspection alone *can* reveal that one is perceiving that God is thus and so. I think this neutralizes the perceived threat in premise 2. At the very least this puts pressure back on our opponent to show why we must think that if introspection immediately justifies the first belief, then it must immediately justify the second.

18.2.2 Rational Support

Let's consider a second objection. If RED is true, then one has reflectively accessible grounds for accepting M-beliefs in the good case that are far superior to anything one has in the corresponding bad case. It isn't immediately obvious, however, how to reconcile that with what I'll call the *Parity Intuition*. Many will find it obvious upon reflection that the subject in the bad case – for whom it is just as if he is in the good case – has just as much *rational support* for accepting the target M-belief as one has in the good case.

Parity Intuition. The subject in the bad case has just as much rational support for accepting the target M-belief as does the subject in the good case.[5]

I'm happy to accept this intuition at face value. There is then the issue of squaring the aforementioned asymmetry with respect to reflectively accessible grounds with this symmetry with respect to rational support.

I don't see that there is any deep tension here. Notice that the subject in the bad case, like the subject in the good case, *believes* themselves to be perceiving that God is thus and so. Now if that is something you actually believe, then I say that you rationally commit yourself to the relevant M-belief. It matters not whether the former belief is true or is itself epistemically supported in some way. Since the M-belief is so clearly entailed by this belief, failure to accept the target M-belief is to commit a rational failing. Put the other way around: accepting this belief gives one rational support for accepting the relevant M-belief. Compare this case: suppose you believe that Jones can fly. That belief may be false and/or epistemically deficient in a thousand ways. Even so, believing it generates rational support for believing that someone can fly. It's certainly the case that to believe the first while disbelieving or withholding judgment about the second is to exhibit a rational failing.[6]

And so, it looks open to the RED to say that the reason there exists the symmetry between the good and bad cases with respect to rational support is that both subjects *believe* that they are perceiving that God is thus and so, and this rationally commits both to the relevant M-belief: it makes this M-belief rationally supported for both. Nevertheless, RED maintains that the nature of the reflectively accessible grounds for a given M-belief is not determined by the degree to which that belief is merely rationally supported. After all, it isn't the subject's *belief* that she is perceiving that God is thus and so that constitutes her reflectively accessible grounds in the good case, but rather the fact constituted by the act of perceiving itself. And so, a subject's having reflective access to factive grounds in the good case is not incompatible with supposing that, at least where mere rational support is concerned, she has no more rational support for accepting the target M-belief as does the subject in the bad case.

---

[5] Support for the parity intuition, sometimes called "the new evil demon intuition," is usually traced to Cohen (1984).

[6] These insights and the example to support them are found in Jim Pryor (2004: 364).

18.3 Advantages: Disposing of a Skeptical Argument and Enlarging on What It Takes to Offer Independent Grounds for Theistic Belief

18.3.1 Resolving the Underdetermination-Based Religious Skeptical Argument

Next, I'll highlight the advantages of RED against other candidate religious epistemologies of theistic perception. The advantages of the view are most easily demonstrated, I think, in connection with the proverbial "theist in the street." This is the theist who is unable to present any good arguments for God, such as versions of the cosmological, teleological, or moral arguments for God's existence. There are two important advantages to highlight here. The first is in overcoming a religious skeptical argument; the second is in making out how one can have independent grounds for theism short of having good arguments.[7]

First, then, I think that unless RED is true it can be hard to show how, in certain skeptical contexts, the theist in the street's M-beliefs are intellectually respectable from her own point of view. We can show that by considering the following religious skeptical argument:

The Underdetermination-Based Religious Skeptical Argument[8]

1. No theist in the street has reflectively accessible grounds that favor her M-beliefs over relevant skeptical hypotheses.
2. Unless the theist in the street has reflectively accessible grounds that favor her M-beliefs over relevant skeptical hypotheses, then, at least in certain skeptical contexts, those beliefs cannot be shown to be intellectually respectable from the subject's point of view.[9]

   ⎯⎯⎯⎯⎯⎯⎯⎯

   Therefore, at least in skeptical contexts, the theist in the street's M-beliefs cannot be shown to be intellectually respectable from the subject's point of view.

I should point out straightaway that premise 2 advances its claim only in relation to *skeptical contexts*. That's important to note. This is a context in

---

[7] There are other advantages of the view that are more easily stated. Suppose empirical epistemological disjunctivism is true. If we would desire a unified theory of reflectively accessible grounds for perceptual belief, then we should adopt religious epistemological disjunctivism as well. Thanks to John Greco for this reminder.

[8] This is a version of the skeptical argument that Pritchard (2016: 133) presents to help display the unique advantages of empirical epistemological disjunctivism.

[9] Even if one lacks such reflectively accessible grounds that favor her M-belief over relevant skeptical hypotheses, those beliefs could still be shown to be intellectually respectable from some third-person point of view. For all that such beliefs might still be the outputs of properly functioning cognitive faculties, reliably produced, etc. I say some more about this later in the chapter. Thanks to Tyler McNabb for helping me clarify.

which the subject herself is actively attending to some relevant "bad case" skeptical scenario: the scenario, for example, in which it only seems to one as though she is perceiving God because she is suffering a religious delusion in a naturalistic world. Premise 2 claims that *only in such contexts* is a subject's M-belief not shown to be intellectually respectable from her own point of view, so long as she lacks available grounds that favor this belief over the known-to-be incompatible skeptical hypothesis.[10]

Now to quickly motivate the argument. Consider, first, premise 1. This premise will draw its support from the Religious NFR Thesis. Suppose James forms the M-belief that God is encouraging him on the basis of a suitable religious experience. This thesis holds that even under ideal circumstances the available grounds for this belief are nonfactive, leaving it entirely open that the skeptical hypothesis may be true. But if so, then it's hard to see how James has access to anything that might adjudicate in favor of the M-belief. In other words, it's hard to see why his grounds should *favor* this belief over the skeptical possibility.

Notice that things might be different if we could count James as having relevant background information – additional grounds, say, in the form of *arguments* for thinking that God more probably exists than not. From James' own point of view such arguments may very well help tip the scales in favor of accepting the relevant M-belief over the skeptical hypotheses. Unfortunately, James is our proverbial theist in the street and so is not in possession of any such argument. One might think to suggest that James at least has additional grounds in the form of testimony from those in James' religious community, or from claims rooted in Scripture. Well, if these sources themselves provide only nonfactive grounds for accepting the relevant truth claims, then we can run similar skeptical arguments as that above. Those arguments will again threaten to show that no beliefs formed from these sources look intellectually respectable from the subject's point of view. But then, certainly, one shouldn't think they can rely on such beliefs to help tip the scales – not when such beliefs cannot themselves be looked upon favorably by the subject herself. One might therefore conclude that so long as the Religious NFR thesis is true, we have solid grounds for accepting premise 1 above.

Turn now to consider premise 2. This premise registers the intuitive verdict that so long as James is locked in the situation described above, *accepting* the relevant M-belief cannot seem, from his point of view, the respectable thing to do, at least not if he's presently attending to the skeptical hypotheses and is just a little concerned to avoid error in his beliefs. That seems eminently

---

[10] This is consistent with allowing that in *nonskeptical* contexts a subject's M-belief might be intellectually respectable from her own point of view, despite not having access to grounds that favor that belief over relevant skeptical hypothesis. Thanks to the editors for prompting this clarification.

plausible. Suppose you believe yourself to be seeing an apple. While you appreciate that this is so only if you're not seeing an artificial apple, you have no identifiable grounds that hint one way or the other. Suppose, for instance, the apparent apple is in a basket way out of reach on top of an apple display at the supermarket. Clearly, your apple belief is not intellectually respectable from your point of view. So long as you're concerned to believe something only if it's true, this looks like a complete shot in the dark. Premise 2, then, seems to enjoy a substantial degree of intuitive epistemic support.

Where does this leave us? Well, it leaves us having to accept that no M-beliefs on the part of the theist in the street are intellectually respectable from her own point of view – not while considering the proposition that these beliefs are simply the result of a religious delusion. *But*, recall, this pertains only if the Religious NFR Thesis is true. If, on the other hand, that thesis is false – if in particular one can have factive grounds for accepting an M-belief on the basis of a religious experience – then the argument falls apart. Then there's no reason to think that one cannot have reflectively accessible grounds that favor an M-belief over the skeptical hypothesis. For in such a case one has grounds that *entail the truth* of the target M-belief, thereby *making it impossible* that one is only suffering a delusory religious experience in a godless world. It's clear how the theist in the street would then have information sufficient to adjudicate in favor of the target M-belief.

Now contrast this result with that delivered by any standard externalist or internalist account in religious epistemology. Take, for example, the view that M-beliefs are warranted just insofar as they are the product of properly functioning cognitive faculties operating within an environment for which they were successfully designed to produce true beliefs (cf. Plantinga 1993a, 2000b). Notice immediately that this is presented as a theory of *warrant*, which Plantinga and followers conceive of as the property that makes the difference between only truly believing something and knowing it. Thus presented, the view is silent concerning the issue that interests us: the nature and/or strength of the reflectively accessible grounds for M-beliefs. So far, then, the view confronts the challenge that while the theist in the street's M-beliefs might be warranted all day long, they cannot, in radical skeptical contexts, be made to seem intellectually respectable from the subject's point of view.

Standard internalist accounts are similarly poorly positioned. Take, for example, the view that suggests that it's not enough for the justification (or warrant, or whatever) of M-beliefs that they are the product of properly functioning cognitive faculties (and other factors); one must also have *evidence* for the M-beliefs. Some will think that such evidence will be easy to come by so long as religious experiences suffice to make it *seem* to the subject that God is thus and so (cf. Tucker 2011). Suppose, as is eminently plausible, that M-beliefs can enjoy such evidence. If the thought here is that the best that a subject can appreciate from her own point of view is that it at least *seems to her* as though God is such and such, then the view falls directly into the hands of the above skeptical argument. These are grounds one might have even if one were suffering a delusory experience in a godless world. Such a view is entirely consistent with the Religious NFR thesis, which is the key support for premise 1. No such view can deliver the result we want. We secure that only by going disjunctivist in our religious epistemology.

At this point one might raise the following objection: if the theist in the street is in the actual world, then the relevant skeptical context at issue is one in which the relevant error possibility is *rationally motivated*.[11] In other words, our theist knows (or should know) that there are others in her community who think that there are reasons for thinking that what she takes to be cases of theistic perception are just delusional religious experiences. In this context, isn't our theist in the street thus precluded from taking for granted that her M-beliefs enjoy factive rational support? I'm not so sure. Certainly, if our theist were impressed enough by the problem of evil to seriously doubt that God exists, then she would be so precluded. But if she knows only that *others* are impressed enough to harbor grave doubts, while she is not, it does not seem to me to have the same effect. Especially if she knows that theists smarter than her in her religious community do not think this problem to be insurmountable. And so, it's not clear to me that the skeptical error possibility remains rationally motivated for our theist, especially if we think she can rely, in this way, on her epistemic community (cf. Wykstra 1998).

18.3.2 Securing Independent Grounds for Theism without Argument

RED secures a second important advantage over alternative views. If true, I think it puts the theist in the street in a position to produce *independent grounds* for believing that God exists. I want to press this point by again considering another argument:

The Argument from Circular Grounds

1. If the theist in the street cannot produce independent grounds for believing that God exists, then she doesn't have a proper rational basis for it.
2. The theist in the street cannot produce independent grounds for believing that God exists.

   ————————

   Therefore, no theist in the street has a proper rational basis for theism.

---

[11] Compare, by contrast, the error possibility that you're not seeing hands because you're a handless brain in a vat. Arguably, this error possibility is never rationally motivated when considered, and we just aren't in a position to acquire any good reason for thinking this true. For further discussion here, see Pritchard (2012: 141–50).

Consider premise 1. Suppose one endeavors to defend the truth of a claim by providing a line of reasoning that is circular or question-begging in nature. Suppose, for example, I offer to defend the claim that an election is taking place by pointing out that Jones over there has just voted. Here I have seemingly offered grounds in support of a conclusion that *I would not have* unless a rational basis for the conclusion were already place. After all, it's only because I have seen Jones mark an X on some paper that I believe he has just voted. And it's hard to see how this constitutes sufficient grounds for believing that Jones has just voted unless I *already have* grounds for thinking that an election is taking place. Therefore, by claiming that Jones over there has just voted, I have offered nothing to show where my rational basis for believing that an election is taking place has originated from. By contrast, if I were able to offer some independent grounds – say, by citing the testimony of the city officials – then we'd be in better shape. But if, as it stands, I can offer only the above line of reasoning, then it would seem that there is something important-antly lacking in the rational basis that I have for the target belief. This serves to illustrate the intuitive support behind premise 1.[12]

Premise 2 states that no theist in the street can produce independent grounds for believing that God exists, that is, grounds that are not circular or question-begging in the way illustrated above. After all, without any good arguments the best she can do is to cite her private religious experiences, or perhaps claims rooted in Scripture. But that will hardly do. Pritchard gives clear expression to this sentiment:

For notice that it is hard to see what specifically rational support is available to the [theist in the street] to justify the foundational status of [their] belief. In particular, the kind of rational support that would immediately leap to mind – e.g., personal religious experience, testimony from peers in one's religious community, the evidence of scripture, and so on – would not be apt to the task since *it already presupposes that one's belief in God's existence is rationally held*. (Pritchard 2011: 145, emphasis added)

Let's focus on religious experience. The claim here is that appealing to claims rooted in religious experiences (e.g., one's M-beliefs) cannot be a way of

---

[12] The election example is taken from Wright (2002: 333). While Wright thinks there is epistemic circularity here, it is *not* the kind defined by Bergmann (2006). According to Bergmann, "an epistemically circular argument's conclusion is such that *its truth is required for warranted belief* in one of the premises" (2006: 181). In Wright's voting example presented here, the circularity obtains *not* because having rational support for the premises requires the *truth* of the target conclusion (that an election is taking place). Rather, the circularity is meant to obtain because having rational support for the premises requires having *rational support* for the target conclusion. The difference here is between what Jim Pryor calls type-2 and type-3 epistemic dependence of a conclusion upon the premises of an argument (Pryor, 2004: 358). Thanks to Tyler McNabb for inviting me to comment on these connections.

producing independent grounds for theism; for any attempt to do so involves offering grounds for theism that one *would not have* unless a rational basis for theism were already somehow in place. Call this the *presupposition thesis.*

Presupposition Thesis. One cannot take religious experience of God at face value without already having in place a suitable rational basis for theism.

Premise 2 above rests for its support on the presupposition thesis. I'll argue that the presupposition thesis rests in turn on the Religious NFT Thesis. Since RED *rejects* that thesis, we can avoid the conclusion of the above argument while unlocking a rather novel idea: that you needn't have to produce an argument for God's existence in order to produce independent grounds for theism. The theist in the street can be shown to have a suitable rational basis for theism after all, despite lacking a suitable argument.[13]

First, I'll show how natural the presupposition thesis can seem within the context of the Religious NFR thesis. It will be helpful to have an example of an exchange to consider. So, suppose James is invited to defend his belief that God exists. Suppose he cites claims whose contents are those of previously formed M-beliefs: "Why think God exists? Well, let me tell you, He's been nothing but present to me all my life, offering among other things tremendous encouragement through life's difficulties." Notice that in citing previously formed M-beliefs, James is appealing to beliefs for which he's never had better than nonfactive grounds for accepting. That follows if the Religious NFR thesis is true. We can model the structure of this line of reasoning, then, as follows:

The (I–II–III) Defense from Religious Experience

GOD (I) Seeming to perceive that God is encouraging me.
GOD (II) God is encouraging me.
GOD (III) Therefore, God exists.
(Since God is encouraging me only if God exists)[14]

We have here, in effect, a defense of GOD (III) by appeal to the supposed rational grounds one enjoys for GOD (II) on the basis of GOD (I). The presupposition thesis says that any grounds one has for accepting GOD (II) on the basis of GOD (I), one has courtesy of having a suitable rational basis for GOD (III) already in place. In other words, the claimed grounds for theism are not enjoyed *independent* of having a suitable rational basis for theism. This seems to me entirely plausible *so long as* the Religious NFR thesis is in place to ensure that one never has better than the nonfactive grounds described in GOD (I) for accepting GOD (II).

---

[13] What follows is a version of the argument I outline in Shaw (2019).
[14] This I-II-III structure is adopted from Wright (2002).

We can press the point in terms of what is needed to surpass the *cognitive locality* that the Religious NFR thesis here creates. The issue is by now familiar. Suppose one has access only to the fact that it *seems to one* that God is encouraging one. How, on so flimsy a basis, can one rightly determine that God is *in fact* encouraging one when, so easily from the subject's point of view, one might just as well be suffering a delusory religious experience in a godless world? To appropriate what Annalisa Coliva says in another context, even if our subject is in the good case, she should still need some "subjectively available reason" for thinking that her religious experiences are more likely caused by real encounters with God than by purely natural causes (Coliva 2015: 25).

In this context it can seem entirely reasonable to suppose that unless one has already in place a suitable rational basis for theism, one cannot take one's religious experiences at face value. For otherwise, doing so would appear far too arbitrary from the subject's point of view. Thus, it can seem entirely reasonable to adopt the presupposition thesis as a way of accounting for the intellectual respectability of taking one's religious experiences at face value. The problem this generates, though, as Pritchard notes above, is that one cannot then go on to cite these religious experiences as a means of providing independent grounds for accepting that God exists.

RED is now a game changer. For suppose that the Religious NFR thesis is false because the available grounds for accepting a target M-belief can be factive, and so of a very different kind than that in GOD (I) above. Then there is no longer an issue of needing to surpass one's cognitive locality with respect to M-beliefs. The relevant "gap" between one's M-belief and the supposed grounds for thinking it true no longer exists. And so, what is arguably the key motivation behind the presupposition thesis falls to the ground, and with it premise 2 of the circularity argument above.

18.4 Conclusion

In this chapter I've explored the prospects for applying epistemological disjunctivism to the religious context. I think those prospects are good. If theistic perception presents no insurmountable metaphysical problems, then I don't see why we cannot conceive of theistic perception as a source of grounds for M-beliefs that are both factive and reflectively accessible to the subject. There is much to gain by doing so. Those beliefs can then be shown to be intellectually respectable from the point of view of the theist in the street, even in skeptical contexts, thus securing an important internalist insight that famously eludes views more in keeping with the status quo. More than that, we are positioned to unlock a view about the epistemology of theistic belief that I have not seen defended before. Within the context of the Religious NFR thesis, it can seem that unless one has some good argument for God, then one's rational basis for theistic belief can seem defective, on account of one's then being unable to produce independent grounds for believing that God exists. That thought misfires if RED is true. For if it is true, then it's no longer clear why appealing to claims rooted in religious experiences cannot be ways of offering independent grounds for theism.

19 Debunking Arguments and Religious Belief

Joshua C. Thurow

Introduction

Imagine you are one of the many people who, in 2016, found a story in your Facebook feed that claimed that Pope Francis had endorsed Donald Trump for president of the United States. The article looks like many other articles in your feed – the writing is similar, the reporting style is similar, and the source is what appears to be a local news channel. Although somewhat surprised by the content, you believe it – after all, there's been lots of weird stuff in the news lately, right? Later, you discover that the source, WTOE 5 News, is not a local television station and that this source has published other false eye-catching claims. This doesn't tell you that the article's claim is false, but it casts serious doubt on the trustworthiness of the source, and so you now refrain from judging, or perhaps even disbelieve, that Pope Francis has endorsed Trump.

In this example, your initial belief that Pope Francis endorsed Trump was debunked by what you later learned about the source you relied on for your belief. In particular, you learned that there was something epistemically fishy about the source of your belief: namely, it isn't as reliable as you had initially assumed.

This is but one simple example of a much broader phenomena – debunking arguments. Later in this chapter, debunking arguments will be analyzed in greater detail, but initially they can be characterized like this: debunking arguments aim to undermine a belief based on epistemically problematic features of how the belief was originally formed or is currently held. Typically debunking arguments offer at least a partial genealogy for the belief and then point out epistemically problematic features of the genealogy.

Religious beliefs have been the target of debunking arguments since at least the time of Hume.[1] Religious beliefs have been thought (i) to be the product of wish fulfillment, (ii) to be an opiate of the masses, (iii) to be a product of enculturation, (iv) to be a byproduct of evolutionarily evolved cognitive mechanisms, and (v) to be a cultural tool to enhance cooperation. These purported influences on religious belief appear to not have any bearing on whether religious beliefs are true. They suggest that humans have religious

---

[1] See Hume (1990 [1779]), Yandell (1990), Kail (2007), and De Cruz (2015).

beliefs for other reasons; once we recognize these real reasons and acknowledge that these real reasons do not indicate that our religious beliefs are true, we should cease to hold our religious beliefs – just as in the above case, you should cease to hold your belief that Pope Francis endorsed Trump. These sorts of debunking arguments have grown in prominence since the late twentieth century, concomitant with the growth of evolutionary psychology and the cognitive science of religion.

The goal of this chapter is to explain how debunking arguments work, present some specific debunking arguments for religious belief, and outline various ways philosophers have attempted to respond to them.

19.1 Debunking Arguments

Debunking a belief differs from other sorts of challenges to a belief, such as a rebuttal or refutation. Unlike debunking, the latter aim to either give reason to think or demonstrate that a belief is false. Compare the debunking arguments for religious beliefs just mentioned to the problem of evil for theism. The problem of evil aims to either give evidence or demonstrate that God does not exist. The above debunking arguments do not do this. Take, for example, the claim that religious belief arises from wish fulfillment. This claim, if true, is not evidence that religious beliefs are false. Rather, this claim, if true, is evidence that religious beliefs are not formed in a way that latches on to the truth. Those beliefs may turn out to be true, for all we know, but our *grounds* for those beliefs do not give us any reason for thinking they are true.

Debunking arguments are a kind of putative undercutting defeater for a belief. Undercutting defeaters knock out the reasons or grounds of the belief by, for example, showing that the reasons do not adequately support the belief or that the grounds are not reliable or do not suffice for a competent belief.[2] The problem of evil is, by contrast, a putative rebutting defeater. Rebutting defeaters for a belief give reason for thinking that the belief is false.[3]

Debunking arguments have two main parts: causal and epistemic. The causal part describes some factors that have influenced the way the belief was formed or has been maintained. The epistemic part draws some epistemic implication from those factors. And the conclusion of a debunking argument states that the belief in question lacks some epistemically valuable status (e.g.,

---

[2] Like Audi (2020), I distinguish reasons from grounds; the former are inferential, whereas the latter are not. Resulting from a perceptual belief-forming mechanism is an example of a ground for a belief.

[3] See Sudduth (n.d.) for an overview on defeaters. It is worth noting that a defeater could in some circumstances be both undercutting and rebutting (McBrayer 2018). So, in principle, a debunking argument could also function as a rebutting defeater, depending on the belief and the defeating factors. Debunking arguments for religious beliefs typically function merely as undercutting defeaters.

the belief is not justified, or is less justified than before, or is not known). Here is a useful schema for debunking arguments:

Debunking Argument Schema

1. S's belief B has been influenced by factor F.
2. Beliefs that are influenced by F do not satisfy epistemic condition R.
3. If B does not satisfy R (or, for some principles, if S is justified in believing that B does not satisfy R), then S lacks epistemic status E in continuing to hold B.

   Therefore,

C. (Once S becomes justified in believing that B does not satisfy R) S's belief B lacks E.[4]

Premise 1 constitutes the causal part of the argument. Premises 2 and 3 together constitute the epistemic part. Premise 3 is the sole purely epistemic premise in the argument. It is an epistemic debunking principle – an epistemic principle that states that certain conditions are sufficient for some sort of debunking.

This is an argument schema, so many different debunking arguments can be generated by filling in different values for B, F, R, and E. Debunking arguments can have different target beliefs, B, they are aiming to debunk; different features, F, of the genealogy of B to which they draw attention; different epistemic conditions, R, that are argued to follow from F (e.g., being not reliably formed, insensitive, unsafe, incompetently formed); and different negative epistemic outcomes for B, E (e.g., being unjustified, being less justified, lacking knowledge). Beliefs that are successfully targeted by a sound debunking argument can be said to be, in some sense, debunked – that is, their epistemic status is not as good as it previously was (or was thought to be), and this loss of status is due to the genealogical information put forward in the argument.

Since we are here concerned with the debunking of religious beliefs, B will be constrained to include only religious beliefs.[5] However, there are many

---

[4] This is slightly modified from Thurow (2018). The parenthetical remarks in premises 3 and 4 are present because some debunking arguments succeed only if the believer becomes justified in believing that their belief does not satisfy R, whereas for other arguments the mere fact that the believer does not satisfy R is enough to debunk their belief regardless of whether they recognize that their belief does not satisfy R. Which kind of argument we are working with depends on R and E.

[5] Debunking arguments have targeted many other sorts of beliefs including, perhaps most famously, moral beliefs (Street 2006; Joyce 2007; Wielenberg 2010; Sauer 2018) as well as mathematical, color, and modal beliefs (see references in Korman 2019). Korman (2019) rightly observes that some debunking arguments are conditional – they argue that given a theorist's set of theoretical commitments, that theorist is committed to regarding certain beliefs as debunked. The most famous example of such an argument is Plantinga's evolutionary argument against naturalism (Beilby 2002; Plantinga 2011).

different religious beliefs, and so even here there might be dozens of different debunking arguments. We cannot consider them all; in any case, recent literature has focused on arguments that aim to debunk belief in gods and other sorts of invisible agents. For the sake of illustration, we will focus on one belief of this sort, namely belief in an invisible, very powerful, very knowledgeable, and morally concerned God – what Norenzayan (2013) calls "Big Gods." The Jewish, Christian, and Muslim God counts as a big god, as does Brahman in monotheistic strands of Hinduism.

Even this narrowly focused target leaves us with many different debunking arguments, as such arguments can appeal to various genealogical features of belief in a big god and rely on different epistemic debunking principles. The next two sections will survey these varieties by, first, summarizing various features that have been used in religious debunking arguments and, second, surveying various epistemic principles that have been used in such arguments. Then, in Section 19.4, we will narrow focus a bit by presenting three prominent debunking arguments from recent literature.

19.2 Genealogical Features of Belief in God

Pascal Boyer, anthropologist and author of *Religion Explained* – one of the most prominent works in the cognitive science of religion – writes, "everybody seems to have some intuition about the origins of religion. Indeed, anthropologists and psychologists ... constantly run into people who think that they already have a perfectly adequate solution to the problem" (Boyer 2001: 5). It would be impossible here to summarize the many accounts of the origin of religion that have been offered (and unnecessary since many are plainly inadequate, as Boyer demonstrates). Instead, we will briefly survey the most prominent explanations that have been developed in the last twenty-five years within the cognitive science of religion.[6] In addition, we will survey a few other potential influences on religious belief.

Today, the most prominent explanations for why humans have religious beliefs are evolutionary in nature. These explanations thus find that religious beliefs (or certain sorts of religious beliefs) were either adaptive, or the byproducts of other adaptive traits, or exaptive – that is, they emerged as byproducts and then became adaptive. Furthermore, these explanations often differ in what they take to be the object of selection: the individual (i.e., individual selection), the group (i.e., group selection), or a concept or idea (i.e., cultural selection).

---

[6] See Preus (1987) for a summary of many classic theories. I'll use "theories" and "explanations" interchangeably in what follows, as these explanations are theories, and they are theories that offer explanations.

According to byproduct explanations, humans have various cognitive features that are adaptive (i.e., humans have these features because these features helped those who had them in their past environment to survive and reproduce better than those that lacked them), and those cognitive features make it very easy to acquire, or even bias humans toward, religious beliefs. One family of byproduct theories are what Hans Van Eyghen calls "preparatory accounts": they do not explain where religious belief came from originally, but they explain why humans would be able to easily entertain religious ideas and find them quite plausible once they are encountered (Van Eyghen 2020: 31). These preparatory accounts appeal to the following features: (i) god concepts are minimally counterintuitive, (ii) humans are intuitive dualists, (iii) humans have an intuitive theory of mind, (iv) childhood development of the theory of mind has children expecting people to be hyperknowers, and (v) humans use their mental resources, including their theory of mind, to make sense of death.

Pascal Boyer has argued that many core religious concepts are minimally counterintuitive – that is, they have at most a couple variations on natural human categories of concepts (Boyer 2001). For instance, *tree* is a natural plant concept, and the category of plant brings along with it certain expectations about how a tree behaves, grows, and reproduces. A change in one or two of these expectations produces a minimally counterintuitive concept (e.g., *invisible tree*). God concepts involve minor variations on the concept of a person – namely, it is a concept of an invisible and highly powerful and knowledgeable person. Minimally counterintuitive concepts spread easily. They are more interesting than intuitive concepts and not as difficult to comprehend as highly counterintuitive concepts. Some of them, such as big god concepts, are also potentially useful for explaining events in the world.

Humans have a set of mental mechanisms devoted to conceiving and understanding agents, which is often called a theory of mind. Our theory of mind enables us to quickly and intuitively understand and conceive of beliefs, motives, concerns, and goals. Furthermore, the theory of mind operates distinct from our intuitive theory of biology. As a result, as Paul Bloom (2005) has argued, humans are intuitive dualists – they naturally understand mental life and biological life to be separate and, in principle, separable features of a person. These traits make it easy for humans to conceive and think about gods, for gods are persons who do not have a body but have a mind and thus have beliefs, goals, and concerns. In addition, young children's theory of mind leads them to think of persons as hyperknowers – that is, as knowing what the children recognize as knowable or worth knowing. Gradually, children come to learn that humans are limited and flawed knowers, but they easily maintain the idea that God is a hyperknower (Barrett 2012). Boyer (2001) argues that the conflicting intuitions between our systems of judgment about biology and mind when we think about dead people makes it easy for us to think that there are invisible disembodied persons who inhabit the world.

The above features all prepare the human mind to entertain and take seriously the idea of a god. They do not explain how humans arrived at the idea of a god. Maybe no such explanation is needed. Humans more or less spontaneously entertain loads of ideas – perhaps it was inevitable that various communities of humans would eventually entertain the idea of a god. However the idea arose, these features, highlighted by the preparatory accounts, explain why humans would find god concepts attractive and plausible.

Other theories of religion, without contradicting the preparatory account, go further by suggesting factors that nudge humans toward, or select for, belief in gods. Justin Barrett (2004) has famously argued that humans possess a hypersensitive agency detection device (HADD) that is set to interpret ambiguous information as evidence of the activity of an agent. For instance, HADD might lead us to think a rustling in a bush is a sign of an animal, or that an odd bang in the house indicates an intruder. Barrett thinks HADD was an evolutionary adaptation, but as a byproduct it will leave us suspecting there is an agent at work in many situations where we can find no other direct evidence of an agent's activity. We will thus have an inclination to think there are invisible agents at work, such as spirits, ghosts, and gods.

Deborah Kelemen and her colleagues have conducted various studies that indicate that humans from various cultures – children, especially – engage in promiscuously teleological thinking. That is, "they reveal a strong tendency to see purpose in nature and generally prefer purpose-based (i.e., teleological) over mechanistic physical explanations as early as preschool, and they generate these types of explanations even when they have not heard them or had them reinforced by others" (Kundert and Edman 2017: 76). These tendencies are shown even in adults when they are made to perform experimental tasks under cognitive load (i.e., quickly, or while performing other tasks, or with distractions). As a result, Kelemen suggests that humans are intuitive theists: "a bias to explain, plus a human predilection for intentional explanation, may then be what leads children, in the absence of knowledge, to a generalized, default view of entities as intentionally caused by someone for a purpose" (Kelemen 2004: 296).

The preceding two explanations fit into the byproduct paradigm for explaining religious belief. Some scholars have argued that some religious beliefs, including belief in big gods, are adaptive. These scholars tend to accept the insights of the preparatory and byproduct accounts. So, they are sympathetic to the idea that a proclivity to accept religious beliefs was initially a byproduct of other adaptive mechanisms. But they think that once on the scene, the acceptance of these beliefs became an adaptation (thus, religious attitudes are exaptations). These adaptationist/exaptationist views regard religious beliefs as adaptive because of how they enable humans to thrive in a social environment. They differ in their explanations of how this works.

One prominent explanation comes from the work of Ara Norenzayan (2013), who argues that belief in big gods is adaptive because the concept of big gods was a tool that large societies came upon to solve the puzzle of big groups.[7] The puzzle is that the survival of big groups requires a high level of social cooperation, but once groups get too big, other mechanisms of rooting out free riders are not effective (e.g., kin selection, reputation management, reciprocity), and so big groups should fall apart. Belief in a big god can solve this puzzle, for if people believe that there is a god who knows everything about what you are doing and thinking, cares that you do what is right and cooperate with others, and will punish you for not doing so or reward you for doing so, then you will be more likely to cooperate. If believers can find ways to signal their belief to each other (and those signals are hard to fake), then believers will find each other, cooperate with each other at a high rate, and reap the benefits. Because of the clear benefits of being part of such a cooperative arrangement, belief in big gods will spread and can be the foundation of very large societies.

The above is just a sampling of some of the theories from the cognitive science of religion of explanatory factors for the widespread prevalence of religious belief.[8] These theories have a couple notable common features. First, all of the theorists who forward these theories grant that more work needs to be done to test and confirm these theories. The theories are promising – their defenders have tested them with various sorts of evidence from history, anthropology, experimental psychology, and behavioral economics. These theories have been far more rigorously formulated and tested than any earlier theory of religion. However, the diversity of theories is one indication that more evidence is needed before any of them can be accepted with confidence. Second, these theories do not explain why any individual person believes in a god. Rather, they explain why belief in gods would develop and become widespread in human communities.

In addition to these more distal evolutionary factors, there are a variety of proximate factors that can influence religious belief in a way that could raise debunking worries. Christian Smith summarizes many of them in his long list of what he calls "cognitive lubricants" for religious attributions (Smith 2017: 183–8). These are common cognitive biases and social psychological effects that can influence people's religious beliefs, including how and when people attribute religious significance, such as the activity of God, to an event. For instance, humans are known to suffer from a confirmation bias that leads

---

[7] For a different adaptationist explanation, see the divine punishment theory of Johnson and Bering (2009) and Bering (2011).

[8] See Stausberg (2009) for a commentary on several contemporary theories and McCauley (2011) for a particularly useful and clear discussion of various factors explaining why religion is natural.

them to focus on confirming evidence for their beliefs, ignore disconfirming evidence, and interpret evidence in a way that conforms to their beliefs. Another example is motivated reasoning. Dan Kahan has found that the political judgments of US adults, especially regarding divisive issues, are strongly influenced by a person's political affiliation. He argues that this is best explained by identity protection: the formation of beliefs to "maintain a person's connection to and status within an identity-defining affinity group whose members are united by shared values" (Kahan 2016: 2).[9] Religious beliefs seem just as, if not more, vulnerable to these influences as other beliefs. The confirmation bias flourishes when there is not clear and decisive experiential evidence available to resolve an issue and beliefs about God are not so clearly and decisively evaluable (even if religious experience provides evidence). And of course, many religious believers have their identity wrapped up in their religious beliefs and affiliations.

There are many other influences on religious belief that we must pass over for lack of space.[10] The influences we have surveyed (and those we have not surveyed) are used to support premise 1 of the schema. We now turn to examine debunking principles that have been used to undergird the epistemic part of the schema.

19.3 Epistemic Debunking Principles

The epistemic part of debunking arguments aims to show that when a belief is influenced in the ways indicated, it does not satisfy an epistemic condition R in virtue of which (or in virtue of the recognition of which) the belief lacks epistemic state E, such as being known or justified or as justified as much as it was before learning about the genealogical features. Various epistemic debunking principles have been used in the literature; in this section we briefly survey them.

Sometimes a broad, somewhat undefined notion of "tracking the truth" is used. One such epistemic debunking principle is as follows:

(TT) If S comes to realize that her belief that p results from a process that does not track the truth regarding p-related beliefs, then S is not justified in believing p.

We want our beliefs to be true, and we want to use methods or processes for arriving at beliefs that track the way the world is. If the process I used to form B does not track the truth and I realize as much, then I have no reason to think that B matches the way the world is. As a result, my belief is unjustified.

---

[9] For a more general skepticism motivated by motivated reasoning, see Carter and McKenna (2020).

[10] See, especially, Luhrmann (2020).

Although TT is plausible, it can be difficult to employ given the vagueness of the notion of "truth-tracking." Various more precise accounts of truth-tracking have been given, although the resulting epistemic principles have proven controversial.[11] The three most popular truth-tracking notions are sensitivity, safety, and reliability.

A person's belief that p, formed using method/process M, is sensitive to the fact that p just in case: if p were false and the person were to use just M in order to investigate whether p, the person would not believe p.[12] Here's one example of a more precise version of TT utilizing sensitivity:

(SensJ) If S comes to realize that S has formed belief that p via a method/process that is not sensitive, then S is not justified in believing p.

Principles like SensJ are either explicitly or implicitly employed in many debunking arguments (Joyce 2007; Thurow 2013; Braddock 2016). They face various challenges, perhaps the most notable of which is that inductive arguments are insensitive, and yet it seems we can have justified beliefs via inductive arguments.[13]

Safety principles have been more popular than sensitivity principles in recent epistemology. A person's belief that p, formed using method/process M, is safe just in case: if the person were to form a belief about p or p-related propositions using M, then p would be true.[14] Here's an example of a more precise version of TT that uses safety rather than sensitivity:

(SafeJ) If S comes to realize that S has formed belief that p via a method/process that is not safe, then S is not justified in believing p.

Safety has also been challenged (although, admittedly, safety as a necessary condition for knowledge has been the typical target, rather than a recognition of unsafety being sufficient for lack of justification).[15]

Reliabilism about knowledge and justification has been widely endorsed. And the notion of reliability seems particularly useful when dealing with defeaters, for even internalist theories of justification and knowledge grant that if I have a justified belief that my belief B is being held on the basis of an

---

[11] See, for instance, White (2010) and Korman and Locke (2020) for critique of various formulations of debunking arguments.

[12] As is typical, sensitivity is here defined in a method-relative way to get around various well-known counterexamples.

[13] See Thurow (2013) and some of the essays in Becker and Black (2012) for discussion of this objection.

[14] There are various formulations of safety principles. This one, like SensJ, makes use of methods to ward off certain objections. The addition of "p-related propositions" is meant to address the problem that most safety principles entail that any true belief about a necessary proposition turns out to be trivially safe.

[15] See Sosa (2007) and Bogardus (2016).

unreliable process, the justification I initially had for B is defeated. Here's an example of a reliability-based debunking principle:

(RelJ) If S comes to realize that S has formed belief that p via a method/process that is not reliable, then S is not justified in believing p.

Although reliability has been difficult to rigorously define, a couple things seem clear. First, reliability of a process should be defined relative to types of propositions and to ordinary situations in which the process is fit to be used (either because it was designed to be used in those situations or because it has evolved to be fit for those situations). Second, reliability is a modal notion – whether a process is reliable depends on how it performs in a range of actual and counterfactual situations. Some have questioned principles like these for reasons related to the classic generality problem for reliabilism. You can get different judgments about whether a process is reliable based on different characterizations of the process; which characterization is the one that matters?[16]

Instead of worrying about whether the target belief results from a truth-tracking process, we might instead worry about whether the target belief was formed in an epistemically virtuous way. Ernest Sosa's virtue epistemology provides one way of developing a virtue-based debunking principle. Sosa's epistemology is focused on the notion of aptness; a belief is apt when it is true because it was formed competently (Sosa 2017). A competence is "a disposition to succeed when one aims at a given objective, in certain (favorable enough) conditions while in (good enough) shape" (Sosa 2017: 193). For Sosa, justification for a belief takes into consideration reflection on whether one's belief was formed aptly. Sosa's system entails the following debunking principle:

(Apt EDP) If I become justified in believing that I might easily have held my belief B, in the way that I have held it, incompetently, then I lack reflective knowledge, knowledge full well, and justified belief that p.[17]

If I become justified in believing that the way that I hold my belief might easily have been incompetent, then I have decent grounds for believing that I do not hold the belief competently. As a result, I cannot aptly recognize that my belief is apt; reflective knowledge requires aptly recognizing my belief is apt, and knowledge full well requires accepting my belief because I recognize its aptness. Thus, I lack reflective knowledge and knowledge full well. Since, on

---

[16] See De Cruz and De Smedt (2015) for an example of this objection and Thurow (2016) for a reply.

[17] See Thurow (2018) for further discussion of (a different phrasing of) this and other debunking principles derived from Sosa's epistemology. This formulation comes from Thurow (2022).

Sosa's view, I should believe in accordance with what my higher-level evidence indicates, I also lack justified belief.

All of the debunking arguments targeting religious belief of which I am aware rest on one of the above principles, or variations on these principles.[18] We now survey some of these arguments.

19.4 Some Debunking Arguments

Relying on the TT principle, Wilkins and Griffiths argue that evolutionary explanations such as those mentioned in Section 19.1 imply that religious beliefs do not track the truth because "none of the leading accounts of the evolution of religious belief makes any reference to the truth or falsity of those beliefs when explaining their effects on reproductive fitness" (2012: 142). Neither byproduct nor adaptationist accounts make any reference to the existence of gods, and so the processes described in these accounts could operate just as well and produce belief in gods whether or not there are any gods. Sometimes this point is put in terms of insensitivity: if there were no god and yet humans were to form a belief about gods using the processes in question, humans would likely still believe in gods (Thurow 2013).[19]

A related argument can be developed using RelJ – call it the "unreliability due to diverse outputs" argument. The evolutionary factors mentioned in the various cognitive science of religion theories can help explain a wide range of beliefs – belief in the Christian, Jewish, Islamic, or Hindu god, or in other polytheistic gods, spirits, and ghosts, for instance. On just about anybody's view, most of these beliefs are false; monotheists think the polytheist (and competing monotheist) gods do not exist. A real generous polytheist could allow that most of these beings exist, but that sort of polytheist is rare. So, then, on most views the factors mentioned by these theories produce mostly false beliefs within the target domain of beliefs about gods, and thus they are unreliable (Braddock 2016). Given RelJ, we should conclude that those of us who are aware of these evolutionary explanations are not justified in holding beliefs in gods.

These two debunking arguments face a couple of challenges that, as we will see shortly, another debunking argument entirely evades. Wilkins and Griffiths' argument attempts to show that the processes that ground beliefs

---

[18] Korman and Locke (2020) defend a different epistemic debunking principle – what they call an explanatory constraint on justified belief. Their principle can generate debunking worries about ethical beliefs but is less clearly threatening to religious beliefs such as belief in God.

[19] Note that the methods formulation of SensJ evades the objection that, on many theistic views, everything depends on God and so if God didn't exist there would be no humans around to form any beliefs (Murray and Schloss 2013). Whether a belief is sensitive depends on what the person would have believed had they used the same method of belief while the belief was false.

in gods do not track the truth. However, truth-tracking, like reliability, should be understood relative to a set of conditions in which the process is fit to operate. Those conditions surely include the conditions that make evolution possible. But now consider the following possibility: God created humans with the intent that they would come to believe in God through the processes in question. If God had done this, then one of the conditions in which the process is fit to operate is that God made it to be used that way. Under that condition, belief in God formed using that process does track the truth. Thus, Wilkins and Griffiths cannot argue that the processes in question do not track the truth without first having an argument that God did not intend for humans to believe in God through them.[20] The unreliability due to diverse outputs argument faces a different objection. Even if many or even most output beliefs of the process are false, the process could still be reliable for a certain general output: there is a divine being of some sort. The argument, as stated, does not give reason to think that this more general belief is unreliably generated.[21] This point can be coupled with the objection to Wilkins and Griffiths' argument: God may well use the processes in question to generate a general sense of the existence of something divine as a step in developing a more intimate relationship with God over time. The argument cannot show that the processes, when used to form this more general belief, are unreliable without first showing that this view about God is false. Note that these objections do not aim to show that belief in God is justified; rather, they aim to show that the above debunking arguments fail in showing that belief in God is not justified.

Whether or not these are good objections to the above debunking arguments, a debunking argument based on Apt EDP evades these objections altogether. According to Apt EDP, if I am justified in thinking that there is a decent chance that the way I formed my belief is incompetent, then I am not justified in holding my belief. If God exists, then a person's belief in him may well be competent if God designed the processes in question to generate belief in him. But if God doesn't exist, then the processes will not be competent, for all the reasons given above in discussion of the previous two debunking arguments. There is at least a decent epistemic chance that God does not exist – a chance I need to take seriously – as there is at least some prima facie strong evidence that he does not exist, namely the problem of evil. This argument does not assume that the problem of evil is in fact strong evidence that God does not exist – just that it is prima facie strong enough to require us to take the possibility of God's nonexistence seriously. But the processes in question that generate belief in God cannot discriminate between whether God

---

[20] This argument is clearly inspired by Plantinga's response to the Marx/Freud objection: it presents no de jure objection to Christian belief in God without a de facto objection (Plantinga 2000b). See Murray and Schloss (2013) and Thurow (2018) for further discussion.

[21] I discuss this move at greater length in Thurow (2013) and Thurow (2018).

exists or does not exist – in either scenario, people will believe that God exists. A believer in God is now left in the following situation: she has some reason to doubt that she is competent and has no way of confirming whether she is competent because her beliefs about God result from a process (the process described by the cognitive science of religion theories) that cannot discriminate whether God exists. She thus is justified in thinking that there is a decent chance she has formed her belief incompetently, and according to Apt EDP, she is thus not justified in believing that God exists.[22]

19.5 Replies to the Debunking Arguments

In the previous section we discussed a couple objections that target specific versions of debunking arguments. In this final section we will briefly present a few objections that, if successful, would undermine many (perhaps all) variations of debunking arguments for belief in God.

19.5.1 The Religious Reasons Reply

We observed that the evolutionary explanations of religious belief explain why humans in general tend to believe in big gods and other invisible agents. They provide, thus, at most a partial explanation of the beliefs of any community or individual. A fuller explanation for why Carol Christian believes in God will involve historical accounts of how Christian belief arose and spread and local explanations for how Carol's parents and friends and neighbors have influenced her, as well as her own individual reflection. For many, if not most, semi-mature religious believers, religious reasons will make their way into this explanation. These reasons needn't take the form of explicitly formulated philosophical arguments; just as when we make predictions about how our friends will react to certain situations based on our extensive history of interaction with them – without explicitly calling to mind various specific incidents or giving arguments – so people may believe in God based on how God's existence makes sense of so many aspects of the world and our lives, without explicitly calling to mind these various aspects or giving arguments. A theist like Carol will have the sense that God makes sense of why there is a universe at all and why it looks designed in various ways. She may have religious experiences while praying or know of others who have had such experiences. She has a sense of how life should be lived that integrates well with her beliefs about God. If she participates in a religious community, she has testimonial evidence about these and other matters from people she has excellent reason to trust. These all amount to reasons for her belief in God on

---

[22] See Thurow (2018) for a deeper discussion of this argument.

which she, in part, bases her belief. Whether her belief is justified, then, depends on whether these are good reasons. The debunking arguments presented above give no reason for thinking these are poor reasons, and thus they cannot undermine Carol's belief.[23]

This reply faces a couple challenges. First, there is a worry about whether debunking arguments can be developed for the religious reasons themselves – perhaps debunking arguments show that believers aren't reliable at assessing these sorts of reasons.[24] Second, Derek Leben has argued that appeal to religious reasons is best explained as a rationalization rather than a real reason for which a person believes (Leben 2014; Hricko and Leben 2018).[25]

19.5.2 The Classic Plantingean Approach

Tyler McNabb derives from Plantinga's work on defeat a general approach to deflecting defeaters:

CPR: S's belief that p can deflect defeater D if S still believes p on the reflection of D and p is the product of properly functioning faculties that are successfully aimed at truth and there is a high objective probability [by objective probability, I <mean> that there is a likelihood of the belief being true in terms of frequency] that the belief produced under these conditions would be true. (McNabb 2019: 31)

So long as a person continues to strongly hold their belief in God, and they are functioning properly, and it is objectively likely that in those conditions their belief is true, then the debunking arguments are deflected. Many religious believers may find themselves in this condition – especially if God, in fact, exists.

It may well be that in these conditions, a person has knowledge that God exists. For instance, on Sosa's view, one can have animal knowledge (i.e., apt belief) while having evidence that one's belief is not apt. But in these circumstances, belief still seems epistemically bad in some way because one is not adequately accounting for higher-order evidence of unreliability or incompetence. If I have evidence that I am not competent or reliable, it seems I should take such evidence into account even if, in fact, I am functioning properly, competent, and reliable. Belief pill and other examples make this claim quite plausible (Joyce 2007; Christensen 2010). Apt EDP-based debunking arguments take into account evidence of incompetence and suggest that I should not continue to hold my belief in these circumstances – it is

---

[23] See Thurow (2013, 2014a, 2014b, 2022) and Jong and Visala (2014) for further discussion of the religious reasons reply.

[24] See Thurow (2013, 2014a, 2014b) and De Cruz and De Smedt (2015) for discussion of this worry.

[25] See Thurow (2022) for a detailed reply to this concern.

unjustified and does not amount to reflective knowledge or knowledge full well. One worry for CPR, then, is that it does not deflect all sorts of debunking arguments.

19.5.3 Epistemic Self-Promotion

Andrew Moon (2021) argues that some theists can deflect debunking arguments because their own religious belief system supports an epistemically self-promoting proposition. For instance, Moon argues, following Plantinga (2000b), that a Christian will often have good reason to believe that "given Christianity's truth, there is a Holy Spirit who is involved in the salvation of human beings . . . which will include their Christian belief formation by way of the Holy Spirit's testimony and instigation" (2021: 794). Since Carol Christian knows both this and that she has formed and sustained her Christian belief in the typical way, she has a defeater-deflector (which prevents something from being a defeater in the first place) for debunking arguments: Carol's belief system itself (provided she is justified in believing it in the first place) gives her reason to think her belief in God is reliable and competent in the circumstances in which she believes. The latter entails that whatever other factors are influencing or have influenced her religious belief do not undermine her reliability or competence. This response involves epistemic circularity but, Moon argues, of a benign sort.[26]

One might worry that this defense is too good – it insulates belief in God so thickly that nothing can undermine it. Moon responds that some people might be subject to a debunking argument if they do not hold their religious belief in the normal way favored by the self-promoting proposition, and that this response does nothing to deflect rebutting defeaters such as the problem of evil. But given the latter point, Moon's response may be ineffective against the Apt EDP-based debunking argument, for presumably a person like us in a situation where God does not exist can also make use of the self-promoting proposition, and so this proposition will not discriminate between the two live possibilities: one in which God exists and superintends the belief-forming process, and one in which he does not.

Arguments that aim to debunk religious belief bring together two fascinating and growing intellectual realms: cognitive evolutionary explanations of religious belief and epistemological reflection on defeat. Both realms are currently flourishing, and so we should expect continued innovations in the evaluation of debunking arguments.

---

[26] Some of the phrasing in this paragraph is inspired by Thurow (2022).

References

Abelson, R. & Kanouse, D. E. 1966. "Subjective Acceptance of Verbal Generalizations," in S. Feldman (ed.), *Cognitive Consistency: Motivational Antecedents and Behavioral Consequents.* New York: Academic Press, pp. 171–197.

Abraham, W. J. 1987. "Cumulative Case Arguments for Christian Theism," in W. J. Abraham and S. W. Holtzer (eds.), *The Rationality of Religious Belief: Essays in Honour of Basil Mitchell.* Oxford University Press, pp. 17–37.

Abrahamov, B. 1993. "Necessary Knowledge in Islamic Theology," *British Journal of Middle Eastern Studies* 20: 20–32.

   2016. "Scripturalist and Traditionalist Theology," in S. Schmidtke (ed.), *The Oxford Handbook of Islamic Theology.* Oxford University Press, pp. 263–279.

'Abd al-Jabbār, Q. 1965a. *Kitāb al-Mughnī fī abwāb al-tawḥīd wa'l-'adl.* Cairo: Dār al-Miṣriyya li'l-Ta'līf wa'l-Tarjama.

   1965b. *Sharḥ Uṣūl al-Khamsa.* Cairo: Maktaba Whaba.

   1988. *Rasā'il al-'adl wa'l-tawḥīd.* London: Dār al-Shurūq.

Adams, R. M. 1987. *The Virtue of Faith and Other Essays in Philosophical Theology.* Oxford University Press.

   2002. *Finite and Infinite Goods: A Framework for Ethics.* Oxford University Press.

Adamson, P. 2022. *Don't Think for Yourself: Authority and Belief in Medieval Philosophy.* Notre Dame, IN: University of Notre Dame Press.

Adler, J. 2002. *Belief's Own Ethics.* Cambridge, MA: MIT Press.

Ahlstrom-Vij, K. & Dunn, J. (eds.). 2018. *Epistemic Consequentialism.* Oxford University Press.

Ahmed, A. 2015. "Hume and the Independent Witnesses," *Mind* 124: 1013–1044.

Aijaz, I. 2018. *Islam: A Contemporary Philosophical Investigation.* New York: Routledge.

al-Azmeh, A. 1988. "Orthodoxy and Ḥanbalite Fideism," *Arabica* 35: 253–266.

al-Baghdādī, A. Q. 2002. *Uṣūl al-Dīn.* Beirut: Dār al-Kutub al-'Ilmiyya.

al-Bāqillāni, A. B. 2000. al-Inṣāf fīmā yajib 'itiqāduhu wa lā yajūz jahl bi. Cairo: al-Maktaba al-Azhariyya li'l-turāth.

Al-Ghazālī, A. H. M. 12th century/1991. *The Alchemy of Happiness,* trans. C. Field. New York: M. E. Sharpe.

al-Juwaynī, A. Y. 1950. *Kitāb al-Irshād ilā Qawāṭi' al-Adilla fī Uṣūl al-I'tiqād.* Baghdād: Maktaba al-Khānjī.

al-Māturīdī, A. M. 2020. *Kitāb al-Tawḥīd.* Istanbul: ISAM.

al-Nasafī, A. M. 2001. *Tabṣirāt al-Adilla fī Uṣūl al-Dīn*. Ankara: Diyanet İşleri Başkanlığı.

2004. *Tebṣıratü'l-edille*. Ankara: Diyanet İşleri Başkanlığı.

al-Rāzī, F. D. 1991. *Kitāb al-muḥaṣṣal*. Cairo: Maktaba Dār al-Turāth.

al-Ṣābūnī, N. D. 2020. *al-Bidāya fī uṣūl al-dīn*, trans. F. A. Khan. Berkeley: Zaytuna College.

Alston, A. J. 1990. *The Thousand Teachings of Shankara*. London: Shanti Sadan.

Alston, W. P. 1982. "Religious Experience and Religious Belief," *Noûs* 16: 3–12.

1986a. "Internalism and Externalism in Epistemology," in *Epistemic Justification: Essays in the Theory of Knowledge*. Ithaca, NY: Cornell University Press, pp. 185–226.

1986b. "Is Religious Belief Rational?" in S. M. Harrison & R. C. Tayler (eds.), *The Life of Religion*, Lanham, MD: University Press of America, pp. 1–15.

1991. *Perceiving God: The Epistemology of Religious Experience*. Ithaca, NY: Cornell University Press.

1996. "Belief, Acceptance, and Religious Faith," in J. Jordan & D. Howard-Snyder (eds.), *Faith, Freedom, and Rationality: Philosophy of Religion Today*. Lanham, MD: Rowman & Littlefield, pp. 3–27.

Altmann, A. 1946. "Translator's Introduction," in *Saadya Gaon: The Book of Doctrines and Beliefs*. Oxford: East and West Library, pp. 11–22.

Anderson, B. 1999. *Contours of Old Testament Theology*. Minneapolis, MN: Augsburg Fortress.

Anderson, C. 2018. "Hume, Defeat, and Miracle Reports," in M. Benton, J. Hawthorne, and D. Rabinowitz (eds.), *Knowledge, Belief, and God: New Insights in Religious Epistemology*. Oxford University Press, pp. 13–28.

Anderson, C. & Pruss, A. 2020. "The Case for Miracles," in M. Peterson and R. VanArragon (eds.), *Contemporary Debates in Philosophy of Religion*, 2nd edn. Hoboken, NJ: Wiley-Blackwell, pp. 113–123.

Anderson, E. 1995. "Knowledge, Human Interests, and Objectivity in Feminist Epistemology," *Philosophical Topics* 23: 27–58.

Andersson, T. 2022. *Kommentar till Sanusi: En systematisk studie i islamisk teologi*. Uppsala: Acta Universitatis Upsaliensis.

Annas, J. 2012. "Ancient Scepticism and Ancient Religion," in B. Morison & K. Ierodiakonou (eds.), *Episteme, etc.: Essays in Honour of Jonathan Barnes*. Oxford University Press, pp. 74–89.

Annas, J. & Barnes, J. (trans.) 2000. *Sextus Empiricus: Outlines of Skepticism*. Cambridge University Press.

Annet, P. 1744. "The Resurrection of Jesus Considered: In Answer to the Tryal of the Witnesses," in J. Earman, 2000. *Hume's Abject Failure: The Argument against Miracles*. Oxford University Press, pp. 113–140.

Anscombe, G. E. M. 2008. "What Is It to Believe Someone?" in M. Geach & L. Gormally (eds.), *Faith in a Hard Ground: Essays on Religion, Philosophy and Ethics by G. E. M. Anscombe*. Charlottesville, VA: Imprint Academic, pp. 1–10.

Anselm of Canterbury. 1979 [1078]. *St Anselm's Proslogion*, trans. M. J. Charlesworth. South Bend, IN: University of Notre Dame Press.

Aquinas, T. 1256–59/1951–54. *Truth (Quaestiones Disputatae De Veritate)*, trans. Robert W. Mulligan, J. V. McGlynn, and R. W. Schmidt, 3 vols., Chicago: Henry Regnery Company.

1975a. *Summa Contra Gentiles: Book One*, trans. A. Pegis. South Bend, IN: University of Notre Dame Press.

1975b. *Summa Contra Gentiles: Book Three*, trans. V. J. Bourke. South Bend, IN: University of Notre Dame Press.

1265–74/1981. *Summa Theologiae, Part II–II (Secunda Secundae)*, trans. Fathers of the English Dominican Province. London: Burns, Oates, and Washbourne. Reprinted by New York: Benziger 1947–48 and Westminster, MD: Christian Classics. www.newadvent.org/summa.

Arnold, D. 2005. *Buddhists, Brahmins, and Belief Epistemology in South Asian Philosophy of Religion*. New York: Columbia University Press.

Askell, A. 2012. "Common Objections to Pascal's Wager." https://askell.io/posts/2012/08/pascal.

Askew, R. 1988. "On Fideism and Alvin Plantinga," *International Journal for Philosophy of Religion* 23: 3–16.

Audi, R. 1991. "Faith, Belief, Rationality," *Philosophical Perspectives* 5: 213–39.

1997. "The Place of Testimony in the Fabric of Knowledge and Justification," *American Philosophical Quarterly* 34: 405–422.

2011. *Rationality and Religious Commitment*. Oxford University Press.

2020. *Seeing, Knowing, and Doing*. Oxford University Press.

Augustine. 1991 [400]. *Confessions*, trans. Henry Chadwick. Oxford University Press.

Babbage, C. 2009. [1838]. *Ninth Bridgewater Treatise*. Cambridge University Press.

Baggett, D. & Walls, J. L. 2016. *God and Cosmos: Moral Truth and Human Meaning*. Oxford University Press.

Baier, A. 1986. "Trust and Antitrust," *Ethics* 96: 231–260. https://doi:10.1086/292745.

Bailey, A. 2002. *Sextus Empiricus and Pyrrhonian Skepticism*. Oxford University Press.

Balasubramanian, R. 1990. "Advaita Vedanta: Its Unity with Other Systems and Its Contemporary Relevance," in *Indian Philosophical Systems*. Calcutta: Ramakrishna Mission Institute of Culture, pp. 15–34.

Baldwin, E. & McNabb, T. 2018. *Plantingian Religious Epistemology and World Religions: Prospects and Problems*. Lanham: Lexington Books.

Barnes, J. 1980. "Socrates and the Jury: Paradoxes in Plato's Distinction between Knowledge and True Belief," *Proceedings of the Aristotelian Society, Supplementary* 54: 193–206.

1997. "The Beliefs of a Pyrrhonist," in M. Burnyeat & M. Frede (eds.), *The Original Sceptics: A Controversy*. Indianapolis, IN: Hackett Publishing, pp. 58–91.

Barrett, C. 1997. "Newman and Wittgenstein on the Rationality of Religious Belief," in I. Ker (ed.), *Newman and Conversion*. South Bend, IN: University of Notre Dame Press, pp. 89–99.

Barrett, J. L. 2004. *Why Would Anyone Believe in God?* Lanham, MD: AltaMira Press.

2012. *Born Believers*. New York: Free Press.

Bartha, P. 2007. "Taking Stock of Infinite Value: Pascal's Wager and Relative Utilities," *Synthese* 154: 5–52.

2012. "Many Gods, Many Wagers: Pascal's Wager Meets the Replicator Dynamics," in J. Chandler & V. S. Harrison (eds.), *Probability in the Philosophy of Religion*. Oxford University Press, pp. 187–206.

Barton, J. Unpublished. "Faith in the Hebrew Bible." Content incorporated into Barton, J. (2022), *Translating the Bible*, London: Penguin.

Basinger, D. 2002. *Religious Diversity: A Philosophical Assessment*. Burlington: Ashgate.

Becker, B. & Black, B. (eds.). 2012. *The Sensitivity Principle in Epistemology*. Cambridge University Press.

Behe, M. 2003. "The Modern Intelligent Design Hypothesis: Breaking Rules," in N. A. Manson (ed.), *God and Design: The Teleological Argument and Modern Science*. London: Routledge, pp. 276–290.

Beilby, J. (ed.) 2002. *Naturalism Defeated?* Ithaca: Cornell University Press.

Bell, R. H. 1995. "Religion and Wittgenstein's Legacy: Beyond Fideism and Language Games," in T. Tessin & M. von der Ruhr (eds.), *Philosophy and the Grammar of Religious Belief*. London: Palgrave Macmillan, pp. 215–248.

Bengson, J. 2020. "Practical Understanding: Skill as Grasp of Method," in C. Demmerling and D. Schröder (eds.), *Concepts in Thought, Action and Emotion*. New York: Routledge, pp. 215–235.

Bennett-Hunter, G. 2019. "Wittgensteinian Quasi-Fideism and Interreligious Communication," in G. Andrejč & D. H. Weiss (eds.), *Interpreting Interreligious Relations with Wittgenstein: Philosophy, Theology and Religious Studies*. Leiden: Brill, pp. 157–173.

Benton, M. A. 2017. "Epistemology Personalized," *The Philosophical Quarterly* 67: 813–834.

2018. "God and Interpersonal Knowledge," *Res Philosophica* 95: 421–447.

Bergmann, M. 2006. *Justification without Awareness*. Oxford University Press.

2008. "Externalist Responses to Skepticism," in John Greco (ed.), *The Oxford Handbook of Skepticism*. Oxford University Press, pp. 504–532.

2015. "Religious Disagreement and Rational Demotion," in J. Kvanvig (ed.), *Oxford Studies in Philosophy of Religion*, vol. 6. Oxford University Press, pp. 21–57.

2017. "Religious Disagreement and Epistemic Intuitions," *Royal Institute of Philosophy Supplement* 81: 19–43.

2018. "Externalist versions of Evidentialism," in K. McCain (ed.), *Believing in Accordance with the Evidence: New Essays on Evidentialism*. Cham: Springer, pp. 109–123.

2021. *Radical Skepticism and Epistemic Intuition.* Oxford University Press.

Bering, J. M. 2011. *The God Instinct.* London: Nicholas Brealey Publishing.

Bernstein, C. 2018. "Is God's Existence Possible?" *The Heythrop Journal* 59: 424–432.

Bhatt, S. R. & Mehrotra, A. 2000. *Buddhist Epistemology.* London: Greenwood Press.

Bird, A. 2010. "Social Knowing: The Social Sense of 'Scientific Knowledge,'" *Philosophical Perspectives* 24: 23–56.

2014. "When Is There a Group That Knows? Scientific Knowledge as Social Knowledge," in J. Lackey (ed.), *Essays in Collective Epistemology.* Oxford University Press, pp. 42–63.

Black, C. C. 2011. *Mark.* New York: Abingdon Press.

Bloom, P. 2005. *Descartes' Baby.* Cambridge, MA: Basic Books.

Bodhi, B. (ed. & trans.) 2012. *The Numerical Discourses of the Buddha: A Translation of Aṅguttara Nikāya.* Boston: Wisdom Publication.

Boespflug, M. 2019. "Locke's Principle of Proportionality," *Archiv für Geschichte der Philosophie* 101: 237–57.

Bogardus, T. 2016. "Only All Naturalists Should Worry About Only One Evolutionary Debunking Argument," *Ethics* 126: 636–661.

BonJour, L. 1992. "Externalism/Internalism" in J. Dancy & E. Sosa (eds.), *A Companion to Epistemology.* Cambridge, MA: Blackwell, pp. 132–136.

Bostrom, N. 2002. *Anthropic Bias: Observation Selection Effects in Science and Philosophy.* London: Routledge.

Bostrom, Nick. 2009. "Pascal's Mugging," *Analysis* 69: 443–445.

Boyer, P. 2001. *Religion Explained: The Evolutionary Origin of Religious Thought.* London: Vintage Press.

Braddock, M. 2016. "Debunking Arguments and the Cognitive Science of Religion," *Theology and Science* 14: 268–287.

Brown, F., Brown, S. R. D. & Briggs, C. A. 1977. "אָמַן (āman)," "אֱמוּנָה ('ĕmûnāh)," in F. Brown, S. R. Driver, & C. Briggs (eds.), *Enhanced Brown-Driver-Briggs Hebrew and English Lexicon.* Oxford: Clarendon Press.

Brueggemann, W. 1986a. *Genesis.* Louisville, KY: Westminster John Knox.

1986b. "The Costly Loss of Lament," *Journal for the Study of the Old Testament* 36: 57–71.

Buchak, L. 2012. "Can It Be Rational to Have Faith?" in *Probability in the Philosophy of Religion*, J. Chandler & V. S. Harrison (eds.), Oxford University Press, pp. 225–247.

Burge, T. 1993. "Content preservation," *Philosophical Review* 102: 457–488.

Byerly, T. R. 2019. "From a Necessary Being to a Perfect Being," *Analysis* 79: 10–17.

Camp, E. 2007. "Thinking with Maps," *Philosophical Perspectives* 21: 145-182.

Campbell, J. 2011. "Why Do Language Use and Tool Use both Count as Manifestations of Intelligence?" in T. McCormack, C. Hoerl, & S. Butterfill (eds.), *Tool Use and Causal Cognition.* Oxford University Press, pp. 169–182.

Canfield, J. 1986. *The Philosophy of Wittgenstein, Volume 9: The Private Language Argument.* New York: Garland.

Cardoso, S. 2010. "On Skeptical Fideism in Montaigne's *Apology for Raymond Sebond*," in J. M. Neto, G. Paganini & J. C. Laursen (eds.), *Skepticism in the Modern Age: Building on the Work of Richard Popkin.* Leiden: Brill, pp. 71–82.

Carroll, T. D. 2008. "The Traditions of Fideism," *Religious Studies* 44: 1–22.

Carter, J. A. & McKenna, R. 2020. "Skepticism Motivated: On the Skeptical Import of Motivated Reasoning," *Canadian Journal of Philosophy* 50: 702–718.

Cerić, M. 1995. *Roots of Synthetic Theology in Islam: A Study of the Theology of Abu Mansur al-Maturidi.* Kuala Lumpur: International Institute of Islamic Thought and Civilization.

Chen, E. & Rubio, D. 2020. "Surreal Decisions," *Philosophy and Phenomenological Research* 100: 54–74.

Chesterton, G. K. 2011. *In Defense of Sanity.* San Francisco: Ignatius Press.

Chignell, A. & Pereboom, D. 2015. "Natural Theology and Natural Religion," in E. Zalta (ed.) *Stanford Encyclopedia of Philosophy.* https://plato.stanford.edu/archives/fall2020/entries/natural-theology/.

Chisholm, R. 1982. "The Problem of the Criterion," in *The Foundations of Knowing.* Minneapolis: University of Minnesota Press, pp. 61–75.

Chouhoud, Y. 2018. *What Causes Muslims to Doubt Islam? A Quantitative Analysis.* Dallas, TX: Yaqeen Institute for Islamic Research.

Christensen, D. 2007. "Epistemology of Disagreement: The Good News," *Philosophical Review,* 116: 187–217. https://doi:10.1215/00318108-2006-035.

  2010. "Higher-Order Evidence," *Philosophy and Phenomenological Research* 81: 185–215.

Chudnoff, E. 2013. *Intuition.* Oxford University Press.

Clark, K. J. (ed.) 1993. *Philosophers Who Believe.* Downers Grove, IL: InterVarsity Press.

Clark, K. J. & Barrett, J. 2010. "Reformed Epistemology and the Cognitive Science of Religion," *Faith and Philosophy* 27: 174–189.

  2011. "Reidian Religious Epistemology and the Cognitive Science of Religion," *Journal of the American Academy of Religion* 79: 1–37.

Clark, S. R. L. 2013. "The Classical Origins of Natural Theology," in R. Manning, J. H. Brooke, & F. Watts (eds.), *The Oxford Handbook of Natural Theology.* Oxford University Press, pp. 9–22.

Clarke, S. 1998 [1705]. *A Demonstration of the Being and Attributes of God and Other Writings.* Cambridge University Press.

Clément, O. (ed.) 1993. *The Roots of Christian Mysticism,* 2nd ed. New York: New City Press.

Clifford, W. K. 1877. "The Ethics of Belief," *Contemporary Review* 29: 289–309.

Clines, D. J. A. 1993. "אָמַן (*āman*)," "אֱמוּנָה (*ʾĕmûnāh*)," in D. J. A. Clines (ed.), *The Dictionary of Classical Hebrew,* vol. 1. Sheffield: Sheffield Academic, pp. 312–316.

Coady, C. A. J. 1992. *Testimony: A Philosophical Study.* Oxford University Press.

Cohen, S. 1984. "Justification and Truth," *Philosophical Studies* 46: 279–96.

Collins, R. 2009. "The Teleological Argument: An Exploration of the Fine-Tuning of the Universe," in Craig & Moreland (eds.), pp. 202–281.

Conee, E. B. & Feldman, R. 2004. *Evidentialism: Essays in Epistemology.* Oxford University Press.

Conee, E. 2010. "Rational Disagreement Defended," in R. Feldman and T. Warfield (eds.), *Disagreement.* Oxford University Press, pp. 69–90.

Coliva, A. 2015. *Extended Rationality: A Hinge Epistemology.* London: Palgrave Macmillan.

Cottingham, J. 2005. *The Spiritual Dimension.* Cambridge University Press.

Cowell, E. B. & Gough, A. E. 1989. *Sarva-darsana-sangraha of Madhavacarya.* Delhi: Parimal Publications.

Craig, W. L. 1979. *The Kalām Cosmological Argument.* New York: Barnes & Noble Books.

　　1989. *Assessing the New Testament Evidence for the Resurrection of Jesus.* Lewiston, NY: Edwin Mellen Press.

　　2001a. *The Cosmological Argument from Plato to Leibniz.* Eugene, OR: Wipf and Stock Publishers.

Craig, W. L. (ed.) 2001b. *Philosophy of Religion: A Reader and Guide.* Edinburgh University Press.

　　2008. *Reasonable Faith: Christian Truth and Apologetics*, 3rd ed. Wheaton, IL: Crossway.

Craig, W. L. & Moreland, J. P. 2009. "Introduction," in Craig & Moreland (eds.), pp. ix–xiii.

Craig, W. L. & Moreland, J. P. (eds.). 2012. *The Blackwell Companion to Natural Theology.* Malden, MA: Wiley-Blackwell.

Crummett, D. 2015. "We Are Here to Help Each Other," *Faith and Philosophy* 32: 45–62. https://doi:10.5840/faithphil20153428.

Cuneo, T. 2016. *Ritualized Faith: Essays on the Philosophy of Liturgy.* Oxford University Press.

Davis, T. 2020. "Dual-Inheritance, Common Sense, and the Justification of Religious Belief," in R. Peels, J. de Ridder, & R. van Woudenberg (eds.), *Scientific Challenges to Common Sense Philosophy.* New York: Routledge, pp. 191–214.

De Cruz, H. 2015. "The Relevance of Hume's Natural History of Religion for the Cognitive Science of Religion," *Res Philosophica* 92: 653–74.

De Cruz, H. & De Smedt, J. 2013. "Reformed and Evolutionary Epistemology and the Noetic Effects of Sin," *International Journal for Philosophy of Religion* 74: 49–66.

　　2015. *A Natural History of Natural Theology.* Cambridge, MA: MIT Press.

Descartes, R. 1988 [1641]. "Meditations on First Philosophy," in *Descartes: Selected Philosophical Writings*, trans. J. Cottingham, R. Stoothoff, & D. Murdoch. Cambridge University Press, pp. 73–122.

DePoe, J. 2020. "A Classical Evidentialist Response to PC," in Depoe & McNabb (eds.), pp. 82–85.

Depoe, J. & McNabb, T. D. (eds.) 2020. *Debating Christian Religious Epistemology: An Introduction to Five Views on the Knowledge of God.* London: Bloomsbury.

de Ridder, J. 2014. "Epistemic Dependence and Collective Scientific Knowledge," *Synthese* 19: 1–17.

2019. "Against Quasi-Fideism," *Faith and Philosophy* 36: 223–43.

Deutsch, E. 1969. *Advaita Vedanta: A Philosophical Reconstruction.* Honolulu: East-West Center Press.

di Ceglie, R. 2017. "Faith and Reason: A Response to Duncan Pritchard," *Philosophy* 92: 231–47.

2022. *God, the Good, and the Spiritual Turn in Epistemology.* Cambridge University Press.

Dietz, C. 2018. "Reasons and Factive Emotions," *Philosophical Studies* 175: 1681–1691.

Dormandy, K. 2018a. "Disagreement from the Religious Margins," *Res Philosophica* 95: 371–395.

2018b. "Resolving Religious Disagreements," *Faith and Philosophy* 35: 56–83. https://doi:10.5840/faithphil201812697.

2020. "The Epistemic Benefits of Religious Disagreement," *Religious Studies* 56: 390–408. https://doi:10.1017/s0034412518000847.

2021. "The Loyalty of Religious Disagreement," in M. Benton & J. Kvanvig (eds.), *Religious Disagreement and Pluralism.* Oxford University Press, pp. 238–270.

Dougherty, T. (ed.). 2011. *Evidentialism and Its Discontents.* Oxford University Press.

Dougherty, T. 2020. "Religious Beliefs Require Evidence," in S. Cowan (ed.) *Problems in Epistemology and Metaphysics: An Introduction to Contemporary Debates.* London: Bloomsbury, pp. 127–139.

Dougherty, T. & Tweedt, C. 2015. "Religious Epistemology," *Philosophy Compass* 10: 547–559.

Doyle, C., Milburn M., & Pritchard, D. (eds.) 2019. *New Issues in Epistemological Disjunctivism,* New York: Routledge.

Draper, P. 2010. "Cumulative Cases," in C. Taliaferro, P. Draper, & P. Quinn (eds.), *A Companion to Philosophy of Religion,* 2nd ed. Malden, MA: Blackwell, pp. 414–424.

Dretske, F. 1981. *Knowledge and the Flow of Information.* Oxford University Press.

Dreyfus, G. B. J. 1997. *Recognizing Reality – Dharmakīrti's Philosophy and Its Tibetan Interpretations.* New York: State University of New York Press.

Duncan, C. 2013. "Religion and Secular Utility: Happiness, Truth, and Pragmatic Arguments for Theistic Belief," *Philosophy Compass* 8: 381–399.

Duncan, M. 2020. "Knowledge of Things," *Synthese* 197: 3559–3592.

Duff, A. 1986. "Pascal's Wager and Infinite Utilities," *Analysis* 46:107–09.

Dunne, J. D. 2004. *Foundations of Dharmakīrti's Philosophy.* Boston: Wisdom Publication.

Earman, J. D. 2000. *Hume's Abject Failure: The Argument against Miracles.* Oxford University Press.

Efird, D. & Worsley, D. 2017. "What an Apophaticist Can Know: Divine Ineffability and the Beatific Vision," *Philosophy & Theology* 29: 205–219.

Elga, A. 2007. "Reflection and Disagreement," *Noûs* 41: 478–502.

El-Tobgui, C. S. 2020. *Ibn Taymiyya on Reason and Revelation.* Leiden/Boston: Brill.

Enoch, D. 2017. "Political Philosophy and Epistemology," in D. Sobel, P. Vallentyne, & S. Wall (eds.), *Oxford Studies in Political Philosophy*, vol. 3. Oxford University Press, pp. 132–65.

Evans, C. S. 1998. *Faith Beyond Reason.* Grand Rapids, MI: Eerdmans.

2010. *Natural Signs and Knowledge of God.* Oxford University Press.

2013. *God and Moral Obligation.* Oxford University Press.

Fagan, M. B. 2012. "Collective Scientific Knowledge," *Philosophy Compass* 7: 821–831.

Fales, E. 2003. "Alvin Plantinga's *Warranted Christian Belief,*" *Noûs* 37: 353–70.

Farkas, K. 2019. "Objectual Knowledge," J. Knowles & T. Raleigh (eds.), *New Essays on Acquaintance.* Oxford University Press, pp. 260–276.

Faulkner, P. 2007. "A Genealogy of Trust," *Episteme* 4: 305–321. https://doi:10.3366/E174236000700010X.

Feldman, R. 2007. "Reasonable Religious Disagreements," in L. Antony (ed.) *Philosophers without Gods: Meditations on Atheism and the Secular.* Oxford University Press, pp. 194–214.

Feldman, R. & Warfield, T. (ed.) 2010. *Disagreement.* Oxford University Press.

Feser, E. 2017. *Five Proofs of the Existence of God.* San Francisco: Ignatius Press.

Festinger, L. 1957. *A Theory of Cognitive Dissonance.* Evanston, IL: Row Peterson.

Fitelson, B. 2001. "A Bayesian Account of Independent Evidence with Applications," *Philosophy of Science* 68: S123–S140.

Flew, A. 1976. *The Presumption of Atheism and Other Philosophical Essays on God, Freedom, and Immortality.* New York: Harper and Row.

1985. "Introduction to Hume," in D. Hume, *Of Miracles.* LaSalle, IL: Open Court Classics.

Fogelin, R. 2003. *A Defense of Hume on Miracles.* Princeton University Press.

Foley, R. 2001. *Intellectual Trust in Oneself and Others.* Cambridge University Press.

Forsthoefel, T. 2002. *Knowing Beyond Knowledge: Epistemologies of Religious Experience in Classical Advaita.* Aldershot: Ashgate.

Fowler, J. 1981. *Stages of Faith: The Psychology of Human Development and the Quest for Meaning.* New York: Harper-Collins.

Frank, R. M. 1989. "Knowledge and Taqlîd: The Foundations of Religious Belief in Classical Ash'arism," *Journal of American Oriental Society* 109: 37–62.

Frankfurt, H. 1998. *Necessity, Volition, and Love.* Cambridge University Press.

Fricker, E. 1994. "Against Gullibility," in A. Chakrabarti & B. K. Matilal (eds.), *Knowing from Words: Western and Indian Philosophical Analysis of*

Understanding and Testimony. Dordrecht: Kluwer Academic Publishers, pp. 125–162.

Fricker, M. 2007. *Epistemic Injustice: Power and the Ethics of Knowing.* Oxford University Press.

Friedman, J. 2017. "Why Suspend Judging?" *Noûs* 51: 302–326.

Gage, L. P. & McAllister, B. 2020. "Phenomenal Conservatism/Response to Critics," in Depoe & McNabb (eds.), pp. 61–81/98–106.

Gambhirananda, S. 1993. *Brahma Sutra Bhasya of Shankaracarya.* Calcutta: Advaita Ashrama.

Ganeri, J. 2018. "Epistemology from a Sanskritic Point of View," in S. Stich, M. Mizumoto, & E. McCready (eds.), *Epistemology for the Rest of the World.* Oxford University Press, pp. 12–21.

Garfield, J. L. 2015. *Engaging Buddhism: Why It Matters to Philosophy.* Oxford University Press.

Gascoigne, N. 2019. *Rorty, Liberal Democracy, and Religious Certainty.* London: Palgrave Macmillan.

Gaus, G. F. 2015. "Public Reason Liberalism," in S. Wall (ed.) *The Cambridge Companion to Liberalism.* Cambridge University Press, pp. 112–140.

Geivett, R. D. 1995. *Evil and the Evidence for God: The Challenge of John Hick's Theodicy.* Philadelphia: Temple University Press.

Gellman, J. 1993. "Religious Diversity and the Epistemic Justification of Religious Belief', *Faith and Philosophy* 10: 345–364.

Gettier, E. 1963. "Is Justified True Belief Knowledge?" *Analysis* 23: 121–123.

Goldberg, S. C. 2007. *Anti-Individualism: Mind and Language, Knowledge and Justification.* Cambridge University Press.

2014. "Does Externalist Epistemology Rationalize Religious Commitment?" in L. Callahan & T. O'Connor (eds.), *Religious Faith and Intellectual Virtue.* Oxford University Press, pp. 279–98.

2021. "How Confident Should the Religious Believer Be in the Face of Religious Pluralism?" in Benton & Kvanvig (eds.), pp. 65–90.

Goldman, A. 1979. "What Is Justified Belief?" in G. Pappas (ed.), *Justification and Knowledge.* Boston: D. Reidel, pp. 1–25.

Goldman, A. I. 1999. *Knowledge in a Social World.* Oxford University Press.

2001. Experts: Which Ones Should You Trust?" *Philosophy and Phenomenological Research* 63: 85–110. https://doi:10.1111/j.1933-1592.2001.tb00093.x.

Goldschmidt, T. 2018. "The Argument from (Natural) Numbers," in J. Walls and T. Dougherty (eds.), *Two Dozen (or So) Arguments for God: The Plantinga Project.* Oxford University Press, pp. 59–75.

2019. "A Proof of Exodus: Yehuda HaLevy and Jonathan Edwards Walk into a Bar," in S. Lebens, D. Rabinowitz, & A. Segal (eds.), *Jewish Philosophy in an Analytic Age.* Oxford University Press, pp. 222–242.

Gomez-Alonso, M. 2021. "Wittgenstein, Religious Belief, and Hinge Epistemology," *Skepsis* 12: 18–34.

Goodman, J. & Salow, B. 2018. "Taking a Chance on KK," *Philosophical Studies* 75: 175–186.

Gottlieb, D. 2017. *Reason to Believe.* Bet Shemesh: Mosaica Press.

Gowans, C. W. 2003. *Philosophy of the Buddha.* London & New York: Routledge.

Graham, P. J. 1997. "What Is Testimony?" *Philosophical Quarterly* 47: 227–232. https://doi:10.1111/1467-9213.00057.

Greco, J. 2009. "Religious Knowledge in the Context of Conflicting Testimony," *Proceedings of the American Catholic Philosophical Association* 82: 61–76.

   2010 *Achieving Knowledge.* Cambridge University Press.

   2021. *The Transmission of Knowledge.* Cambridge University Press.

Grice, P. 2001. *Aspects of Reason.* Oxford University Press.

Guerrero, L. 2013. *Truth for the Rest of Us: Dharmakīrti's Philosophy of Language.* PhD dissertation, University of New Mexico.

Gutschmidt, R. 2021. "The Religious Dimension of Skepticism," *International Philosophical Quarterly* 61: 77–99.

Gutting, G. 1982. *Religious Belief and Religious Skepticism.* South Bend, IN: University of Notre Dame Press.

Habermas, G. 1996. *The Historical Jesus.* Joplin, MO: College Press.

Habgood-Coote, J. 2020. "Group Knowledge, Questions, and the Division of Epistemic Labour," *Ergo* 6: 925–966.

Hájek, A. 2003. "Waging War on Pascal's Wager," *The Philosophical Review* 112: 27–56.

   2007. "The Reference Class Problem Is Your Problem Too," *Synthese* 156: 563–585.

   2008. "Are Miracles Chimerical?" *Oxford Studies in Philosophy of Religion* 1: 82–103.

   2018. "Pascal's Wager," in E. Zalta (ed.) *The Stanford Encyclopedia of Philosophy.* https://plato.stanford.edu/entries/pascal-wager/.

Halbfass, W. 1990. *India and Europe: An Essay in Philosophical Understanding.* Delhi: Motilal Banarsidass.

Hallaq, W. 1991. "Ibn Taymiyya on the Existence of God," *Acta Orientalia* 52: 49–69.

Halvorsson, H. 2018. "A Theological Critique of the Fine-Tuning Arguments," in M. Benton, J. Hawthorne, & D. Rabinowitz (eds.), *Knowledge, Belief, and God: New Insights in Religious Epistemology.* Oxford University Press, pp. 122–135.

Hardwig, J. 1985. "Epistemic Dependence," *Journal of Philosophy* 82: 335–349.

   1991. "The Role of Trust in Knowledge," *Journal of Philosophy* 88: 693–708.

Harrison, V. S. 2006. "Internal Realism and the Problem of Religious Diversity," *Philosophia* 34: 287–301.

   2019. *Eastern Philosophy.* London & New York: Routledge.

   2022. *Eastern Philosophy of Religion.* Cambridge University Press.

Hartshorne, C. 1962. *The Logic of Perfection.* La Salle, IL: Open Court.

Harvey, P. 1996. *An Introduction to Buddhism.* Cambridge University Press.

2009. "The Approach to Knowledge and Truth in the Theravāda Record of the Discourses of the Buddha," in W. Edelglass & J. Garfield (eds.), *Buddhist Philosophy: Essential Readings*. Oxford University Press, pp. 175–85.

Harvey, R. 2021. *Transcendent God, Rational World: A Māturīdī Theology.* Edinburgh University Press.

Hawley, K. 2014. Trust, Distrust and Commitment. *Noûs* 48(1): 1–20.

Hawthorne, J. & Dunaway, B. 2017. "Skepticism," in W. Abraham & F. Aquino (eds.), *The Oxford Handbook of the Epistemology of Theology.* Oxford University Press, pp. 290–308.

Hawthorne, J. & Isaacs, Y. 2018. "Fine-Tuning Fine-Tuning," in M. Benton, J. Hawthorne, & D. Rabinowitz (eds.), *Knowledge, Belief, and God: New Insights in Religious Epistemology.* Oxford University Press, pp. 136–168.

Hawthorne, J., Isaacs, Y., & Lasonen-Aarnio, M. 2021. "The Rationality of Epistemic Akrasia," *Philosophical Perspectives* 35: 206–228.

Hawthorne, J. & Magidor, O. 2018. "Reflections on the Ideology of Reasons," in D. Star (ed.), *The Oxford Handbook of Reasons and Normativity.* Oxford University Press, pp. 113–142.

Hayes R. P. 1988. *Dignāga on the Interpretation of Signs.* Dordrecht: Kluwer Academic Publishers.

Healey, J. P. 1992. "Faith: Old Testament," in D. Freedman (ed.) *The Anchor Yale Bible Dictionary, D–G: Volume 2.* New York: Doubleday, pp. 744–749.

Heer, N. 1993. "The Priority of Reason in the Interpretation of Scripture: Ibn Taymīya and the Mutakallimūn," In M. Mir & J. E. Fossum (eds.), *Literary Heritage of Classical Islam. Arabic and Islamic Studies in Honor of James A. Bellamy.* Princeton: Darwin Press, pp. 181–195.

Helm, P. (ed.) 1999. *Faith and Reason* (Oxford Readers). Oxford University Press.

Hetherington, S. (ed.) 2019. *Epistemology: The Key Thinkers.* 2nd ed. New York: Bloomsbury Press.

Hick, J. 1966. *Faith and Knowledge.* Ithaca, NY: Cornell University Press.

1989. *An Interpretation of Religion.* New Haven: Yale University Press.

Hieronymi, P. 2008. "The Reasons of Trust," *Australasian Journal of Philosophy* 86: 213–236. https://doi:10.1080/00048400801886496.

Hinchman, E. S. 2005. "Telling as Inviting to Trust," *Philosophy and Phenomenological Research* 70: 562–587. https://doi:10.1111/j.1933-1592.2005.tb00415.x.

Hoitenga, D. 1991. *Faith and Reason from Plato to Plantinga: An Introduction to Reformed Epistemology.* State University of New York Press.

Holder, J. 2013. "A Survey of Early Buddhist Epistemology," in S. Emmanuel (ed.) *A Companion to Buddhist Philosophy.* Oxford: Wiley-Blackwell, pp. 223–240.

Holton, R. 1994. "Deciding to Trust, Coming to Believe," *Australasian Journal of Philosophy* 72: 63–76. https://doi:10.1080/00048409412345881.

Hoover, J. 2007. *Ibn Taymiyya's Theodicy of Perpetual Optimism.* Leiden: Brill.

2019; Ibn Taymiyya. London: Oneworld Academic.

Howard-Snyder, D. 2013. "Propositional Faith: What It Is and What It Is Not," *American Philosophical Quarterly* 50: 357–372.

2016. "Does Faith Entail Belief?" *Faith and Philosophy* 33: 142–162.

2017a. "Markan faith," *International Journal for Philosophy of Religion* 81: 31–60.

2017b. "The Skeptical Christian," *Oxford Studies in Philosophy of Religion* 8: 142–167.

2019. "Can Fictionalists Have Faith? It All Depends," *Religious Studies* 55: 447–468.

Howard-Snyder, D. & McKaughan, D. J. 2020. "Faith and Humility: Conflict or Concord?" in M. Alfano, M. Lynch, & A. Tanesini (eds.), *Handbook on the Philosophy of Humility*. New York: Routledge, pp. 212–224.

2022. "Faith and Resilience," *International Journal for Philosophy of Religion* 91: 205–241.

Hricko, J. & Leben, D. 2018. "In Defense of Best-Explanation Debunking Arguments in Moral Philosophy," *Review of Philosophical Psychology* 9: 143–160.

Huemer, M. 2007. "Compassionate Phenomenal Conservatism," *Philosophy and Phenomenological Research* 74: 30–55.

Hume, D. 1975 [1748]. *Enquiries Concerning Human Understanding*, ed. L. A. Selby-Bigge, 3rd ed. Oxford: Clarendon Press.

1990 [1779]. *Dialogues Concerning Natural Religion*. London: Penguin Books.

2000 [1777]. "Of Miracles," in B. Davies (ed.) *Philosophy of Religion: A Guide and Anthology*. Oxford University Press, pp. 430–436.

Hyman, J. 1999. "How Knowledge Works," *Philosophical Quarterly* 49: 433–451.

Ibn Qudāma, M. D. 1962. *Taḥrīm al-Naẓar fī Kutub ahl al-Kalām*, trans. George Makdisi as *The Censure of Speculative Theology of Ibn Qudama*. Cambridge: Gibb Memorial Trust.

Ibn Taymiyya, Taqī al-Dīn. 1972. *Majmū'āt al-Rasā'il al-Kubrā*, vol 2. Beirut: Dār iḥyā' al-turāth al-'arabī.

1979. *Dar' ta'āruḍ al-'aql wa-l-naql*. Riyadh: Jāmi'at al-Imām Muḥammad b. Sa'ūd al-Islāmiyya.

1995. *Majmū' Fatāwā Shaykh al-Islām Aḥmad b. Taymiyya*. Mujamma' al-Malik Fahd.

2005. *al-Radd' 'ala al-Manṭiqiyyīn*. Beirut: Mu'assasa al-Rayyān.

2014. *al-Intiṣār li-ahl al-athar (naqḍ al-mantiq)*. Mecca: Dār 'ālam al-Fawā'id.

2018. *Amrāḍ al-qulūb wa-shifā'uhā*. Cairo: al-Maṭba'a al-Salafiyya.

Ibrahim, M. D. 2013. "Immediate Knowledge according to al-Qāḍī 'Abd al-Jabbār," *Sciences and Philosophy* 23: 101–115.

Jackson, E. In press a. "A Permissivist Defense of Pascal's Wager," *Erkenntnis*.

In press b. "An Epistemic Version of Pascal's Wager." *Journal of the American Philosophical Association*.

2023. "Faithfully Taking Pascal's Wager," *The Monist* 106: 35–45.

Jackson, E. & Rogers, A. 2019. "Salvaging Pascal's Wager," *Philosophia Christi* 21: 59–84.

Jackson, F. 1982. "Epiphenomenal Qualia," *Philosophical Quarterly* 32: 127–136.

Jackson, S. 2009. Islam and the Problem of Black Suffering. New York: Oxford University Press.

James, W. 1896 (1979). "The Will to Believe," in F. Burkhardt et al. (eds.), *The Will to Believe and Other Essays*. Cambridge, MA: Harvard University Press, pp. 2–32.

Jayatilleke, K. N. 1963. *Early Buddhist Theory of Knowledge*. London: George Allen & Unwin Ltd.

Jepsen, A. 1977. "אָמַן (*āman*)," in G. J. Botterweck, H. Ringgren, & Heinz-Josef Fabry (eds.), *Theological Dictionary of the Old Testament*, revised ed., vol. 1, trans. D. Green & J. T. Willis. Grand Rapids, MI. Eerdmans, pp. 292–323.

Johnson, D. 1999. *Hume, Holism, and Miracles*, Ithaca: Cornell University Press.

Johnson, D. & Bering, J. 2009. "Hand of God, Mind of Man: Punishment and Cognition in the Evolution of Cooperation," in J. Schloss & M. Murray (eds.), *The Believing Primate: Scientific, Philosophical, and Theological Reflections on the Origin of Religion*. Oxford University Press, pp. 26–43.

Jones, K. 2012. "Trustworthiness," *Ethics* 123: 61–85. https://doi:10.1086/667838.

Jones, W. 1998. "Religious Conversion, Self-Deception, and Pascal's Wager," *Journal of the History of Philosophy* 36: 167–188.

Jong, J. & Visala, A. 2014. "Evolutionary Debunking Arguments against Theism, Reconsidered," *International Journal for Philosophy of Religion* 76: 243–258.

Jordan, J. 1991. "The Many-Gods Objection and Pascal's Wager," *The International Philosophical Quarterly* 31: 309–17.

1998. "Pascal's Wager Revisited," *Religious Studies* 34: 419–431.

2006. *Pascal's Wager: Pragmatic Arguments and Belief in God*. Oxford University Press.

2007. "Pascal's Wagers and James's Will to Believe," in W. Wainwright (ed.), *The Oxford Handbook of Philosophy of Religion*. Oxford University Press, pp. 168–187.

Joyce, R. 2007. *The Evolution of Morality*. Cambridge, MA: MIT Press.

Kahan, D. 2016. "The Politically Motivated Reasoning Paradigm, Part I," in R. Scott, M. Buchmann, & S. Kosslyn (eds.), *Emerging Trends in the Social and Behavioral Sciences*. Wiley-Blackwell. https://doi.org/10.1002/9781118900772.etrds0417.

Kahn, Y. 2017. *Va-etchanan: Remembering Sinai*. [Online] Available at: https://etzion.org.il/en/tanakh/torah/sefer-devarim/parashat-vaetchanan/va-etchanan-remembering-sinai [Accessed 08 12 2021].

Kahneman, D. 2011. *Thinking, Fast and Slow*. New York: Farrar, Straus and Giroux.

Kail, P. 2007. "Understanding Hume's Natural History of Religion," *The Philosophical Quarterly* 57: 190–211.

Kalupahana, D. J. 1992. A *History of Buddhist Philosophy: Continuities and Discontinuities*. Honolulu: University of Hawai'i Press.

Kant, I. 1998 [1781]. *Critique of Pure Reason*, trans. P. Guyer and A. W. Wood. Cambridge University Press.

2018 [1793] *Religion within the Bounds of Mere Reason*, revised ed., trans. & ed. A. Wood and G. Di Giovanni. Cambridge University Press.

Karunadasa, Y. 2017. *Early Buddhist Teachings: The Middle Position in Theory and Practice*. Sri Lanka: Buddhist Publication Society.

Keith, A. B. 1989, *The Religion and Philosophy of the Upanishads*, vol. 2, Delhi: Motilal Banarsidass. First published 1925, Cambridge, MA: Harvard University Press.

Kelemen, D. 2004. "Are Children 'Intuitive Theists'?: Reasoning About Purpose and Design in Nature," *Psychological Science* 15: 295–301.

Keller, L. J. 2018a. "Divine Ineffability and Franciscan Knowledge," *Res Philosophica* 95: 347–370.

2018b. "The Argument from Intentionality (or Aboutness): Propositions Supernaturalized," in J. Walls & T. Dougherty (eds.), *Two Dozen (or So) Arguments for God: The Plantinga Project*. Oxford University Press, pp. 11–28.

Kelly, T. 2005. "The Epistemic Significance of Disagreement," *Oxford Studies in Epistemology* 1: 167–196. https://doi.org/10.1002/9781119420828.ch17.

2010. "Peer Disagreement and Higher Order Evidence," in R. Feldman & T. Warfield (eds.), *Disagreement*. Oxford University Press, pp. 111–174.

2014a. "Evidence," in E. Zalta (ed.) *Stanford Encyclopedia of Philosophy*. https://plato.stanford.edu/entries/evidence/.

2014b. "Evidence Can Be Persmissive," in M. Steup, J. Turri, & E. Sosa (eds.), *Contemporary Debates in Epistemology*. Oxford: Wiley Blackwell, pp. 298–311.

Kienzler, W. 2006. "Wittgenstein and John Henry Newman on Certainty," *Grazer Philosophische Studien* 71: 117–138.

Kierkegaard, S. 1983 [1843]. *Fear and Trembling*, trans. H. V. Hong & E. H. Hong. Princeton University Press.

Kim, J. 1994. "Explanatory Knowledge and Metaphysical Dependence," *Philosophical Issues* 5: 51–69.

King, N. L. 2012. "Disagreement: What's the Problem? Or a Good Peer Is Hard to Find," *Philosophy and Phenomenological Research* 85: 249–272. https://doi:10.1111/j.1933-1592.2010.00441.x.

Kitcher, P. 1991. "Socializing Knowledge," *Journal of Philosophy* 88: 675–676.

Koons, R. C. 2018. "The General Argument from Intuition," J. Walls & T. Dougherty (eds.), *Two Dozen (or So) Arguments for God: The Plantinga Project*. Oxford University Press, pp. 238–260.

Korcz, K. A. 2021. "The Epistemic Basing Relation," in E. Zalta (ed.), *Stanford Encyclopedia of Philosophy*. https://plato.stanford.edu/archives/spr2021/entries/basing-epistemic/.

Korman, D. 2019. "Debunking Arguments," *Philosophy Compass* 14: e12638.

Korman, D. & Locke, D. 2020. "Against Minimalist Responses to Moral Debunking Arguments," *Oxford Studies in Metaethics* 15: 309–332.

Kundert, C. & Edman, R. O. 2017. "Promiscuous Teleology: From Childhood Through Adulthood and from West to East," in R. Hornbeck et al. (eds.), *Religious Cognition in China.* Switzerland: Springer, pp. 79–96.

Kusch, M. 2002. *Knowledge by Agreement: The Programme of Communitarian Epistemology.* Oxford University Press.

Kvanvig, J. 2018. *Faith and Humility.* Oxford University Press.

Lackey, J. 2008. *Learning From Words: Testimony as a Source of Knowledge.* Oxford University Press.

  2014. "Taking Religious Disagreement Seriously," in L. Callahan & T. O'Connor (eds.), *Religious Faith and Intellectual Virtue.* Oxford University Press, pp. 300–317.

  2017. "The Epistemology of Testimony and Religious Belief," in W. Abraham & F. Aquino (eds.), *The Oxford Handbook of the Epistemology of Theology.* Oxford University Press, pp. 203–220.

Lasonen-Aarnio, M. 2010. "Unreasonable Knowledge," *Philosophical Perspectives* 24: 1–21.

Leben, D. 2014. "When Psychology Undermines Belief," *Philosophical Psychology* 27: 328–350.

Lebens, S. 2020a. "Pascal, Pascalberg, and Friends," *International Journal of Philosophy of Religion* 87: 109–130.

  2020b. *The Principles of Judaism.* Oxford University Press.

  2021. "Proselytism as Epistemic Violence: A Jewish Approach to the Ethics of Religious Persuasion," *The Monist* 104: 376–392.

  In press. "Amen to Da'at: On the Foundations of Jewish Epistemology," *Religious Studies.*

Leftow, B. 2007. "Ontological Arguments," in W. Wainwright (ed.) *The Oxford Handbook of Philosophy of Religion.* Oxford University Press, pp. 80–111.

  2012. *God and Necessity.* Oxford University Press.

  2022. *Anselm's Argument: Divine Necessity.* Oxford University Press.

Leibniz, G. 1991 [1714]. *The Monadology.* University of Pittsburgh Press.

Leonard, N. 2021. "Epistemological Problems of Testimony," in E. Zalta (ed.), *Stanford Encyclopedia of Philosophy.* https://plato.stanford.edu/entries/testimony-episprob/.

Levin, J. 2021. "Functionalism," in E. Zalta (ed.), *The Stanford Encyclopedia of Philosophy.* https://plato.stanford.edu/archives/win2021/entries/functionalism/.

Licona, M. R. 2010. *The Resurrection of Jesus: A New Historiographical Approach.* Downers Grove, IL: InterVarsity Press.

Ljiljanaa, R. & Slavišab, K. 2017. "Religious Hinge Commitments: Developing Wittgensteinian Quasi-Fideism," *Belgrade Philosophical Annual* 30: 235–256.

List, C. 2005. "Group Knowledge and Group Rationality: A Judgment Aggregation Perspective," *Episteme* 2: 25–38.

Locke, J. 1979 [1689]. *An Essay Concerning Human Understanding,* ed. P. Nidditch, Oxford: Clarendon Press.

Long, T. 2010. "*De jure* Objection to Religious Belief," *Religious Studies* 46: 375–394.

Longino, H. 1990. *Science as Social Knowledge: Values and Objectivity in Scientific Inquiry.* Princeton University Press.

Lopes, D. M. 2005. *Sight and Sensibility: Evaluating Pictures.* Oxford: Clarendon Press.

Lougheed, K. 2018. "Recognition and Epistemic Injustice in the Epistemology of Disagreement," *Philosophical Forum* 49: 363–377. https://doi:10.1111/phil.12197.

Lowe, E. J. 2002. *A Survey of Metaphysics.* Oxford University Press.
  2010. "John Locke," in S. Bernecker & D. Pritchard (eds.), *Routledge Companion to Epistemology.* London: Routledge, pp. 687–696.

Luhrmann, T. M. 2020. *How God Becomes Real.* Princeton University Press.

Lycan, W. & Schlesinger, G. 1989. "You Bet Your Life: Pascal's Wager Defended," in J. Feinberg (ed.) *Reason & Responsibility: Readings in Some Basic Problems of Philosophy*, 7th ed. Belmont, CA: Wadsworth, pp. 80–90.

Mackie, J. L. 1982. *The Miracle of Theism: Arguments for and against the Existence of God.* Oxford University Press.

Maharshi, R. 1995. *Who Am I?* trans. T. M. P. Mahadevan. Tiruvannamalai: Sri Ramanasramam.

Malcolm, N. 1960. "Anselm's Ontological Arguments," *Philosophical Review* 69: 41–62.

Marsh, J. 2013. "Darwin and the Problem of Natural Nonbelief," *Monist* 96: 349–376.

Martin, M. 1975. "On Four Critiques of Pascal's Wager," *Sophia* 14: 1–11.
  1990. *Atheism: A Philosophical Justification.* Philadelphia: Temple University Press.

Matilal, B. K. 1986. *Perception: An Essay on Classical Indian Theories of Knowledge.* Oxford: Clarendon Press.

Mavrodes, G. I. 1989. "Enthusiasm," *International Journal for Philosophy of Religion* 25: 171–86.

Mawson, T. J. 2005. *Belief in God: An Introduction to the Philosophy of Religion.* Oxford University Press.

Mayeda, S. 1992. *A Thousand Teachings: The Upadesasahasri of Shankara.* Albany, NY: State University of New York Press.

McAllister, B. 2020. "Evidence Is Required for Religious Belief," in M. Peterson & R. VanArragon (eds.), *Contemporary Debates in Philosophy of Religion*, 2nd edn. Hoboken: Wiley Blackwell, pp. 269–278.

McBrayer, J. 2014. "The Wager Renewed: Believing in God Is Good for You," *Science, Religion & Culture* 1: 130–140.
  2018. "The Epistemology of Genealogies," in H. Van Eyghen et al. (eds.), *New Developments in the Cognitive Science of Religion: The Rationality of Religious Belief.* Switzerland: Springer, pp. 157–169.

McCain, K. 2012. "The Interventionist Account of Causation and the Basing Relation," *Philosophical Studies* 159: 357–382.

2014. *Evidentialism and Epistemic Justification.* New York: Routledge.

2015. "Explanationism: Defended on All Sides," *Logos & Episteme* 6: 333–349.

2018. "Explanationist Aid for Phenomenal Conservatism," *Synthese* 195: 3035–3050.

2022. *Understanding How Science Explains the World.* Cambridge University Press.

McCain, K. & Moretti, L. 2021. *Appearance and Explanation: Phenomenal Explanationism in Epistemology.* Oxford University Press.

McCauley, R. 2011. *Why Religion Is Natural and Science is Not.* Oxford University Press.

McDowell, J. 1982. "Criteria, Defeasibility, and Knowledge," *Proceedings of the British Academy* 68: 173–192.

1994. "Knowledge by Hearsay," in B. Matilal & A. Chakrabarti (eds.), *Knowing from Words: Western and Indian Philosophical Analysis of Understanding Testimony.* Dordrecht: Kluwer Academic Publishers, pp. 195–224.

1995. "Knowledge and the Internal," *Philosophy and Phenomenological Research* 55: 877–893.

McGinn, C. 1984. *Wittgenstein on Meaning: An Interpretation and Evaluation.* Oxford: Blackwell.

McGinn, M. 1989. *Sense and Certainty: A Dissolution of Skepticism.* Oxford: Blackwell.

McGrew, T. & McGrew, L. 2009. "The Argument from Miracles: A Cumulative Case for the Resurrection of Jesus of Nazareth," in Craig & Moreland (eds.), pp. 593–662.

McGuckin, J. 2011. *Prayer Book of the Early Christians.* Brewster, MA: Paraclete Press.

McKaughan, D. J. 2013. "Authentic Faith and Acknowledged Risk: Dissolving the Problem of Faith and Reason," *Religious Studies* 49: 101–124.

2016. "Action-Centered Faith, Doubt, and Rationality," *Journal of Philosophical Research* 41: 71–90.

2017. "On the Value of Faith and Faithfulness," *International Journal for Philosophy of Religion* 81: 7–29.

2018. "Faith Through the Dark of Night: What Perseverance Amidst Doubt Can Teach Us About the Nature and Value of Religious Faith," *Faith and Philosophy* 35: 195–218.

McKaughan, D. J. & Howard-Snyder, D. 2022. "Theorizing about Faith and Faithfulness with Jonathan Kvanvig," *Religious Studies* 58: 628–648. https://doi:10.1017/S0034412521000202.

In press a. "Faith and Faithfulness," *Faith and Philosophy.*

In press b. "Perseverance in the Religious Life," in N. King (ed.), *Endurance.* Oxford University Press.

McKim, R. 2001. *Religious Ambiguity and Religious Diversity.* Oxford University Press.

McMyler, B. 2011. *Testimony, Trust, and Authority.* Oxford University Press.

McMyler, B. & Ogungbure, A. 2018. "Recent Work on Trust and Testimony," *American Philosophical Quarterly* 55: 217–230.

McNabb, T. D. 2019. *Religious Epistemology.* Cambridge University Press.

McPherson, D. 2020. *Virtue and Meaning: A Neo-Aristotelian Perspective.* Cambridge University Press.

Medina, J. 2013. *The Epistemology of Resistance: Gender and Racial Oppression, Epistemic Injustice, and the Social Imagination.* Oxford University Press.

Meier, J. P. 1991. *A Marginal Jew: Rethinking the Historical Jesus.* New York: Doubleday.

Menssen, S. & Sullivan, T. D. 2007. *The Agnostic Inquirer.* Grand Rapids: Eerdmans.

   2021. "The Argument from Ramified Natural Theology," in C. Ruloff & P. Horban (eds.), *Contemporary Arguments in Natural Theology: God and Rational Belief.* London: Bloomsbury Academic, pp. 311–325.

   2022. "Can I Be Obliged to Believe?" *Religions* 13: 1159.

Menzel, C. 2018. "The Argument from Collections." in J. Walls & T. Dougherty (eds.), *Two Dozen (or So) Arguments for God: The Plantinga Project.* Oxford University Press, pp. 29–58.

Mihirig, A. A. 2022a. "Typologies of Scepticism in the Philosophical Tradition of Kalām," *Theoria* 88: 13–48.

   2022b. "Analogical Arguments in the Kalām Tradition: Abū'l-Ma'ālī al-Juwaynī and Beyond," *Methodos: Savoirs Et Textes* 22.

Miller, B. 2015. "Why Knowledge Is the Property of a Community and Possibly None of Its Members," *Philosophical Quarterly* 65: 417–441.

Miller, C. 2016. "Is Theism a Simple Hypothesis? The Simplicity of Omni-Properties," *Religious Studies* 52: 45–61.

Millican, P. 2011. "Twenty Questions about Hume's 'Of Miracles'," *Royal Institute of Philosophy Supplement* 68: 151–92.

Mitchell, B. 1973. *The Justification of Religious Belief.* London: Macmillan.

Moberly, R. W. L. 1997. "אמן (*'āman*)," in W.A. VanGemeren (ed.) *New International Dictionary of Old Testament Theology and Exegesis*, vol. 1. Grand Rapids, MI: Zondervan, pp. 427–433.

de Montaigne, M. 2003 [1576]. *Apology for Raymond Sebond*, trans. R. Ariew & M. Grene. Indianapolis, IN: Hackett.

Moon, A. 2012. "Warrant *Does* Entail Truth," *Synthese* 184: 287–297.

   2017. "Plantinga's Religious Epistemology, Skeptical Theism, and Debunking Arguments," *Faith and Philosophy* 34: 449–470.

   2021. "Circular and Question-Begging Responses to Religious Disagreement and Debunking Arguments," *Philosophical Studies* 178: 785–809.

Mooney, J. 2019. "From a Cosmic Fine-Tuner to a Perfect Being," *Analysis* 79: 449–452.

Moran, R. A. 2005. "Getting Told and Being Believed," *Philosophers' Imprint* 5: 1–29.

Moreland, J. P. 2008. *Consciousness and the Existence of God: A Theistic Argument*. London: Routledge.

Morgan, T. 2015. *Roman Faith and Christian Faith: Pistis and Fides in the Early Roman Empire*. Oxford University Press.

Moser, P. K. 2008a. "Religious Scepticism," in J. Greco (ed.) *The Oxford Handbook of Skepticism*. Oxford University Press, pp. 200–224.

   2008b. *The Elusive God: Reorienting Religious Epistemology*. Cambridge University Press.

   2010. *The Evidence for God: Religious Knowledge Reexamined*. Cambridge University Press.

Mougin, G. & Sober, E. 1994. "Betting against Pascal's Wager," *Noûs* 28: 382–95.

Mother Teresa. 2007. *Come Be My Light: The Private Writings of the "Saint of Calcutta."* New York: Doubleday.

Mulhall, S. 2007. *Wittgenstein's Private Language: Grammar, Nonsense, and Imagination in Philosophical Investigations, §§ 243-315*. Oxford: Clarendon Press.

Mulhall, S. & Swift, A. 1996. *Liberals & Communitarians*. 2nd ed. Malden, MA: Blackwell Publishing.

Murray, M. 2009. "Scientific Explanation of Religion and the Justification of Religious Belief," in Schloss & Murray (eds.), pp. 168–178.

Murray, M. & Goldberg, A. 2009. "Evolutionary Accounts of Religion: Explaining and Explaining Away," in Schloss and Murray (eds.), pp. 179–199.

Murray, M. J. & Schloss, J. 2013. "Evolutionary Accounts of Religion and the Justification of Religious Belief," in J. P. Moreland et al. (eds.), *Debating Christian Theism*. New York: Oxford University Press, pp. 242–260.

Mustafa, A. R. 2013. *On Taqlīd: Ibn al-Qayyim's Critique of Authority in Islamic Law*. Oxford University Press.

Nagasawa, Y. 2017. *Maximal God: A New Defence of Perfect Being Theism*. Oxford University Press.

Ñāṇamoli, B. & Bodhi, B. (eds. and trans.) 1995. *The Middle Length Discourses of the Buddha: A New Translation of the Majjhima Nikaya*. Boston: Wisdom Publication.

Nelson, L. H. 1993. "Epistemological Communities," in *Feminist Epistemology*. New York: Routledge, pp. 121–160.

Neuhaus, R. J. 2000. *Death on a Friday Afternoon: Meditations on the Last Words of Jesus from the Cross*. New York: Basic Books.

Newman, J. H. 1979 [1870]. *An Essay in Aid of a Grammar of Assent*, Notre Dame, IN: University of Notre Dame Press.

Nguyen, C. T. 2018. "Echo Chambers and Epistemic Bubbles," *Episteme* 17: 141–161. https://doi:10.1017/epi.2018.32.

   2023. "Trust as an Unquestioning Attitude," *Oxford Studies in Epistemology*.

Nielsen, K. 1967. "Wittgensteinian Fideism," *Philosophy* 42: 191–209

Norenzayan, A. 2013. *Big Gods*. Princeton University Press.

O'Donnell, D. S. 2021. *"O Woman, Great Is Your Faith!": Faith in the Gospel of Matthew*. Eugene, OR: Pickwick Publications.

Oppy, Graham. 1991. "On Rescher on Pascal's Wager," *The International Journal for Philosophy of Religion* 30: 159–68.

2006. *Arguing about Gods*. Cambridge University Press.

2007. *Ontological Arguments and Belief in God*. Cambridge University Press.

Pace, M. & McKaughan, D. J. 2022. "Judaeo-Christian Faith as Trust and Loyalty," *Religious Studies* 58: 30–60.

Page, B. 2020. "Arguing to Theism from Consciousness," *Faith and Philosophy* 37: 336–362.

Paley, W. 1802. *Natural Theology or Evidences of the Existence and Attributes of the Deity*. London: R. Faulder.

Pandeya, R. C. 1989. *The Pramāṇavārttikam of Ācārya Dharmakīrti with the Commentaries Svopajñavtti of the Author and Pramāṇavārttikavrtti of Manorathanandin*. Delhi: Motilal Banarsidass.

Pargament, K. I. & Exline, J. J. 2022. *Working with Spiritual Struggles in Psychotherapy: From Research to Practice*. New York: Guilford Press.

Parsons, K. M. 2013. "Perspectives on Natural Theology from Analytic Philosophy," in R. Manning, J. Brooke, & F. Watts (eds.), *The Oxford Handbook of Natural Theology*. Oxford University Press, pp. 248–261.

Pascal, B. 1662/1958. *Pensees*, trans. W. Trotter. New York: J. M. Dent Co., fragments 233–241.

Peirce, C. S. 1965 [1908]. "A Neglected Argument for the Reality of God," in C. Hartshorne & P. Weiss (eds.), *Collected Papers of Charles Sanders Peirce*, vol. 6. Cambridge, MA: Harvard University Press, pp. 452–85.

Penelhum, T. 1983a. *God and Scepticism: A Study in Scepticism and Fideism*. Dordrecht, Netherlands: D. Reidel.

1983b. "Scepticism and Fideism," in M. Burnyeat (ed.) *The Skeptical Tradition*. University of California Press, pp. 287–318.

2010. "Fideism," in C. Taliaferro, P. Draper, & P. Quinn (eds.), *A Companion to Philosophy of Religion*, 2nd ed. Oxford: Blackwell, pp. 441–448.

Pessagno, M. J. 1979. "Intellect and Religious Assent," *The Muslim World* 69:18–27.

Phillips, D. Z. 1976. *Religion Without Explanation*. Oxford University Press.

Philipse, H. 2012. *God in the Age of Science?* Oxford University Press.

Pittard, J. 2019. *Disagreement, Deference, and Religious Commitment*. Oxford University Press.

Plantinga, A. 1974. *The Nature of Necessity*. Oxford: Clarendon Press.

1980. "The Reformed Objection to Natural Theology," *Proceedings of the American Catholic Philosophical Association* 15: 49–62.

1983. "Reason and Belief in God," in A. Plantinga & N. Wolterstorff (eds.), pp. 16–93.

1985. "Self-Profile," in J. Tomberlin & P. van Iwagen (eds.), *Alvin Plantinga*. Dordrecht: D. Reidel Publishing Company, pp. 3–97.

1991. "Theism, Atheism and Rationality," *Truth: An Interdisciplinary Journal of Christian Thought* 3.

1993a. *Warrant and Proper Function.* Oxford University Press.

1993b. *Warrant: The Current Debate.* Oxford University Press.

1998. "Religion and Epistemology," in E. Craig (ed.) *Routledge Encyclopedia of Philosophy.* London: Routledge. https://doi:10.4324/9780415249126-K080-1.

2000a. "Pluralism: A Defense of Exclusivism," in K. Meeker & P. L. Quinn (eds.), *The Philosophical Challenge of Religious Diversity.* Oxford University Press, pp. 172–192.

2000b. *Warranted Christian Belief.* Oxford University Press.

2011. *Where the Conflict Really Lies: Science, Religion, and Naturalism.* Oxford University Press.

2015. *Knowledge and Christian Belief.* Grand Rapids, MI: Eerdmans.

2018 [1986]. "Two Dozen (or so) Theistic Arguments," in J. Walls & T. Doughterty (eds.), *Two Dozen (or so) Arguments for God: The Plantinga Project.* Oxford University Press, pp. 461–479.

Plantinga, A. & Wolterstorff, N. (eds.) 1983. *Faith and Rationality: Reason and Belief in God.* Notre Dame, IN: University of Notre Dame Press.

Pojman, L. 1986. "Faith Without Belief?" *Faith and Philosophy* 3: 157–176.

Popkin, R. 1992. "Fideism, Quietism, and Unbelief: Skepticism for and against Religion in the Seventeenth and Eighteenth Centuries," in M. Hester (ed.) *Faith, Reason, and Skepticism.* Philadelphia, PA: Temple University Press, pp. 121–154.

2003. *The History of Scepticism from Savonarola to Bayle.* Oxford University Press.

Poston, T. 2014. *Reason and Explanation: A Defense of Explanatory Coherentism.* New York: Palgrave-MacMillan.

2018. "The Argument from (A) to (Y): The Argument from So Many Arguments," in J. Walls & T. Dougherty (eds.), *Two Dozen (or So) Arguments for God: The Plantinga Project.* Oxford University Press, pp. 372–388.

Potter, K. 1981. *Advaita Vedanta up to Shankara and His pupils.* Delhi: Motilal Banarsidass.

Preus, J. 1987. *Explaining Religion.* New Haven: Yale University Press.

Pritchard, D. H. 2011. "Wittgensteinian Quasi-Fideism," *Oxford Studies in the Philosophy of Religion* 4: 145–159.

2012. *Epistemological Disjunctivism.* Oxford University Press.

2015a. *Epistemic Angst: Radical Skepticism and the Groundlessness of Our Believing.* Princeton University Press.

2015b. "Wittgenstein on Faith and Reason: The Influence of Newman," in M. Szatkowski (ed.) *God, Truth and Other Enigmas.* Berlin: Walter de Gruyter, pp. 141–164.

2016. *Epistemology*, 2nd ed. New York: Palgrave Macmillan.

2017a. "Faith and Reason," *Philosophy* 81: 101–118.

2017b. "Wittgenstein on Hinge Commitments and Radical Scepticism in *On Certainty*," in H.-J. Glock & J. Hyman (eds.), *Blackwell Companion to Wittgenstein*. Oxford: Blackwell, pp. 563–575.

2018. "Quasi-Fideism and Religious Conviction," *European Journal for Philosophy of Religion* 10: 51–66.

2019a. "Wittgensteinian Epistemology, Epistemic Vertigo, and Pyrrhonian Scepticism," in J. Vlasits & K. M. Vogt (eds.), *Epistemology After Sextus Empiricus*. Oxford University Press, pp. 172–192.

2019b. "Wittgenstein's *On Certainty* as Pyrrhonism in Action," in N. de Costa & S. Wuppuluri (eds.), *Wittgensteinian (adj.): Looking at Things from the Viewpoint of Wittgenstein's Philosophy*. Dordrecht: Springer, pp. 91–106.

2021. "Sceptical Fideism and Quasi-Fideism," *Manuscrito* 44: 3–30.

2022a. "Exploring Quasi-Fideism," in D. Moyal-Sharrock & C. Sandis (eds.), *Extending Hinge Epistemology*. London: Anthem, ch. 2.

2022b. "Quasi-Fideism and Epistemic Relativism," *Inquiry*. https://doi.org/10.1080/0020174X.2022.2135820.

In press a. "Honest Doubt: Quasi-Fideism and Wittgensteinian Epistemology,"in D. H. Pritchard & N. Venturinha (eds.), *Wittgenstein and the Epistemology of Religion*. Oxford University Press.

In press b. "Pyrrhonism and Wittgensteinian Quietism," in L. Perissinotto & B. R. Cámara (eds.), *Ancient Scepticism and Contemporary Philosophy*. Milan, Italy: Mimesis International.

Pritchard, D. H. & Richmond, A. 2012. "Hume on Miracles," in A. Bailey & D. O'Brien (eds.), *The Continuum Companion to Hume*. London: Continuum, pp. 227–245.

Pruss, A. R. 2001. "Śaṃkara's Principle and Two Ontomystical Arguments," *International Journal for Philosophy of Religion* 49: 111–120.

2010. "The Ontological Argument and the Motivational Centres of Lives," *Religious Studies* 46: 233–249.

Pryor, J. 2001. "Highlights of Recent Epistemology," *British Journal for the Philosophy of Science* 52: 95–124.

2004. "What's Wrong with Moore's Argument?" *Philosophical Issues* 14: 349–378.

Quinn, P. L. 2000. "Toward Thinner Theologies: Hick and Alston on Religious Diversity," in K. Meeker & P. L. Quinn (eds.), *The Philosophical Challenge of Religious Diversity*. Oxford University Press, pp. 226–243.

Quong, J. 2011. *Liberalism without Perfection*. Oxford University Press.

Radhakrishnan, S. 1992. *The Principal Upanishads*. Atlantic Highlands, NJ: Humanities Press International.

Rasmussen, J. 2009. "From a Necessary Being to God," *International Journal for Philosophy of Religion* 66: 1–13.

Rath, B. 2017. "Christ's Faith, Doubt, and the Cry of Dereliction," *International Journal for Philosophy of Religion* 81: 161–169.

Ratzsch, D. 2003. "Perceiving Design," in N. Manson (ed.) *God and Design*. New York: Routledge. pp. 124–144.

Rawls, J. 1996. *Political Liberalism* New York: Columbia University Press.

 2001. *Justice as Fairness: A Restatement*. Cambridge, MA: Harvard University Press.

Rea, M. (ed.) 2009. *Oxford Readings in Philosophical Theology: Trinity, Incarnation, Atonement*, vol. 1. Oxford University Press.

Rea, M. 2018. *The Hiddenness of God*. Oxford University Press.

Rea, M. C. 2021. "Protest, Worship, and the Deformation of Prayer," in *Essays in Analytic Theology: Volume 2*. Oxford University Press, pp. 193–210.

Reppert, V. 2009. "The Argument from Reason," in Craig & Moreland (eds.), pp. 344–390.

Rhoads, D. M. 2004. *Reading Mark: Engaging the Gospel*. Minneapolis, MN: Fortress.

Ribeiro, B. 2009. "Sextus, Montaigne, Hume: Exercises in Skeptical Cartography," *The Modern Schoolman* 87: 7–34.

 2021. *Sextus, Montaigne, Hume: Pyrrhonizers*, Leiden: Brill.

Rini, R. 2017. "Fake News and Partisan Epistemology," *Kennedy Institute of Ethics Journal* 27: E-43-E-64. https://doi:10.1177/1326365X17702268.

Ritchie, A. 2012. *From Morality to Metaphysics: The Theistic Implications of Our Ethical Commitments*. Oxford University Press.

Rockwood, N. 2020. "Locke on Reason, Revelation, and Miracles," in J. Gordon-Roth & S. Weinberg (eds.), *The Lockean Mind*. London: Routledge, pp. 545–553.

Rogers, K. A. 2021. "The Argument from Certainty," in C. Ruloff & P. Horban (eds.), *Contemporary Arguments in Natural Theology: God and Rational Belief*. London: Bloomsbury Academic, pp. 179–194.

Rolin, K. 2007. "Science as Collective Knowledge," *Cognitive Systems Research* 9: 115–124.

Rota, M. 2016a. "A Better Version of Pascal's Wager," *American Catholic Philosophical Quarterly* 90: 415–439.

 2016b. *Taking Pascal's Wager: Faith, Evidence, and the Abundant Life*. Downers Grove, IL: InterVarsity Press.

 2017. "Pascal's Wager," *Philosophy Compass* 12: 1–11.

Rowe, W. 1979 "The Problem of Evil and Some Varieties of Atheism," *American Philosophical Quarterly* 16: 335–341.

Russell, B. 1912. *The Problems of Philosophy*. London: Williams and Norgate; New York: Henry Holt and Company.

Ryle, G. 1949. *The Concept of Mind*. University of Chicago Press.

Sacks, J. 2020. *Morality: Restoring the Common Good in Divided Times*. New York: Basic Books.

Sauer, H. 2018. *Debunking Arguments in Ethics*. Cambridge University Press.

Saul, J. 2013. "Scepticism and Implicit Bias," *Disputatio* 37: 243–263.

Schellenberg, J. L. 2005. *Prolegomena to a Philosophy of Religion*. Ithaca, NY: Cornell University Press.

2007. *The Wisdom to Doubt*. Ithaca, NY: Cornell University Press.

Schliesser, B. 2022. "Shades of Faith: The Phenomenon of Doubt in Early Christianity," *Religious Studies* First View. https://doi:10.1017/S0034412522000105.

Schloss, J. & Murray, M. (eds.). 2009. *The Believing Primate: Scientific, Philosophical, and Theological Reflections on the Origin of Religion*. Oxford University Press.

Schmemann, A. 1973. *For the Life of the World*. Yonkers, NY: St. Vladimir's Seminary Press.

Schroeder, M. 2012. "Stakes, Withholding, and Pragmatic Encroachment on Knowledge," *Philosophical Studies* 160: 265–285.

Schönbaumsfeld, G. 2016. *The Illusion of Doubt*. Oxford University Press.

Seel, N. M. 2012. "Fowler Faith Stages," in N. M. Seel (ed.), *Encyclopedia of the Sciences of Learning*. New York: Springer, pp. 1323–1324.

Senor, T. 2020. "Religious Beliefs Do Not Require Evidence/Response to Dougherty," in S. Cowan (ed.) *Problems in Epistemology and Metaphysics: An Introduction to Contemporary Debates*. London: Bloomsbury, pp. 139–154.

Shanahan, M. 2015. *The Technological Singularity*. Cambridge, MA: MIT Press.

Sharpe, A. 1909. "Doubt," in *The Catholic Encyclopedia*, vol. 5. New York: Robert Appleton Company. www.newadvent.org/cathen/05141a.htm.

Shaw, K. 2016. "Religious Epistemological Disjunctivism," *International Journal for Philosophy of Religion* 79: 261–279.

2019. "A Plea for the Theist in the Street: A Defense of Liberalism in the Epistemology of Religious Experience," *Faith and Philosophy* 36: 102–128.

Siderits, M. 1980. "The Madhyamaka Critique of Epistemology I," *Journal of Indian Philosophy* 8: 307–335.

1981. "The Madhyamaka Critique of Epistemology II," *Journal of Indian Philosophy* 9: 121–160.

2007. *Buddhism as Philosophy*. Indianapolis: Hackett Publishing.

Siderits, M., Tillemans, T., & Chakrabarti, A. (eds.) 2011. *Apoha: Buddhist Nominalism and Human Cognition*. New York: Columbia University Press.

Sluga, H. 2004. "Wittgenstein and Pyrrhonism," in W. Sinnott-Armstrong (ed.), *Pyrrhonian Skepticism*. Oxford University Press, pp. 99–117.

Smith, C. 2017. *Religion: What It Is, How It Works, and Why It Matters*. Princeton University Press.

Smith, N. 2021. "How to Hang a Door: Picking Hinges for Quasi-Fideism," *European Journal for Philosophy of Religion* 13: 51–82.

Solomon, S., Greenberg, J., & Pyszczynski, T. 1991. "A Terror Management Theory of Social Behavior: The Psychological Functions of Self-Esteem and Cultural Worldviews," *Advances in Experimental Social Psychology* 24: 93–157.

Sorensen, R. 1983. "Hume's Scepticism Concerning Reports of Miracles," *Analysis* 43: 60.

Sosa, E. 1997. "Reflective Knowledge in the Best Circles," *The Journal of Philosophy* 94: 410–430.

2007. *A Virtue Epistemology*. Oxford University Press.

2017. *Epistemology*. Princeton University Press.

Spevack, A. 2020. "Continuing Conversations: Later Sunni Kalām-Theology's Ongoing Engagement with Philosophy," in A. Shihadeh and J. Thiele (eds.), *Philosophical Theology in Islam: Later Ash'arism East and West*. Leiden/Boston: Brill.

Staal, F. 1979. "The Meaninglessness of Ritual," *Numen* 26: 2–22.

Stausberg, M. (ed.) 2009. *Contemporary Theories of Religion*. London: Routledge.

Stcherbatsky, T. 1930, 1932. *Buddhist Logic*, 2 vols. Leningrad: Bibliotheca Buddhica 26. Reprinted The Hague: Mouton and Co., 1958.

Stoltz, J. 2009. "Buddhist Epistemology: The Study of Pramāṇa," *Religion Compass* 3/4: 537–548.

2021. *Illuminating the Mind: An Introduction to Buddhist Epistemology*. Oxford University Press.

Strawson, P. F. 1974. *Freedom and Resentment, and Other Essays*. London: Methuen.

1985. *Skepticism and Naturalism: Some Varieties*. New York: Columbia University Press.

1994. "Knowing from Words," in B. K. Matilal & A. Chakrabarti (eds.), *Knowing from Words: Western and Indian Philosophical Analysis of Understanding and Testimony*. Dordrecht: Kluwer, pp. 23–27.

Stroud, S. 2006. "Epistemic Partiality in Friendship," *Ethics* 116: 498–524.

Street, S. 2006. "A Darwinian Dilemma for Realist Theories of Value," *Philosophical Studies* 127: 109–166.

Stump, E. 2000. "Francis and Dominic: Persons, Patterns, and the Trinity," *Proceedings of the American Catholic Philosophical Association* 74: 1–25.

2010. *Wandering in Darkness: Narrative and the Problem of Suffering*. Oxford University Press.

2012. "*Wandering in Darkness:* Further Reflections," *European Journal for Philosophy of Religion* 4: 197–219.

Sudduth, M. n.d. "Defeaters in Epistemology," in J. Feiser & B. Dowden (eds.), *The Internet Encyclopedia of Philosophy*. https://iep.utm.edu/defeaters-in-epistemology/.

Swain, M. 1988. "Alston's Internalistic Externalism," *Philosophical Perspectives* 2: 461–473.

Swinburne, R. 2003. *The Resurrection of God Incarnate*. Oxford: Clarendon Press.

2004. *The Existence of God*, 2nd ed. Oxford University Press.

2005. *Faith and Reason*, 2nd ed. Oxford University Press.

2018. "The Argument from Colors and Flavors," in Walls & Dougherty (eds.), pp. 293–302.

Tennant, F. R. 1930. *Philosophical Theology, Volume II, the World, the Soul, and God*. Cambridge University Press.

Thakchöe, S. 2007. *The Two Truth Debate: Tsongkhapa and Gorampa on the Middle Way*. Boston: Wisdom Publication.

2011. "Prāsaṅgika Epistemology in Context," in *The Cowherds: Moonshadows: Conventional Truth in Buddhist Philosophy*. Oxford University Press, pp. 39–55.

2012. "Candrakīrti's Theory of Perception: A Case for Non-Foundationalist Epistemology in Madhyamaka," *Acta Orientalia Vilnensia* 11: 93–125.

2013. "Prāsaṅgika Epistemology: A Reply to sTag tsang's Charge against Tsongkhapa's Use of Pramāṇa in Candrakīrti's Philosophy," *Journal of Indian Philosophy* 41: 1–27.

Thagard, P. 1997. "Collaborative Knowledge," *Noûs* 31: 242–261.

The Qur'an (Oxford World Classics), trans. M. A. S. Abdel Haleem. Oxford University Press, 2008.

Theokritoff, E. 2009. *Living in God's Creation*. Yonkers, NY: St. Vladimir's Seminary Press.

Thurow, J. C. 2013. "Does Cognitive Science Show Belief in God to Be Irrational? The Epistemic Consequences of the Cognitive Science of Religion," *International Journal for Philosophy of Religion* 74: 77–98.

2014a. "Does the Scientific Study of Religion Cast Doubt on Theistic Beliefs?" in M. Bergmann & P. Kain (eds.), *Challenges to Moral and Religious Belief: Disagreement and Evolution*. Oxford University Press, pp. 277–294.

2014b. "Some Reflections on Cognitive Science, Doubt, and Religious Belief," in R. Trigg, & J. L. Barrett (eds.), *The Roots of Religion: Exploring the Cognitive Science of Religion*. Farnham, UK: Ashgate Press, pp. 189–207.

2016. "Book Review of De Cruz & De Smedt, *A Natural History of Natural Theology*," *Faith and Philosophy* 33: 370–374.

2018. "Debunking and Fully Apt Belief," *Filosofia Unisinos* 19: 294–301.

2022. "Rationalization, Reasons, and Religion," in D. Machuca (ed.), *Evolutionary Debunking Arguments*. London: Routledge, pp. 129–159.

Tillemans, T. J. F. 1999. *Logic, Language, Scripture*. Boston: Wisdom Publications.

2011. "Buddhist Epistemology (*pramāṇavāda*)," in W. Edelglass & Jay L. Garfield (eds.), *The Oxford Handbook of World Philosophy*. Oxford University Press, pp. 233–244.

2021. "Dharmakīrti," in E. Zalta (ed.), *The Stanford Encyclopedia of Philosophy* (Spring 2021 Edition). https://plato.stanford.edu/archives/spr2021/entries/dharmakiirti/.

Timpe, K. 2022. "Toward an Account of Lamenting Well," in O. Crisp, J. Arcadi, & J. Wessling (eds.), *Analyzing Prayer: Theological and Philosophical Essays*. Oxford University Press, pp. 95–115.

Tolhurst, W. 1998. "Seemings," *American Philosophical Quarterly* 35: 293–302.

Tucker, C. 2011. "Phenomenal Conservatism and Evidentialism in Religious Epistemology," in K. J. Clark & R. VanArragon (eds.), *Evidence and Religious Belief*. Oxford University Press, pp. 52–73.

Tucker, C., ed. 2013. *Seemings and Justification: New Essays on Dogmatism and Phenomenal Conservatism.* Oxford University Press.

Tuggy, D. 2017. "Jesus as an Exemplar of Faith in the New Testament," *International Journal for Philosophy of Religion* 81: 171–191.

Tuomela, R. 2004. "Group Knowledge Analyzed," *Episteme* 1: 109–127.

Turner, J. B. 2021. "An Islamic Account of Reformed Epistemology," *Philosophy East and West* 71: 767–792.

Urban, H. B. 2015. *New Age, Neopagan, & New Religious Movements.* Oakland: University of California Press.

Uslu, F. 2007. "Knowledge and Volition in Early Ash'arī Doctrine of Faith," *Journal of Islamic Studies* 18: 163–182.

VanArragon, R. 2020. "Evidence Is Not Required for Religious Belief," in M. Peterson & R. VanArragon (eds.), *Contemporary Debates in Philosophy of Religion*, 2nd ed. Hoboken: Wiley-Blackwell, pp. 279–287.

Van Eyghen, H. 2020. *Arguing from Cognitive Science of Religion.* London: Bloomsbury.

Van Inwagen, P. 1994. "Quam Dilecta," in T. V. Morris (ed.) *God and the Philosophers: The Reconciliation of Faith and Reason.* Oxford University Press, pp. 31–60.

van Inwagen, P. 2009. "Listening to Clifford's Ghost," *Royal Institute of Philosophy Supplement* 65: 15–35. https://doi.org/10.1017/S1358246109990038.

Vidyabhusana, M. S. C. (trans.). 1975. *The Nyaya Sutras of Gotama*, 2nd ed. New Delhi: Oriental Books Reprint Corporation.

Visala, A. 2020. "Cultural Evolution and Debunking Arguments: A Response to Davis," in R. Peels, J. de Ridder, & R. van Woudenberg (eds.), *Scientific Challenges to Common Sense Philosophy.* New York: Routledge, pp. 215–222.

Wainwright, W. J. 1994. "Skepticism, Romanticism, and Faith," in T. V. Morris (ed.), *God and the Philosophers.* Oxford University Press, pp. 77–87.

Walls, J. & Dougherty, T. (eds.). 2018. *Two Dozen (or so) Arguments for God: The Plantinga Project.* Oxford University Press.

Walshe, M. (ed. and trans.) 1995. *The Long Discourse of the Buddha: A Translation of Digha Nikāya.* Boston: Wisdom Publication.

Ware, K. (Metropolitan Kallistos of Diokelia). 2013. "Through Creation to the Creator," in J. Chryssavgis & B. Foltz (eds.), *Toward an Ecology of Transfiguration: Orthodox Christian Perspectives on Environment, Nature, and Creation.* New York: Fordham University Press, pp. 86–105.

Weger, U. & Wagemann, J. 2021. "Towards a Conceptual Clarification of Awe and Wonder a First Person Phenomenological Enquiry," *Current Directions in Psychology* 40: 1386–1401. https://doi.org/10.1007/s12144-018-0057-7.

Westerhoff, J. 2009. *Nāgārjuna's Madhyamaka: A Philosophical Introduction.* Oxford University Press.

2010. *The Dispeller of Disputes: Nāgārjuna's Vigrahavyāvartanī.* Oxford University Press.

2018. *The Golden Age of Indian Philosophy.* Oxford University Press.

Whitcomb, D., Battaly, H., Baehr, J., & Howard-Snyder, D. 2017. "Intellectual Humility: Owning Our Limitations," *Philosophy and Phenomenological Research* 94: 509–539.

White, R. 2010. "You Just Believe That Because . . ." *Philosophical Perspectives* 24: 573–615.

Whittaker, J. H. 2010. "Wittgensteinian Philosophy of Religion," in C. Taliaferro, P. Draper & P. Quinn (eds.), *A Companion to Philosophy of Religion*. Oxford: Blackwell, pp. 659–666.

Wielenberg, E. 2010. "On the Evolutionary Debunking of Morality," *Ethics* 120: 441–464.

Wilkins, J. & Griffiths, P. 2012. "Evolutionary Debunking Arguments in Three Domains: Fact, Value, and Religion," in G. Dawes & J. Maclaurin (eds.), *A New Science of Religion*. New York: Routledge, pp. 133–146.

Williams, M. 1991. *Unnatural Doubts: Epistemological Realism and the Basis of Skepticism*. Oxford: Blackwell.

In press. "Fideism, Skepticism and 'Hinge' Epistemology," in D. H. Pritchard & N. Venturinha (eds.), *Wittgenstein and the Epistemology of Religion*. Oxford University Press.

Williamson, T. 1997. "Knowledge as Evidence," Mind 106: 1–25.

2000. *Knowledge and Its Limits*. Oxford University Press.

2007. *The Philosophy of Philosophy*. Oxford University Press.

2017. "Ambiguous Rationality," *Episteme* 14: 263–274.

In press. "Justification, Excuses and Sceptical Scenarios," in F. Dorsch and J. Dutant (eds.), *The New Evil Demon*. Oxford University Press.

Wittgenstein, L. 1966. *Wittgenstein's Lectures and Conversations on Aesthetics, Psychology and Religious Belief*, ed. C. Barrett. Oxford: Basil Blackwell.

1969. *On Certainty*, eds. G. E. M. Anscombe & G. H. von Wright, trans. D. Paul & G. E. M. Anscombe. Oxford: Blackwell.

1980. *Culture and Value*, trans. P. Winch, ed. G. H. von Wright. University of Chicago Press.

Wolterstorff, N. 1976. *Reason within the Bounds of Religion*, Grand Rapids, MI: Eerdmans.

1983a. "Can Belief in God Be Rational if It Has No Foundations?" in Plantinga & Wolterstorff (eds.), pp. 135–186.

1983b. "Introduction," in Plantinga & Wolterstorff (eds.), pp. 1–15.

1995a. *Divine Discourse*. Cambridge University Press.

Wolterstorff, N. 1995b. "On Being Entitled to Beliefs about God," revised and reprinted in Wolterstorff 2010, pp. 313–333.

1996. *John Locke and the Ethics of Belief*. Cambridge University Press.

Wolterstorff, N. 1999. "Epistemology of Religion," revised and reprinted in Wolterstoff 2010, pp. 144–172.

Wolterstorff, N. 2001a. "Reformed Epistemology," revised and reprinted in Wolterstoff 2010, pp. 334–349.

2001b. *Thomas Reid and the Story of Epistemology*. Cambridge University Press.

2010. *Practices of Belief*, Terence Cuneo (ed). Cambridge University Press.

2015. *The God We Worship*. Grand Rapids, MI: Eerdmans.

2016. "Knowing God Liturgically," *Journal of Analytic Theology* 4: 1–16.

Wray, K. B. 2007. "Who Has Scientific Knowledge?" *Social Epistemology* 21: 337–347.

Wright, C. 2002. "(Anti-)Sceptics Simple and Subtle: G. E. Moore and John McDowell," *Philosophy and Phenomenological Research* 65: 330–348.

2004. "Warrant for Nothing (and Foundations for Free)?" *Proceedings of the Aristotelian Society, Supplementary* 78: 167–212.

Wright, L. 2013. *Going Clear: Scientology, Hollywood, and the Prison of Belief*. New York: Vintage Books.

Wykstra, S. J. 1989. "Towards a Sensible Evidentialism: On the Notion of 'Needing Evidence,'" in W. Rowe & W. Wainwright (eds.), *Philosophy of Religion: Selected Readings*. Oxford University Press, pp. 481–491.

2001. "On behalf of the Evidentialist," in D. Z. Phillips & T. Tessin (eds.), *Philosophy of Religion in the 21st Century*. New York: Palgrave, 64–84.

2002. "Not Done in a Corner: How to Be a Sensible Evidentialist About Jesus," *Philosophical Books* 43: 81–135.

Wynn, M. 1997. "Beauty, Providence, and the Biophilia Hypothesis," *Heythrop Journal* 38: 283–299.

Yandell, K. 1990. *Hume's "Inexplicable Mystery": His Views on Religion*. Philadelphia: Temple University Press.

Yao, Z. 2004. "Dignāga and Four Types of Perception," *Journal of Indian Philosophy* 32: 57–79.

Zagzebski, L. 1993. "Religious Knowledge and the Virtues of the Mind," in L. Zagzebski (ed.) *Rational Faith: Catholic Responses to Reformed Epistemology*. Notre Dame: University of Notre Dame Press, pp. 199–225.

2012. *Epistemic Authority: A Theory of Trust, Authority, and Autonomy in Belief*. Oxford University Press.

Index

For EU product safety concerns, contact us at Calle de José Abascal, 56–1°, 28003 Madrid, Spain or eugpsr@cambridge.org.